## CSWE's Core Competencies and Practice Behavior E

Practice Behavior

| Practice Behavior | |
|---|---|
| **Professional Identity (2.1.1)** | |
| *Practice Behavior Examples...* | |
| Advocate for client access to the services of social work | |
| Practice personal reflection and self-correction to assure continual professional development | 3, 5, 6 |
| Attend to professional roles and boundaries | 4 |
| Demonstrate professional demeanor in behavior, appearance, and communication | 1, 3 |
| Engage in career-long learning | 3 |
| Use supervision and consultation | 3 |
| **Ethical Practice (2.1.2)** | |
| *Practice Behavior Examples...* | |
| Recognize and manage personal values in a way that allows professional values to guide practice | 3, 4 |
| Make ethical decisions by applying standards of the National Association of Social Workers Code of Ethics and, as applicable, of the International Federation of Social Workers/International Association of Schools of Social Work Ethics in Social Work, Statement of Principles | 3, 4, 6, 13 |
| Tolerate ambiguity in resolving ethical conflicts | 4 |
| Apply strategies of ethical reasoning to arrive at principled decisions | 3, 4, 6 |
| **Critical Thinking (2.1.3)** | |
| *Practice Behavior Examples...* | |
| Distinguish, appraise, and integrate multiple sources of knowledge, including research-based knowledge, and practice wisdom | 1, 2, 3, 4, 5, 6, 7, 8, 9, 10, 11, 12, 13 |
| Analyze models of assessment, prevention, intervention, and evaluation | 1, 2, 3, 4, 5, 6, 7, 9, 11, 13 |
| Demonstrate effective oral and written communication in working with individuals, families, groups, organizations, communities, and colleagues | |
| **Diversity in Practice (2.1.4)** | |
| *Practice Behavior Examples...* | |
| Recognize the extent to which a culture's structures and values may oppress, marginalize, alienate, or create or enhance privilege and power | 4 |
| Gain sufficient self-awareness to eliminate the influence of personal biases and values in working with diverse groups | 3, 4 |
| Recognize and communicate their understanding of the importance of difference in shaping life experiences | 1, 2, 3, 4, 8, 9, 12, 13 |
| View themselves as learners and engage those with whom they work as informants | |
| **Human Rights & Justice (2.1.5)** | |
| *Practice Behavior Examples...* | |
| Understand the forms and mechanisms of oppression and discrimination | 4 |
| Advocate for human rights and social and economic justice | 4 |
| Engage in practices that advance social and economic justice | 4 |

## CSWE's Core Competencies and Practice Behavior Examples in This Text

| Practice Behavior | Chapter |
|---|---|
| **Research-Based Practice (2.1.6)** | |
| *Practice Behavior Examples...* | |
| Use practice experience to inform scientific inquiry | 1, 2, 3, 4, 6, 10, 11, 12, 13 |
| Use research evidence to inform practice | 1, 2, 3, 4, 6, 7, 8, 10, 11, 12, 13 |
| **Human Behavior (2.1.7)** | |
| *Practice Behavior Examples...* | |
| Utilize conceptual frameworks to guide the processes of assessment, intervention, and evaluation | 3, 4, 13 |
| Critique and apply knowledge to understand person and environment. | 1, 2, 3, 4 |
| **Policy Practice (2.1.8)** | |
| *Practice Behavior Examples...* | |
| Analyze, formulate, and advocate for policies that advance social well-being | |
| Collaborate with colleagues and clients for effective policy action | |
| **Practice Contexts (2.1.9)** | |
| *Practice Behavior Examples...* | |
| Continuously discover, appraise, and attend to changing locales, populations, scientific and technological developments, and emerging societal trends to provide relevant services | |
| Provide leadership in promoting sustainable changes in service delivery and practice to improve the quality of social services | |
| **Engage, Assess, Intervene, Evaluate (2.1.10(a)–(d))** | |
| *Practice Behavior Examples...* | |
| (A) ENGAGEMENT<br>Substantively and effectively prepare for action with individuals, families, groups, organizations, and communities | 1, 2, 3, 4, 8, 9, 10, 11, 12, 13 |
| Use empathy and other interpersonal skills | 1, 2, 3, 4, 8, 9, 10 |
| Develop a mutually agreed-on focus of work and desired outcomes | 1, 2, 3, 4, 7, 8, 10, 11, 12, 13 |
| (B) ASSESSMENT<br>Collect, organize, and interpret client data | 1, 2, 3, 4, 5, 6, 7, 8, 9, 10, 11, 12, 13 |
| Assess client strengths and limitations | 1, 2, 3, 4, 5, 6, 8, 10, 11, 12 |
| Develop mutually agreed-on intervention goals and objectives | 1, 2, 3, 4, 5, 6, 8, 10, 11, 12 |
| Select appropriate intervention strategies | 1, 2, 3, 4, 5, 6, 7, 10, 11, 12 |
| (C) INTERVENTION<br>Initiate actions to achieve organizational goals | 3 |
| Implement prevention interventions that enhance client capacities | |
| Help clients resolve problems | 1, 2, 3, 4, 5, 6, 7, 9, 10, 11, 12, 13 |
| Negotiate, mediate, and advocate for clients | |
| Facilitate transitions and endings | 11 |
| (D) EVALUATION<br>Critically analyze, monitor, and evaluate interventions | 1, 2, 3, 4, 5, 6, 7, 8, 9, 10, 11, 12, 13 |

# Outcome-Informed Evidence-Based Practice

John G. Orme
University of Tennessee

Terri Combs-Orme
University of Tennessee

**PEARSON**

Boston Columbus Indianapolis New York San Francisco Upper Saddle River
Amsterdam Cape Town Dubai London Madrid Milan Munich Paris Montreal Toronto
Delhi Mexico City São Paulo Sydney Hong Kong Seoul Singapore Taipei Tokyo

**Editorial Director:** Craig Campanella
**Editor in Chief:** Dickson Musslewhite
**Executive Editor:** Ashley Dodge
**Editorial Product Manager:** Carly Czech
**Director of Marketing:** Brandy Dawson
**Executive Marketing Manager:** Jeanette Koskinas
**Senior Marketing Manager:** Wendy Albert
**Marketing Assistant:** Jessica Warren

**Production Manager:** Meghan DeMaio
**Creative Director:** Jayne Conte
**Cover Designer:** Suzanne Duda
**Cover Design:** Yuri Arcurs/Shutterstock
**Interior Design:** Joyce Weston Design
**Editorial Production and Composition Service:**
　Ravi Bhatt/PreMediaGlobal
**Printer/Binder/Cover Printer:** R. R. Donnelley & Sons

Many of the designations by manufacturers and seller to distinguish their products are claimed as trademarks. Where those designations appear in this book, and the publisher was aware of a trademark claim, the designations have been printed in initial caps or all caps.

**Library of Congress Cataloging-in-Publication Data**

Orme, John G.
　Outcome-informed evidence-based practice / John G. Orme, Terri Combs-Orme.
　　p. cm.
　Includes bibliographical references and index.
　ISBN-13: 978-0-205-81628-6 (alk. paper)
　ISBN-10: 0-205-81628-2 (alk. paper)
　1. Evidence-based social work.　2. Social services—Outcome assessment.　I. Combs-Orme, Terri.
II. Title.
　HV10.5.O763 2012
　361.3'2—dc23

　　　　　　　　　　　　　　　　　　　　　　　2011019616

ISBN-10: 0-205-81628-2
ISBN-13: 978-0-205-81628-6

# Contents

---

## 3. Why Measure, Monitor, and Modify?    29

---

## 4. Assessment: The Early Stages of Outcome-Informed Practice    51

# PART II: MONITORING AND INTERPRETING CLIENT PROGRESS

## 5. Charting Your Client's Progress   72

## 9. Standardized Scales   165

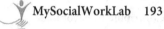

## 10. Individualized Rating Scales    194

## 13. Summing Up    243

# Preface

The contemporary view of evidence-based practice is that it is "a process for making practice decisions in which practitioners integrate the best research evidence available with their practice expertise and with client attributes, values, preferences, and circumstances" (Rubin, 2008, p. 7). Evidence-based practice is one of the most important developments in social work, medicine, and other social service and allied health care professions in recent times because it holds such promise for improving the well-being of our clients.

Measuring and monitoring each client's progress is an important part of evidence-based practice because, as Sir Winston Churchill wryly observed in a different context: "However beautiful the strategy, you should occasionally look at the results." In this book, we provide practical tools for measuring and monitoring each client's progress, so you'll know if and when to modify your evidence-based strategy in order to ensure the best possible results for every one of your clients.

We call the approach we present in this book *outcome-informed practice*, and it's an important element of evidence-based practice, hence the title of the book: *Outcome-Informed Evidence-Based Practice*. We didn't coin the term *outcome-informed practice*, but our take on it is fairly broad given the scope of social work practice (e.g., Mizrahi & Davis, 2008; Roberts, 2009) and our integration of related ideas from different disciplines. Other disciplines employ different terms to describe similar methods of practice.

In the context of psychotherapy, Barry Duncan, Scott Miller, and their colleagues use the term *client-directed outcome-informed therapy* to describe an approach that has much in common with what we have in mind (e.g., Duncan, Miller, & Sparks, 2004; Duncan, Miller, Wampold, & Hubble, 2010). Similarly, Lambert and his colleagues (e.g., Lambert, 2010b) have conducted methodologically rigorous research on the effects of measuring and monitoring client outcomes and using this feedback to guide psychotherapy practice. Bickman (2008) refers to such methods as *measurement feedback systems*.

In the context of education, measuring and monitoring client outcomes and using this feedback to guide interventions is referred to as *response to intervention* (Clark & Alvarez, 2010; Riley-Tillman & Burns, 2009), and among behaviorists this approach is referred to frequently as *response-guided experimentation* (e.g., Edgington, 1983; Ferron & Jones, 2006). Last but not least, in the context of social work, Bloom, Fischer, and Orme (2009) refer to this approach as *evaluation-informed practice*. At the risk of arguing with ourselves, we prefer the term *outcome-informed practice* because it places the focus clearly and squarely on ongoing client progress.

# Introduction

We've tried to bring the concepts presented in this book alive with cases that highlight the diversity of clients encountered by social workers. You'll see cases in nearly all of the chapters, integrating the concepts of outcome-informed practice. We aim to provide enough detail to illustrate the important principles in these case examples, but obviously it's not possible to present all of the facts that are important to any case. Whereas you may see clients meet their goals in a relatively short time in the cases we present here, we know that most cases require more time and may involve a series of stops and starts. We hope you will accept these limitations for pedagogical purposes.

Part I of this book, "Foundations of Outcome-Informed Practice," includes Chapters 1 through 4. Chapter 1 consists of two cases that illustrate the basics of outcome-informed practice. One case involves a foster child and her family, a classic area for social work practice and one that is complex and often messy. The other case involves a Saudi Muslim university student whose depression is related to adjusting to a new culture. Both cases demonstrate how measuring and monitoring client progress, and modifying interventions accordingly, can guide you to make the best decisions at each step in working with a client. They also provide concrete real-world contexts for formally introducing the concepts of outcome-informed practice in Chapter 2.

In Chapter 2, we discuss basic concepts of outcome-informed practice and relate these general concepts back to the specifics of the cases presented in Chapter 1. Outcome-informed practice is practice in which you: (1) measure your client's outcomes at regular, frequent, predesignated intervals, in a way that is sensitive to and respectful of the client; (2) monitor those outcomes to determine if your client is making satisfactory progress; and (3) modify your intervention plan as needed. An *outcome*, as we use the term, is the status of a client's problem before, during, or after intervention along some dimension, such as the frequency or severity of the problem. *Outcome measures* are tools for measuring the status of clients' problems. *Progress monitoring* is the process of measuring client outcomes at regular, frequent, predesignated intervals to obtain real-time feedback about client progress. Finally, *client progress* is defined in reference to the client's *goals*, which are general and abstract statements of desired outcomes for which an intervention is implemented, and *objectives*, which are more specific and concrete statements detailing desired outcomes of an intervention along with measurable criteria used to define and evaluate client success.

Given all the research that supports evidence-based practices, we think it's only fair that in Chapter 3 we answer the question: "Why should you systematically measure and monitor your clients' outcomes at regular, frequent intervals?" Evidence-based practice, or indeed any kind of social work, psychology, psychiatry, counseling, or other practice, is time-consuming and complicated. Why are we giving you one more thing to think about? We hope you will see why and agree with us about the importance of measuring and monitoring your clients' progress after you read Chapter 3, if you do not already. The reasons are compelling and go to the heart of our work.

Chapter 4 discusses assessment, a complex process that we believe involves both science and art. Volumes have been written about conducting good assessments, and we find valuable information in nearly every account we read. We do not pretend to present the final word on this difficult topic here. Instead, our discussion emphasizes details that contribute to an assessment that provides the foundation for carefully measuring and monitoring clients' progress. We do not discount qualitative data that should be considered in every good assessment. Years of experience probably make you more sensitive to these qualitative data, and they are valuable for your understanding of your clients. These important qualitative data should be integrated, however, with data that are as objective as possible, and sifted through a lens of critical thinking. The combination should provide the tools you need to conduct an assessment that will maximize the chances that your clients will achieve their goals.

Part II of this book, "Monitoring and Interpreting Client Progress," includes Chapters 5 through 7. In these chapters, we show you how to graph, analyze, and interpret your clients' progress. Chapter 5 discusses how to construct simple line graphs to visually represent client progress, and our companion website contains Microsoft Word templates you can download and use to create these graphs easily. In these graphs, notice that the horizontal axis represents the chronological progression of equal time periods (e.g., days, weeks), and the vertical axis represents numerical values of the outcome measure (e.g., number of times a behavior occurs). Each data point represents the intersection of a time period and a numerical value of the outcome measure (e.g., number of times a behavior occurs on a given day), and successive data points connected with lines give a picture of client changes over time and under different conditions (before, during, and after intervention). Throughout this book, for the most part, we present graphs in their final forms. In practice, however, you should graph outcome data regularly and analyze them as you go along, using this practice-based evidence to make decisions to effectively and efficiently help your clients achieve their goals.

In Chapter 6, we discuss how to visually analyze the type of graphs discussed in Chapter 5. We don't discount the usefulness of statistical analyses, at least in research, but we're skeptical about whether the benefits of most statistical analyses outweigh the costs in practice, and so for the most part we leave discussion of statistical analyses to others. Visual analysis, although not without limitations, enables you to answer the critical questions about ongoing, unfolding client change in a relatively simple straightforward way: Is your client changing? Is that change for the better or worse? Are the pace and amount of change sufficient?

In this chapter, we show you how to analyze your clients' progress in real time and use this practice-based evidence as you go along, making evidence-based practice decisions to help your clients in a dynamic process. Again, critical thinking is required to use all your data, including your graphs of client outcomes, to make appropriate decisions: Continue the intervention as is? Modify the intervention some around the edges? Throw it out and start over with another intervention altogether? Even if you are not aware of it, you make these decisions every time you see a client. This chapter provides the tools to make those decisions deliberately and with as little bias and confusion as possible.

In Chapter 7, we discuss different single-case designs that you'll find useful in practice, as well as how to interpret the results from these different designs. Single-case designs are a family of evaluation and research designs characterized by the systematic repeated measurement of a client's outcome(s) at regular, frequent, predesignated intervals under different conditions (e.g., before, during, and after intervention). Single-case designs let you monitor client progress, identify intervention effects, and more generally, learn when, why, how, and the extent to which client change occurs.

For example, in the simple A-B design, there is a pre-intervention baseline phase (A) during which an outcome is measured repeatedly in the absence of an intervention, followed by an intervention phase (B). You can use the baseline phase to confirm or disconfirm that a client problem actually exists, establish the extent of the problem, develop and explore hypotheses that might prove useful for intervention planning, and begin to build an alliance with your client. You can use the design itself to determine whether your client is changing over time, whether changes are for the better or worse, whether the pace of change is satisfactory, and whether the amount of change is sufficient. You can also use the design to determine the extent to which your intervention is related to client change, but not to determine the extent to which your intervention *was responsible for* client change. We discuss other designs in this chapter that allow you to do this.

Part III of this book, "Practical Methods for Measuring Client Progress," includes Chapters 8 through 12. In these chapters we discuss measurement issues that influence the quality of the information you and your client collect. Chapter 8 discusses how to select and develop measures for monitoring client progress that are practical, yet as free of error as realistically possible in practice. It also discusses how to develop an overall plan for measuring and monitoring client outcomes, and how to engage clients in the development and implementation of the measurement plan. Knowledge is produced by humans, and there's no doubt that we will always "see through a glass darkly." We see clients for only a short time and in unusual circumstances, and we will never have complete information. But the principles in this chapter will help you select and construct the best measures for collecting information, use the information appropriately, understand and weigh the weaknesses and strengths of your information, interpret the data you have about your clients, and integrate what you know to make the best decisions for and with your clients.

The topic of Chapter 9 is standardized scales. Appendix A contains examples of standardized scales, and Appendix B contains a current list of online and published resources for standardized scales. Standardized scales are important for constructing your understanding of what is happening with a client because usually the scales have been thoroughly tested, and they come with information that allows you to understand their strengths and limitations. In addition, you can usually compare your clients' scores on these measures to populations, such as individuals who have been diagnosed with specific disorders. These facts help you integrate the data you get from standardized scales with other types of data such as subjective impressions and qualitative data.

Standardized scales usually contain multiple statements, questions, or other types of items rated along some dimension (e.g., a 7-point scale ranging from "strongly disagree" to "strongly agree"), items that require the selection of one option from several available (e.g., multiple choice), or items that require some form of a "yes" or "no" response. Responses to these items are combined into an overall score to measure constructs such as depression, self-esteem, or interpersonal functioning. Rather than developing standardized scales yourself, you select them from the many standardized scales already available. There are far too many standardized scales to discuss them all in this chapter, but we do recommend and describe exemplars of standardized scales. However, the focus of this chapter is on helping you select and use standardized scales to measure and monitor client progress.

In Chapter 10 we discuss individualized rating scales (IRSs). All IRSs are constructed in a similar way: the client's problems are identified, and then a scale is developed to measure the degree, magnitude, or intensity of each problem. For example, you might ask a client to rate her degree of satisfaction with her marriage, job, spouse, or child using the following scale: (1) extremely dissatisfied, (2) very dissatisfied, (3) somewhat dissatisfied, (4) mixed, (5) somewhat satisfied, (6) very satisfied, (7) extremely satisfied. IRSs are easy to develop and use with a wide range of clients to identify and quantify individualized client problems and to monitor client progress in a way that is especially sensitive to the unique perceptions of individual clients. However, they must be developed with care to maximize accuracy and utility for helping your clients reach their goals. This chapter provides the information to help you develop IRSs that are as accurate as possible, while representing directly the client's specific concerns.

In Chapter 11 we discuss direct observation of client behavior—that is, observation by an outside observer. Behavior refers to what people *do* (e.g., expressions of criticism and contempt), in contrast to what people *have* (e.g., depression). It includes how people move and what they say, think, and feel. The range of behaviors social workers attempt to change is immense, for example, bullying, fighting, and other forms of physical aggression; exercising; and binge eating and purging. Others include self-injurious thoughts and behaviors; panic attacks; expressions of criticism, contempt, and praise; truancy; homework completion; property destruction; theft; excessive alcohol consumption; and illegal drug use. Observation of these behaviors provides a unique window into the client's concerns that cannot be obtained in any other way.

In Chapter 12 we discuss self-monitoring. Self-monitoring is the systematic observation and recording by a person of his or her own behavior or other experiences. In its most basic form, self-monitoring consists simply of a person's identifying an experience (e.g., activity, thought, feeling) and recording how frequently it occurs, how long it lasts, or its degree, magnitude, or intensity. Frequently, self-monitoring is expanded to include the collection of information about the conditions under which the experience occurs, and this is called a *client log* or *structured diary*. Client logs can help you and the client generate working hypotheses about the mechanisms causing and maintaining client problems, and develop and implement interventions based on these hypotheses. Again, this information provides a valuable perspective that you cannot get in any other way.

Finally, Chapter 13 wraps up by returning to some of the cases used in previous chapters.

## Companion Website

We created a companion website for this book that contains a rich source of materials that we think you will find useful for outcome-informed evidence-based practice: http://ormebook.com/. This website contains a core set of elements for each chapter:

- PowerPoint presentation.
- List of recent relevant published articles and books for additional reading.
- Chapter tables and figures in Microsoft Word so readers can open, explore, and use these documents for their own purposes (e.g., forms for behavioral observation and self-monitoring).
- Internet resources.

Also, this website contains material specific to the following chapters:

**Chapter 2:** Single-case design bibliography; bibliography of evidence-based practice texts; online resources for evidence-based practices.

**Chapter 5:** Microsoft Word 2007 templates for constructing single-case design graphs and instructions for using these templates.

**Chapter 9:** Excel program for scoring the Center for Epidemiological Studies Depression Scale (CES-D); Excel program for scoring the Walmyr Assessment Scales; Microsoft Word document that provides information for determining clinically significant change for the Walmyr Assessment Scales; Excel program for calculating reliable change; Microsoft Word document describing how to determine a clinical cutoff.

Finally, this will be a living website. We will update it and include new materials on a regular basis. Also, we hope that you will contribute ideas and materials for this website that you think useful and, accordingly, we will maintain a list of contributors to this website.

## Acknowledgements

Special thanks go to Martin Bloom and Joel Fischer for allowing us to use material from *Evaluating Practice: Guidelines for the Accountable Professional* (2009). Two better scholars, colleagues, and friends could not be found.

We also want to thank the authors of the measures presented in Appendix A for allowing us to reproduce their measures, and for kindly answering our questions about their measures: Jussara Bittencourt, Patricia Chamberlain, Mark J. Macgowan, A. John Rush, Joachim Stöber, and Jerome Yesavage.

We want to express appreciation to our dean, Karen Sowers, of the College of Social Work at the University of Tennessee, for her support of this and numerous other projects. We also want to thank the anonymous reviewers of this book for their valuable contributions. We especially want to thank Dr. Kathleen Jordan for her valuable suggestions, and the kind and thoughtful spirit in which they were offered.

Finally, we want to thank our students for all that we've learned from them, and for all of the things they do as social workers to make the world a better place. It has been and continues to be a real pleasure to be part of all that.

# 1

# Outcome-Informed Practice in Practice

## Two Case Examples

| Advancing Core Competencies in This Chapter | | | | |
|---|---|---|---|---|
| ✖ Professional Identity | ■ Ethical Practice | ✖ Critical Thinking | ✖ Diversity in Practice | ■ Human Rights & Justice |
| ✖ Research-Based Practice | ✖ Human Behavior | ■ Policy Practice | ✖ Practice Contexts | ✖ Engage, Assess, Intervene, Evaluate |

In this chapter, we illustrate outcome-informed evidence-based practice using two cases. These two cases illustrate the basic elements of outcome-informed practice. They also provide concrete real-world contexts for formally introducing the concepts of outcome-informed practice in Chapter 2, and we hope that these cases bring these concepts alive.

As you read the following two cases, you might make note of several issues:

- Describe the specific steps taken to enhance the social workers' understanding of their clients' problems and goals. You might recognize steps that you have used in your own work with clients, as well as some you have not used.
- Think about how the social workers' interventions in these cases might be different if they did not take those specific steps. In particular, look at how the social workers monitor their clients' problems during intervention. Do you see specific intervention decisions and actions based on that monitoring that would be possible without this monitoring? Do you think the clients' outcomes would be different, either for better or for worse?

# CASE 1: A FOSTER CHILD'S PROVOCATIVE BEHAVIOR

Sandra, a 16-year-old who was sexually abused for 7 years until she was placed in foster care 2 years ago, has lived with the Grant family for 6 months. The foster family has consulted an agency social worker because of Sandra's provocative behavior toward her foster father. (She was removed from her first foster home for this reason.) Sandra, her social worker, Gayle, and the foster parents, Diane (age 35) and Greg (age 34), meet in Gayle's office. The couple also has a 2-year-old daughter, Emily. Gayle serves as Sandra's case manager, organizing and managing Sandra's services from various providers, monitoring Sandra's progress in therapy in collaboration with the therapist, and acting as liaison with the court and Sandra's birth parents.

## Session 1

Gayle begins the assessment by asking the foster parents to explain what they mean by *provocative behavior*. Together, Diane and Greg produce this list of problematic behaviors:

- Sandra often walks around the house in just a bath towel or skimpy pajamas, even though she's been asked to wear a robe.
- Sandra kisses Greg on the mouth, sits on his lap, often when scantily dressed, and rubs against him unnecessarily.
- Sandra's tone of voice is often suggestive when she speaks to Greg. (The adults have a hard time describing what they mean by this, so Diane role-plays some examples.)
- Sandra makes racy jokes and comments to Greg.
- Sandra exhibits these behaviors both when Diane is present and when she is not.

When prompted by Gayle, both foster parents agree that Sandra's behavior in other ways is good. She is obedient, is loving and protective of Emily, and does her chores and homework without complaint. Both Diane and Greg have talked to Sandra about these problems before, but she claims not to understand what they mean. "That's just me," she says in the session. "I just sound flirty. I'm not trying to come on to Greg, for heaven's sake! He's my dad now!" She states that, as far as she is concerned, there are no problems between her and her foster parents.

Gayle asks all family members to state their goals. Both Diane and Greg say, "Sandra will just act like a regular member of the family—a daughter, not a sexpot." Sandra's goal is "to make this placement work because I want to stay here."

In the next step, Gayle seeks more details and an estimate of how serious these problems are before discussing intervention: How frequently do these events occur? When and where do they happen? How uncomfortable are Greg and Diane at these times? She asks them and Sandra to help her construct a picture of the previous week. To measure discomfort, she proposes a rating scale from 1 (not at all uncomfortable) to 3 (somewhat uncomfortable) to 5 (uncomfortable) to 7 (extremely uncomfortable) for each event, as shown in Table 1.1. They also define the labels used to describe the numbers on the rating scale according to Greg's

| Table 1.1 | Greg's Discomfort Rating Scale. | | | | | | |
|---|---|---|---|---|---|---|---|
| Greg's scale for rating his degree of discomfort | | | | | | | |
| 1 | 2 | 3 | 4 | 5 | 6 | 7 |
| Not at all uncomfortable | | Somewhat uncomfortable | | Uncomfortable | | Extremely uncomfortable |

experiences so they will all be in agreement. For example, Greg describes the most uncomfortable he has ever felt in such a situation, and that defines a 7 on the scale.

They then discuss the activities of each day of the previous week using a calendar to prod everyone's memory, noting when and where inappropriate events occurred and how uncomfortable Greg was. Sandra expresses surprise that the specific events described caused such extreme discomfort. She was just being herself—what is the problem?

Sandra's question leads to a discussion of the abuse she experienced in her early life and how it may have affected her attitudes about normal behavior between fathers and daughters. She seems genuinely confused about what is wrong with her behavior. It seems that it will be difficult to get past her confusion to change her behavior until she is able to understand the meaning of these behaviors to Greg and Diane. Therefore, Gayle suggests that the family collect data about the problem in the next week.

Gayle notes that today's discussion may actually change Sandra's (and her foster parents') behavior slightly, but suggests that Greg keep a daily diary of inappropriate behaviors and his level of discomfort in the next week. She explains that the purpose of gathering baseline data before intervention is to determine the extent of the problem, to develop and explore hypotheses that might prove useful for intervention planning, and to monitor how the behaviors change over time as they work on the problem to ensure that sufficient progress is being made. Figure 1.1 on page 4 is an example of a simple form for gathering data that Greg will use.

## Session 2

In the first week of observation (Figures 1.2 and 1.3 on page 4 and 5), Greg's completed chart shows between 1 and 3 uncomfortable interactions with Sandra each day; his highest level of discomfort ranges from 3 to 5 on most occasions and 7 only once (when a male neighbor was in the home with Greg and Sandra came in inappropriately dressed). Greg comments that there were fewer occasions than he expected and says he felt less uncomfortable this week because he realizes now that Sandra's past experiences probably have something to do with what's happening. Diane remains extremely uncomfortable (data not shown).

**Engage, Assess, Intervene, Evaluate**

***Practice Behavior Example:*** *Collect, organize, and interpret client data*

**Critical Thinking Question:** What are the advantages of carefully measuring the behaviors and feelings selected for intervention in Sandra's case instead of relying on Sandra, Diane, and Greg's informal impressions?

**Figure 1.1** • General Format for Client Log, Prepared for Greg's Use.

| Client: Greg Grant | | Day and date: Week 1 |
|---|---|---|
| Time | Client records important event/uncomfortable interactions with Sandra | Client records reactions to event/discomfort rating |
| | | |
| | | |
| | | |
| | | |
| | | |
| | | |
| | | |
| | | |
| | | |
| | | |
| | | |

**Figure 1.2** • Daily Number of Greg's Uncomfortable Interactions with Sandra (session 1).

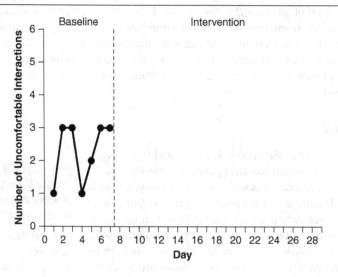

**Figure 1.3** • Greg's Highest Level of Discomfort in Interactions with Sandra (session 1).

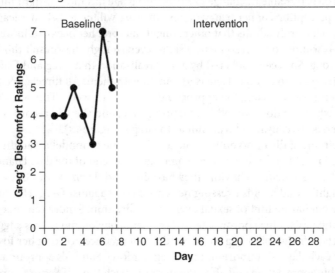

Based on the data, the group talks about what Sandra meant to convey on each occasion (affection, gratitude, playfulness), as opposed to Greg's perceptions. Sandra is shocked at Greg's accounts, offering benign explanations for each event. Only the occasion with the neighbor makes sense to her, because she was embarrassed herself. Gayle asks Greg and Diane to describe one other occasion, and as they talk, she writes down a very detailed account of Sandra's behavior (e.g., what Sandra was wearing, what she said and in what tone, how she touched Greg) and what bothered Greg about it (e.g., what he was thinking, how he felt). They spend about 15 minutes going over this event in very specific detail.

Based on this discussion, Gayle offers a tentative conceptualization of the case: As a result of long-standing sexual abuse by her birth-father, Sandra has not learned the kinds of normal behaviors that are typical between fathers and daughters. Although she is not attempting to seduce Greg, her behaviors suggest otherwise and embarrass her foster parents profoundly. Greg and Diane now have a better understanding of Sandra's experiences and sympathize with her, but they are unwilling to allow her to continue to behave this way in their home. Moreover, they fear that her behavior may extend to other males in other settings, and that the behavior could put her in danger. The foster parents' objectives (for this behavior to stop) and Sandra's objectives (to maintain the placement) are compatible, so Greg and Diane readily agree with this conceptualization, and Sandra reluctantly says, "Yea, maybe."

Gayle suggests two possible evidence-based interventions to reach both goals: cognitive behavior therapy (CBT) to help Sandra develop better understanding of what her behavior means to and how it affects other people (delivered by Sandra's therapist in consultation with Gayle) and behavioral skills training with Gayle and the family to teach Sandra how to behave more appropriately. Gayle is unable to find any evidence of uses of these interventions with this type of problem, but both interventions have been shown effective with many other types of problems.

The family agrees to a combination of the two interventions. Greg and Diane feel that Sandra will be better able to change her behavior if she has more insight into her motives and others' perceptions of her behavior, and they are willing to help her learn new behaviors. Sandra reluctantly admits that others might interpret her behavior in ways she doesn't intend and is willing to learn some new skills, even though she doesn't think she is doing anything wrong. She seems sobered by a new realization that Greg and Diane are serious about requiring her to change if she is to remain with them. All three agree to continue to monitor their progress using the approach they used last week. This week Greg also will tell Sandra when she does something inappropriate, and she will record what happened from her perspective, using a form similar to Greg's (Figure 1.1).

To begin the skills intervention, Gayle asks Diane to model a daughter's appropriate hug and kiss of her father when he comes in at the end of the day. Diane does so, and they describe the specific behaviors they have in mind: Diane kisses Greg on the cheek, hugs him lightly, and avoids pressing her entire body against Greg. Her tone of voice is affectionate but has no hint of sexual overture or flirtation. Sandra rehearses the behavior and the group praises the appropriate parts of her behavior and makes suggestions about other aspects. For the following week, Sandra will practice greeting her foster father appropriately each day. It's important that Greg reinforce Sandra's appropriate behavior by expressing his appreciation and affection in return each time. If Sandra's greeting is inappropriate, he will ignore her, in hopes of extinguishing the behavior.

## Session 3

The graphs shown in Figures 1.4 and 1.5 indicate that Sandra's inappropriate behaviors in the week after beginning the intervention have reduced, and Greg and Diane report feeling more comfortable. They say they have felt closer to Sandra and more spontaneous in interactions with her because they are less worried that she will embarrass them.

**Figure 1.4** • Daily Number of Greg's Uncomfortable Interactions with Sandra (session 2).

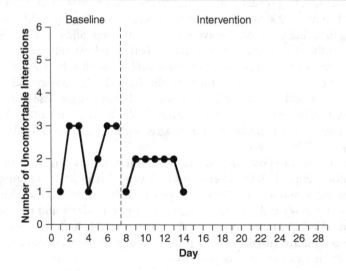

**Figure 1.5** • Greg's Highest Level of Discomfort in Interactions with Sandra (session 2).

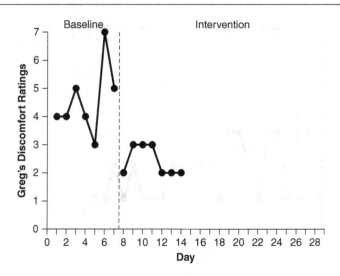

The group discusses several occasions that did make Greg feel uncomfortable in the previous week and how Sandra could have avoided that. Greg admits that maybe he was too touchy on one occasion because he was in a bad mood. They reenact that situation, and Sandra's behavior is perfect. Sandra beams and spontaneously hugs them both appropriately.

Diane asks if Sandra also has made changes in her behavior at school. "I've been thinking," she says. "I think I've been acting all-like-giggly and silly with the boys at school all the time." She reports that she has deliberately toned that down, but now the boys are ignoring her. "They used to tease me a lot and want to be around me, you know like in the halls and at lunch and whatever." She feels ignored now, especially since she doesn't have close female friends. "And if I'm not giggly and flirty, like how should I be? All serious and stuff? I totally don't know how to do that." Diane tentatively adds to her case conceptualization: Perhaps Sandra's past abuse have made it difficult for her to learn appropriate social skills in general? It rings true. The four of them then help Sandra practice friendly behavior to use with both boys and girls at school, including reflective listening and asking interested questions.

The family agrees to another week of monitoring, and Sandra also agrees to monitor her behavior at school and the responses of others. (Sandra will use a form similar to that shown in Figure 1.1, with columns for time and place, her actions, and other kids' responses. For the sake of simplicity and space, we do not show those data here.)

## Session 4

For the third week of observation, Figures 1.6 and 1.7 show continued improvement at home. Sandra says she feels more loved because Greg and Diane are not backing off from her. She also says she is doing better at being friendly at school without being so flirtatious

**Figure 1.6** • Daily Number of Greg's Uncomfortable Interactions with Sandra (session 3).

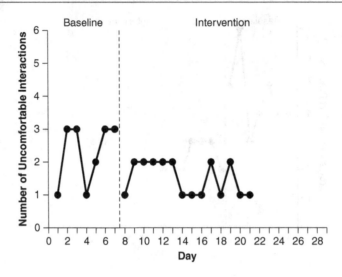

**Figure 1.7** • Greg's Highest Level of Discomfort in Interactions with Sandra (session 3).

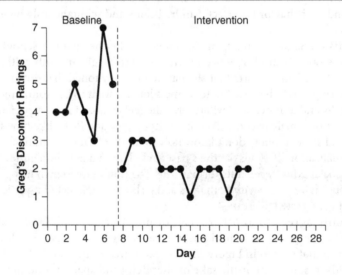

and she likes how people are responding. Now the girls talk to her, too, and she doesn't feel so ridiculous. Some of the boys actually talk to her, rather than just goofing around. She recounts one long conversation with a boy in her English class about a poem they both liked.

The family feels that they will soon be ready to terminate the intervention but would like to monitor for one more week, hoping to see a pattern of stability in their data.

## Session 5

The last week of observation indicates that the family has achieved its objectives, and everyone is satisfied with his or her progress. They review the data in Figures 1.8 and 1.9 and discuss the steps they have taken to make the changes. They agree to terminate, but Gayle will check in with the family monthly, as is customary for the agency, and they will discuss how things are going then.

**Figure 1.8** • Daily Number of Greg's Uncomfortable Interactions with Sandra (session 4).

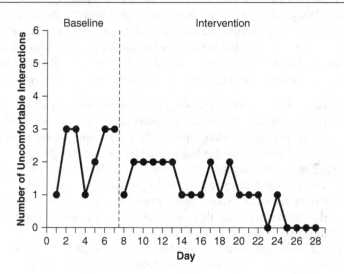

**Figure 1.9** • Greg's Highest Level of Discomfort in Interactions with Sandra (session 4).

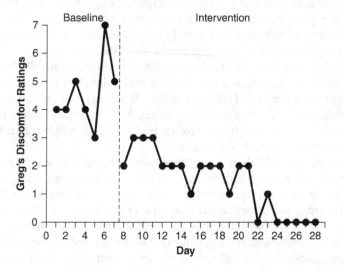

# CASE 2: A DEPRESSED UNIVERSITY STUDENT

## Session 1

Mark is a licensed clinical social worker (LCSW) who works in a university counseling center. His client is Dahlia, a 20-year-old Muslim junior from Saudi Arabia. (It is important to note that Dahlia originally requested a Muslim therapist, but none was available. Mark has some training and experience working with Muslim clients and feels comfortable doing so, so he was assigned and Dahlia agreed.)

Dahlia came to the center complaining of sadness, weepiness, insomnia, and trouble concentrating. Her grades have fallen from nearly all A's to C's this semester. This is of great concern to Dahlia, because she is a premed major, and she may not be accepted to medical school if she isn't able to improve her grades quickly. When asked what she thinks is going on, Dahlia says that she is afraid she has a terrible illness and is dying.

Mark probes for details, and they discuss her problem more concretely:

- Dahlia has had trouble getting to sleep and staying asleep for about 3 months. In the past week, she has experienced this every night, and she estimates she sleeps about 3 hours per night, waking up every hour or so and having trouble going back to sleep. Recently, she has begun napping during the day.
- She experiences difficulty studying every day, partly because she is exhausted and sleepy, and as a result did poorly on an important exam this week.
- She describes herself as "weepy" and reports that she finds herself crying at odd times. She did this every day this past week, including once when she had to leave class. She doesn't know why she was crying.
- She says that she feels worthless and bad, that she is letting down her parents who are sacrificing so much to send her to school, and that poor grades reflect badly on her family as well as the Muslim community.

The assessment process further reveals that Dahlia has few friends, though she is a member of a local mosque that is active on campus. She has always been an introvert and does not enjoy group activities, preferring to study when she is not in class, but she has become friendly with two American girls in her dorm. They eat dinner together nearly every evening and sometimes study together in one of their rooms.

Dahlia's family in Saudi Arabia has urged her by telephone to talk about her problems with her imam, but she is uncomfortable doing that. Her family is very religious and assures her that prayer and religious study will help her, but she is comfortable with Western medicine and feels it is more likely to help her. "My family is more religious than I am," she says, "and besides, I have a medical problem, not a religious one. Why would I talk to the imam about a medical problem?"

From the beginning, Mark suspects clinical depression, but he resists committing himself to that diagnosis. His research and experience tell him that many Muslims equate mental illness to physical illness, but it is possible that Dahlia does have a physical illness. Dahlia has not used the term *depression*, so he doesn't either. He asks Dahlia if she has had a physical exam lately to rule out possible physical causes. She confirms that she had an exam recently, with no clinical findings; the exam ruled out anemia and thyroid problems, two issues Mark was thinking about. Dahlia cannot recall any specific incident that precipitated her current feelings.

Mark administers the Quick Inventory of Depressive Symptomatology (QIDS; Rush et al., 2003) to Dahlia. This is a standardized scale that is reproduced in Appendix A. He chooses this measure because it is short (16 items, 5–10 minutes), easy to administer and interpret, and has excellent reliability and validity (topics we discuss in Chapter 8). Moreover, the symptom items on the measure seem especially pertinent in Dahlia's case. There are forms for both the client and the practitioner to complete. Mark refers to the website www.ids-qids.org for scoring and interpretation information and a copy of the measure, as well as a semistructured interview format. He has some concern about the lack of evidence of use of the measure with Muslims, but he decides to go ahead and use it with caution. Dahlia's English is flawless, and she shows no hesitation that might indicate poor understanding. Nevertheless, he will use the data with caution, as he understands that experiences of symptoms are embedded in culture.

The QIDS asks a series of questions about the respondent's feelings and behavior in the previous 7 days. Dahlia's score of 13 (out of 27) at this first session is categorized as "moderate depression." Mark scores Dahlia at 14 on his version after the session. Table 1.2 provides guidelines for interpreting QIDS scores, and we'll have more to say about this in Chapter 9.

Mark explains that the questionnaire she just completed, as well as her reports and his impressions, indicate that Dahlia is clinically depressed and confirms that she understands what this means. He is careful to refer to depression as an *illness*, since this is the way Dahlia refers to her problem. When asked why she thinks she has become depressed, Dahlia says she does not know, but Mark perceives that she is holding something back. "What has changed? What is different now?" Mark asks. Dahlia just shakes her head. "Nothing, really."

Aware that many Muslims find suicide so repugnant that they are reluctant to admit suicidal ideation, Mark asks Dahlia if she has wished God would let her die. She says yes, she has felt this way for over a month. "Sometimes I think about doing it myself," she says, eyes on her lap and so quietly that Mark almost cannot hear her, "but I would never do that."

Dahlia's treatment goals are to feel well again, to be able to study hard as she always has before, and to "feel at peace." They work to make the goals more specific and concrete so that they will have measurable criteria to define and evaluate Dahlia's progress and ultimate success:

- Dahlia gets a full night's sleep daily and awakens fully rested.
- Dahlia is able to concentrate and study productively for long hours as she did before.

**Table 1.2 Interpreting QIDS Scores.**

| QIDS interpretation | QIDS score |
| --- | --- |
| No depression | ≤5 |
| Mild depression | 6–10 |
| Moderate depression | 11–15 |
| Severe depression | 16–20 |
| Very severe depression | ≥21 |

- Dahlia no longer cries and feels sad every day.
- Dahlia feels good about herself and the work she is doing.
- Dahlia's score on the QIDS remains at 5 or below ("no depression").

Mark offers an early, incomplete case conceptualization: Dahlia's symptoms of sadness, crying, poor sleep, inability to concentrate, and negative self-image indicate that she is clinically depressed, but what is not clear, he tells her, is what is causing her depression. There is no family history, and there have been no recent losses. They will have to think and talk about that. Mark explains that research has shown two interventions to be effective with depression: CBT, a way of changing dysfunctional thoughts that lead to depression, and antidepressant medication. He has read the literature indicating that many Muslims find antidepressants to be the most acceptable option because of their view that depression is a sickness (http://ssrdqst.rfmh.org/cecc/index.php?q=node/25, retrieved February 21, 2010), so he wants to offer both options. He adds that some research has found CBT to be effective for depression with Muslims (Hodge, 2006).

Mark suggests that Dahlia might be a candidate for medication and suggests a referral to the psychiatrist in the student health center, as well as a week of baseline data collection about her sleep and study, since these are two major facets of her depression. Dahlia agrees and wants to see a psychiatrist immediately. She is also interested in CBT.

Before ending this first session, Mark and Dahlia sign a contract that she will call him before harming herself in any way, and he gives her his cell phone number. In addition, they make plans to monitor Dahlia's problems; she will record the number of hours she sleeps, aiming for 8 hours nightly, and how many hours she studies daily, aiming for at least 4. In addition, each night she will estimate how sad she feels on a scale from 1 (not at all sad) to 3 (a little sad) to 5 (quite sad) to 7 (as sad as she has ever felt), as shown in Table 1.3. Dahlia's objective is a 2 or below.

## Session 2

Dahlia completes the QIDS in the lobby before her appointment, and her score is 14, indicating no real change from last week. Mark will complete the QIDS after their session (see Figure 1.10, session 2). They go over her sadness, sleep, and studying data together, and Mark constructs graphs so it will be easy to monitor Dahlia's progress over time. In this case, we present only the completed graphs to conserve space, but remember that in session 2, Dahlia and Mark are working with only the first (baseline) 7 days of sleep and studying data (see Figures 1.11 and 1.12, days 1–7).

| Table 1.3 | Dahlia's Sadness Rating Scale. |

| Dahlia's scale for rating her degree of sadness | | | | | | |
| --- | --- | --- | --- | --- | --- | --- |
| 1 | 2 | 3 | 4 | 5 | 6 | 7 |
| Not at all sad | | A little sad | | Quite sad | | As sad as she has ever felt |

**Figure 1.10** • Dahlia (●) and Mark's (○) QIDS Scores.

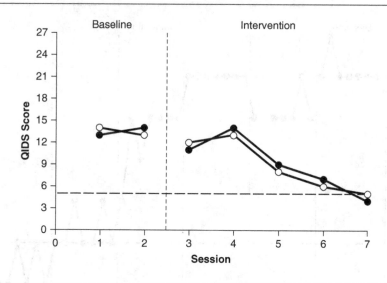

**Figure 1.11** • Daily Number of Hours Sleeping (●) and Studying (○).

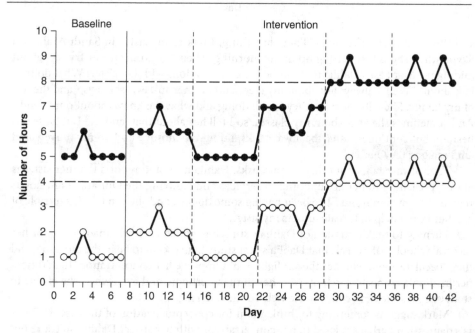

They discuss each of the items on the graph, beginning with Dahlia's sadness, which appears to be fairly stable at a high level. Nevertheless, she reports no suicidal urges or feelings in the past week. As for sleep, Mark notes that clearly Dahlia is not sleeping enough to function well. He asks about her sleep routine: what time she goes to bed, what she does right before sleep, and so on. "I usually study after dinner until about 11 or so,

**Figure 1.12** • Daily Ratings of Sadness.

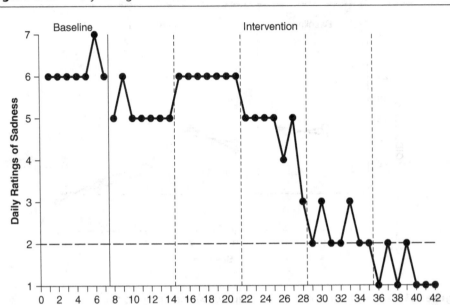

and then I shower," she says. "Then, last thing, I talk to my sister in Saudi Arabia on Skype when she is just getting up in the morning. Then I go to sleep—or try to—about midnight." Mark asks Dahlia to describe her conversations with her sister. What do they talk about? "Well, I always ask about my niece and brother-in-law," she says, "and the rest of my family. She tells me what they are all doing and what she knows about our friends. And sometimes she asks about my classes, so I tell her about that, and …" Dahlia seems hesitant but continues, "and she always asks did I go to mosque and do my prayers and am I reading the Qur'an."

"You always talk about that?" Mark asks. Dahlia nods and reports that her sister is always preaching to her about going to services and studying the Qur'an. "I am not as religious as my family, and I've been having some doubts, and she can tell. It's terrible of me, but I can't help it. It really upsets my sister."

Turning to the discussion of Dahlia's studying, which is clearly inadequate for her medical school goal, reveals that Dahlia's best study hours seem to be in the morning, and they speculate about whether the sunlight might improve her concentration. In addition, her insomnia seems to catch up with her in the afternoon, and even when she is able to study she says she can't concentrate well, so she often naps.

Mark suggests something to think about for conceptualization of the case: Is Dahlia's depression perhaps related to her conversations with her sister? Dahlia isn't sure but doesn't reject the idea. They also question whether the reason for her depression could be broader: Dahlia is changing, as anyone in a new culture and getting an education changes, but these changes contribute to feelings of loneliness and alienation from her family. They discuss her religious doubts a little more and how the doubts contribute to negative self-thoughts. Dahlia describes the negative thoughts and says she has them constantly.

Mark asks Dahlia whether she would like to start CBT or wait until her antidepressant medication begins to work. Dahlia says she would like to start CBT right away. She will continue graphing for another week. Mark suggests adding negative self-thoughts to her monitoring, and Dahlia will use the memo application on her new iPad to record. She will note any negative self-thoughts when she sits down to eat each day. They spend a few moments discussing how to identify and record her negative thoughts. (These data are not included here in the interest of space and simplicity.)

## Session 3

Going over her data (see Figure 1.10, session 3, and Figures 1.11 and 1.12, days 8–14), Mark and Dahlia note some improvements in sleep and studying, though Dahlia is far from her objectives. "I think I have hope now that I can be cured, though," she says. Mark asks about suicidal thoughts, and Dahlia says there have been none.

Dahlia has had some difficulty charting her negative thoughts (data not shown), because they are so frequent, but she says she realized this week as she was monitoring that they nearly always relate to her sister. Dahlia's sister always wants to talk about religion and what Dahlia is doing at the mosque and seems to disapprove of any nonreligious activities except classes. Dahlia tries to change the subject to talk about her 3-year-old niece but is not always successful. Mark asks Dahlia, "What do you think it is about talking to your sister that causes you to feel so bad about yourself?"

Reluctantly, Dahlia admits that she is questioning her Muslim beliefs, acculturating and enjoying Western culture, and even feeling more equal to men. She is horrified at her religious doubts, though, and is telling herself that she is terrible for questioning her beliefs, especially after communicating with her sister, who is very devout. "I've even been thinking of not wearing the hijab anymore, but I haven't told anyone. My family and some of the people at the mosque would be horrified."

Mark has done some research about effective methods for dealing with depression related to religious questions, finding that Islamic beliefs and principles can be effectively integrated with CBT, and that there is some research showing effectiveness for such a modified model (Hodge, 2006). Knowing his own bias against any type of religion and hoping to avoid letting that interfere in his work with Dahlia, Mark is determined to be especially vigilant in monitoring Dahlia's progress, and he also consults the literature about Arab culture (e.g., Al-Krenawi & Graham, 2000). He is aware that for many Muslims, faith is an integral part of every aspect of life (Graham, Bradshaw, & Trew, 2011) and that effective social work with these clients must include attention to their religious needs. Dahlia will monitor again, this time noting for each negative self-thought whether it is related to religion and how upsetting the thoughts are to her. Next week, they will examine how rational Dahlia's negative thoughts are and write some corrective thoughts that Dahlia can use to counter the negative ones. Mark and Dahlia also discuss her belief that it is wrong to question her religion and that doing so is dishonoring her family.

Mark asks Dahlia to pay attention to her interactions with her dorm friends this week, too, and to think about her feelings after each occasion. As part of his evolving case conceptualization, Mark wonders if social isolation and loneliness are helping to maintain Dahlia's depression, as she feels alienated from her family and her culture. He suggests that she has moved away from the interaction and reinforcement of her old life but has not yet replaced those things in her new life. Dahlia agrees to think about that.

## Session 4

Graphs show Dahlia's depression symptoms to be worse in the past week, especially sadness and difficulty getting to sleep (see Figure 1.10, session 4, and Figures 1.11 and 1.12, days 15–21), and she admits to Mark that she has thought about dying. She has not considered suicide, however. She quit monitoring her negative self-thoughts early in the week because she said they happened "all the time." She has had no interactions with her dorm friends this past week because school has not been in session and both are out of town. She also did not go to mosque this week. "I had a fight with my sister on the phone about religion—she scolded me for not attending services—and we haven't talked or emailed since." In addition, Dahlia has not managed to study enough, although she feels that her concentration might be better. Could it be the medication? Mark agrees that it's possible.

Mark asks whether she has felt lonely this week, with no conversations with her sister and her friends gone, and she says "yes." He suggests that they modify her intervention to address her isolation. They discuss ways she can increase her social interactions, including participating in her mosque's women's groups and accepting her dorm friends' invitations to do volunteer work with them at a local homeless shelter. Dahlia admits that she especially likes the latter idea because one religious belief she does not question is the admonition to help others. On the other hand, she says she feels somewhat uncomfortable in the women's groups at her mosque because most of the women there are very conservative. Dahlia will keep monitoring the other items and try volunteering at least once this week.

## Session 5

Dahlia comes to her session all smiles, reporting major improvements in her symptoms (see Figure 1.10, session 5, and Figures 1.11 and 1.12, days 22–28). She has volunteered twice this week, enjoying the first time so much that she has signed up to do it three times a week. She reports enjoying the interaction there and feeling very in touch with God through the experience. "I am thinking about which parts of my religion are meaningful to me and which are not," she says. "I have not talked to my sister about this yet, but I will eventually."

Dahlia also suggests that she quit taking her antidepressants, feeling that she has solved her own problems and doesn't need them now. Mark cautions that they do not know what role the antidepressants have played in her new feelings of wellness, and points out that he and Dahlia would work closely with her psychiatrist on this question in any case. He suggests that Dahlia continue the medication until she feels that she has satisfactorily resolved her issues with her sister, allow her mood to stabilize for a while, and then talk with her psychiatrist about gradually discontinuing the medication. She agrees.

Is one reason Dahlia feels better that she is enjoying time with other people? Dahlia thinks Mark might be right. "I look forward to having dinner with my friends at the dorm most evenings, and I really enjoy volunteering

**Professional Identity**

***Practice Behavior Example:*** *Advocate for client access to the services of social work*

**Critical Thinking Question:** What are the advantages of monitoring Dahlia's progress at regular, frequent, predesignated intervals instead of waiting until termination to determine her progress?

with them." She and her sister are talking a few times a week now, but carefully staying away from the topic of religion.

Mark tells Dahlia about a new support group for students who are struggling with spiritual and religious issues. Several members of the group (including one Jewish boy and one Christian girl) are also questioning their beliefs and having feelings similar to Dahlia's. Perhaps they can be helpful to one another. Participation in the group also can provide another social outlet for Dahlia. Dahlia is not certain but agrees to think about it and continues monitoring.

**Research-Based Practice**

***Practice Behavior Example:*** *Use practice experience to inform scientific inquiry*

**Critical Thinking Question:** What are the advantages of modifying the interventions for Sandra and Dahlia based on carefully measuring and monitoring progress in these two cases, instead of just assuming that evidence-based interventions will be effective?

## Session 6

Dahlia arrives for her session without her hijab and smiling broadly. Her graphs show that she is doing well, still volunteering, studying hard, and pulling her grades back up to A's (see Figure 1.10, session 6, and Figures 1.11 and 1.12, days 29–35). She feels certain that she is "well now," but has decided she is not ready to discontinue psychotherapy. She also has decided to join the support group Mark mentioned to her.

## Session 7

Dahlia arrives feeling well and happy, as shown by her graphs (see Figure 1.10, session 7, and Figures 1.11 and 1.12, days 36–42). She has joined the support group and attended one meeting. She enjoyed the meeting and feels that it will be a good resource for her in learning to deal with her family. She was surprised to see another young Muslim woman at the group, and they have had lunch together once since that time and seem to have much in common. She takes a deep breath and tells Mark that she thinks she is ready to discontinue therapy, as long as she can call him if she becomes depressed again. "I think I will continue taking the medication for a few months, though." Together, Mark and Dahlia review Dahlia's charts, discussing the progress she has made. Dahlia says she might continue monitoring her sleep and studying hours for a while, "just to be sure."

# CONCLUSIONS

Each of these cases exemplifies outcome-informed evidence-based practice. In both, the practitioners follow the steps of evidence-based practice, but clearly it is the clients' progress toward their goals and objectives that drive decision-making and actions at each step—not a commitment to the specific intervention or faith that the methods will work. It should be clear that this approach is possible only when you carefully measure and monitor the client's outcomes consistently, frequently, and systematically. Chapter 2 will refer back to these cases as we explain the terminology and important aspects of outcome-informed practice.

## PRACTICE TEST

**PRACTICE TEST** The following questions will test your knowledge of the content found within this chapter and help you prepare for the licensing exam by applying chapter content to practice. For more questions styled like the licensing exam, visit **MySocialWorkLab.com**

1. Which of the following is illustrated by Sandra's case:
   a. Client problems should be defined after intervention begins
   b. Qualitative information is not important
   c. Client progress should be monitored during, but not before intervention
   d. Measurable criteria should be used to define and evaluate client success

2. It is clear in Dahlia's case that she improved
   a. Because of antidepressant medication
   b. Because of CBT
   c. Over the course of intervention
   d. Because of participation in a support group

3. Which of the following is the most important reason a social worker should monitor a client's progress:
   a. Demonstrate the effectiveness of an intervention
   b. Ensure that the client's goals are achieved
   c. Provide evidence to funding sources
   d. Develop knowledge for use with future clients

4. Evidence-based interventions
   a. Do not guarantee client success
   b. Guarantee client success when the evidence is strong
   c. Guarantee client success when implemented properly
   d. Guarantee client success when implemented by trained social workers

5. A social worker is working with an adult, Adam, who was sexually abused as an adolescent. Adam blames himself for the abuse and is angry at himself. In collaboration with Adam, the social worker selects an evidence-based intervention that he thinks will help Adam. How could you measure and monitor Adam's progress?

6. A social worker is working with Adam, the client described in the previous question. What kind of information would make you change the evidence-based intervention implemented by the social worker?

## SUCCEED WITH

Visit **MySocialWorkLab** for more licensing exam test questions, and to access case studies, videos, and much more.

# 2

# Introduction to Outcome-Informed Practice

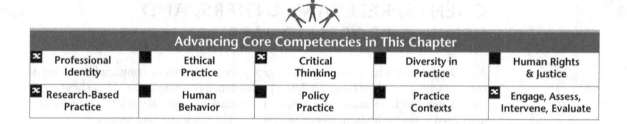

| Advancing Core Competencies in This Chapter | | | | |
|---|---|---|---|---|
| Professional Identity | Ethical Practice | Critical Thinking | Diversity in Practice | Human Rights & Justice |
| Research-Based Practice | Human Behavior | Policy Practice | Practice Contexts | Engage, Assess, Intervene, Evaluate |

In Chapter 1, we provided case examples of our vision of how outcome-informed practice works. In this chapter, we return to those examples to provide a basic introduction to outcome-informed practice.

## BASIC CONCEPTS OF OUTCOME-INFORMED PRACTICE

Outcome-informed practice is practice in which you (1) *measure* your client's outcomes at regular, frequent, predesignated intervals, in a way that is sensitive to and respectful of the client; (2) *monitor* those outcomes to determine if your client is making satisfactory progress; and (3) *modify* your intervention plan as needed. These are the key ingredients in outcome-informed practice as illustrated in Figure 2.1. Now, let's go into a little more detail and discuss the basic concepts of outcome-informed practice illustrated in the case examples presented in Chapter 1.

**Figure 2.1** • Key Ingredients in Outcome-Informed Practice.

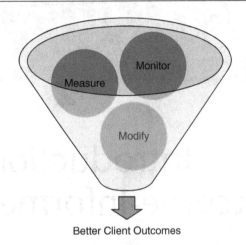

Better Client Outcomes

# CLIENTS, RELEVANT OTHERS, AND HELPING PROFESSIONALS

A *client* is an individual, couple, family, group, organization, or community seeking assistance with a problem from a helping professional. Sometimes we call a client a *case*. Clients also may be referred to as *patients* in medical and psychiatric settings or *residents* in assisted living facilities, independent living facilities, and nursing homes.

Typically, clients are part of an interrelated network of people—a system, as are we all. Often this network is important to the effective delivery of services, for example Sandra and her foster parents. We refer to people who are important to a client's life or well-being as *relevant others* or sometimes *significant others*. Borrowing from Bloom et al., where appropriate we refer to *client systems* to call attention to clients as part of the many systems in which they live.

*Helping professionals* include social workers, psychologists, psychiatrists, counselors, nurses, physical and occupational therapists, and other allied health care or social service professionals. The focus of this book is on social workers who provide direct services to clients, not only in clinical settings but in a broad array of settings such as schools, health care, social service agencies, and residential facilities.

## Client Problems and Outcomes

Outcome-informed practice begins with assessment, discussed in detail in Chapter 4. The first part of assessment, of course, involves identifying the client's problems. A client *problem*, as we use this term, is a specific situation, condition, or concern that needs to be addressed in order to achieve a desired goal. Problems usually include difficulties or deficiencies to be remediated or prevented. For example, a client might be depressed and seek help to eliminate depression. In other cases, a client may not identify a problem as such but may open the conversation with a goal, such as "I want to have more friends," indicating a desire to enhance assets or strengths. Generally, it is quite feasible to design and implement appropriate interventions directly from such goals without re-framing them as problems, but often detailed discussion will lead to the articulation of specific problems.

An outcome is the status of a client's problem along some dimension, such as fre-quency (e.g., Sandra's inappropriate behaviors) or severity (e.g., Dahlia's depression symptoms as measured by the QIDS [Quick Inventory of Depressive Symptomatology]). It can be the status of a client's problem before, during, or after intervention. Sometimes others use *outcome* to mean the final status of a client's problem after intervention, but in this book we use it to refer to the status of a problem at any time.

## Selecting Client Goals and Defining Objectives

As the famous and erudite baseball player/philosopher Yogi Berra said, "If you don't know where you're going, you might wind up someplace else." You and your client need a goal to know where you're going and when you've arrived so you won't need to con-stantly ask "Are we there yet?"

A client's progress is judged against a *goal*, the desired outcome upon comple-tion of intervention. For example, a client's goal might be to change behavior, as with Sandra, or to return to functionality, as with Dahlia. Goals should be tailored to the unique circumstances and needs of each client, and they should indicate change in real-world functioning or quality of life that is sufficient and meaningful to the cli-ent, relevant others, and/or society at large. As Huff observed in his wonderful book entitled *How to Lie with Statistics* (1954, p. 58), "a difference is a difference only if it makes a difference." Even if improvement occurs over time in a client's problem, you can't necessarily conclude that the change is sufficient or meaningful. Of course, this is, or already should be, a routine part of social work practice, and it isn't unique to outcome-informed practice (Garvin, 2009).

Goals are usually relatively abstract statements that provide only general guid-ance in evaluating client progress. For example, Sandra's goal is to stay with her foster parents, and her foster parents' goals are to feel more comfortable around her. *Objec-tives* are more specific, concrete statements along with measurable criteria that can be used to define and evaluate client success. For example, Sandra and her foster parents' objectives might be to re-duce the specific problematic behaviors that are endan-gering her placement to near zero.

Often it is also helpful to specify intermediate goals or objectives, that is, goals or objectives that are achieved before the ultimate ones. For example, Dahlia's first ultimate goal is to feel well again, so we might set intermediate goals of feeling well enough within three weeks to study more each day and to increase her amount of sleep each night. (Intermediate objec-tives might specify the number of hours of sleep and study-ing.) Intermediate goals and objectives provide benchmarks

**Engage, Assess, Intervene, Evaluate**

***Practice Behavior Example:*** *Develop mutually agreed-on intervention goals and objectives*

**Critical Thinking Question:** What problems and associated goals and objectives might be appropriate in working with a 13-year-old gay student who reports being bullied at school?

that can be useful for demonstrating to a client that although the ultimate goal has not been reached, he or she is making definite progress toward that goal. Goals and objectives are discussed in more detail in Chapter 4.

## Measuring Client Outcomes

*Outcome measures* are tools for measuring the status of clients' problems along various dimensions. For example, we might use a standardized scale to measure severity of depression, so the numerical score serves as an indicator of the severity of the depression. The *measurement plan* is the overall strategy used to measure the status of each problem. A good measurement plan starts with the selection or development of reliable, valid, and sensitive (yet practical and efficient) outcome measures from among different types of measurement methods and measurement instruments. For example, Mark chooses two methods (standardized scales and individualized rating scales) and a specific measure (the QIDS) to work with Dahlia. A good measurement plan also specifies how to obtain the information (e.g., paper versions of the QIDS and computer recording of Dahlia's sadness and studying); who will provide the information (e.g., Dahlia for most data, augmented by Mark's completion of the therapist version of the QIDS); and where (e.g., at treatment sessions for the QIDS and in her dorm for Dahlia's self-report data) and how often (daily and weekly) the information should be collected. Everything is planned so that nothing is forgotten or left to chance.

## Monitoring Client Progress

*Progress monitoring* is the process of systematically using relevant outcome measures to provide immediate feedback about client progress. It begins before intervention as part of assessment whenever practical, continues during intervention, and may continue after intervention concludes with follow-up data.

Progress monitoring is something that social workers and other helping professionals already do—in a way we are just arguing for doing it more systematically and collecting higher-quality outcome data, for example by using more reliable and valid outcome measures. Progress monitoring lets you know right away if your client is making satisfactory progress, so if he or she is off track, you can do something about it sooner, rather than later. For example, we hope weekly monitoring of Sandra's behavior and her foster parents' discomfort with her behavior will prevent a crisis and her move to a new foster home. More generally, in contrast to pretest and posttest outcome measurement, progress monitoring makes it easier to learn how, why, and when change occurs, not just whether change has occurred after the intervention concludes. Measure early and measure often—that's our advice.

We want to clearly distinguish between evaluation and progress monitoring. The term *evaluation* means systematic investigation of the value, quality, or importance of something or someone in relationship to a set of standards. Although there are many kinds of evaluation, often

**Engage, Assess, Intervene, Evaluate**

*Practice Behavior Example:* Collect, organize, and interpret client data

**Critical Thinking Question:** What methods could you use to measure and monitor progress of a 13-year-old gay student who reports being bullied at school, and how could you engage this client in the development of this measurement plan?

the term is used to refer to a process at the conclusion of a case or program: Did the client achieve his or her goals? Outcome-informed practice stresses monitoring progress throughout intervention in order to make adjustments when they are needed, a process sometimes referred to as *formative evaluation*.

## Managing Client Outcomes

There is one reason for measuring and monitoring client outcomes: you can use this feedback to modify the intervention plan along the way, if needed, to improve the quality of the intervention and the client's outcomes. This is referred to as *outcomes management*. Again, in a way, this is something that social workers and other helping professionals do already; we are just arguing for doing it more systematically by adding feedback based on high-quality, yet practical and efficient, outcome measures.

This process is analogous to cooking a sauce. We begin by selecting the freshest high-quality ingredients and a proven recipe (evidence-based practices), and then we taste the sauce continuously (measure the outcomes). Perhaps it needs a bit more tanginess (doesn't achieve our goal), so we add lemon juice (adjust the intervention). Then we continue tasting it (monitoring outcomes) to be sure that it tastes the way we prefer (is making progress toward the goal) by adding salt or thickening it at times. In some cases, we may have to throw out the sauce and start over, as you may completely change interventions when you see that you are on the wrong track altogether.

Just as we do when cooking a sauce, you use the real-time feedback provided by outcome monitoring to continuously guide decision-making about whether to continue, change, or end interventions. This feedback gives you a road map to guide you and your client in your journey toward accomplishing the client's goals. The process will help you accomplish the client's goals in a more effective, timely, and efficient way. For example, Dahlia's data on depression symptoms might suggest in a few short weeks the need for another therapeutic intervention or even another antidepressant. In response to a cumulative pattern of outcomes suggesting deterioration (because drawing a conclusion with a single data point is more prone to error), you might examine whether you and your client are adhering to the treatment plan consistently—perhaps Sandra is inconsistent with her new behaviors or Greg is inconsistent with his praise and affection. Maybe you need to try a different intervention—Dahlia may decide that the antidepressant is all she wants right now. You may even return to the assessment and case formulation stage—perhaps Dahlia's depression symptoms are not due to dysfunctional thinking at all but due to something else entirely. How much better is it to know this in a short amount of time, rather than after months have passed and her grades have been irreparably damaged, or even after she begins seriously contemplating suicide?

## Ensuring Intervention Fidelity

An *intervention* is a specific planned action by a helping professional that is designed to achieve a goal, prevent an undesirable outcome, or otherwise bring about beneficial change in a targeted client. Usually interventions are referred to as *treatments* when they are designed to relieve a pathological or otherwise undesirable condition. Interventions should be linked logically and clearly to a client's problems and goals—they should be relevant to the problem at hand, so, for example, Mark focuses on Dahlia's depression symptoms and does not implement a treatment designed to enhance her self-esteem. (In Chapter 4, we will discuss how you should be able to use your knowledge of human behavior and change to explain exactly how you expect an intervention to reach the goals; this is part of case conceptualization.)

Evidence-based practice involves not only making sure you select interventions that are most likely to lead to client success but also making sure that these interventions are implemented accurately. What if your client is not making satisfactory progress? One thing to consider when this happens is whether the intervention has been delivered exactly as designed and planned, that is, whether the intervention is being delivered with fidelity. You can't assume an intervention to be ineffective unless you know that the intervention with all critical features has been implemented as planned. Of course you might not be alerted to the fact that your intervention is not being implemented faithfully if you do not monitor the client's outcomes continuously. Consider a simple example: If Dahlia does not see a diminution in her depressive symptoms after several weeks on the antidepressant, her psychiatrist might want to clarify that she is taking the medication correctly and in the right dosage, before moving to a different medication.

Conversely, if a client is making satisfactory progress, but you haven't implemented the intervention with fidelity, you can't attribute this happy state of affairs to the intervention and, if problems reemerge later, you might inadvertently reinstitute an ineffective intervention. For example, if Greg and Diane continue to be uncomfortable with Sandra, is that because they have not been using the new behaviors as instructed, or could it be because their discomfort actually originates from something other than Sandra's behavior? We won't know if we don't assess the fidelity of the intervention.

Therefore, to the extent possible and practical, it is a good idea to systematically and continually document and track the extent to which you are implementing your intervention as designed and planned. This is known as *intervention monitoring*, and it is used to ensure the fidelity of an intervention, including the extent to which the client is following the prescribed intervention regimen, which is commonly referred to as *intervention adherence*. The process of determining the extent to which an intervention was implemented with fidelity is referred to as an *implementation assessment*; it is used to improve the quality of care provided to clients.

Practically speaking, intervention monitoring is more commonly seen in research, and we have not seen good guidelines that practitioners can use for this purpose. One exception to this generality is Parent–Child Interaction Therapy (PCIT; Eyberg, 2010), a highly standardized, well-researched intervention for parents and their young children with behavior problems. The PCIT package includes a form with a checklist indicating use of the most important elements of the intervention protocol to be completed by the therapist after each session. Other treatment manuals also might provide such checklists, but in the absence of such standardized forms, practitioners should review their work frequently to be sure that the intended intervention is indeed being used as intended.

## Determining Intervention Effects

Sometimes it is not enough to know simply that a client's goals were achieved. At times you will also want to know if it was the intervention or something else that caused the change. For example, as mentioned earlier, if something other than the intervention caused the observed client change, it might not have lasting effects or, if the problem re-emerges later, you might inadvertently reinstitute an ineffective intervention. For example, if Dahlia's depression lifts, is it because of the antidepressant or the CBT (cognitive behavior therapy)? This may be important if Dahlia later decides to discontinue one of the two interventions.

In these situations, if ethical and practical, try to find out what portion of the change in client outcomes, if any, can be attributed uniquely to the intervention rather than to other influences; that is, try to determine the *intervention effect*. This is known as an *outcome evaluation*, and it includes identification of unintended intervention effects (side effects), including harmful, undesired, inadvertent intervention effects (adverse effects). To do this, you need evaluation designs that go beyond collection of outcome data during baseline and intervention. (We'll have more to say about this in Chapter 7.)

## SUMMING UP

When you finish with your intervention, as part of the termination process, you will sum up the extent to which the intervention goals have been achieved. For example, upon completion of the intervention, are the scores of Sandra's foster parents on the individualized measure of discomfort at or below the desired level? In the program evaluation literature this is referred to as a *summative evaluation*. However, outcome-informed practice is more than a judgment about ultimate success or failure of efforts to help the client achieve his or her goals. More importantly, it is used to inform and guide your unfolding practice efforts. Outcome-informed practice is first and foremost a process, not a product.

The basic elements of outcome-informed practice as we see it are: Measure and monitor client outcomes in a relatively objective yet practical way that is tailored to the particular circumstances of each client, and use this *practice-based evidence* in concert with evidence-based practice to modify your intervention plan as needed in order to improve the quality and outcomes of your interventions. It can, and we argue should, be an approach to practice used by all frontline helping professionals in partnership with clients.

## INTERVENTION RESEARCH AND OUTCOME-INFORMED PRACTICE

How is outcome-informed practice different from the intervention research on which much of evidence-based practice is based? Outcome-informed practice does draw on the tools, logic, and language of intervention research (e.g., Fraser, Richman, Galinsky, & Day, 2009; Nezu & Nezu, 2008):

- Reliable, valid, and sensitive measures are used systematically to quantify and draw conclusions about client outcomes.
- Attention is given to ensuring that the intervention is delivered appropriately, including making sure that the client is following the prescribed intervention regimen, although typically these procedures are much more intensive and formalized in intervention research.
- Adverse and other side-effects are of concern.

- Final conclusions are drawn about the extent to which an intervention has had the desired effect, including concern regarding whether a change in a client's real-world functioning or quality of life that is sufficient or meaningful to the client, relevant others, and/or society at large has occurred. More emphasis is placed on the latter concern in outcome-informed practice.

However, although outcome-informed practice borrows from intervention research, it is different from it in important ways. First and foremost, the primary purpose of outcome-informed practice with a client is to improve the well-being of *that particular client*. We are talking about a way to practice, not about research. Consequently, outcome-informed practice begins with and is tailored to the emerging problems, goals, needs, characteristics, and circumstances of each particular client without regard to the extent to which results will generalize to other clients. Outcomes are selected for their importance to each specific client, not for theoretical reasons, although theory is important to the process of conceptualizing a case and selecting an intervention. Information about the role of an intervention in causing observed change is important only insofar as it is useful in helping the client being served. Designs and measurement plans are tailored to specific clients, and interventions are changed midstream, if need be, in response to client progress, which is continually monitored and tracked over time using a systematic stream of outcome data. This is not to say that outcome-informed practice cannot inform practice with future clients or add to our knowledge about interventions, because it can (Barkham, Hardy, & Mellor-Clark, 2010). And it's not to say that these issues are unimportant, because they are. These are just not the primary reasons for outcome-informed practice.

Intervention research, on the other hand, usually is initiated to inform practice for future clients through developing generalized causal knowledge about interventions that will contribute to a scientific body of knowledge through professional publications and presentations. Consequently, benefits to participants are of secondary importance; intervention research begins with and flows from an interest in developing generalized causal knowledge about the intervention. Designs and measures are not tailored to individual participants; in fact, great care is taken to ensure that interventions are delivered in the same way to all participants regardless of individual needs or circumstances. Interventions are not changed over time in response to client progress. Certainly, researchers and research participants don't work together to understand and interpret client outcomes. Because of the focus on the intervention rather than the client, intervention research often is conducted on homogenous samples quite dissimilar in important ways to the clients you may see in practice. Moreover, requirements for informed consent for conducting research differ from those for informed consent for conducting treatment (Del Carmen & Joffe, 2005; Reamer, 2009).

# SINGLE-CASE DESIGNS

Intervention research typically involves the collection and aggregation of data across people or cases for the purpose of discovering general principles or theories that characterize the average person or case, for example comparison of the mean level of a relevant outcome variable in experimental and control groups in randomized clinical trials (Solomon, Cavanaugh, & Draine, 2009). This type of research, known as *nomothetic research*, studies groups of people or cases for the purpose of examining how an intervention works in general. The focus is on outcomes at the group level with the "average" person or case.

Idiographic research, in contrast, focuses on the description and understanding of the unique and lawful characteristics, qualities, and responses of a particular person or case. This type of research addresses the question of how an intervention works with a particular person or case. There is a relatively large body of intervention research in which outcomes are measured for individual cases at regular, frequent, and predesignated intervals under different conditions (such as baseline and intervention) in order to monitor client progress, identify intervention effects, and more generally, learn if, when, why, and how client change occurs. This body of intervention research uses a family of research and evaluation designs known as single-case designs. These designs are also known as *single-system designs*, *N = 1 designs*, or sometimes *time series* or *interrupted time series designs* (e.g., Bloom et al., 2009; Kazdin, 2011). We use the conventional term *single-case design* in this book, although with the recognition that a case can be an individual, couple, family, group, organization, or even community. Outcome-informed practice draws heavily on the tools, logic, and language of this type of intervention research, and the cases in Chapter 1 and throughout this book illustrate this approach.

Often single-case designs are used to develop generalized causal knowledge that contributes to scientific knowledge through professional publications and presentations. Other times single-case designs are used with a specific client to improve the well-being of that particular client. Oftentimes there is considerable overlap in these two uses of single-case designs. We have published a bibliography of published single-case design articles on our companion website, and you can also see an annotated bibliography in Janosky, Leininger, Hoerger, and Libkuman (2009). In this book, we focus on using single-case designs to benefit each particular client being served in the tradition of Bloom et al. (2009), Di Noia and Tripodi (2008), Thyer and Myers (2007), and others.

## Research-Based Practice

***Practice Behavior Example:*** *Use research evidence to inform practice*

**Critical Thinking Question:** What kinds of research evidence could you use to develop an intervention for a 13-year-old gay student who reports being bullied at school, and what practice-based evidence could you use to determine this client's progress?

# CONCLUSIONS

This chapter has presented definitions and explanations of the terminology you will see in this book, as well as the processes you observed in the two cases presented in Chapter 1. Remember that you can always turn to the glossary or the companion website for more information about these terms.

**PRACTICE TEST** The following questions will test your knowledge of the content found within this chapter and help you prepare for the licensing exam by applying chapter content to practice. For more questions styled like the licensing exam, visit **MySocialWorkLab.com**

1. A social worker and her client mutually agree that the client needs to reduce her anxiety, and this is what they hope to achieve at the completion of their work together. Anxiety reduction is an example of a/an

   **a.** Objective

   **b.** Goal

   **c.** Outcome measure

   **d.** Measurement method

2. A social worker is working with an adolescent girl who binges and purges. The objective is to eliminate these behaviors. The main reason the social worker should measure and monitor these outcomes at regular, frequent, predesignated intervals is to

   **a.** Determine whether the intervention is effective

   **b.** Research the effectiveness of the intervention

   **c.** Demonstrate accountability to funding sources

   **d.** Ensure that the client's goals are achieved

3. Which of the following is a characteristic of single-case designs:

   **a.** Outcomes are measured for individual cases at regular, frequent, predesignated intervals under different conditions

   **b.** Intervention effects are more important than outcomes

   **c.** Groups of people are studied for the purpose of discovering general principles or laws that characterize the average person

   **d.** Intervention effects are examined with a particular person or case

4. Outcome-informed practice is like intervention research in which of the following ways:

   **a.** Improvement in the well-being of each particular client is of paramount concern

   **b.** Generalization of intervention effects across clients is of paramount concern

   **c.** Reliable, valid, and sensitive outcome measures are used

   **d.** Designs and measurement plans are tailored to specific clients

5. A social worker meets with a 4-year-old Hispanic boy, Chico, and his father. The boy was referred to the social worker because of "behavioral problems" at preschool. What would the social worker need to know before developing a plan to measure and monitor Chico's progress?

6. A social worker is working with Chico, the client described in question 5. The social worker, in collaboration with Chico's father and teachers, selects an evidence-based intervention for this problem. After a few weeks of intervention, there is no improvement in Chico's behavioral problems. Before trying another intervention, what should the social worker consider?

## SUCCEED WITH

Visit **MySocialWorkLab** for more licensing exam test questions, and to access case studies, videos, and much more.

**3**

# Why Measure, Monitor, and Modify?

| Advancing Core Competencies in This Chapter | | | | |
|---|---|---|---|---|
| ☒ Professional Identity | ☒ Ethical Practice | ☒ Critical Thinking | ☒ Diversity in Practice | ◼ Human Rights & Justice |
| ☒ Research-Based Practice | ◼ Human Behavior | ◼ Policy Practice | ☒ Practice Contexts | ☒ Engage, Assess, Intervene, Evaluate |

**E**ve is a 32-year-old HIV-positive client in a hospital outpatient clinic. She is referred to Gordon, a social worker, because of nonadherence to her retroviral medication regimen. Imperfect adherence to retroviral medication is a critical problem; it increases an individual's viral load, leads to drug resistance, and makes it more likely that a patient will infect others with HIV; therefore, the medication regimen may be discontinued if a patient cannot achieve near-perfect adherence to it (Cox, 2009).

Eve lives with a partner of 7 years (Joe) and their 7-year-old daughter (Susan), who are not HIV positive. She has a bachelor of fine arts degree in music and works occasionally playing piano in restaurants or bars. She would like to work more, but her illness makes it hard for her to do so. The family struggles with finances, and Eve and Susan are on Medicaid. Eve experiences a great deal of stress and has no social support except her partner and daughter. She also states that her side effects interfere with her ability to work and to care for her daughter.

# WHY: TO OBTAIN THE BEST CLIENT OUTCOMES

We are confident that all social workers want the best possible outcomes for their clients. We want our depressed clients to enjoy life, our abusive-parent clients to be reunited with their children and the families to thrive, and our probation clients to become productive, solid citizens. Motivation is not the issue.

Unfortunately, the desire to help clients does not guarantee success. Ever since the early 1970s when Mullen, Dumpson, and Associates (1972) reviewed the effectiveness of social work interventions and Joel Fischer (1973) asked "Is casework effective?" social work has been somewhat on the defensive about research showing our services to be ineffective. Indeed, "treatment failure" is not uncommon in social work, as illustrated particularly by the frequency of clients who simply never return after the first visit (Meyer, 2001). Even more distressing is evidence that some fairly well-known interventions cause harm to clients (Lilienfeld, 2007).

Failure is not unique to social workers, of course. In fact, the first earth-shaking announcement that psychotherapy did not work occurred in psychology in the 1950s (Eysenck, 1952). Slade, Lambert, Harmon, Smart, and Bailey (2008) estimated that 5–10% of all adult mental health clients deteriorate while in treatment, and 40–60% show no significant benefit. Similarly, Warren, Nelson, Mondragon, Baldwin, and Burlingame (2010) found that 14–24% of children receiving mental health services deteriorate while in treatment, and over 30% show no significant benefit.

Today, there is a large and ever-increasing body of research demonstrating that many interventions are indeed effective at ameliorating client problems; see, for example, the compendium of recent books on evidence-based practice on our companion website and the list of related websites. Consequently, despite the fact that we know that some clients will not improve, or will deteriorate, we might assume that evidence-based practices will lead to better outcomes for our clients; after all, research shows them to be effective—often a lot of rigorous research. Yet, as Proctor and Rosen (2008) state, "even when empirically supported intervention knowledge is available, the provider is still left with considerable uncertainty regarding how effective a given intervention will be with a given client" (p. 287). Moreover, evidence-based practices have been demonstrated with samples of clients who might very well be quite different from your own clients, and adaptations are often necessary. Given the risks of diminishing the effectiveness of an intervention when you implement changes, careful measurement and constant monitoring of client outcomes are crucial. In fact, even when you implement an intervention exactly as the protocol specifies, you need to verify that it is effective for this specific individual (Mullen & Streiner, 2004). Bloom and Orme (1993) call this not just helping a client, but *demonstrably* helping. Evidence-based practice is a *means*, not the goal (Rubin, 2008).

Moreover, despite your efforts to find the best methods, there is also some surprising credible evidence that the therapist's treatment modality is not related to client outcomes (Cnaan & Dichter, 2008; Lambert & Barley, 2001; Okiishi, Lambert, Eggett, Nielsen, & Dayton, 2006), although many would not agree with this. For example, see the debate presented in Norcross, Beutler, and Levant (2006). Graybeal (2007) reviews the available evidence put forth by Lambert and many others and estimates that only about 15% of the variability in psychotherapy outcome is accounted for by specific intervention methods.

## What Does Contribute to Client Outcomes?

Lambert (2007) suggests that the single most important predictor of psychotherapy outcome is initial client functioning: severity, somatization, comorbidity, complexity of disorder, and the like. Graybeal (2007) agrees, attributing about 40% of the variance to these factors.

Individual therapist effects are also important. Good client outcomes are not randomly distributed among practitioners; research shows large and significant differences (Lambert, 2007; Okiishi et al., 2006), despite the fact that most research designs in psychotherapy are constructed to neutralize effects due to individual therapists, treating them as a nuisance factor. Research provides no evidence of clear benefits to clients whose therapists have more experience and training (Sapyta, Riemer, & Bickman, 2005). Neither do gender nor therapist discipline influence client outcomes (Okiishi et al., 2006). Even with the use of highly systematic interventions such as written protocols and manuals, there is a large therapist effect on outcomes (Graybeal, 2007).

The term *common factors* is often used to refer to factors that are common across all theories and methods, including placebo effects or the expectancy for change; Graybeal (2007) estimated that these factors account for about 15% of the variance. Therapist allegiance to a particular intervention and characteristics of the therapist such as empathy, warmth, and acceptance are estimated by both Graybeal (2007) and Saggese (2005) to account for about 30% of the variance. In practice, it's difficult to disentangle such therapist characteristics from the therapeutic alliance, that is the joint collaboration of client and practitioner.

Numerous studies and meta-analyses demonstrate that the alliance or relationship is the single most important common factor for predicting clinical outcomes in psychotherapy (Lambert & Barley, 2001). Duncan et al.'s (2003) review of over 1,000 studies demonstrated that the strength of the therapist–client alliance is one of the best predictors of outcome, and the amount of change attributable to the alliance is over seven times that attributable to the specific method employed in therapy. Whatever the exact impact of relationship on outcome, certainly considerable evidence points to its importance, and there are research-based practice guidelines that clinicians of any orientation can use to optimize the therapeutic alliance (Muran & Barber, 2011), including careful monitoring of the quality of the alliance along with client outcomes. Chapter 9 provides several practical measures you can use to do this.

## Contributions of Feedback to Outcome

There is an emerging, methodologically strong body of evidence demonstrating that— at least for outpatient mental health care—ongoing, relatively objective feedback to the practitioner reduces deterioration and treatment dropout, improves overall outcome, and leads to fewer treatment sessions with no worsening of outcome for clients who are making progress. That is, feedback increases cost-effectiveness (e.g., Anker, Duncan, & Sparks, 2009; Lambert, 2010b; Reese, Norsworthy, & Rowlands, 2009; Shimokawa, Lambert, & Smart, 2010).

The beneficial effect of feedback on client outcomes may be especially pronounced for clients who are not doing well in psychotherapy. Lambert and his colleagues have conducted a program of research about the utility of weekly feedback to therapists using clients' self-reports, which is summarized in Lambert (2010b) and Shimokawa et al. (2010). Clients completed the Outcome Questionnaire-45 (OQ-45) that measures overall functioning (symptoms of psychological disturbance, interpersonal problems, social role functioning, and quality of life) at each appointment. Then, each client's session-by-session progress was compared to his or her predicted progress based on initial level of functioning and norms from a large database of similar cases. Therapists received feedback on each client at each appointment, with an "alarm" system for those who were deteriorating relative to the predicted pattern of progress. After a decade of research and five large randomized controlled studies involving 20,000 clients, Lambert (2010a) states unequivocally that "it is time for clinicians to routinely monitor treatment outcomes" (p. 239).

---

**B**efore his first meeting with Eve, Gordon reviews the literature following the steps outlined by Rubin (2008) and finds little about interventions for medication adherence with HIV patients specifically, though there is some research with other diseases such as diabetes and hypertension. More specifically, Gordon searches the following free websites for systematic reviews and syntheses:

- Campbell Collaboration: http://www.campbell collaboration.org/
- Guide to Community Preventive Services: http://www.thecommunityguide.org/
- U.S. Department of Health and Human Services, Agency for Healthcare Research and Quality: http://www.ahrq.gov/clinic/index.html

Then, he searches the following free websites for abstracts and summaries of systematic reviews and specific interventions:

- U.S. Department of Health and Human Services, Substance Abuse and Mental Health Services Administration (SAMHSA), National Registry of Evidence-Based Programs and Practices (NREPP): http://nrepp.samhsa.gov/
- U.S. Department of Health and Human Services, SAMHSA, Center for Mental Health Services: http://mentalhealth.samhsa.gov/cmhs/communitysupport/toolkits/about.asp

Finally, he searches the following free bibliographic databases and web search engines:

- Google Scholar: http://scholar.google.com/
- PubMed: http://www.ncbi.nlm.nih.gov/pubmed/

He is concerned about the lack of sample diversity in the research he finds anyway, especially the dearth of evidence about interventions for HIV-positive women.

A recent review suggests a number of risk factors for poor HIV medication adherence (Martin, Haskard-Zolnierek, & DiMatteo, 2010), including complexity of regimens, lack of understanding of the regimen, poor social support, and side effects, and Gordon plans to discuss these issues with Eve. Martin et al. advocate a patient-centered approach to medication adherence that focuses on the individual's circumstances, values, and resources. This approach emphasizes self-management by the patient and thus promotes self-efficacy as an important tool, and is consistent with a successful multifaceted intervention program reported by Dieckhaus and Odesina (2007). This program combined a number of interventions based on a comprehensive assessment, including education, dosing calendars, organized pill boxes, auxiliary social work and other services, telephone follow-ups, and other individual services as needed.

Although nearly half of the patients in this study were female, and patients in the study improved their compliance from 89.1% to 96.9%, results were not presented by gender, and no control group was used. Patient viral load improved significantly. The best available evidence thus suggests an approach based on individualized assessment, and so Gordon resolves to carefully assess Eve's specific circumstances.

# WHY: TO AVOID NATURAL BIASES

But why is systematic monitoring necessary? Can't we tell how our clients are doing? Most social workers begin each session with a check-in such as "How has your week been?" partly as a way to break the ice and spark discussion. Nelsen (1994) describes the "fairly unsystematic ways" that most social workers use to monitor their clients' progress: "they notice clients' functioning in treatment sessions and periodically ask clients what is happening in regard to their presenting problems or other agreed-upon goals" (p. 140). And, of course, a small number of social workers do engage in systematic monitoring (e.g., Cnaan & Dichter, 2008; Collins, Kayser, & Platt, 1994).

But it is unrealistic to expect practitioners to be able to determine how a client is responding to intervention based on these unsystematic approaches. Clearly, there are strong confirmation biases working when you appraise your client's progress: *You care deeply about your work and really want this client to get better.* Years of research show that your tendency is to see improvement, whether it exists or not. There is evidence, at least in the area of mental health, that practitioners tend to overestimate improvement and underestimate deterioration, in relation to clients' self-reports (Worthen & Lambert, 2007). In the area of psychotherapy, practitioners have much more confidence in their abilities to judge clients' progress than is warranted by the data (Hannan et al., 2005; Lambert et al., 2003). Much as we might like to think of ourselves as highly perceptive, evidence demonstrates that most therapists cannot accurately determine how clients are responding to intervention (Lambert et al., 2003), except perhaps for changes in demeanor during sessions, without the aid of objective measures.

At the first session, Gordon assesses Eve's circumstances, resources, and needs in order to identify possible areas for intervention. Eve indicates that she understands her complicated medication regimen; she does not need more education about it. She admits she just often forgets to take her pills, especially when she is feeling stressed. Eve states that her stress is a major reason she misses doses of her medication; her finances are a mess, work is sporadic, and she never feels that she devotes enough time to her daughter. In addition, her partner Joe is her only social support, and he works long hours, often 70 hours a week. Finally, Eve states that the side-effects of her drugs are unpleasant. She has been able to reduce the side-effects to some extent, but she remains slightly nauseated and fatigued much of the time.

Eve claims that she takes her pills "most of the time," but hasn't monitored to see how often, so Gordon suggests that she start recording her medication as a first step and provides a form for her to use (Figure 3.1). Eve will check off each dose as she takes it, and she and Gordon will chart the average number of doses taken each week (percent compliance). Blood tests will monitor her viral load. Eve's goal is to take her medication appropriately 100% of the time.

Gordon decides to pursue the stress issue, because it appears to be closely related to her forgetting her medication (at least at this point, before they have baseline data to review). He hypothesizes that better coping with her stress might help her remember her medication better. Eve agrees, so Gordon explains how self-monitoring could be helpful for confirming that this is true. She is not sure that she can monitor all these things but agrees to try. She and Gordon develop an individualized 7-point measure of coping with stress to be completed

*(continued)*

**Figure 3.1** • Eve's Medication Compliance and Coping With Stress.

| Date | Morning meds by 8:00 | Noon meds by 1:00 | Bedtime meds | Coping with stress* | Comments |
|------|----------------------|-------------------|--------------|---------------------|----------|
|      |                      |                   |              |                     |          |
|      |                      |                   |              |                     |          |
|      |                      |                   |              |                     |          |
|      |                      |                   |              |                     |          |
|      |                      |                   |              |                     |          |
|      |                      |                   |              |                     |          |
|      |                      |                   |              |                     |          |
|      |                      |                   |              |                     |          |

*1, completely overwhelmed; 3, very stressed but maintaining some control; 5, in control most of the time; 7, coping effectively nearly all day

**Overall compliance:** _____   **Average coping:** _____

each evening on her medication compliance form (Figure 3.1). Eve will record 1 for feeling completely overwhelmed by her stress that day; 3 for being very stressed but maintaining some control; 5 for being in control most of the time; and 7 for coping effectively nearly all day. Eve's goal is to maintain a 5. A column for comments is provided for Eve to note daily events that might be related to her stress.

# WHY: TO IMPROVE CLINICAL DECISION-MAKING

We are not always aware of it, but social work involves constant decision-making. From what data to elicit during assessment and how, to what intervention to implement, to when and how to terminate services, and everything in between, there are constant decisions to be made. How do we make these decisions? Evidence-based practices are a valuable tool for the social worker, but they are not always informative for every decision that must be made, as Eve's case illustrates.

Indeed, although the evidence-based practice literature places great emphasis on the important decision of what interventions to apply to specific client problems and there is a great deal of attention paid to how to articulate an answerable question and to locate and evaluate the evidence, there is less focus on other important decisions.

For example, social workers' decisions during assessment include where to start the discussion, what questions to ask, which comments by the client merit follow-up and additional discussion, how much information to share with the client about possible interventions and the evidence about those interventions, and many others. O'Hare (2009) points out that we make decisions all the time about how serious clients' problems are, and that this is an essential step toward setting priorities and intervention planning.

Perhaps most important, practitioners must decide in each session whether to continue the current intervention as is, modify it, or move to a different intervention altogether, as we see in Eve's case. Each of these decisions takes the intervention in a different direction.

Garb (2005) presented research showing that a majority of psychologists in practice do not follow rules about considering and asking about all the DSM (*Diagnostic and Statistical Manual of Mental Disorders*) criteria and placing equal emphasis on all the different criteria when they are diagnosing clients; apparently, they make decisions about diagnosis using idiosyncratic approaches, rather than following the instructions. His review also demonstrated that practitioners almost never use all routinely available data to make judgments about client personality and psychopathology; instead, they are selective in attending to certain criteria, with causally related ones apparently receiving more attention. These variations in how psychologists make diagnoses amount to their making different *decisions*, and they

**A**t the second session, Eve is shocked to see from her diary (Figure 3.2) that she has taken her medication only about 76% of the time. Her stress-coping levels vary widely, and she and Gordon are able to pinpoint some of her biggest stressors and discuss how she can plan ahead for them. This week she forgot her medication when unusual, stressful events occurred: Susan's being ill and needing to be picked up from school, a parent–teacher meeting for which she was late, and her performing at a restaurant two evenings.

Gordon decides to focus on how Eve copes with her stress, and Eve admits she really has no specific ways of coping. Gordon describes several evidence-based interventions for stress reduction, but Eve already feels overwhelmed and doesn't want anything else on her plate. She does agree to spend a few minutes learning deep breathing, and Gordon also gives her a pamphlet about a free yoga class at the community center. Eve will continue to monitor her coping, as well as her medication adherence.

**Figure 3.2** • First Week of Self-Monitoring by Eve.

| Date | Morning meds by 8:00 | Noon meds by 1:00 | Bedtime meds | Coping with stress* | Comments |
|------|----------------------|-------------------|--------------|---------------------|----------|
| 3/1 | √ | √ | | 3 | Late to work |
| 3/2 | √ | | √ | 4 | Susan sick—picked up early from school |
| 3/3 | √ | √ | | 2 | Late for parent-teacher meeting |
| 3/3 | | √ | √ | 4 | |
| 3/4 | √ | | √ | 3 | Evening restaurant job |
| 3/5 | √ | √ | | 2 | Evening restaurant job |
| 3/6 | √ | | √ | 4 | Exhausted |
| 3/7 | √ | | √ | 5 | Exhausted |

*1, completely overwhelmed; 3, very stressed but maintaining some control; 5, in control most of the time; 7, coping effectively nearly all day

Session 2: Overall compliance: 76%   Average coping: 3.9

might account for the poor inter-rater reliability of diagnoses made in practice. We cannot help but believe that those decisions affected much more than just the diagnostic process.

But isn't decision-making easier with "manualized" interventions? With a manual, the practitioner simply follows the protocol, right? There should be fewer decisions to make. In fact, however, Garb's (2005) review shows widespread failure to follow specific and widely supported "best practice guidelines." He cites the treatment of schizophrenia as an example. It is impossible to know, but we might hope that these failures to follow guidelines are in fact modifications based on practitioners' reasoned decisions based on monitoring of their clients' outcomes, rather than biases or heuristics based on convenience and efficiency (American Psychological Association Presidential Task Force on Evidence-Based Practice, 2006). In any case, this example clearly demonstrates the ubiquitous nature of decision-making in intervention.

---

**A**t session 3, Eve's coping is a bit better (Figure 3.3, week 2). She has complied with her medication regimen 86% of the time and says her compliance wasn't better because of unpleasant side effects and stress over losing a job. Eve's physician joins Gordon and Eve for a moment to report that her blood work is not good. Although he acknowledges her improved compliance this week, if Eve's compliance does not improve significantly next week—to near perfect—he wants to take her off the antiretroviral regimen due to the risk of making her disease worse.

Gordon and Eve review her diary (Figure 3.4) closely and talk about the times she forgot her medication in the past week. She connects two of the three forgotten doses to a harassing call from her landlord about overdue rent and an argument with Joe. She is having trouble sleeping, and Susan has become anxious about her parents' arguments. Gordon suggests asking Joe to join them in their next session, explaining that his support could be very helpful, but Eve demurs. She will make do on her own. Gordon reviews the instructions for deep breathing with Eve, and they close the session.

---

**Figure 3.3** • Eve's Average Weekly Percentage of Medication Adherence (•) and Ability to Cope With Stress (o).

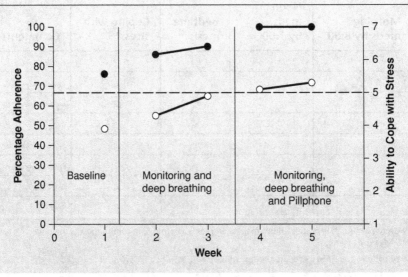

**Figure 3.4** • Second Week of Self-Monitoring by Eve.

| Date | Morning meds by 8:00 | Noon meds by 1:00 | Bedtime meds | Coping with stress* | Comments |
|------|----------------------|-------------------|--------------|---------------------|----------|
| 3/8 | | √ | √ | 3 | Susan late to school |
| 3/9 | √ | | √ | 3 | |
| 3/10 | √ | √ | √ | 4 | Long walk |
| 3/11 | √ | √ | √ | 6 | Yoga class |
| 3/12 | √ | | √ | 5 | Dr. appointment |
| 3/13 | √ | √ | √ | 4 | Headache all day |
| 3/14 | √ | √ | √ | 5 | Yoga class |

*1, completely overwhelmed; 3, very stressed but maintaining some control; 5, in control most of the time; 7, coping effectively nearly all day

Session 3: Overall compliance: 86%   Average coping: 4.3

It is reasonable to ask how constant monitoring of client outcomes influences decision-making. Lambert et al. (2003) find indications that practitioners who monitor are clearly more attentive to clients who are not making satisfactory progress. Feedback that a client is not improving or is even deteriorating offers a number of options, including changing projected dates for achievement of goals, adjusting goals, or focusing on additional intermediate goals (Patrick, Mozzoni, & Patrick, 2000). One also may change interventions, as Eve's case shows, or even return to the case conceptualization.

Several authors provide suggestions for using monitoring data to make decisions about intervention. Riley-Tillman and Burns (2009) present a table (p. 16) for making intervention decisions based on monitoring data. Chorpita, Bernstein, and Daleiden (2008) also present a rationally determined framework to inform each decision point in intervention. Lambert, Harmon, Slade, Whipple, and Hawkins (2004) constructed a color-coded alert system based on comparisons of monitoring data for individual clients to a large database. For example, a client who is not making expected progress and for whom there is a high chance for a negative outcome may have a red sticker adhered to his or her chart.

Extending the research showing the benefits of feedback to therapists about client outcomes, Lambert and his colleagues have moved to provide Clinical Support Tools (CST) that therapists can use to improve outcomes with clients who are not progressing (Lambert, 2010b; Shimokawa et al., 2010). The CST are based on research deconstructing the most important variables in clinical outcome, including client rating of the therapeutic alliance, motivation, perceptions of social support, and errors in diagnostic and treatment planning. The CST package includes a decision tree, measures of the first three variables above with cutoff scores indicating problems, and a list of suggested interventions for each variable. Lambert's review of the limited research on use of the CST indicates

At the fourth session, Eve's compliance is about 90% (Figure 3.3, week 3), and her physician wants to discontinue the antiretroviral medication. She is adamant that she can do better, though, and points out that her coping improved again. She states that she really likes the deep breathing and uses it often. Her diary (Figure 3.5) shows that she is using some new methods of coping with her stress.

Three weeks of data provide suggestive practice-based evidence that Eve's problems with taking her medication result from high levels of stress and poor coping skills, but Gordon is frustrated at Eve's lack of progress and concerned about her health. Gordon again suggests that he teach Eve systematic relaxation and focus more on other means of coping, but she continues to resist, saying there must be another way. She just does not want any other interventions or things to practice.

Gordon suggests changing tracks altogether. Progress is too slow to continue on this course, even if stress is indeed the major cause of Eve's noncompliance, he tells her. Gordon suggests they try a technological intervention: Pill Phone, an application provided by many cell phone providers that sends reminders about medications via cell phone calls (https://www. pillphone.com/PillLogin.htm). Interventions using cell phones for this purpose are relatively new, so there is not a body of research support, but Gordon finds a number of references to successful use in small studies (e.g., Armstrong et al., 2009; Quinn et al., 2008; Strandbygaard, Thomsen, & Backer, 2010).

The Pill Phone application allows the user to program his or her medications and when they are due and to set the phone to call, vibrate, or both at those times. The user replies to the call that the medication is taken (or pushes a "snooze" button to be reminded again), and the data are maintained on a server (they can be sent to others if desired, as well). The service is inexpensive ($4 a month for Eve's provider), and Gordon and Eve set up the application on her phone before she leaves the office. (Because Pill Phone interacts with a medication database, telephone reminders also display pictures of the specific medications that are due. Gordon is glad to build in this way of reducing the probability of medication errors.)

**Figure 3.5 •** Third Week of Self-Monitoring by Eve.

| Date | Morning meds by 8:00 | Noon meds by 1:00 | Bedtime meds | Coping with stress* | Comments |
|------|----------------------|-------------------|--------------|---------------------|----------|
| 3/15 | √ | √ | √ | 5 | Yoga class |
| 3/16 | √ |   | √ | 4 | Noon job |
| 3/17 | √ | √ | √ | 5 | Good day |
| 3/18 | √ | √ | √ | 4 | Yoga class |
| 3/19 | √ | √ | √ | 5 | Dr. appointment |
| 3/20 | √ | √ | √ | 4 |  |
| 3/21 | √ | √ | √ | 4 | Yoga class |
| 3/22 | √ |   | √ | 3 | Job canceled |

*1, completely overwhelmed; 3, very stressed but maintaining some control; 5, in control most of the time; 7, coping effectively nearly all day

Session 4: Overall compliance: 90% Average coping: 4.9

significant improvement over treatment as usual, and we can expect much more research about this potentially exciting development soon.

Greenhalgh (2009) also recounts several ways that regular self-report feedback from patients in medical settings may improve patients' health. Self-reports provide material for productive discussion during doctor–patient meetings, possibly leading patients to assume more responsibility for their own health, as Eve's case demonstrates. Rubin (2008) also suggests that clients' commitment to change might be enhanced by looking at their data with their social workers. This may, in turn, lead to better adherence to treatment and increased satisfaction. Similarly, ongoing systematic feedback allows social workers and their clients to analyze changes in target problems as they relate to both the intervention and the changes in the clients' lives and to take appropriate steps. In this way, regular systematic feedback is likely to provide excellent material for therapeutic discussions.

## WHY: TO PREVENT CLIENT DETERIORATION

The possibility of deterioration by clients while receiving services is one that receives short shrift in the literature. Although large randomized controlled trials (RCTs), meta-analyses, and sophisticated statistics are hailed as invaluable tools for identifying the most effective interventions, these methods in fact do nothing to help us understand, predict, or handle deterioration. Yet, as mentioned earlier, research shows that 5–10% of adult (Slade et al., 2008) and 14–24% of child (Warren et al., 2010) clients deteriorate while receiving services.

Lambert and his colleagues have demonstrated that consistent feedback to the therapist using a short measure of client functioning (OQ-45) completed at each session can reduce rates of deterioration, partly by reducing rates of dropout from therapy (Lambert, 2010b; Shimokawa et al., 2010). Since that time they and others have extended this research in two important ways that hold promise for further improvements. First, using computerized data about client outcomes for thousands of clients, actuarial data have been used to compare clients' outcomes to expected rates of change and to provide "alarms" to therapists of impending failure. (See Chapter 9 for a description of these systems.)

Second, as described earlier, Lambert and his colleagues (Whipple et al., 2003) have designed resources (CST) for use with clients who are deteriorating or not progressing, based on preexisting research. Use of feedback and the CST was related to fewer cases of deterioration and more cases of reliable positive change in clients (Harmon et al., 2007; Whipple et al., 2003).

## WHY: TO BRIDGE THE GAPS IN EVIDENCE-BASED PRACTICE

If you are using the best, state-of-the-art empirically supported treatment model, do you really need to evaluate your practice in an ongoing, systematic manner? *Yes.* Winston Churchill said it best: "However beautiful the strategy, you should occasionally look at the results." (We got this wonderful quotation from Lambert, 2010a.)

Fraser, Richman, Galinsky, and Day (2009) define an evidence-based intervention as one "that has been evaluated using scientific methods with cumulative findings from several evaluations demonstrating effectiveness" (p. 183). In evidence-based practice, empirical research is evaluated based on a hierarchy, with RCTs as the most highly valued research. We would argue that although the use of evidence-based practice is the place to start, it is not sufficient for the following four reasons.

## Meaning of the Evidence

First, RCTs compare mean scores of individuals in an intervention group to mean scores of individuals in a control or placebo group, but interventions typically are delivered to individuals (Mullen & Streiner, 2004). As Mullen and Streiner explain, this means that a proportion of people in the intervention group get worse, whereas a proportion of people in the control group get better. There is always variability around the mean. Of course as Rosen and Proctor (2003) note, "The essence of the dilemma of idiographic application of empirical generalizations is that empirically derived professional knowledge, be it descriptive, explanatory, or control oriented (how to influence human behavior), is knowledge fraught with uncertainty, even when obtained through optimal research designs. This uncertainty is related to the probabilistic nature of all scientific inferences and conclusions" (p. 200). RCTs tell us whether interventions are efficacious and effective with the *average* client, but the practitioner needs to know if the intervention is effective with *this* client (Proctor & Rosen, 2008). Significant group effects do not guarantee positive effects for individuals.

## Focus of the Evidence

Whereas it is a fundamental of social work practice to work with the whole person in his or her environment, evidence-based research often emphasizes the problem or diagnosis, such as depression, and the intervention, such as cognitive behavior therapy (CBT). This approach may shortchange the importance of the multiple contextual variables that explain and maintain human behavior and social problems.

Group data cannot account for individual circumstances, strengths, and resources. In fact, we would argue that selecting treatments for individual clients based on group data may be a fine example of the *ecological fallacy*, that is, drawing inferences about individuals related to group-level data. (See Patrick et al., 2000, for a good discussion of this issue in the history of single-case design in medicine.) This is particularly troubling given that in order to decrease variance based on client characteristics, most RCTs intentionally study homogenous samples that are quite unlike many or even most of your clients (Morgan & Morgan, 2009; Proctor & Rosen, 2008). You may find yourself in the ironic position of applying an intervention to a client who would have been disqualified from the studies on which its efficacy and effectiveness are based!

Even in a meta-analysis that demonstrates a significant strong effect size for an intervention (unusual, almost by definition) including dozens of practitioners and perhaps thousands of clients, a considerable proportion of clients do not benefit from the intervention, and up to 10% deteriorate. With the more frequently reported small or medium effect sizes, a sizable proportion of clients may not benefit and/or may even deteriorate. Whether this is because of the failure to consider all the important demographic (e.g., race, gender, SES [socioeconomic status]) and contextual factors, or to more idiographic factors, it compels us to be vigilant. A demonstrably successful intervention is not successful with everyone.

Moreover, few randomized experiments or meta-analyses are able to take into account diversity issues related to culture, ethnicity, age, gender, sexual orientation, and social class, not to mention possible interactions among all of these and other relevant factors (McBeath, Briggs, & Aisenberg, 2010). We know that all of these factors and others are critical influences in people's lives, and professional consensus is clear that these factors influence treatment effectiveness, and yet historically very few minorities have been included in the evidence-based practice research (Aisenberg, 2008). For example, we know very little about the effectiveness of interventions with people from different racial or ethnic backgrounds (Sue & Zane, 2006), people who are lesbian, gay, bisexual, or transgender (Brown, 2006), or people with disabilities (Olkin & Taliaferro, 2006). If we go to the evidence and select the modality with the strongest scientific support for a client's problem, but which has not been demonstrated to be effective with diverse clients, we cannot assume that the modality will be effective with individual clients, especially those from diverse backgrounds (Furman, 2009; Rodgers & Potocky, 1997). Proctor and Rosen (2008) forthrightly state that especially when there is doubt about goodness of fit for a particular client, but even when that is not the case, "a recursive evaluation–feedback loop should be adopted to determine whether the intervention as implemented attains the predicted results or whether it should be further modified or abandoned" (p. 289).

### Critical Thinking

***Practice Behavior Example:*** *Distinguish, appraise, and integrate multiple sources of knowledge, including research-based knowledge, and practice wisdom*

**Critical Thinking Question:** Go to the Campbell Collaboration web page (http://www.campbellcollaboration.org/). Then (1) select The Campbell Library; (2) enter African-American as a search term; (3) select All text and search; (4) select View All and Sort by Year; (5) read through the list of reviews; and (6) open and read a recent review of interventions that includes information about African-Americans. What evidence do you see of interventions that have been shown to be effective specifically with African-Americans?

## Methods of the Evidence

Third, there is also reason for healthy skepticism about evidence-based practice itself. What is *evidence*, and who decides what evidence is most valid? A hierarchy that places RCTs at the top of the list of reliable evidence will certainly favor certain types of interventions that lend themselves most easily to such designs, especially micro-level interventions that fit neatly into the model (Furman, 2009). (See Donaldson, Christie, & Mark, 2009, for several viewpoints on this issue.) What about cases where interventions with larger systems are warranted? Many social work clients have problems due to societal discrimination, lack of opportunity, and social injustice. We do not see many evidence-based practices for these issues (McBeath et al., 2010). Whereas Mullen and Streiner (2004) claim that evidence-based practice is for clients at all system levels, they acknowledge the dominance of one-on-one social work in the evidence-based practice literature.

In addition, some have questioned the methodologies relied most heavily on in the evidence-based practice literature, including meta-analyses. Meta-analyses quantitatively combine a large number of studies, using *effect sizes*, which are standardized measures of effectiveness across studies (Littell, Corcoran, & Pillai, 2008). For example, Thomas and

**A**t session 5, Eve is proud to demonstrate 100% compliance with her medication, despite some stressful events over the week. Eve's blood work also shows a slight decrease in her viral load. She has been practicing deep breathing and is sleeping better and says that knowing she is on track with her medication has actually helped her feel less stressed.

She and Gordon review the graph of her data (Figure 3.3, week 4) and her compliance diary (Figure 3.6) to sum up her success so far and agree that technology seems to be the most effective way for her to achieve compliance with her antiretroviral medication regimen. They will have one final session to be sure Eve's compliance is stable and set up a monitoring plan Eve can maintain on her own with Pill Phone, including specific criteria for contacting Gordon if she feels she needs to.

**Figure 3.6** • Fourth Week of Self-Monitoring by Eve.

| Date | Morning meds by 8:00 | Noon meds by 1:00 | Bedtime meds | Coping with stress* | Comments |
|------|----------------------|-------------------|--------------|---------------------|----------|
| 3/23 | √ | √ | √ | 5 | Yoga class |
| 3/24 | √ | √ | √ | 5 | Job at noon |
| 3/25 | √ | √ | √ | 5 | Job canceled |
| 3/26 | √ | √ | √ | 6 | Yoga class |
| 3/27 | √ | √ | √ | 4 | Dental appointment |
| 3/28 | √ | √ | √ | 5 | Quiet day |
| 3/29 | √ | √ | √ | 6 | Yoga class |

*1, completely overwhelmed; 3, very stressed but maintaining some control; 5, in control most of the time; 7, coping effectively nearly all day

Session 5: Overall compliance: 100%     Average coping: 5.1

Zimmer-Gembeck (2007) compared the effectiveness of Parent–Child Interaction Therapy and the Triple P Positive Parenting Program across 24 different studies. The ability to examine the effectiveness of an intervention or program across many different studies is seductive, but criticisms have been issued about both the logic (Pawson, 2002) and the statistical methods (Nugent, 2009) used in meta-analyses. In the future, perhaps this will be less of a problem, as the amount of research increases and large studies are able to demonstrate effects on specific subgroups of individuals.

## Availability of the Evidence

Finally, evidence-based practices are not available for every client problem you encounter (Persons, 2008), much less for every set of client characteristics, circumstances, and resources. Fischer (2009) dares to suggest that evidence-based interventions are not available for *most* of the complex cases social workers see. In particular, there is little research that factors in comorbidity (Rubin, 2008), although it is far from rare for our clients to have more than one diagnosis or problem (Springer & Tripodi, 2009). Taylor and Gray (2010) report that the *British Medical Journal Clinical Evidence* database has evaluated more than 2,500 psychiatric interventions and concluded that 46% are of unknown effectiveness. McBeath et al. (2010) draw similar conclusions about empirically supported interventions for social work practice. The evidence just isn't there for a lot of available interventions.

Moreover, resource constraints impose realistic barriers on the implementation of evidence-based practice in many settings (Barratt, 2003). Patrick et al. (2000) sum up what we often do in these situations: "In the absence of clear direction, the practitioner calls on experience, peers, and clinical lore" (p. 61). In these circumstances, with this degree of uncertainty, it is especially important to monitor clients' outcomes closely.

It is important to acknowledge that although meta-analyses and RCTs are privileged, evidence-based practice requires that we use the best *available* evidence. Often this evidence comes from quasi-experimental data, single-case designs, or even case studies. (Recall that Gordon did not find much in the research specific to female HIV-positive clients.) In such cases especially, the limitations of evidence-based practice demand that we pay attention to *whether this particular client is moving toward his or her goal at this time*. Only careful measurement and monitoring of each client's outcomes at regular frequent intervals lets you determine if your particular client is making satisfactory progress and, more importantly, do something about it if not.

# WHY: TO IMPROVE YOUR RELATIONSHIPS WITH YOUR CLIENTS

How does ongoing case evaluation improve your relationship with your client?

First, it demonstrates your respect for your client by giving him or her an important voice. This is not to say that you do not respect your clients if you do not engage in ongoing outcome monitoring, but the *demonstration* of your respect, through the collection of regular data and the willingness to adjust the intervention when those data do not indicate progress, makes a clear statement of your respect for your client's experience. Bloom and Orme (1993) emphasize that evaluation is done *with*, not *to* the client. They also emphasize the importance of not just help, but *demonstrable help*. There is no better demonstration of your help than objective evidence of change in your client's life.

Second, ongoing evaluation demonstrates conscientiousness on your part, and may enhance your client's confidence in you (Campbell, 1988). Your client's confidence also contributes to expectancy effects in treatment, that is the client's expectation that intervention will be effective (Greenberg, Constantino, & Bruce, 2006). Indeed, Andrews (2007) suggests that building the client's hope and expectancy of change may be a critical part of effective intervention.

Client expectancy and improved client-therapist relationship may be the reasons for the evidence that ongoing feedback reduces treatment dropout. (See the review of factors related to dropout by Barrett, Chua, Crits-Christoph, Gibbons, & Thompson, 2008.) You cannot provide effective services to clients who leave treatment. And you can't know your approach is failing unless you systematically measure and monitor your client's outcomes at regular frequent intervals to determine if your particular client is making satisfactory progress. Recall how surprised Eve was when she learned how poor her medication compliance was.

# WHY: TO ENHANCE YOUR DEVELOPMENT AS A PRACTITIONER

Though its most important use is for the benefit of the client, monitoring outcomes over your practice also will improve your skills. Feedback on your clients reinforces and clarifies what you have learned and allows you to generalize to the specific types of clients you serve.

## Skills and Expertise

All practitioners are not created equal. The vast majority of research studies focus on interventions, paying little if any attention to the intervener, be it the teacher, therapist, or farmer (Wampold, 2010). Yet evidence shows huge differences in client outcomes among therapists (Hubble, Duncan, Miller, & Wampold, 2010), even when using the same intervention methods. "Simply put, some therapists are more effective than others" (Brown & Minami, 2010, p. 280). Interestingly, these differences hold up even when medication is the intervention being delivered! And such effects are not confined to psychotherapy; O'Hare (2009) states that "because of generally loose standards in social work education and in the mental health and social services fields, practitioners can continue for years providing substandard work as long as such work does not attract the attention of state health authorities or practice negligence does not come to light in a civil suit" (p. 347).

Research has not provided much information on the reasons for different providers' different outcomes. Sapyta et al.'s (2005) review of the effects of feedback on mental health therapists revealed that client outcomes are not related to therapist training or experience; O'Hare (2009) also argues that experience does not guarantee expertise. Sapyta et al. suggest that one reason for the poor ability of training and experience to predict client outcomes is that neither education nor experience necessarily informs therapists about which of their actions are effective and which are not. These authors liken clinical practice without ongoing feedback to learning archery while wearing a blindfold; your skills are unlikely to improve if you cannot see where the arrow is landing.

The kind of "feedback loop" that is part of outcome-informed practice enables you to begin to accumulate a knowledge base about the effects of the evidence-based practices you select on the types of clients you see in practice, avoiding overcommitment to an intervention method without regard to specific clients' needs (Proctor & Rosen, 2008). We do learn from experience, but only when that experience includes knowledge of the results of our actions. Systematically monitoring client outcomes allows you to hone your skills based on real-time data about the outcomes of your actions (Okiishi et al., 2006).

## Critical Thinking

***Practice Behavior Example:*** *Analyze models of assessment, prevention, intervention, and evaluation*

**Critical Thinking Question:** Go to the websites http://nrepp.samhsa.gov/ and http://mentalhealth.samhsa.gov/cmhs/communitysupport/toolkits/about.asp and search for other interventions that might be useful for Eve. Which interventions did you choose? Why would these be effective for Eve?

Throughout his work with Eve, Gordon has shared her outcome data with his supervisor, discussing the rationales for the decisions he has made. They discussed his decision to focus on Eve's stress, for example, based on an apparent connection between stressful events and noncompliance with her medical regimen; his decision to urge (unsuccessfully) Eve to try more targeted stress-reduction interventions; and his decision to suggest the technological intervention when the first approach appeared to be a failure.

Gordon regrets that it took so long to get Eve's medication adherence to the required level and feels that he should have realized earlier that Eve was not making sufficient progress so he could have acted sooner. Gordon's supervisor compliments him on his effective use of the scientific method and suggests that collecting data each week provided him the practice-based evidence he needed to help Eve make this important change. Without this practice-based evidence, he could have continued to pursue a course with Eve that might have endangered her life.

## Supervision

Most social workers and psychologists in agencies work under the guidance of licensed, experienced supervisors, or sometimes in peer-supervision groups. Does such supervision obviate the need for regularly and systematically monitoring one's clients? No, it does not. The primary reason, of course, is that outcome-informed practice focuses first on client outcome, and supervision may or may not directly affect client outcomes; research provides no clear answer to this question (Worthen & Lambert, 2007).

But this is not the only reason that supervision cannot stand in lieu of regular systematic evaluation. First, in addition to the fact discussed earlier that practitioners are not good judges of their clients' progress, Worthen and Lambert's (2007) review of the available research suggests that neither do supervisors appear to be effective at such subjective judgments. This is due in part to the fact that your supervisor can only evaluate your cases using the information you present. In general, supervision is conducted through discussion of individual clients (perhaps using case notes), occasional viewing of tapes of sessions, and (probably rare) live observation; rarely are data on client outcomes part of the supervision process (Kadushin & Harkness, 2002; Worthen & Lambert, 2007). Although such methods may be helpful to social workers in reflecting on and discussing their actions, the subjective nature of the process may or may not enhance individual clients' outcomes. Moreover, not all social workers and other practitioners have close supervision. Independent practitioners in particular must guard against the bias that comes from wanting to help and expecting to see improvement.

Greenhalgh (2009) also emphasizes the usefulness of regular client self-reports in multidisciplinary teams. Such reports provide a common focus and language for the different disciplines and may provide a more clear picture of the client's well-being than individual specialists are likely to have. In particular, Marshall, Haywood, and Fitzpatrick (2006) emphasize that patient-reported outcomes feedback is likely to prod physicians to think beyond the specific disease to a more holistic view of the patient's health. Similar advantages should accrue to peer-supervision groups that focus on client outcomes.

# WHY: TO BE ACCOUNTABLE

As helping professionals, social workers are accountable to a number of stakeholders: our supervisors and agency, funding sources including managed care and insurance organizations, the profession itself, ourselves, and, of course, our clients. Clients have a right to expect the best services we can provide.

Accountability is frequently mentioned as a major reason for using evidence-based practices (Baker, Stephens, & Hitchcock, 2010), as many funding sources now require evidence that the most empirically supported interventions are being used in order to justify further funding. For example, Bolen and Hall (2007) document the growing accountability requirements of managed care organizations, whereas Franklin, Kim, and Tripodi (2009) discuss accountability issues for social work in public education settings. In the United Kingdom, where evidence-based practice is more widely disseminated than in the United States, the National Health Service enforces explicit requirements for the delivery of evidence-based interventions (Gilgun, 2005).

What has been missing until very recently is accountability to funders based on client outcomes. Brown and Minami (2010) make a convincing case that at least for psychotherapy services, outcome-based accountability is coming—and soon. These authors provide a discussion of the complex issues driving this move, including an increase in providers and a decrease in demand for psychotherapy. They provide data showing that as a percentage of overall health care spending, spending for psychotherapy has been decreasing since the 1990s; this is due in part to a preference for medication, based on public perceptions that it is faster and more effective than psychotherapy, especially for depression. As Brown and Minami explain, these conditions have led to initiatives by a number of large managed care organizations to provide differential reimbursement based on client outcomes. United Behavioral Health (UBH), which provides mental health services to 22 million subscribers through a network of 60,000 providers, is now promoting outcome-informed care. We cannot provide extensive detail here about the initiatives currently being implemented or considered, but we are convinced that this is a trend that demands our attention.

Changes brought about by managed care already include reductions in the number of sessions most clients can expect to have covered by private insurance. This change calls for a laser focus on client outcomes so that clients are able to make as much progress as

At the sixth and final session, Eve again has been 100% compliant with her medication, and her coping remains stable (diary data not shown, but see Figure 3.3, week 5). Her blood work is also good. As Eve and Gordon review her progress and plan for her continued use of Pill Phone, she acknowledges that although the deep breathing and the yoga class have been helpful for coping better with the stress in her life, the telephone reminders have been the key. She still has stress, and she hopes to continue to improve her coping ability.

Alone, Gordon reviews what he has learned. He resolves not to make assumptions about the application of evidence-based practices to specific clients, especially when his client's special circumstances have not been well accounted for in the research. The collection of practice-based evidence in this case enabled him to focus on his client's outcomes, rather than committing himself to an intervention that was not acceptable to his client, and to locate resources that were consistent with his client's specific needs and goals.

possible within the allotted time frame. At the same time, public agencies face reduced budgets and cuts in personnel that may limit access to services there, as well. Monitoring client outcomes constantly and modifying the intervention as needed provides an important tool for achieving clients' goals in as short a time as possible and conserving limited resources.

# WHY: LAST, BUT NOT LEAST—TO MEET YOUR ETHICAL OBLIGATIONS

Values are preferences for those things we believe to be good, and values have always been a foundation of the social work profession. Out of our values grow our ethics, that is our moral actions. Social work is a profession that was originally grounded in values, though some say that as the foundation of the profession, values have been replaced by knowledge (Furman, 2009). Bisman (2004) asserts that this shift began in 1970s with the "scientist practitioner" movement.

An understanding of the values of the profession on which our ethics are based informs our understanding of our ethical obligations to evaluate our work with clients. The Preamble of the National Association of Social Workers Code of Ethics (1996, revised 2008) states unequivocally: "Social workers' primary responsibility is to promote the well-being of clients. In general, clients' interests are primary." The overriding importance of the clients' interests may at times be called upon to compete with issues of accountability to organizations or a commitment to science, but commitment to client well-being unequivocally is paramount.

The Preamble lists six core values that grow from this primary responsibility: service, social justice, dignity and worth of the person, importance of human relationships, integrity, and competence. Each of these values might dictate that we carefully monitor our work with clients, but one speaks most directly to the issue: service.

The ethical principle in the Preamble flowing from the service value ("Social workers' primary goal is to help people in need and to address social problems") moves us to specific actions that relate to both evidence-based and outcome-informed practice. The principle reminds us that research, science, and the particular treatment modalities we use are *tools*, not ends in themselves. We use evidence-based methods as a means of enhancing our clients' outcomes, not because of an adoration of science. We are thus obligated to demonstrate the effectiveness of our tools (evidence-based practices) for promoting the well-being of specific clients. (We are taking this admonition to be specific to each client.)

Specific guidelines in the Code do refer to both evidence-based practice (Section 4.0.1: "(c) Social workers should base practice on recognized knowledge, including empirically based knowledge, relevant to social work and social work ethics") and progress monitoring (Section 5.0.2: "Social workers should monitor and evaluate policies, the implementation of programs, and practice interventions"). Particularly in light of the primacy of clients' well-being as declared in the Preamble, it is clear that the purpose of these two guidelines is *to enhance client outcomes*. Indeed, we suggest that the term *empirically based knowledge* in Section 4.0.1 of the Code also should include timely information about the client's status throughout the delivery of services. Andrews (2007) has called this *practice-based evidence*. (Other authors use this term in other ways, but we use Andrews's meaning to emphasize that specific evidence about a client's outcomes is at least as important as general evidence about interventions.)

The Council on Social Work Education's (2008) required competencies for master's level social workers underscores the importance of monitoring clients' progress, stating that social workers "engage in research-informed practice and practice-informed research" (Educational Policy 2.1.6). The document elaborates:

Social workers use practice experience to inform research, employ evidence-based interventions, evaluate their own practice, and use research findings to improve practice, policy, and social service delivery. Social workers comprehend quantitative and qualitative research and understand scientific and ethical approaches to building knowledge. Social workers

- use practice experience to inform scientific inquiry and
- use research evidence to inform practice.

At this point, it's good to remember that outcome-informed practice as we propose it is *not* research, but rather an essential part of practice. Much discussion about the ethics of single-case designs is devoted to a number of ethical dilemmas (e.g., Mechling & Gast, 2010; Nelsen, 1994) centering around evaluation using single-case designs that is conducted for the purpose of research and publication. Most of the issues in these discussions, such as informed consent and delay of treatment to obtain a sufficient baseline, do not pertain to outcome-informed practice, which is conducted for the purpose of decision-making and improving outcomes for individual clients. In outcome-informed practice, the ethical issues are practice issues.

For example, Nelsen (1994) discusses the most frequent objection to the use of single-case designs in social work practice: delay of intervention to obtain a stable baseline. As we emphasize throughout this book, outcome-informed practice does not recommend delay of the intervention unless such a delay is in the best interests of a specific client. Often, as Eve's case illustrates, the matter is too urgent to take the time to collect extended baseline data before beginning to intervene in some way. Nevertheless, some baseline information is useful for case conceptualization and for other practice-related reasons, as discussed in more detail in Chapter 6.

### Diversity in Practice

***Practice Behavior Example:*** *Recognize the extent to which a culture's structures and values may oppress, marginalize, alienate, or create or enhance privilege and power*

**Critical Thinking Question:** Go to Google Scholar (http://scholar.google.com/). Search for a recent meta analysis of research evidence concerning the effectiveness of an intervention of interest to you. Was the intervention effective with diverse clients? If so, how? What, if any, evidence showed a lack of effectiveness?

Staudt (1997) discussed a number of such *pseudo-issues* in practice evaluation, using the term to indicate that these issues are often presented as evaluation issues, when they are in fact practice issues. She discussed the delay or withdrawal of treatment to establish causality, cultural competence and sensitivity (issues that attach to practice itself and are important in every case, irrespective of evaluation), and gender and ethnic bias (again always important). She also discusses criticisms that single-case designs may inadequately capture the complexities of clients' lives and social work practice itself, noting as we do that this is always an issue in social work practice. Should such difficulties release social workers from the obligation to ensure that their clients are progressing toward achieving their goals? We think not. Proctor (1990) points out that such issues may be clarified

G ordon's work with Eve is clearly guided by his primary ethical obligation to focus on her well-being. This case is unusual in that failure could actually endanger the client's survival, but our obligations are no less serious when this is not the case.

Gordon acts on his ethical obligation by first conducting scientific inquiry to locate the best intervention methods for his specific client and her specific circumstances (rather than simply using the methods with which he is most comfortable). Taking special note of the lack of research about HIV-positive women, he proceeds with caution and carefully monitors Eve's outcomes. It is not unusual to have a client whose circumstances and problems are not covered by evidence-based interventions; ethics compel us in these cases to be especially vigilant in selecting interventions and monitoring outcomes.

Gordon's literature review suggests a number of other stress-reduction methods that have been shown to be effective (e.g., systematic relaxation), but Eve chooses not to take advantage of these interventions, and on this issue, Gordon respects her right to self-determination. This situation is especially frustrating to Gordon as he observes evidence from her data that her medication compliance continues to be dangerous to her health.

Finally, Gordon is committed to Eve's well-being, not to evidence-based practices, so when monitoring of Eve's outcomes demonstrates lack of sufficient progress using the intervention with the best research support he can locate, Gordon suggests a new intervention based on Eve's specific needs. You may note that we cite little evidence of the effectiveness of the technological intervention Gordon finally implements (the Pill Phone) for her problem, and there are certainly no meta-analyses of randomized clinical trials; in this case, Gordon is using the best available evidence he has: the data showing effectiveness with his client.

by returning to the purpose of the evaluation. In outcome-informed practice, that purpose is always *to improve this client's outcomes*.

## CONCLUSIONS

In reality, outcome-informed practice is nothing new. The social work profession was founded on the desire to improve the lives of our clients, whether we practice with individuals, families, groups, communities, or societies. Evidence-based practice is intended to enhance our efforts to do this, and the enthusiastic proponents of evidence-based practice certainly discuss evaluation of outcomes with individual clients (e.g., Rubin, 2008). We are simply endeavoring to elaborate on these issues and to provide tools to make it easy for you to monitor your clients' outcomes.

Our emphasis on client outcomes also recognizes reality. The simple fact is that most practitioners use one method with which they are familiar and in which they are (we hope) well trained and experienced. Probably most often that model is somewhat eclectic, though perhaps based primarily in one camp, such as CBT. It is not practical to expect social workers to be well trained and competent in a wide range of treatment models; most schools of social work teach a limited number of models. Even if one could reach competence in a handful of models, most practice contexts are not conducive to staying well informed about current research on multiple models. We hope that you will select a model that has been shown by research to be sound, but at the very least (and even with the most highly researched models) we hope you will carefully monitor your clients' outcomes to be sure that they are moving toward their goals. This is the heart of social work.

**PRACTICE TEST** The following questions will test your knowledge of the content found within this chapter and help you prepare for the licensing exam by applying chapter content to practice. For more questions styled like the licensing exam, visit **MySocialWorkLab.com**

1. There are numerous reasons to measure and monitor each client's progress in a relatively objective way. Which of the following is the most important?
   a. Develop knowledge about the effectiveness of interventions
   b. Demonstrate accountability to funders and other stakeholders
   c. Enhance your relationship with your clients
   d. Improve client outcomes

2. Ongoing, relatively objective feedback about client progress is especially beneficial for psychotherapy clients who are doing
   a. Better than expected
   b. As well as expected
   c. Worse than expected
   d. As well as expected in some ways but not others

3. Social workers are most likely to
   a. Overestimate client progress
   b. Underestimate client progress
   c. Accurately estimate client progress
   d. Neither underestimate nor overestimate client progress

4. RCTs are especially useful for
   a. Demonstrating whether interventions are effective with the average client
   b. Testing the effects of almost all interventions of interest to social workers
   c. Demonstrating whether interventions are effective with a particular client
   d. Accounting for the effect of culture, ethnicity, age, gender, sexual orientation, and social class on client outcomes

5. A social worker selects an intervention for an Asian-American client who is questioning her gender identity and is depressed. There is considerable evidence from randomized clinical trials that the intervention the social worker selects is effective for alleviating depression. Yet, the client deteriorates during intervention. What are possible reasons for this deterioration?

6. A social worker is working with the client described in question 5. The social worker doesn't think that he has the time to measure and monitor this client's progress, but it seems to the social worker as if the client is progressing satisfactorily. Unexpectedly, the client drops out of treatment. How could the social worker have been so mistaken?

# SUCCEED WITH

Visit **MySocialWorkLab** for more licensing exam test questions, and to access case studies, videos, and much more.

# 4

# Assessment

## The Early Stages
## of Outcome-Informed Practice

| Advancing Core Competencies in This Chapter | | | | |
|---|---|---|---|---|
| ✖ Professional Identity | ✖ Ethical Practice | ✖ Critical Thinking | ✖ Diversity in Practice | ✖ Human Rights & Justice |
| ✖ Research-Based Practice | ✖ Human Behavior | ■ Policy Practice | ✖ Practice Contexts | ✖ Engage, Assess, Intervene, Evaluate |

Roland Jackson is referred to Susan, a hospital social worker, after his second visit to the emergency department (ED) for troubled breathing, rapid heartbeat, and panic. Tests have ruled out medical reasons for his symptoms. He is a 35-year-old married African-American with two sons, ages 10 and 13. He is employed in a manufacturing plant, one of few employers in his small town offering good wages and benefits.

At Susan's first appointment with Mr. Jackson, she reads his hospital record and asks him to describe the experiences that led him to the ED, paying special attention to his affect as he speaks and seeking details about what happened on those occasions. She also asks him to describe a typical day, including highlights ("breakfast and dinner with my wife and boys") and lowlights ("interactions with my boss"). His wife attends this session, and she provides a description of when her husband's problems became apparent to her and how he is different now than he was before.

Noticing that Mr. Jackson becomes anxious when he talks about work, Susan asks him if there are problems there. He relates that his boss is extremely critical and disrespectful of him and other employees, frequently shouting and using racist remarks and epithets. "I worry all the time about losing my job. I can hardly sleep for wondering how I could support my family—how we would survive—if that happened. Sometimes I think about that all night."

Assessment is the systematic collection, organization, and interpretation of data related to a client's functioning in order to make decisions or recommendations about intervention or other services. Social work scholars clearly recognize the importance of assessment; there are multiple treatises on the subject, and schools of social work without exception emphasize assessment in coursework and field experiences. Agencies usually require completion of lengthy assessment forms to be placed in clients' records, and supervision often includes placing assessment under a microscope. Every model or framework of social work practice addresses the assessment process, and though each model emphasizes different aspects, consensus exists about the importance of a competent assessment for effective practice.

At its most basic and least controversial, the purpose of assessment is to collect the information needed to help clients reach their goals. Jordan and Franklin (2011) elaborate that assessment is "ongoing analysis and synthesis of information about the client and his or her social environment for the purpose of formulating a diagnosis or coherent intervention plan to help the client" (p. 4). O'Hare (2005) highlights further the complexities of assessment, when he characterizes it as "a form of problem analysis" (p. 14), explicitly adding reflection and reasoning to the assembly of facts.

Our review of multiple social work texts leads us to conclude that all approaches to assessment expect that it will contribute to forming good working relationships; identifying client problems and goals; integrating understanding of clients' social contexts, obstacles to change, and strengths or resources; and informing intervention plans. Beyond these universal generalities, assessment occurs within the context of an agency or practice setting (which may prescribe or delimit the process), as well as the practitioner's understanding of human development and behavior and approach to practice.

Therefore, consistent with Berlin and Marsh (1993), we emphasize assessment as a series of judgments wherein the social worker integrates a great deal of information of various types from different sources to inform efforts to help the client reach his or her goals, at the same time building a relationship with the client by demonstrating compassionate understanding.

In this chapter, we do not attempt to lay out everything you need to know to do a good assessment; there are already several excellent texts for that purpose (e.g., Corcoran & Walsh, 2010; Franklin & Jordan, 2011). Moreover, we do not provide detail about the qualitative data all competent social workers incorporate into their understanding of their clients: data about the client's appearance (disheveled? neat? poorly or well groomed? poorly nourished?), manner (calm? nervous? angry?), speech (articulate? confused?), and the hundred other important details we can gain through observation. Other qualitative data are gleaned from agency intake forms, conversation, and other methods, and we certainly do not advocate dismissing such narrative information. Particularly when these data come from multiple sources and are combined with expertise, experience, and objective data, they are invaluable. In this book, however, we emphasize the aspects of assessment that are critical to outcome-informed practice, with particular focus on methods of reducing subjectivity and bias.

# OUTCOME-INFORMED PRACTICE: THE SCIENTIFIC METHOD AND CRITICAL THINKING

Our approach to practice and assessment is rooted in science. As Mary Richmond (and before her, our Charity Organization Societies ancestors) emphasized, assessment is scientific; that's what distinguishes it from sitting with a friend at Starbucks discussing her problems with her boyfriend. Reid (2003) reminds us, however, that there are two distinct applications of science in social work practice. The first is the application of scientific knowledge—as demonstrated in the evidence-based practice movement, for example. We do not just randomly try things to see what happens, but prefer interventions for which there is some external evidence of effectiveness (be it research or personal experience).

The second and somewhat more neglected aspect of science, and one that can be and is also used in practice models that do not claim to be evidence-based, is use of the scientific method, that is a method of practice wherein we systematically construct hypotheses (*Perhaps this client is particularly vulnerable to discrimination due to childhood experiences*), test those hypotheses (*Tell me about other experiences you've had in your life with prejudice and discrimination*), and revise those hypotheses in light of new knowledge (*Mr. Jackson says he has experienced the usual day-to-day experiences, such as being watched closely while he is shopping, but believes he handles these experiences well. Perhaps his responses to what is happening now are not related to previous experiences of racism*). And the process begins again.

Use of the scientific method means that our understanding of our clients is always tentative. Gilgun (2005) calls this "holding [our] knowledge lightly" (p. 59). It recognizes the complexity of human behavior and explicitly rejects the notion that we can completely understand another's perspective. *I may mostly work within the cognitive behavior therapy framework, but I cannot approach every client I see with the untested assumption that his or her problem is a problem of dysfunctional thinking. I must hypothesize and gather data (particularly from the client, who is the expert on his or her situation, although we recognize that this won't be possible with all clients, e.g., very young children).*

The scientific method bids us engage in reflection about what clients and others tell us and what we observe, based on our understanding of human behavior. We seek both confirmatory and disconfirmatory information. Moreover, the scientific method involves comparing alternatives for goodness of fit.

The scientific method is directly connected to critical thinking, which though often discussed in the context of evidence-based practice (e.g., Gambrill, 2005) is completely comfortable in many approaches to practice. A full discussion of critical thinking is beyond the scope of this chapter, but a brief review is in order.

Gambrill's (2005) application of critical thinking to social work practice emphasizes practice as a series of judgments made under conditions of uncertainty and many potential sources of error. "Critical thinking involves clearly describing and carefully evaluating our claims and arguments, no matter how cherished, and considering alternative views when needed to arrive at decisions that do more good than harm" (pp. 11–12). She emphasizes paying attention to the process of making practice judgments, examining the context in which problems occur, asking questions from different points of view, identifying and questioning our assumptions, and considering the different consequences of different beliefs and actions.

Later, we discuss assessment from such a critical, scientific approach. We highlight aspects of assessment that are crucial to the outcome-informed practice approach to social work practice, rather than covering the basic essential skills of open-ended questions, reflective listening, and the like, which are covered in most basic social work practice texts.

# DEFINING THE PROBLEMS

A case usually begins with a presenting complaint or problem that explains why the client is seeking professional services. Often, of course, the presenting complaint turns out *not* to be the problem you and the client will tackle in the intervention, but it is the best starting point for the process of inquiry and engagement with a client. An assessment should be efficient: as comprehensive as necessary, and as parsimonious as possible, incorporating everything you hear from and observe about a client, as well as any collateral sources you have. Especially critical is understanding of the various contexts in which your clients live, since it is there that you may find the causes and most certainly will identify obstacles and resources related to resolution of clients' problems.

## Practice Models Provide Guidance

Although there are many commonalities, specific practice models focus differentially on specific aspects of assessment. For example, solution-focused intervention minimizes historical data except as it concerns occasions characterized by the absence of the identified problem (Corcoran, 2005). Behaviorally-based intervention models focus on functional analyses of behavior, which operationalize clients' behaviors and interactional patterns to shed light on the purposes served by problem behavior (Cooper, Heron, & Heward, 2007).

Such differences in focus are inevitable because models employ their own unique ideas about how behavior develops and changes to organize information into useful chunks—to form order out of chaos (Howe, 2002). The scientific method reminds us, however, to be cautious and tentative in our use of such frameworks, to try out other ways of thinking

In an effort to fully understand Mr. Jackson's problems, Susan seeks as much detail as possible about his stress at work, worry, and panic attacks. She begins with his physical symptoms as documented in the ED record, but also explores how he experiences the panic attacks ("What are you thinking about? What emotions are you feeling?"), how he feels about the troublesome interactions with his boss, the content of his worries ("What thoughts run through your mind when you can't sleep?"), and how all these things influence his behavior and how he feels about himself.

Susan is well trained and experienced in cognitive behavior therapy and believes that many emotional problems result from dysfunctional thinking, but she does not assume that dysfunctional thinking is the cause of Mr. Jackson's problems. She also believes that his affect (sad, somewhat impatient) is consistent with both anxiety and clinical depression, but she does not begin to attach either of these labels. Depression and anxiety instead are hypotheses she will explore, along with other possibilities.

about the information we receive from clients, and to be open to the idea that our models and frameworks may not be right for every case. For example, cognitive behavior therapy is not appropriate as the sole method for dealing with unemployment, poverty, and homelessness, although it may be useful for specific tasks related to intervention.

Social workers use different tools to collect information systematically. Some use eco-maps (Hartman, 1995) or genograms (McGoldrick, Gerson, & Shellenberger, 1999) to provide a framework for discussing context and social resources with clients (though we know of no empirical evidence demonstrating that such methods yield better outcomes for clients than any other method). Others simply begin with "How can I help you today?" and engage in conversation, following up on answers that seem important and then filling in gaps. Some social workers (few, according to Richey, Blythe, & Berlin, 1987) begin with standardized screening measures and then follow up on potential issues indicated by clients' scores.

All of these methods can be fruitful for generating data to guide assessment. However, outcome-informed practice is characterized by the attempt to maximize the objectivity of the data collected—without rejecting the types of more subjective, qualitative data discussed earlier—and the interpretations of those data through use of the scientific method. This effort to maximize objectivity is the first major hallmark of outcome-informed practice and is exemplified through the use of outcome measures, discussed later.

A problem that is common to all methods of social work practice, and indeed to the efforts of all helping professionals, is the client who is unable to gather data, for reasons of developmental or cognitive disability, poor literacy, or other reasons. Young children can provide some information, but that information may be limited in various ways. In all cases, however, practitioners must have accurate, relevant data to provide competent services.

In most cases, clients who cannot provide data come to us with others who can: parents of young children, family members of the disabled, and often nurses or other personnel in nursing homes, for example. We can think of no instance in which competent services can be provided in the complete absence of data about clients' problems, goals, strengths, and outcomes. The fact that outcome-informed practice emphasizes constant monitoring of client outcomes merely calls attention to this universal fact.

When clients cannot provide information directly, other sources (including the examples listed earlier) must provide the information you need, although you will be lacking the client's subjective self-reports of outcomes, for example of negative self-thoughts and sad mood. You will be missing his or her goals as well, and all of these are important. In all cases, we seek a variety of data from various sources, and in these cases, we will be especially vigilant to get as many sources of different types of data as possible. Ethics require us to protect the client's self-determination as much as possible, so we take special care when clients cannot provide direct input.

There are also clients (usually called *mandated* or *involuntary*) who do not want services but are required by law to be in your office. Clearly, it is a challenge to get the kind of data needed to provide competent outcome-informed practice with these individuals. However, we see this as a practice issue, irrespective of the methods you use; you simply cannot work with a client unless the client enters into a working relationship with you. See Rooney (2009) and Trottera (1999) for detailed discussions of methods for working with mandated clients.

**Engage, Assess, Intervene, Evaluate**

***Practice Behavior Example:*** *Select appropriate intervention strategies*

**Critical Thinking Question:** What practice models might be useful for Mr. Jackson's assessment, and what are the potential advantages and disadvantages of these practice models for this particular case?

## The Problem List

The first goal of assessment is a list of the problems identified by the client, stated as precisely as possible, and based on as much pertinent information as you can gather. *Problems* are specific situations, conditions, or concerns that need to be addressed in order to achieve desired goals, including difficulties or deficiencies to be remediated or prevented, as well as assets and strengths to be enriched. The problem list, which may be modified many times and should be considered a draft, consists of the problems identified by the client, in the client's own words where appropriate, in language as specific as possible.

The process of moving from a client's initial problem statement (*I've been having these terrible attacks*) to the working problem list is a matter of adding more and more specificity and detail to the client's articulation of his or her problems, and this process involves the basic skills of reflective listening, hypothesis-generation, and hypothesis-testing.

One issue that is related to the social worker's practice model as well as his or her unique practice style is whether the problem list should be comprehensive or more circumscribed. Some models, such as solution-based casework, compile a short list of the most urgent issues to be addressed immediately (Antle, Barbee, Christensen, & Martin, 2008), whereas others begin with a more comprehensive list and proceed to set priorities for immediate intervention. Both approaches have merit; the short-list approach enables intervention to begin more quickly and perhaps to be more focused. The latter approach, on the other hand, may provide a richer context that is helpful for goal-setting and intervention. For example, although Mr. Jackson may not want to address the problem with you, it might be wise to be aware of it if he is estranged from his extended family.

Working from the scientific method frequently requires you to check your hypotheses by seeking the client's confirmation or disconfirmation: "Mr. Jackson, I am forming an idea of your situation here, but I might not be right. As I see it right now, we can state your problems like this: First, you have been having panic attacks (explaining to him what panic attacks are if necessary), which are frightening and very unpleasant; second, you are worrying constantly about losing your job; third, you are experiencing a great deal of stress at work, particularly when you interact with your boss. Finally, worry and these events at work are causing you other problems, including difficulty sleeping and eating and behaving the way you want to with your family. Is that an accurate picture? Have I left anything out?" (Note the tentative language. At this point, you want your client to be able to feel comfortable saying "No! That isn't it at all.")

If Mr. Jackson confirms these generally stated problems as the ones he'd like to work on, you still need a way of pinning down the frequency, duration, and severity of his problems and the circumstances impinging on intervention, both positive and negative. Measurement helps us achieve this important goal of specificity in assessment and moves us closer to helping him set priorities for intervention. It is simply a systematic process of assigning labels (usually numbers) to characteristics of people, objects, or events using explicit and consistent rules, so, ideally, the labels accurately represent the characteristic measured.

Every social work assessment includes measurement of the client's problems, of course (see Nelsen, 1994). Some methods are relatively subjective and "loose": *Mr. Jackson is more stressed when he must talk to his boss about problems than when they meet in the break room.* Others are relatively more objective, that is relatively less influenced by personal feelings, beliefs, experiences, interpretations, or other biases or prejudices, and concrete: *Every one of the 5–10 daily interactions with his boss causes Mr. Jackson to*

**M**r. Jackson confirms Susan's general impression of his problems, but she needs more information to test the hypotheses she is forming. First, she asks him to complete several standardized measures, including the Penn State Worry Questionnaire—Past Week (PSWQ-PW) (Meyer, Miller, Metzger, & Borkovec, 2008; Stöber & Bittencourt, 1998), the Panic Disorder Severity Scale (PDSS) (Shear et al., 1997, 2008), and the Quick Inventory of Depressive Symptomatology—Self-Report (QIDS-SR) (Rush et al., 2003, 2006; Trivedi et al., 2004). These measures will help her understand the severity of his problems, and she also can use the scores to measure his progress as they work together over the coming weeks. (The PSWQ-PW, the QIDS-SR, and other standardized scales are reproduced in Appendix A.)

Second, Susan works with Mr. Jackson to construct an individualized measure of the stress produced by his interactions with his boss at work (see Chapter 10), and they discuss his interactions with his boss in the past week using this individualized scale. He will carry a small spiral notebook in his pocket and rate each interaction for the next week. They construct a scale from 1 (pleasant or neutral, no stress at all) to 3 (mildly stressful) to 5 (moderately stressful) to 7 (extremely stressful) and go through the scale to agree on the meaning of each score to Mr. Jackson by linking each data point to specific previous interactions:

- 1 (pleasant or neutral, no stress at all): "I haven't had an interaction like this with him in a long time. I guess when he first came and we'd just pass in the hall it was like this. Nothing had happened yet and we'd be like—you know—'Hey, how ya' doin'?' "

- 3 (mildly stressful): "I guess it's a 3 now when I just pass him in the hall. Even when it's a 'hey-how-ya'-doin' thing now, so much has happened that I tense up just seeing him. My neck and shoulders get tight and I breathe a little fast."

- 5 (moderately stressful): "Yesterday we had to talk about a problem on the production floor, and I'm pretty sure he thought the slowdown was my fault, although he didn't say that. My hands got sweaty, I could tell I was red in the face, and my voice didn't sound normal. I felt like a dope, and then I thought about how stupid I looked all afternoon. That's a 5."

- 7 (extremely stressful): "Two weeks ago he blew up at one of my guys on the floor—he isn't supposed to deal with them directly—and he used the 'N' word. My guy was humiliated. I was so upset I thought I might pass out, but I couldn't say anything to my boss. I went in the bathroom and threw up. That's a 7."

*sweat, hyperventilate, and feel sick to his stomach.* More objective measurement involves operational definitions (as you see earlier on the individualized scale), that is definitions that assign meaning to the problem in terms of the activities or operations used to measure it, ideally in a way that contains relevant features of the problem and excludes irrelevant features. Outcome-informed practice is characterized by combining the qualitative data all social workers collect (i.e., narrative information gathered through observation, conversation, and clinical methods) with more objective and concrete data, that is the use of numbers. Ideally, when possible, it also involves collaborating with the client to understand and interpret his or her progress as indicated by the numerical outcome data.

## Quantifying the Client's Problems

"But I collect a rich tapestry of data that gives me a comprehensive view of my client as *she* describes it," you might say. "My client can tell me how miserable she is and how intense the fights have been with her husband, and I can see that when she recounts those fights. I *understand*. What do numbers add?"

The essential components provided by numbers are specificity, a degree of objectivity, and the ability to monitor client progress. Let's be clear: Most social workers are good people who *really* want their clients to get better. And our clients usually come to us in great distress, and they *really* want to feel better. Moreover, they appreciate our help, and oftentimes they *really* want to please us. Such a situation is a perfect setup for bias, particularly when there is ambiguity, as there always is in clinical decision-making. Hunsley and Mash (2008) call assessment a process in which practitioners "must interactively formulate and test hypotheses by integrating data that are often incomplete or inconsistent" (p. 4).

Bias is simply a leaning based on emotion: *I want my client to get better, so, especially if there is any ambiguity, I tend to see improvement.* It is normal and natural—but it is not scientific and can obscure reality and your client's chances of reaching her goals. Confirmatory bias, *where I see what I want or expect to see* (Nickerson, 1998), is especially insidious, as shown in Figure 4.1.

Confirmatory bias is the tendency to perceive and pay more attention to data that confirm an original impression. We all have a tendency to believe in our initial judgments, even when we learn that those judgments were based on inaccurate information (Gambrill, 2005). Moreover, after making a judgment (*Mr. Jackson is less anxious and upset this week*), our tendency is to seek evidence confirming the accuracy of that judgment (*He looks more rested. I was right—he's better!*)

Of course seeking confirmatory evidence is a good thing, but it may be even more important to seek *disconfirming* evidence, that is to engage in *falsification*, to minimize bias. Gilgun (2005) defines falsification as seeking "information that challenges our own understandings and an openness to contradictory evidence" (p. 52). So if Susan and Mr. Jackson believe he has felt less anxious this week, she should also be especially alert to evidence that contradicts those impressions. For example, did Mr. Jackson's wife observe edginess or shortness of temper at home? Perhaps coming to Susan's office gives him hope so that he discounts the anxiety he has felt in the last week, or perhaps he wants to please her by appearing to feel better and so convinces himself that he does. We counter that bias by seeking evidence to disconfirm our impressions. Monitoring his condition with appropriate outcome measures is an effective way to do this.

**Figure 4.1 •** Confirmatory Bias.

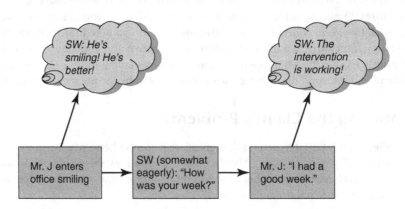

Subsequent chapters in this book provide details on five types of outcome measures for monitoring your clients' progress, and so we only summarize here. Collecting data with these measures at the initial appointment not only will provide more detail—and more *objective* detail—on your client's situation, but also will give you a baseline for comparison in subsequent sessions.

## Standardized Scales

Standardized scales like those Susan uses with Mr. Jackson measure constructs that are common to many individuals, such as depression, through administration of the same items, such as statements or questions, to different people. The same procedures for administering, scoring, and interpreting the measure are used with all respondents. Information is usually available about the reliability and validity of standardized scales, that is whether they are really and accurately measuring what you want to measure, and norms make it possible to compare individual scores to population scores. With some scales, research also allows you to determine if individual scores fall into a clinical range. (See Chapter 9 for more details about selecting, using, and interpreting data from standardized scales, as well as where you can go to find these resources. In particular, note the process that Susan would go through to select measures that have shown good properties with African-Americans. In Chapter 1, Mark goes through the same process to select appropriate measures for his Muslim client.)

## Individualized Rating Scales

Quantitative measurement does not mean exclusively standardized measures. It is also often useful to collaborate with your client to construct individualized measures to tap the exact issues of concern to your client, such as the severity of Mr. Jackson's negative encounters with the boss each day. Often this may be your only choice. We believe that even when you employ good standardized measures, it is helpful to use individualized measures as well, because they emphasize the "front and center" role of the client's perceptions and experiences. (See Chapter 10 for more detail about constructing and using individualized rating scales.)

## Behavioral Observation

In many cases, targets for intervention involve behavior, either overt or covert. Observation and recording of the frequency and/or duration of these behaviors provide important data for specifying problems and goals, as well as monitoring client progress during intervention. Direct observation (see Chapter 11) is conducted by another party. Recall Greg's behavioral observation of the number of inappropriate interactions with his foster daughter and Dahlia's self-monitored hours of sleeping and studying in Chapter 1, as well as Eve's self-monitoring of taking her medication and coping with stress in Chapter 3.

## Self-Monitoring

Self-monitoring is similar to behavior observation, but the client records his or her own behavior (see Chapter 12). It thus provides unique information often available only from the client, for example measures of depressed mood, negative thoughts, and behaviors that occur in private.

# Triangulation

*Triangulation* is an engineering term that describes a process of collecting data from several nearby locations to verify the location of a geographical point. In assessment, triangulation means that we collect data from several sources (client self-report, records, observations by others, etc.) and use different methods (standardized scales, individualized rating scales, daily logs, behavioral observation by client and others, practitioner observation, and expertise) to home in on the problems.

Triangulation is valuable for several reasons. First, it helps avoid "method bias," which is the tendency for data collected in the same way or from the same source to be in agreement. A pessimistic client's reports may always lean toward a negative view, for example, although others may be able to recount examples of improvement they have observed. In fact, this discovery based on your collection of data from different sources might lead to discussions with the client and identification of the client's negativity as either a problem or an obstacle to achieving his or her goals.

Second, using different methods and sources of information improves the validity of information because each has its own weaknesses, so that the combination should be stronger than any single one. For example, behavioral observations are subject to misinterpretation by observers, although standardized measures may contain social desirability bias. Moreover, different methods provide different angles on problems. Standardized scales tell us that Mr. Jackson's anxiety is in the clinical range; our observations and in-depth discussions with him inform us about the meaning of his problems to him. Our discussions with his wife suggest that changes in his behavior (distractibility, negative mood, lack of self-confidence in making decisions) have been apparent and getting worse for about a year, since his boss moved to that position, whereas he was not aware of those gradual changes. Thyer and Myers (2007) invoke the folk tale of several blind men who describe an elephant by touch when they talk of triangulation in assessment; one man describes the long trunk that moves constantly back and forth, another describes the shape of the large ears, and a third describes the short, thin tail. Just as each of the individuals was able to thoroughly and accurately describe one part of the elephant, each aspect of

---

After about an hour's observation and discussion with both Mr. Jackson and his wife, reading his hospital records, and looking at the measures Susan and Mr. Jackson have completed, Susan feels that they are ready to construct a working list of problems (though she knows that this list may change over time as she continues to assess and measure):

- He has been experiencing panic attacks of increasing severity for about 3 months, with the last two resulting in ED visits in the last 2 weeks.

- He is highly anxious at work when he talks with his boss, resulting in sweating, hyperventilating, trembling, and nausea.

- He is afraid he will be fired and worries constantly about how disastrous this would be for his family.

- As Mr. Jackson's worries have begun to intrude into other parts of his life, he is cross with his wife and children and has difficulty sleeping and eating.

Mr. Jackson agrees that this list is accurate and wants to focus on the second problem first, believing that reducing his anxiety at work is likely to help him with the other related problems.

assessment contributes a unique perspective on a case, and the information is enhanced by combining those perspectives.

## Setting Goals

Often we may be tempted to jump from the problem list directly to the intervention: *You're anxious? There is an excellent treatment protocol for anxiety using cognitive behavior therapy that has been shown to be very effective. Let's get right to it.* In fact, the evidence-based practice literature appears to move directly from diagnosis to intervention; that is, it is usually organized by either diagnosis (evidence-based practices for depression, for anxiety, etc.) or practice model (cognitive behavior therapy, behavior modification).

But, first, it's important to establish exactly how the client wants things to be different, that is to establish goals or desired outcomes. Going through the process of goal-setting honors the client's right to self-determination, avoids false assumptions, increases his or her motivation to change, and enhances his or her self-efficacy (Hepworth, Rooney, Rooney, Strom-Gottfried, & Larsen, 2006). Perhaps most critical, goals bring focus to our work with clients and prevent us from falling into the trap of simply ruminating endlessly about problems in the absence of moving toward change.

In addition, although goals naturally emerge from discussions about client problems, it is important to keep these two ideas distinct. *Problems* are specific situations, conditions, or concerns that need to be addressed in order to achieve desired goals. *Goals* are general and abstract statements of desired outcomes for which an intervention is implemented. Often, of course, goals are mirror images of problems (e.g., problem = constant worrying about getting fired, goal = stop or reduce worrying), but this is not always true (e.g., problem = loneliness, goal = engage in more pleasant social interactions). In many cases, however, problem reversal is not the goal of intervention (Proctor & Rosen, 2003).

The range of different types of goals demonstrates how they go well beyond the reversal of problems. Goals also can be preventive (e.g., prevent alcoholism and related problems), protective (e.g., protect current level of health), promotional (e.g., promote healthy family relationships and interactions), or rehabilitative (e.g., complete court-mandated class after arrest for driving and drinking). Goals can be formulated in terms of increasing something positive (e.g., expressions of warmth, empathy, praise) or decreasing something negative (e.g., expressions of criticism). Although there is considerable agreement that they should be expressed in positive terms whenever possible, we find that in the vast majority of cases clients tend to express their goals in negative terms; that is, they want to remove or reduce their problems. In any case, goals should indicate change in a client's real-world functioning or quality of life that is sufficient or meaningful to the client, significant others, and/or society at large. Many social workers begin goal-setting by asking questions such as "How will you know when you have solved these problems? How will that look?" This also can be posed as the "miracle question": *Suppose you woke up in the morning and a miracle had occurred overnight, and your problem was completely gone. How would you know that? How would you be different?*

Finally, goals are important because they allow us to monitor clients' progress in light of what they hope to accomplish. They also allow us to regularly measure "where the client is" compared to where he or she wants to be.

**M**r. Jackson has some difficulty with setting goals. Susan asks him, "How will things be different if our work together is successful?" and at first he replies, "My boss will treat me and the other employees with respect." Susan explains that his goals must be about *him*: what *he* will do and how *he* will feel. It isn't possible for the two of them to change his boss's behavior or attitudes.

After more discussion, he sets the following goals:

- I will feel normal—not nervous—when I talk to my boss. I will be able to talk to my boss without physical symptoms of anxiety (sweating, rapid heartbeat and breathing).

- I will be relaxed and easygoing at home, like I used to be (or restated as "I will be pleasant and patient with my wife and children like I was before").

- I will be able to sleep and eat normally again.

- I won't worry about getting fired all the time.

There are a number of practice considerations involved in establishing goals. Goals should be linked clearly to the target of intervention; for example, successfully applying for promotion would not be an appropriate goal for Mr. Jackson now, although preserving positive job evaluations for future promotion might be appropriate. Goals should be emotionally compelling to the client, not harmful to others if achieved, attainable, and legal (Garvin, 2009). In addition, the selection of goals often involves personal values, which are sometimes in conflict, such as between husband and wife, parent and child, individual and society, even social worker and client. Therefore, goal-setting may require a process of discussion and negotiation among different involved parties in much the same way that targets for intervention are selected. Consequently, when establishing and pursuing goals in practice, due consideration should be given to a client's racial and ethnic identity, national origin, cultural background, gender, age, sexual orientation, disability status, religion, extent of spirituality, and socioeconomic status.

## Considerations in Goal Formulation

Goals are central to engaging in effective practice in that they provide a standard for ongoing monitoring of client progress and a basis for evaluating ultimate client success. Therefore, they provide ongoing guidance about whether an intervention should be

**I**t is possible to conceive of a number of goals that might alleviate Mr. Jackson's problems and yet be completely unacceptable: killing his boss, for example. Our preference might be to file a discrimination suit due to his boss's racist remarks or to report him to his superiors for same, in hopes that he will be removed from his authority over Mr. Jackson. However, Mr. Jackson rejects these goals because the boss is the son of the owner and others have been fired for criticizing him. Another goal might be to find another job, but this is unacceptable to Mr. Jackson because he enjoys wages and seniority at his company that exceed those he could command elsewhere. He also rejects any notion of mediation or discussion with his boss of their communication difficulties; such actions are not consistent with his upbringing or temperament, and he's sure they wouldn't work.

continued, changed, or terminated. For goals to be useful for outcome-informed practice, they should be well-defined, specific, and measurable.

First, goals should be stated in terms of outcomes for the client, for example the client's adherence to an exercise program, self-injurious thoughts and behaviors, illegal drug use, or binge drinking. It would, for example, not be an appropriate goal statement to say, "I will provide cognitive behavior therapy to help Mr. Jackson feel less anxious." Decreasing anxiety is an excellent goal, but providing therapy designed to decrease anxiety is part of the intervention plan, not the goal. As fundamental as this principle appears to be, it is not uncommon to see goals expressed as provision of services. Moreover, as illustrated in the case example, the goal should be stated according to the client's behavior, not the behavior of others. An obvious and extreme example involves work with an abusive husband, whose goal would be "to handle my anger nonviolently," rather than "my wife won't make me mad."

Second, goal statements should specify what clients will be doing to show that they have achieved goals. For example, *Mr. Jackson will be able to talk to his boss without feeling anxious; will be patient and pleasant with his wife and children; and will sleep well*. It is not at all uncommon for clients to express their goals initially very vaguely: *I want to feel better* or *We want to get along better*. However, an important part of a successful assessment is to narrow that down as much as possible. Working with the abusive husband in the earlier paragraph, we might hope to further specify his goal of acting nonviolently as *to take a time-out when I get angry and then discuss the issue, rather than hitting*.

So although we hope Mr. Jackson will feel better after intervention, the more specific his goals are, the more likely he is to achieve success. We might work with him to operationalize his goal, that is, define it in terms of the activities or operations used to measure it: *Mr. Jackson will remain relaxed and pleasant in interactions with his boss* and *Mr. Jackson will not worry about work when he is at home*. Or he might wish to define his goals even more specifically: *When Mr. Jackson talks to his boss he will feel and act as he does in a conversation with others at work, or as he did with his previous boss. When he is at home he will not worry about work or losing his job*.

Third, goal statements should specify when, where, and with whom clients will do something. For example, the goal might be for a client to spend more time with his or her children at home on the weekend, ask more questions in algebra class, or eliminate negative self-statements at work. Mr. Jackson might want to distinguish between business-related conversations and mere social exchanges with his boss, or he may want to differentiate between routine work issues and conflicts/problem areas. He certainly has different goals for his behavior and feelings at home as opposed to the work setting. Setting goals according to specific circumstances, such as at home with family, at work with co-workers, and at work with authority figures, provides details that are important for good intervention plans and ongoing monitoring of outcomes. This process also can demonstrate for the client that he is successful in some arenas and perhaps suggest tactics for use in other arenas.

## Setting Objectives

Let's return for a moment to the three M's: measure, monitor, and modify the intervention as needed. Well-stated, specific goals point us in the right direction to accomplish these tasks. However, we need to do more than go in the right direction when we take a journey. Objectives provide the road signs to keep us on the right path.

It is important to differentiate goals from objectives. As described earlier, *goals* are most often stated in a client's own words and, at least in the early stages of intervention, tend to be more general; *objectives* are stated more specifically and involve quantification (i.e., numbers) in some way. Although there are many definitions for both of these terms, there is some consensus for our differentiation of *goals* and *objectives*.

At his first session, Mr. Jackson may express his goal as *to feel better* or *to be like I was before*. The wise social worker will work with him to be more specific about what he means, perhaps clarifying his goal as *to be free of anxiety* or *to feel healthy and relaxed at work and at home*. Although these goals are stated more specifically than his initial goal statement, they are still somewhat general. Nevertheless, it is important to use his own words here, if only to indicate our respect for and understanding of his desires. To construct useful objectives for these goals, we will use numbers. For example, an objective for Mr. Jackson might be to reduce his score on a standardized anxiety measure to the non-clinical range or to a specific benchmark score. This is just one more way that we reduce the subjectivity and possibility of bias as we monitor his progress.

## Intermediate Goals and Objectives

It can be overwhelming for clients to think about their ultimate goals and objectives, so effective social workers typically also collaborate with clients to form intermediate goals or objectives. These are smaller goals or objectives that must be accomplished in order

---

Susan and Mr. Jackson take his goals and form measureable objectives, so that it will be easier to monitor his progress:

- Goal: I will feel normal—not nervous—when I talk to my boss. Objective: Using a checklist constructed with my social worker, I will reduce the unpleasant symptoms I have when I talk to my boss from an average of five per interaction to two. Alternatively, we might work with Mr. Jackson to create a single item to describe his nervousness in interactions with his boss, with the objective of reducing his score from 5 on a 7-point scale to 3 for most interactions.

- Goal: I will be relaxed and easygoing at home, like I used to be. Objective: I will reduce the number of thoughts I have about work while I'm at home from five per evening (the baseline at start of intervention) to two. For this objective, it might be valuable to measure his family's perceptions of his behavior as well as his own.

- Goal: I will be able to sleep and eat normally again. Objective: I will go to sleep within

20 minutes of lying down and sleep at least 8 hours per night. I'll eat three meals a day, enough so I don't feel hungry. They may go further to specify Mr. Jackson's first goal and objective even more. For example, he agrees that it is normal for him to feel somewhat anxious when talking to a superior at work. He was raised to respect authority, and he recognizes and respects his boss's status. Using his single-item individualized rating scale, he suggests that a measure of 1 (same relaxed physical state as speaking with family and friends) is not realistic, but a 2 (somewhere between not stressed at all to mildly stressed) during routine conversations with his boss seems appropriate. When he must discuss conflictual issues, such as a problem with one of his crew or a snafu on the production line, he would be satisfied with a 3 (mildly stressed). He had a good working relationship with his former boss, and describes the interactions with him as satisfactory and consistent with these standards.

to achieve the ultimate desired outcomes. For example, before tackling his anxiety during discussions with his boss about problem issues, Mr. Jackson might want to achieve an intermediate goal of feeling comfortable during social and routine discussions; an objective might specify a specific score on an individualized or standardized measure. When he begins to feel more comfortable in these interactions, he may extend his expectations to more difficult situations. Intermediate goals thus may be less overwhelming and provide a sense of success to facilitate moving to more difficult goals.

**Engage, Assess, Intervene, Evaluate**

*Practice Behavior Example:* Collect, organize, and interpret client data

**Critical Thinking Question:** What specific problems were identified in Mr. Jackson's assessment, what corresponding goals and objectives were identified for each problem, and what other problems, goals, or objectives should you consider in collaboration with Mr. Jackson?

This is a good time to emphasize again that the purpose of regularly monitoring clients' outcomes in light of their goals and objectives is to use that information to adjust the intervention plan, if needed, and to do so in a timely fashion. In Mr. Jackson's case, weekly monitoring of intermediate goals may allow us to move faster than we might have expected (e.g., if he makes rapid progress on his intermediate goals and his progress seems to be generalizing), to change the intervention plan (e.g., if he is unable to achieve even the smallest change in his interactions with his boss), or even to go back to problem formulation (e.g., if he makes progress on the intermediate goals but finds that he feels no closer to his goal of feeling less anxiety over all). This approach is consistent with Hunsley and Mash's (2008) discussion of evidence-based assessments as a means for testing whether interventions have brought about meaningful changes in the client's life, either for better or worse.

## CASE CONCEPTUALIZATION

It might appear from the layout of this chapter that you begin and conclude formulating problems, and then you do the same with formulating goals and objectives, and then you move to case conceptualization. This is not true; assessment is a recursive process, particularly if done scientifically and with constant monitoring of client outcomes. Social work practice, like human nature, is messy and filled with ambiguity, so to some degree the assessment process is, too.

We mentioned earlier the pitfalls of moving directly from client problems to diagnosis to intervention, emphasizing that setting explicit goals provides focus and avoids misconstruing the client's wishes. Another step—or way of thinking about the entire process of assessment perhaps—is called *case conceptualization* or *case formulation* (Berman, 2010; Proctor & Rosen, 1983). Case conceptualization can bring added value to assessment and make it just a little less messy.

Persons (2008) describes case conceptualization as a way of integrating theory with the individual aspects of a case, or going from *nomothetic* to *idiographic* (Hunsley & Mash, 2008). A nomothetic formulation and treatment plan are general: for example, anxiety results from faulty thinking that attaches danger to certain situations, resulting in the physiological stress response, so an intervention is delivered according to a protocol to change the client's thinking and thus eliminate the inappropriate stress response. An idiographic case formulation and treatment plan describes the mechanisms that are causing and maintaining a particular client's symptoms, disorders, and problems and the plan for treating them in a particular individual. The case conceptualization is a set of hypotheses about the mechanisms causing and maintaining Mr. Jackson's symptoms, disorders, and problems.

Case conceptualization integrates a theory or model of human behavior to describe the client's problems and disorders, proposes mechanisms for the causes of the problems and the recent precipitants of current issues, and describes the origins of the problem. The result is an idiographic formulation of the case that is far more useful for intervention planning and monitoring than a simple diagnosis or problem list, and that provides a shared understanding for client and practitioner (Berlin & Marsh, 1993). Alter and Egan (1997) also include explicit statements of how the intervention will bring about the desired goals, given the theory or model being used. (Alter and Egan's use of the term *logic model* appears to be equivalent to *case conceptualization*, and they emphasize the critical thinking required for this step.) For example, if Susan chooses to address Mr. Jackson's case using cognitive behavior therapy, she would need to state how thought stopping or any other specific strategy would be expected to help him change his thinking and how she expects this change in thinking to eliminate or reduce his anxiety. In this way, the case conceptualization is useful for highlighting gaps in the social worker's logic when selecting an intervention.

Kuyken, Padesky, and Dudley (2009) consider case conceptualization to be a higher order of thinking in assessment that has hypothesis-testing as a central feature. Meier (2003) specifically asserts that inclusion of alternative explanations or theories provides one guard against ubiquitous confirmation bias. Austrian (2009) refers to this process as *inferential thinking*, a process wherein the social worker looks at the raw data obtained from the client to determine its meaning, "an intellectual process that retains the client's individual situation and also moves the case from what has been presented to one that is part of a class of cases" (p. 377). The result is a greater possibility of integrating and using theoretical knowledge to enhance client outcomes. For example, if Mr. Jackson's problems are common to African-Americans who must deal with racism on the job, there may be a whole body of literature to suggest useful tools for dealing with these problems. (We will not, of course, put aside our understanding of Mr. Jackson as an individual.) Indeed, there is a growing body of research demonstrating the effects of racism and discrimination on the mental health of African-American men (Watkins, Hudson, Caldwell, Siefert, & Jackson, 2011).

Perhaps the most useful aspect of case conceptualization is the way it explicitly incorporates diversity (Meier, 2003). Cultural identities (racial and ethnic minorities, gender, sexual orientation, etc.) encompass common developmental experiences, strengths, and other issues that can be proposed as hypotheses for understanding clients and explored for usefulness in designing and implementing interventions (Berman, 2010). You can see how our case conceptualization in the example of Mr. Jackson recognizes the central role of the racism he is experiencing in his problem. This may be the most important use of case conceptualization, since the evidence-based practice movement has generally assigned an "adjust after-the-fact" role to culture and diversity, rather than incorporating it from the start of the process of developing and testing interventions (Kazdin, 2008).

Case conceptualizations also can call attention to important lifespan issues that are part of understanding client problems and planning interventions. For example, Berman (2010) discusses important issues specific to stages of development for children that inform case conceptualization. Although she does not discuss adult developmental stages, they are clearly important to fully understanding and conceptualizing a case with a client. If Mr. Jackson were an unmarried man in his early 20s, his different developmental stage and situation might suggest different methods for intervening.

**B**uilding on the earlier stated problems list and all the data she has about Mr. Jackson, Susan conceptualizes this case:

Mr. Jackson suffers from intense anxiety and worry that originated in stressful interactions with his boss and have spilled over into his home life to affect his relationships and physical health. He must deal with his boss's insults, racial epithets, and lack of respect frequently in his daily work, but does not feel that he can take action to challenge his boss's inappropriate behavior. Mr. Jackson's main goal is to reduce his worry and anxiety to more normal levels at work, to return to his prior relaxed state away from work, and to eliminate the physical symptoms he is experiencing.

Mr. Jackson has many resources he can draw on to achieve his goals, including a supportive family, a wide circle of friends in which he is held in high regard, a history of excellent performance evaluations, and the respect of his peers at work. He is intelligent, highly motivated to solve his problems, and willing to make changes to achieve his goals. Susan feels that a significant obstacle to success is the effect of the racism and discrimination he is experiencing on his self-concept, but his experience with and attitude toward the routine discrimination he has experienced throughout his life will probably serve as a resource; he is not bitter and is able to see other people's racism as *their* problem, not his. At the same time, in most situations he protects his and his family's rights and interests competently and with self-respect.

Susan may look at interventions specifically designed to reduce anxiety, perhaps through systematic relaxation, or she may suggest a cognitive behavior therapy method to help Mr. Jackson change his thinking and reactions to his boss's inappropriate behavior (e.g., Butler, Fennell, & Hackmann, 2008). In any case, she will be aware of discrimination and oppression as significant aspects of his problems; like most African-Americans he must deal with the memories of other victimization experiences, and he lives in a society that permits the boss to behave as he does. Finally, Mr. Jackson's felt helplessness about dealing directly with his boss's behavior is realistic but surely provides an obstacle to successful achievement of his goals.

## When Case Conceptualization Is Especially Important

According to Persons (2008), there are certain situations in which case conceptualization can be particularly useful for resolving specific assessment and intervention problems. These include:

- *Multiple disorders and problems:* Few clients present with just one problem (Springer & Tripodi, 2009). In fact, it is probably the accumulation of problems that motivates most people to take the big step of seeking professional assistance; most of us have the resources to handle things that are thrown at us one at a time. A case conceptualization allows a practitioner to view problems in a way that provides a richer understanding of the client's contexts.
- *Multiple providers:* Many clients are involved with multiple providers, such as health care providers and nursing home or residential treatment center staff. A comprehensive case conceptualization can provide common understanding and a good organizing point for multiple providers. The case conceptualization can be invaluable for a multidisciplinary team for visualizing and remaining aware of the total picture of the client's case (Alter & Egan, 1997).
- *Situations not found in any intervention protocols:* Not every problem lends itself to diagnosis or simple description. Certainly, social work with community groups and organizations is outside this clinical approach and may benefit from a conceptualization that provides a good base for intervention planning.

- *Situations for which there are no evidence-based practices:* Research has not been conducted to determine the most effective interventions for every client problem, and sometimes interventions must be borrowed from related problems or client groups. For example, the literature on discrimination might give us some hints about specific ways Mr. Jackson can handle it at work without risking his job.
- *Treatment failure:* After verifying that the intervention was implemented correctly and that the client has followed through as intended, the next action to take when an intervention fails is to return to the case conceptualization. Have we failed to pay sufficient attention to important contexts of the client's life? Have we failed to use significant available resources or plan for likely barriers to success? Meier (2003) states, "Thorough reconceptualization of the case should be one of the first techniques attempted when treatment failure becomes apparent" (p. 45).
- *Multiple evidence-based practices:* For some diagnoses, multiple intervention protocols exist. How do we select the most likely to succeed? Case conceptualization may provide guidance.

## Considerations for Case Conceptualization

Meier (2003) urges humility in the construction of the case conceptualization (i.e., using the scientific method). It is an ongoing process; hypotheses may be confirmed or rejected at any point. Kuyken et al. (2009) also caution against forcing a case to fit a particular model of human behavior because we are comfortable with that model, citing the "Procrustean dilemma." Procrustes was a mythical character who was famous for inviting guests from far and wide to stay in his home with the claim that his guest bed would fit anyone. He did not tell potential guests that it might be necessary to cut off their legs or stretch them on a rack to make them fit the bed! We do well not to approach every case as an example of the method with which we are most comfortable, so case conceptualization may be an excellent place to try out alternatives. We might construct Mr. Jackson's problems in several ways, including faulty thinking, physiological reactions to stress, or any number of other possibilities.

If an intervention appears to have no effect at all, one of the most important steps to take (earlier, rather than later) is to return to the case conceptualization to determine if we may have forced the case into a model that does not fit. For example, we may attempt to take a cognitive behavior approach to working with Mr. Jackson, perhaps teaching him to change his thoughts about his boss's behavior. If he demonstrates proficiency at controlling his thoughts, and our graphs indicate he is doing so regularly, but his complaints and symptoms have not abated, we might want to return to the case conceptualization to consider another practice model.

### Human Behavior

**Practice Behavior Example:** *Critique and apply knowledge to understand person and environment*

**Critical Thinking Question:** What theories or models of human behavior might be useful for conceptualizing Mr. Jackson's case, and what questions and decisions should you consider when you apply these nomothetic theories or models specifically to Mr. Jackson?

Because it integrates the individual and the theoretical model, case conceptualization should give explicit consideration to the client's resources *in relation to the planned intervention*. That is, what resources are necessary for a client to successfully implement intervention X? Does this client have or can he develop those resources?

For example, if we are working within a cognitive behavior framework to help a client learn to monitor and change his or her thoughts, we need to be sure that the client has the cognitive capacity and inclination to understand and follow instructions, including monitoring procedures (Berman, 2010). Another model (such as operant conditioning) might be more useful for a client whose cognitive functioning is limited.

# DIAGNOSIS: A LIMITED BUT OFTEN NECESSARY TOOL

The *Diagnostic and Statistical Manual of Mental Disorders* (DSM; 2000) is a publication of the American Psychiatric Association that provides criteria for the classification of mental disorders, such as substance-related disorders, schizophrenia and other psychotic disorders, mood disorders, and anxiety disorders. It includes specific required symptoms and how long they must be present for each diagnosis, as well as additional information, for example, subtypes and/or categories, numerical codes and other information for recording diagnoses, associated features and disorders, specific culture, age, and gender features, prevalence, course, familial pattern, and differential diagnosis.

*DSM* was designed for use in clinical, educational, and research settings by health and mental health professionals. It is a fact of life: whether or not you believe in psychiatric diagnoses, if you are practicing in the mental health field, agency and managed care regulations require that you understand and employ the system of classification laid out in *DSM*. It is important to realize, however, that a diagnosis is not an assessment. Diagnosis may establish eligibility for services, facilitate discussion with other professionals across disciplines, and suggest bodies of literature for you to consult, but it is not sufficient for selecting and implementing an intervention plan. In fact, a diagnosis may not even be very informative for intervention.

Because much of the evidence-based practice literature is organized around diagnoses or problems (Corcoran & Walsh, 2010; Kirk & Reid, 2002), though, it can be easy to forget that a diagnosis is simply a social construction designed to facilitate talking to other

---

**S**usan is reluctant to assign a psychiatric diagnosis to Mr. Jackson, as she feels that his problems are entirely environmental and his reactions normal. Her agency, however, and his insurance company, both require a diagnosis. She discusses the problem, which she considers to be an ethical dilemma, with her supervisor.

Susan is already uncomfortable with not dealing directly with Mr. Jackson's boss's behavior, she notes; her preference would be to conceptualize the case as a response to racism and blatant discrimination and to move to stop that behavior. She is clear that her professional and ethical obligation is to pursue her client's goals, so she puts those preferences aside, but this is a source of irritation to her. Susan feels it would be dishonest and unethical to assign a psychiatric diagnosis because it conveys pathology, but after much discussion, she and her supervisor agree on a diagnosis of Adjustment Disorder Unspecified (309.9, "psychological response to an identifiable stressor or stressors that results in the development of clinically significant emotional or behavior symptoms" (American Psychiatric Association, 2000, pp. 679–680). If the insurance company refuses to accept that diagnosis, she and her supervisor will revisit the issue.

professionals. A diagnosis allows you to tell your supervisor that you are having difficulties with your depressed client, rather than your client "who is sad, tearful, lethargic and uninterested in things that once gave him pleasure, is unable to sleep or eat, and has had these symptoms for longer than 6 months." It is, in fact, an overly simplistic method that omits important information, not just about context but also about symptoms, strengths, and relevant circumstances and history.

Because knowledge is often organized around diagnosis, we can come to believe that it tells us more than it does. *DSM* implies nothing about etiology, meaning, client strengths, or barriers to effective intervention. (See Kirk & Reid, 2002, for a comprehensive history and discussion of the *DSM*.) Even the *DSM-TR* (text revision; American Psychiatric Association, 2000) itself cautions against making too much of diagnosis. Although the evidence-based practice literature frequently focuses on clinical diagnosis as a key term in the search for appropriate interventions (see Corcoran & Walsh, 2010), most experts agree that diagnosis does not really point to specific appropriate interventions (Persons, 2008).

In two aspects, evidence-based practice may place insufficient attention on the assessment process, at least in how it is presented in the literature. First, at least in many major publications, evidence-based practice often treats assessment minimally and as if diagnosis is the goal, since diagnoses are the jumping-off points for selecting interventions. This is logical, since evidence-based practice knowledge tends to be organized around diagnosis, mirroring the medical model (Proctor & Rosen, 2003). That is, medical practice often starts from diagnosis (strep throat) and then indexes that diagnosis to treatments (antibiotics) to reverse the problem (cure the disease).

Second, in some cases the drive to reach a valid diagnosis in order to construct the appropriate literature research question might displace the assembly of other important information. Should the search for the appropriate intervention for Mr. Jackson center around his diagnosis (309.9, Adjustment Disorder Unspecified), his demographic group (middle-aged, working-class, male, African-American), his goals (positive functioning at work and home), or even perhaps his experiences (racial prejudice and discrimination)? Clearly, one unintended consequence of an approach that emphasizes diagnosis may be failure to place a client in a context that aids in understanding and thus intervention planning. To be fair, evidence-based practice advocates do not explicitly suggest that diagnosis is all that's needed for selecting interventions—we just believe that more elaboration is needed on the other aspects that are involved.

Despite these serious limitations of diagnosis, we would argue that the process can be made more valid through the use of the scientific method. Constructing a list of possible diagnoses to rule out and taking a falsification approach is not only liable to produce a better diagnosis, but the process will also contribute to your overall assessment.

## CONCLUSIONS

Outcome-informed practice does not call for an entirely new way of assessing clients. Rather, it focuses our attention on conducting an assessment that is more directed toward being able to monitor client outcomes during intervention so that the intervention plan can be modified as needed. In the long run, we think you will find that more specificity and objectivity not only help you monitor your clients' outcomes more effectively, but also help you deliver more successful interventions.

**PRACTICE TEST** The following questions will test your knowledge of the content found within this chapter and help you prepare for the licensing exam by applying chapter content to practice. For more questions styled like the licensing exam, visit **MySocialWorkLab.com**

1. Assessment is the systematic collection, organization, and interpretation of data related to a client's functioning, and it serves different purposes. However, the ultimate purpose is to
   a. Inform and improve the quality of supervision
   b. Enhance the quality of the relationship between the social worker and client
   c. Document characteristics of agency clients
   d. Help clients reach their goals

2. A social worker and his client mutually agree that the client needs to spend at least 3 hours a week helping his son with his homework. The desired amount of time the father spends helping his son with his homework is an example of a/an
   a. Problem
   b. Goal
   c. Objective
   d. Measure

3. A social worker asks her client to systematically observe and record the amount of time he spends studying each day. Which measurement method is the client being asked to use?
   a. Standardized scale
   b. Self-monitoring
   c. Direct observation
   d. Individualized rating scale

4. Case conceptualization integrates a theory or model of human behavior to do the following?
   a. Propose mechanisms for the causes of the problems and the recent precipitants of current issues
   b. Prescribe a specific intervention for the identified problems and disorders
   c. Identify a method for measuring the identified problems and disorders
   d. Determine who should measure and monitor the client's outcomes

5. A social worker meets with a 14-year-old Latino/African-American, Dominick, and his parents. Dominick's grades have declined recently and his parents are concerned. What theory or model of human behavior might be useful for conceptualizing this case and, following from this, what information should the social worker collect during the assessment?

6. A social worker is working with Dominick, the client described in question 5, and his parents. The social worker is confident that she can determine Dominick's progress without formally measuring his progress. What problems might the social worker encounter in taking this approach, and what are potential disadvantages of this approach?

# SUCCEED WITH

Visit **MySocialWorkLab** for more licensing exam test questions, and to access case studies, videos, and much more.

# 5

# Charting Your Client's Progress

## Advancing Core Competencies in This Chapter

| | | | | |
|---|---|---|---|---|
| ■ Professional Identity | ■ Ethical Practice | ☒ Critical Thinking | ■ Diversity in Practice | ■ Human Rights & Justice |
| ☒ Research-Based Practice | ■ Human Behavior | ■ Policy Practice | ■ Practice Contexts | ☒ Engage, Assess, Intervene, Evaluate |

**A**s a school social worker in a rural community, Keisha frequently works with students whose home lives challenge their abilities to learn. Stephen is one such child. A fourth grader, he is a bright, charming child with above-average test scores, but his grades are poor because he frequently does not do his homework. Stephen lives with his father, who works long hours as a farm laborer to support the family, and younger sister, for whom Stephen carries much of the responsibility. Stephen wants to do better and has even mentioned going to college someday; this is an idea planted and nourished by Stephen's father, who desperately wants better lives for his children. So both Stephen and his father are motivated to work with Keisha.

In this chapter, we will see how graphing can be helpful in Keisha's work with Stephen as he strives to get his homework done, improve his grades, and preserve his opportunities for a better life.

Charting your client's progress is critical to delivering effective outcome-informed practice. Single-case design graphs provide visual feedback about a client's progress that allows you to interpret client outcomes effectively and efficiently as you monitor and make decisions about client progress, as we've illustrated in previous chapters. However, you need to understand the basic elements of single-case design graphs to interpret them. You also need to understand the stylistic conventions used for constructing these graphs so you can produce graphs that are easily and accurately interpreted. This is not just a matter of producing more attractive graphs, but a matter of creating effective tools that enhance your clients' chances of achieving their goals.

In this chapter, we first discuss the standard elements of good single-case design graphs and the stylistic conventions used to construct them. Then, we briefly discuss graphing more than one data series (e.g., showing two different outcomes) on a single graph. Finally, we show you how to construct your own single-case design graphs with Microsoft Word. We will see how useful graphing can be in Keisha's work to help Stephen reach his goal of completing his homework and improving his grades.

Throughout this chapter, and for the most part throughout this book, we present graphs in their final form, but in practice you should graph outcome data regularly and analyze them as you go along, thus allowing you to use this practice-based evidence to make the decisions most likely to improve your client's outcomes.

# CONSTRUCTING GOOD SINGLE-CASE DESIGN LINE GRAPHS

Using standard conventions as you construct your graph results in graphs that are neat, easy to understand, and more directly useful to your work. Moreover, well-done graphs illustrate clients' progress in ways that enhance your work together and reinforce client progress. A snapshot of one's progress toward achieving a goal is dramatic and can inspire a client to make difficult changes. Think of posting a photograph of yourself in a bathing suit on the refrigerator. Does that ice cream look as good to you now?

Keisha has several options for the type of graphs she can use to represent Stephen's single-case design data, including line graphs, bar graphs, and scatter plots. Line graphs are the most common and useful. (See Cooper et al., 2007, and Spriggs & Gast, 2010, for comprehensive discussions of single-case design graphs.)

In a line graph, successive data points (e.g., measures of an outcome at particular times) connected with lines show changes in the value of a variable (e.g., client outcomes), usually over time. Later, we discuss the important elements of constructing good line graphs—and by *good*, we mean easy to construct and interpret and useful for your work. Often it's useful to annotate single-case design graphs, too, so we briefly discuss annotation as well.

Let's illustrate the basic elements of a single-case design graph with a hypothetical example that will demonstrate how proper use of the conventions helps make the graph more useful and interpretable. Figure 5.1 shows a graph with baseline and intervention conditions, that is an A-B design, after Keisha has been working with Stephen for 10 weeks. Stephen's problem is clear from looking at the baseline; when he and Keisha begin their work together, he is completing very few homework assignments. The *outcome* in the graph is percentage of completed homework assignments per week; the *outcome measure* is the teacher's report of the percentage of completed homework assignments per week, aggregated each week from daily report cards sent to Stephen's father by email from Stephen's teacher (e.g., Kelley & Jurbergs, 2009). Stephen's goal is to

**Engage, Assess, Intervene, Evaluate**

***Practice Behavior Example:*** *Develop a mutually agreed-on focus of work and desired outcomes*

**Critical Thinking Question:** What would you tell Stephen, his father, and his teacher to explain why it is important to graph Stephen's progress each week?

**Figure 5.1** • The Effect of Contingent Reinforcement on the Percentage of Homework Assignments Completed by Stephen.

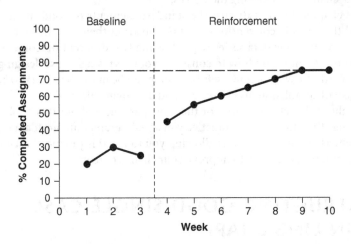

**Figure 5.2** • The Effect of Contingent Reinforcement on the Percentage of Homework Assignments Completed by Stephen, With Elements of a Single-Case Design Line Graph Identified.

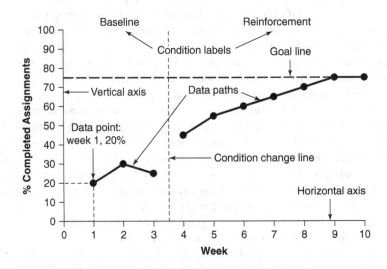

increase the percentage of completed homework assignments; the objective, agreed to by Stephen, his father, the teacher, and Keisha (i.e., our client system in this case), is for Stephen to complete 75% of his homework assignments each week; and the intervention is reinforcement for completing homework assignments. Stephen's reinforcer is extra time using the educational computer games he enjoys at school.

Figure 5.2 identifies the basic elements of a single-case design graph illustrated with our hypothetical example. Let's turn to a discussion of these elements, and as we discuss each element, you can look back at Figure 5.2 and identify it.

# Horizontal Axis (X-axis)

The *horizontal axis*, also called the *X-axis*, is a solid horizontal line. From left to right, the horizontal axis represents the chronological progression of equal time periods: week 1, 2, 3, and so on. Sometimes units other than time are used, such as intervention sessions.

A brief label, centered below and parallel to the horizontal axis, indicates the time periods represented on the horizontal axis—weeks in this case. Specific time periods are labeled (e.g., 0, 1, 2), but you may label only some of them if you are working with a large number of time periods, labeling only weeks 2, 4, 6, and so on. Characters other than numbers also can be used to label time periods, such as *M, T, W,* and *Th.*

Sometimes, as with follow-ups, there are discontinuities in time intervals represented on the horizontal axis. Discontinuities are represented by breaks in the horizontal axis. This is illustrated in Figure 5.3 where the teacher reported Stephen's percentage of completed assignments at a follow-up in week 14, one month after the intervention ended at week 10. We also would show discontinuities in this way if the intervention is stopped for a time due to a school vacation or extended illness that keeps Stephen out of school.

# Vertical Axis (Y-axis)

The *vertical axis*, also called the *Y-axis*, is a solid vertical line starting at the left end of the X-axis. It represents a range of numerical values of the outcome measure. Equal intervals represent equal quantities (e.g., 10–20%, 20–30%), and lower to higher values are arranged from bottom to top.

A brief label, centered to the left of and parallel to the vertical axis, indicates the outcome (e.g., completed assignments) and dimension on which it's measured (e.g., percentage completed). The values are labeled, but again you may choose not to label all of them if there are many values.

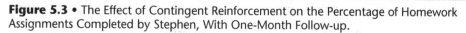

**Figure 5.3** • The Effect of Contingent Reinforcement on the Percentage of Homework Assignments Completed by Stephen, With One-Month Follow-up.

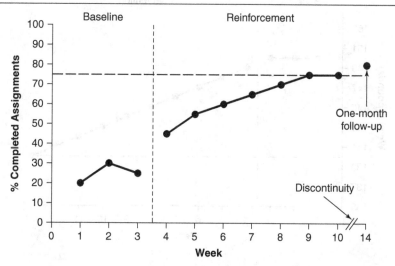

The range of values on the vertical axis should be sufficient to accommodate the full range of data. However, you might try different ranges to determine which portrays your data most accurately and is most likely to lead to accurate conclusions. Increasing the range magnifies variability; this is useful when small changes are important. Decreasing the range minimizes the portrayal of variability; this is useful when only larger changes are important. For example, suppose that you're working with an adolescent client whose goal is to lose 10 pounds (150 to 140 pounds) at a healthy rate of 1 pound per week. You collect 3 weeks of baseline and 10 weeks of intervention data.

Figures 5.4 and 5.5 show the same data for this hypothetical example, and both graphs accommodate the full range of data. However, Figure 5.4 has a narrow range (135–155) on the vertical axis and Figure 5.5 has a wide range (0–165). Figure 5.4 clearly indicates the small but meaningful weekly weight loss starting with the implementation of the intervention. Figure 5.5 suggests little change in weight after the implementation of the intervention; it misses important changes over time. Figure 5.4 would probably be more rewarding and motivating for the client, even though both figures illustrate the same data.

Generally, it's a good idea for the vertical axis to be about two-thirds the size of the horizontal axis; for example, you might use 4″ for the vertical axis and 6″ for the horizontal axis. A higher ratio might overemphasize variability in the data, and a lower one might underemphasize it. You might need to modify this ratio if multiple graphs are stacked on top of each other on a single page, for example if you have multiple baseline designs (discussed in Chapter 7) or if there are a large number of time periods plotted on the horizontal axis.

Finally, occasionally there are zeros in the outcome data, for example if Stephen completes none of his homework assignments. In these cases, Keisha may find it useful to have the horizontal axis cross the vertical axis at a point slightly below zero on the vertical axis. This is illustrated in Figure 5.6, where you'll notice that the three baseline data points are 0, 2, and 0, and the zeros do not fall on the horizontal axis. This keeps values of zero

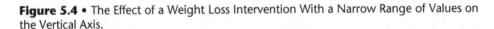

**Figure 5.4** • The Effect of a Weight Loss Intervention With a Narrow Range of Values on the Vertical Axis.

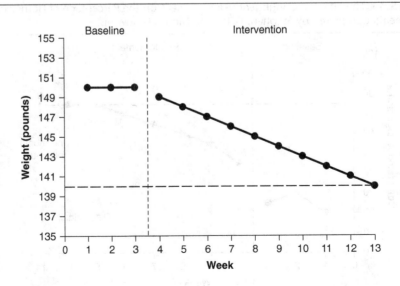

**Figure 5.5** • The Effect of a Weight Loss Intervention With a Wide Range of Values on the Vertical Axis.

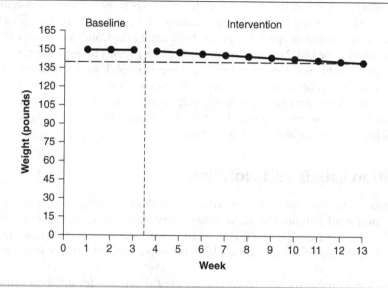

**Figure 5.6** • The Effect of Contingent Reinforcement on the Percentage of Homework Assignments Completed by Stephen, With Y-Axis Crossing Below Zero.

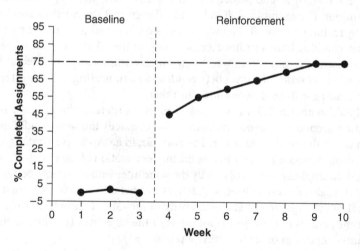

from falling directly on the horizontal axis and permits Keisha to distinguish zero values from values close to zero.

## Condition Change Lines

A *condition* is the environmental arrangement in effect at a given time in a single-case design, for example the baseline or the intervention. A *phase* is a period of time within a single-case design (Cooper et al., 2007). For example, in an A-B-A-B design, there are two conditions (baseline and intervention) and four phases (two baseline and two intervention).

*Condition change lines* show the point when a change is made from one condition to the next, for example from baseline to intervention. This point is clearly identified with a dashed vertical line drawn upward from the horizontal axis. Condition change lines are centered between the last data point in one condition (week 3 in our example) and the first data point in the next condition (week 4 in our example), so that data points on either side clearly fall in one condition or another. Sometimes you may want to distinguish between minor changes within a condition, such as a training phase within an intervention condition. In these cases, use dashed lines to separate the minor changes in conditions and solid lines to separate the major changes.

## Condition Labels and Notation

*Conditions* are labeled with single words such as *Baseline*, brief descriptive phrases such as *Contingent Reinforcement*, or, if necessary, abbreviations such as *A* for baseline (but stay away from *FU* as an abbreviation for *Follow-up*). Condition labels are located along the top of the graph, parallel to the horizontal axis, and centered over the condition.

Often letters and subscripts (*notation*) are used as symbols for different conditions, especially when discussing different types of designs. For example, you may use A-B design, or A-B-A-B design, where the single dash (-) separates adjacent conditions. Baseline is always represented by *A*, and subsequent letters (*B*, *C*, etc.) stand for different but specific interventions. For example, *A-B* indicates a design that starts with a baseline *A* and is followed by an intervention *B*. To indicate the simultaneous presence of two different interventions, combine letters without a dash. For example, *A-BC* indicates a design that starts with a baseline *A* and is followed by two interventions implemented at the same time, *BC*. Note the absence of a dash between *B* and *C*, indicating that the interventions occur at the same time instead of one after the other.

Subscripts also are used along with letters to label different phases; these subscripts refer to the first, second, and so on implementation of exactly the same condition, and the sequence in which the conditions occur. For example, in an $A_1$-$B_1$-$A_2$-$B_2$ design, the first baseline is $A_1$ and the second is $A_2$, whereas the implementation of the intervention the first time is $B_1$ and the implementation of exactly the same intervention the second time is $B_2$.

Superscripts also are used along with letters to label different phases, such as A-$B_1$-$B_2$-$B_3$ to indicate changes in either the intensity of the intervention (e.g., time-out for a child with time periods of 5, 10, and 15 minutes) or the objectives (exercise lasting 30, 45, and 60 minutes per day in order to receive a reinforcer).

## Goal Line

A *goal line* is a dashed line that represents the objective, for example Stephen's goal of 75% completed homework assignments, as quantified by the outcome measure, in this case his teacher's report of percentage of completed assignments. Figures 5.1 through 5.6 show horizontal goal lines. Goal lines provide a visual aid for easily monitoring and evaluating client progress. They are not a standard element of single-case design graphs, but they are nothing new and are used by others (e.g., Riley-Tillman & Burns, 2009, p. 89). We like the way they call attention to what the client is hoping to accomplish.

Horizontal goal lines portray the objective, but they don't indicate the time frame for the objective to be realized. In some circumstances, it's possible and useful to specify the goal and the time you hope it will take to reach the goal (e.g., Clark & Gilmore, 2010; Riley-Tillman & Burns, 2009). For example, suppose that Keisha is an intern working with Stephen toward the goal of 75% completed homework assignments. She wants him to achieve this goal by the end of the 7 weeks she has left in her internship, and she has already collected 3 weeks of baseline data. Figure 5.7 illustrates a goal line that portrays the goal of 75% completed homework assignments and the time line to reach that goal.

Here's how you construct and plot a time line for achieving a goal, which is also sometimes called an *aim line* (Riley-Tillman & Burns, 2009, pp. 89–93):

- Construct a graph that includes baseline data and time periods on the horizontal axis extending out to the time you want the goal to be achieved.
- Compute the median of the last three baseline data points, in this example the only three. (A *median* is the middle value in a set of numbers ordered from lowest to highest.) In our example, the baseline values are 20, 25, and 30, ordered from lowest to highest, so the median equals 25% completed homework assignments.
- Put a mark on the graph where the median of the last three data points (25%) intersects the middle baseline time period (week 2).
- Put a mark on the graph where the goal intersects the time period by which you want the goal to be achieved, in this case week 10, the seventh week of intervention.
- Connect these two marks with a straight dashed line.

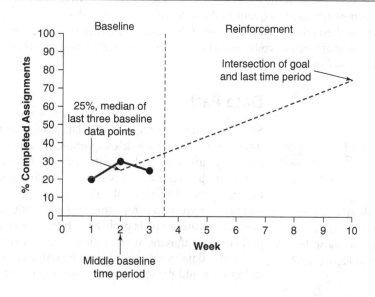

**Figure 5.7** • The Effect of Contingent Reinforcement on the Percentage of Homework Assignments Completed by Stephen, With Baseline Data and Time Line.

**Figure 5.8 •** The Effect of Contingent Reinforcement on the Percentage of Homework Assignments Completed by Stephen, With Baseline and Intervention Data and Goal Line.

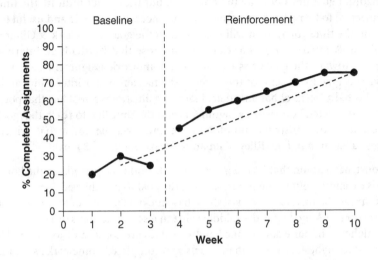

Figure 5.7 portrays Keisha's time line for achieving the goal of 75% completed homework assignments. It should be clear how the goal line can serve as a nice guide that may be motivating for Stephen to continue his progress. Figure 5.8 portrays what actually happens. As shown in Figure 5.8, Stephen is "ahead of schedule" every week except the last, when the objective is achieved.

## Data Points

Each *data point* represents the intersection of a time period (e.g., week 1) and a numerical value of the measure used to quantify the outcome (e.g., 20%), that is the percentage of homework Stephen completed each week. Oftentimes a solid circle is used to represent data points, although other symbols can be used, too (e.g., ●, Δ). These symbols are sometimes called *data markers*.

**Engage, Assess, Intervene, Evaluate**

***Practice Behavior Example:*** *Critically analyze, monitor, and evaluate interventions*

**Critical Thinking Question:** What questions would you have and what practice decisions would you make each week in response to Stephen's progress illustrated in Figure 5.8?

## Data Paths

Solid lines connecting consecutive data points within a condition create a *data path*. It's important to connect the data points because data paths are the main focus of attention in the interpretation and visual analysis of line graphs. Notice in Figure 5.8 that the solid line dramatically illustrates Stephen's progress in completing his homework. Seeing his progress on this graph is probably reinforcing for Stephen, perhaps as reinforcing as extra computer game time.

Some data points should not be connected because doing so would provide a misleading picture of the data path. Specifically, we don't connect data points (1) across conditions (see any figure in this book); (2) before and after a missing data point; or (3) across time periods during which data were collected using different time intervals than the rest of the design (see the follow-up period in Figure 5.3).

Let's look at the data paths in our example as illustrated in Figure 5.1. During baseline, Stephen's percentage of completed assignments was always below 30, well below the goal; there is clearly a problem warranting intervention. The discrepancy between the goal (75%) and the baseline level or median (25%) indicates the extent of the problem. In addition, we see no discernable trend toward improvement or deterioration during baseline, suggesting that this problem will not get better or worse without intervention. (Of course with only three data points, this might be a risky prediction.) During intervention, Stephen's percentage of completed assignments increases relative to what we would expect from baseline, and we see no overlapping data points in the baseline and intervention conditions; this pattern provides convincing evidence of change from baseline to intervention. The increase in percentage of completed assignments doesn't occur until after Keisha implements the intervention with Stephen, and the increase starts immediately after the onset of intervention; both of these facts further suggest the possibility that the intervention is the cause of the increase. The goal is attained, suggesting a change in real-world functioning that is sufficient and meaningful for the client system: Stephen, his father, and his teacher.

Do the data paths indicate that Keisha's intervention *caused* the change in the percentage of homework assignments Stephen completed, that is can we claim that there is an intervention effect? That's one good possibility. However, we don't know the extent to which it is the intervention or an extraneous variable that coincided with the implementation of the intervention that caused the improvement. For example, something else may have occurred in Stephen's life at about the same time the intervention was implemented that caused the change. It would take a different type of design to answer this question with any degree of certainty. (We'll have more to say about this in Chapter 7.)

## Annotations

Sometimes it's useful to add brief descriptions or explanations called *annotations* on graphs so the graph provides a more complete picture of what's going on. For example, it might allow Keisha's supervisor to interpret the graph without much explanation. In such cases, unplanned or notable events that occur, such as Stephen's winning the class spelling bee or having an emergency appendectomy, can be identified with small arrows or other symbols next to the relevant data points. Client information also can be placed in a box in the lower right corner of the graph. Figure 5.9 shows an example of annotations.

## Figure Caption

The *figure caption* is located below the graph flush left. The figure is captioned with a concise statement that, in combination with axis and condition labels, gives sufficient information to identify the intervention(s) and outcome(s). In addition, the caption explains any symbols used in the graph and clarifies any potentially confusing features of the graph. The resulting graph is clear enough to be useful to Stephen's father, teacher, or principal, or Keisha's supervisor, without extensive additional information. Think of it as a photograph that shows Stephen's progress so far toward his goal.

**Figure 5.9 •** The Effect of Contingent Reinforcement on the Percentage of Homework Assignments Completed by Stephen, With Annotations.

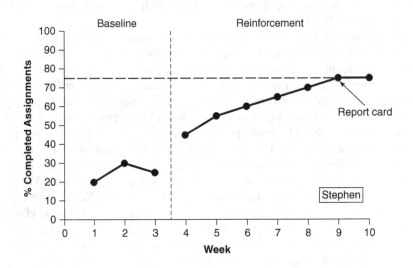

# GRAPHING MULTIPLE DATA SERIES

A *data series* is a set of related data points plotted on a graph, for example data from one outcome, such as percentage of completed assignments, or data from one source, such as a single teacher. Figures 5.1 through 5.9 illustrate one data series per graph.

Sometimes it's useful to plot two or more data series on the same graph. For example, Keisha might plot Stephen's completed homework assignments and his grades on the same graph. This will allow her to visually analyze how the two outcomes are related over time and check her assumption that completing homework leads to better grades; it will also illustrate this for Stephen. Similarly, you might want to plot your ratings and a client's ratings of the quality of the therapeutic alliance on the same graph to identify discrepancies that might need to be discussed and resolved. In the same way, you might want to plot a client's ratings of depression and anxiety on the same graph to visually analyze effects of your intervention on both outcomes.

Plotting multiple data series on the same graph is easy. Use different symbols for data points associated with different data series (e.g., ●, ○, Δ), and identify different data series with arrows drawn to the data series, or a legend or figure caption identifying the different symbols. Figure 5.10 illustrates this. Notice that there is no label on the Y-axis in Figure 5.10 because both outcomes are plotted on the same Y-axis. Instead, the figure caption indicates the symbol associated with each data series.

---

✕⭝✕

**Engage, Assess, Intervene, Evaluate**

***Practice Behavior Example:*** *Critically analyze, monitor, and evaluate interventions*

**Critical Thinking Question:** What difference would it make in terms of your ability to monitor Stephen's progress each week if you graphed the following data from Figure 5.10: (1) percentage of completed homework assignments—A: 20, 30, 25; B: 45, 55, 60, 65, 70, 75, 75 and (2) grades—A: 35, 40, 35; B: 55, 65, 70, 75, 75, 85, 80?

**Figure 5.10** • The Effect of Contingent Reinforcement on the Percentage of Stephen's Completed Homework Assignments (●) and Grades (○).

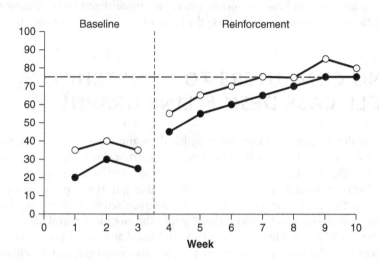

**Figure 5.11** • The Effect of Contingent Reinforcement on the Percentage of Stephen's Completed Homework Assignments (●) and Grade Point Average (○).

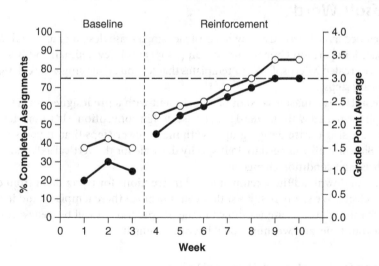

If data for different series are on different scales, for example percentage of completed homework assignments with a potential range from 0 through 100 and grade point average with a potential range from 0 through 4, use two vertical axes, one on the left and another on the right. Figure 5.11 illustrates this.

Of course, just because it's possible to plot multiple data series on a single graph doesn't mean it's always a good idea. Graphs with multiple data series are more complicated to interpret and communicate. Don't plot more than two or at most three different data series on one graph, because the amount of information might be difficult to understand.

# USING COMPUTERS TO CONSTRUCT SINGLE-CASE DESIGN LINE GRAPHS

Single-case design graphs can be drawn by hand on graph paper. However, we strongly suggest that you invest time in learning how to construct single-case design graphs with a computer. This will take a small investment of time, maybe a few hours depending on your skill with computers and how you go about doing it. It will pay off handsomely in the long run, though, in terms of reducing the time required to construct graphs, improving the quality of your graphs, and making graphs that are more useful for your clients.

Microsoft Word and Excel are available and familiar to most people who use computers, and it is relatively easy to construct single-case design graphs with either software application. We created most of the graphs in this book with Microsoft Word 2007, and you can download these files from our companion website and experiment with editing them in different ways to make your own graphs if you have access to a computer with Microsoft Word 2007.

## Microsoft Word

We developed a relatively easy way to construct single-case design graphs with Microsoft Word based, in part, on Grehan and Moran (2005) and Riley-Tillman and Burns (2009). That is, we created Microsoft Word templates that let you create single-case design graphs in a few easy steps.

A template is a master version of a document with a predesigned format, such as a line graph formatted with standard single-case design conventions. It's a shortcut you can use to create single-case design graphs with many fewer steps than if you started from scratch. Basically, all you need to do is specify the scale for the vertical axis and enter your data, labels, and condition change line(s).

You can download these templates and instructions for using them from our companion website. We strongly suggest that you download these templates and instructions and work through the examples shown in the instructions. It will be well worth a couple hours of your time, and we think you'll have fun doing it.

## Microsoft Excel and PowerPoint

You also can create single-case design graphs easily with Microsoft Excel, although probably not as easily as with Microsoft Word unless you already know a little bit about Microsoft Excel. The CD that accompanies Bloom et al. (2009) includes numerous Microsoft Excel files that provide examples of single-case design graphs and calculation of a wide range of statistics for single-case design data. In addition, Riley-Tillman and Burns

(2009) and Dixon et al. (2009) provide excellent descriptions of how to create single-case design graphs, and Riley-Tillman and Burns also demonstrate how to analyze single-case design data with Microsoft Excel. Finally, Barton, Reichow, and Wolery (2007) provide a good discussion of how to create single-case design graphs with PowerPoint.

## CONCLUSIONS

Social work practice is one of those areas in life where you don't just want to change something; you want that change to be apparent. Graphs are some of the best tools for demonstrating change—to the client, relevant others in the client's life, and your supervisor, at least. Moreover, if done well, graphing your clients' outcomes can help "keep you honest," making it more difficult for bias to create the false impression of positive change when it has not in fact occurred. So we strongly advise you to spend a little time learning to create graphs that can be extremely useful in your practice. The next chapter will help you use and interpret your graphs to inform your decision-making when working with your clients.

**PRACTICE TEST** The following questions will test your knowledge of the content found within this chapter and help you prepare for the licensing exam by applying chapter content to practice. For more questions styled like the licensing exam, visit **MySocialWorkLab.com**

---

**1.** Single-case design graphs are useful for different purposes. However, in terms of outcome-informed practice, the most important purpose is to

   **a.** Determine the effectiveness of the intervention

   **b.** Provide evidence concerning the effectiveness of the intervention

   **c.** Ensure that the client's goals are achieved

   **d.** Demonstrate accountability to funding sources

**2.** Solid lines should be used to connect consecutive data points:

   **a.** Within conditions

   **b.** Across conditions

   **c.** Before and after a missing data point

   **d.** Across time periods during which data were collected using different time intervals than the rest of the design

**3.** Goal lines provide a visual aid for determining which of the following:

   **a.** Origins of the client's problems

   **b.** Degree to which the intervention caused change in the client's problem

   **c.** Whether client improvement will be lasting

   **d.** Degree to which the objective is achieved

**4.** An A-B-A-B design has

   **a.** Four conditions and two phases

   **b.** Two conditions and four phases

   **c.** Two conditions and two phases

   **d.** Four conditions and four phases

**5.** A social worker is working with a 22-year-old Army private first class, Linda, who is being sexually harassed at work and wants to eliminate this harassment. Linda reports the following number of harassment incidents per week: baseline—5, 4, 3; intervention—2, 1, 0, 0; and follow-up—0, 0. How would you interpret these data each week and overall?

**6.** Download and use the single-case design Microsoft Word templates and associated instructions from our companion website to graph the data of Linda, the client described in question 5. How would you interpret these graphed data each week and overall, and are your interpretations different before and after you graphed these data?

---

## SUCCEED WITH

Visit **MySocialWorkLab** for more licensing exam test questions, and to access case studies, videos, and much more.

# 6

# Visually Interpreting Your Client's Progress

| Advancing Core Competencies in This Chapter | | | | |
|---|---|---|---|---|
| ■ Professional Identity | ■ Ethical Practice | ✂ Critical Thinking | ■ Diversity in Practice | ■ Human Rights & Justice |
| ✂ Research-Based Practice | ■ Human Behavior | ■ Policy Practice | ■ Practice Contexts | ✂ Engage, Assess, Intervene, Evaluate |

In Chapter 5, we presented the guidelines for constructing good single-case design graphs. We illustrated the guidelines showing social worker Keisha's work with Stephen, a fourth grader who is having trouble completing his homework. We'll continue to talk about Stephen in this chapter, showing how we might interpret different patterns of data that might emerge as Keisha monitors Stephen's progress.

Single-case design data typically are graphed and analyzed visually (Cooper et al., 2007; Gast & Spriggs, 2010; Johnston & Pennypacker, 2009; Kazdin, 2011; Riley-Tillman & Burns, 2009). Visual analysis is a systematic process for interpreting results of single-case design data that involves visually examining graphed data within and between different conditions, for example between baseline and intervention. It is a search for patterns in outcome data over time and under different conditions and the interpretation of those patterns. Thus, visual analysis is a critical tool for monitoring your client's outcomes for the purpose of informing your intervention and, most important, improving your client's outcomes.

Visual analysis enables you to answer questions about ongoing, unfolding client change. It allows you to analyze your client's progress in real time and use this practice-based evidence as you go along to make the right decisions to help your clients in a dynamic process.

We begin by discussing how to visually analyze results from the simplest A-B design; this will help you understand how to analyze most other designs because most of the guidelines for A-B designs also apply to the more complicated designs. It isn't possible to lay out all possible patterns, so we explain and illustrate basic principles here.

A reading of the literature over the past 30 years will show that many employ statistical analysis for single-case design data. We use visual analysis because we believe it is the most practical method for practitioners in busy settings and because we believe it provides the means for determining whether interventions make real-world differences to clients. The use of statistics in the analysis of single-case design data is a complicated and controversial area, to say the least, however. For recent discussions of the use of statistics to analyze single-case design data, see Bloom et al. (2009), Campbell and Herzinger (2010), Houle (2009), Nugent (2010), and Satake, Jagaroo, and Maxwell (2008). SING-WIN, designed by Charles Auerbach, David Schnall, and Heidi Heft Laporte for and included with *Evaluating Practice* (Bloom et al., 2009), is an easy-to-use Windows-based computer program that does many of the statistical analyses discussed in the literature.

# IDENTIFYING CHANGE AND MAKING DECISIONS

Clients hope their problems will change for the better as a result of your work together, as do you. Figure 6.1 illustrates questions about change that you and your client should ask and answer continuously as you work together:

- Is change occurring?
- If change is occurring, is it change for the better—are the client's problems getting better or worse?
- If change is occurring, and it is change for the better, is the pace of change sufficient—is change happening rapidly enough, based on previous research, theory, experience, or other considerations?
- If change is occurring, and it is in the desired direction, is the change large enough—is the change meaningful and sufficient to the client?

Answers to these questions have implications for how you and your client move forward. If change is unfolding in the desired direction at a pace sufficient to reach your client's objective in a reasonable time, success is on the way and you might just want to continue doing what you're doing. If in the end the amount of change is sufficient and meaningful to your client and others with a stake in the client's progress, success has been achieved and you should plan for consolidating and maintaining the gains that have been made, anticipating potential setbacks, collecting follow-up data to be sure the change lasts, and/or refocusing on other client problems needing attention.

If no change is occurring, or if change is in an undesirable direction, or if it is occurring too slowly to reach your client's objective in a reasonable time, at some point you need to modify the intervention plan to change course. Changing course might involve one or more of the following:

- Trying a different intervention or modifying the current intervention. For example, Keisha might try a different method of reinforcing Stephen for appropriate

**Figure 6.1** • Flowchart Illustrating Decisions About Client Change.

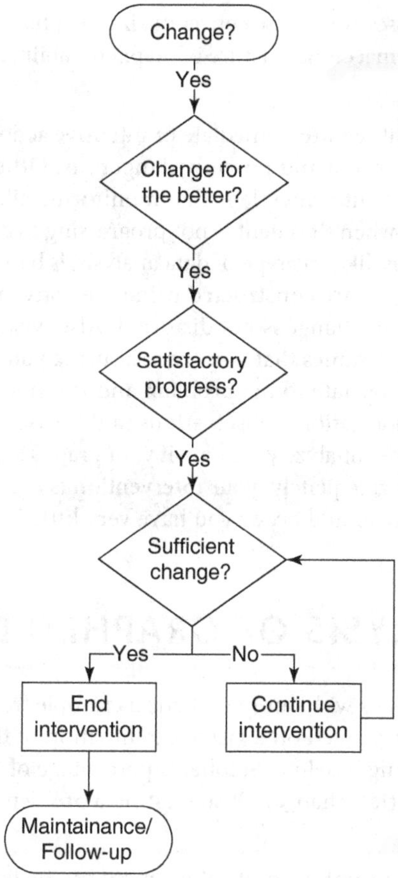

behavior, perhaps giving him time to read books of his choice rather than using the computer to play games.

- Checking the status of the "helping alliance," "client motivation to change," and environmental and biological factors in the client's life, including social support. For example, how is the relationship between Keisha and Stephen? Is he still enthusiastic about doing better with his homework? Is an illness or family problem making it hard for Stephen to do his homework?
- Extending the date for goal achievement if progress is being made toward resolving the problem, albeit too slowly. For example, Stephen may need a few more weeks for change to really set in.
- Revising the goal or objective, if it turns out to be unreasonable or impossible to reach. For example, maybe Stephen's home life simply makes it unrealistic to expect him to consistently finish 75% of his homework.
- Refocusing your efforts on other problems that may need to be resolved first. For example, perhaps Keisha needs to work with Stephen's father to help him find suitable child care in the evenings to free Stephen up to do his homework.

- Collecting more information. For example, is Stephen depressed? Does he need glasses?
- Returning to the assessment/case conceptualization phase. For example, Keisha may have a totally inaccurate picture of Stephen's abilities, home life, or motivation.

Some situations might require immediate or intensive action, for example if a client's depression is becoming severe and possibly dangerous. Other situations might allow more time, but the important principle is that monitoring allows you to make changes sooner, rather than later, when the client is not progressing as expected.

Finally, visual analysis, like any type of data analysis, is based on certain assumptions. It assumes that your graphs are constructed using the conventions discussed in Chapter 5 so the picture of client change is not distorted. Also, visual analysis, or any type of analysis for that matter, presumes that you are measuring your outcome accurately, that your intervention is appropriate to the problem and is implemented with fidelity, and that you have enough information—observations in this case—to draw accurate conclusions. After all, how can you analyze your data if your graphs are poorly constructed, your outcomes are measured inadequately, your intervention isn't appropriate to the problem or isn't implemented as it should be, or you have very little information about your client's progress?

## VISUAL ANALYSIS OF GRAPHED DATA

Let's illustrate visual analysis with our hypothetical example from Chapter 5. Our analysis of the data from Chapter 5 based on a visual examination of the graphed data is shown again in Figure 6.2. During baseline, Stephen's percentage of completed assignments is well below the objective (less than 30%), suggesting a problem warranting intervention.

**Figure 6.2** • The Effect of Contingent Reinforcement on the Percentage of Homework Assignments Completed.

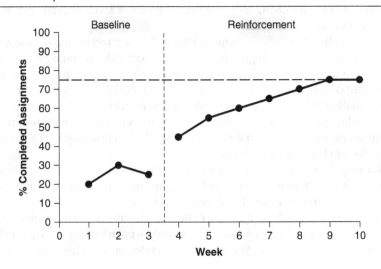

The discrepancy between the objective, 75%, and the baseline level (e.g., median), 25%, indicates the extent of the problem. In addition, we can detect no discernable trend toward improvement or deterioration during baseline; this suggests that the problem isn't likely to get better or worse without intervention, although with only three data points we can't be certain.

Looking at the total course of intervention, you can see that during intervention Stephen completes a greater percentage of assignments than you would expect from the baseline, and there are no overlapping data points in the baseline and intervention conditions; this pattern provides convincing evidence of change from baseline to intervention. The percentage of completed assignments doesn't increase until after Keisha implements the intervention, and the increase starts immediately after the onset of intervention; both of these facts further suggest the possibility that the intervention is the cause of the increase. Stephen achieves his objective, and the outcome appears to show sufficient and meaningful change in real-world functioning.

Do the data paths indicate that Keisha's intervention is the cause of the change in Stephen's percentage of completed homework assignments? That is, to what extent is there an intervention effect? It's certainly a good possibility that the change occurred because of the intervention. What is not clear, though, is how much of the change is due to the intervention, as opposed to something else happening in Stephen's life at about the same time. Perhaps Stephen started working with a tutor in week 4 or his father changed jobs and is now able to help him with his homework in the evening. It would take a different type of design to answer this question with any degree of certainty, and we have more to say about this in Chapter 7.

**Engage, Assess, Interven**

***Practice Behavior Example:*** *Critically analyze, monitor, and evaluate interventions*

**Critical Thinking Question:** What questions would you need to consider when deciding how much change is sufficient and meaningful in Stephen's case and in other cases?

## Within-Phase Patterns

Change can occur within a phase or between conditions, and both are important. However, change between conditions is interpreted primarily in reference to patterns of outcome data within phases. That is, we have to consider how things are changing within phases in order to interpret change that happens between conditions, so we will begin there.

### Level

Level is the value on the vertical axis around which a series of outcome data converge (Cooper et al., 2007). This is illustrated in Figure 6.3, which shows two possible different levels for baseline and intervention, as well as a data series without any discernable level.

Sometimes it may be useful to characterize the overall level of a phase by a single value such as the mean or median, but at times this can be misleading. For example, in Figure 6.3, a mean or median would obscure the variability in the baseline and intervention data represented by ▲. The last two or three data points in a phase are especially important indicators of level if they are higher or lower than the overall level. For example, in Figure 6.2, the level at the end of intervention for the two data paths with discernable levels is higher than at the beginning—there was a change for the better in level within

**Figure 6.3** • Two Possible Different Within-Condition Levels of Completed Homework Assignments (lowest level = ●, highest level = ○) and One Data Series With No Discernable Level (▲).

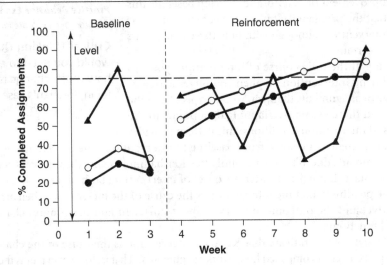

this phase. Therefore, the percentage of completed homework assignments for the last 2 weeks of intervention (75%) gives a more accurate picture of the final level for this phase than, say, the median (65%) for the entire intervention phase. To some degree, this is a matter of judgment, and you will need to think critically.

## Trend

Trend is the overall direction of a data path within a phase. Figure 6.4 illustrates three types of trend: (1) no trend; (2) negative trend, also referred to as *descending* or *decelerating* because values are decreasing over time; and (3) positive trend, also referred to as *ascending* or *accelerating* because values are increasing over time.

In our example with Stephen, higher values are more desirable, that is a higher percentage of completed assignments is a good thing, so a positive trend is an improving trend and a negative trend is a deteriorating trend. If higher values are undesirable, indicating, for example, greater depression, a positive trend would indicate deterioration and a negative trend would indicate improvement. Obviously, you need to know which way is "up" before concluding that your client is getting better or worse.

Trends are common. Parker, Cryer, and Byrns (2006) reviewed 165 published A-B comparisons and found that 41% of baseline phases showed an improving trend, 45% a deteriorating trend, and only 15% no discernable trend. So as much as we appreciate a nice stable baseline, for reasons we'll discuss later, we need to learn to deal with trends because we will see them frequently.

The slope of a line indicates the typical amount of change in an outcome from day to day, week to week, or whatever unit is involved. It indicates the pace of change within a phase. For example, in Figure 6.4, the percentage of completed homework assignments

**Figure 6.4** • Three Types of Trend (no trend = ●, negative/descending/deteriorating trend = ○, positive/ascending/improving trend = ▲).

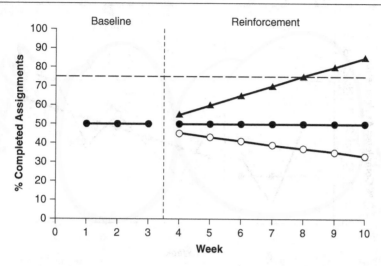

goes up by 5 each week (55, 60, 65, etc.) for the positive trend, and down by 2 (45, 43, 41, etc.) for the negative trend. The steeper the slope (e.g., 5 vs. 2), the greater the change over time and the stronger the trend.

Finally, although we often think of trends as linear, falling on a straight line as illustrated in Figure 6.4, they can take other forms. For example, as illustrated in Figure 6.2, the intervention trend is slightly curvilinear. Or, for example, in psychotherapy, clients oftentimes exhibit rapid improvement initially, followed by continued but slower improvement. It's also interesting to note that this pattern predicts a positive final outcome (Lambert, 2007; Lutz, Stulz, & Kock, 2009).

## Variability

Variability is the degree to which data points deviate from the overall trend. It is the extent to which data fall within a relatively narrow range around the overall trend. Figure 6.5 shows baseline and intervention patterns with and without variability, although variability is a matter of degree, and it's the norm rather than the exception.

A *stable baseline* occurs when data exhibit relatively little variability over time and little or no trend during baseline; this is illustrated in Figure 6.5 in the flat baseline pattern. In contrast, a *variable baseline* has data that are scattered around a relatively larger range of values around a horizontal line, as illustrated in Figure 6.5 in the variable baseline pattern. A stable baseline is ideal for determining change from baseline to intervention, and more generally from one condition to the next, but, unfortunately, most baselines show improving or deteriorating trends to some degree (Parker et al., 2006). This is why it's so important that you learn to interpret patterns of client data that include trend.

Variability that exhibits a sequence of alternating patterns, for example both upward and downward trends, is known as a *cyclical pattern*. For example, in the variable baseline data illustrated in Figure 6.5, notice that Stephen completes a relatively higher percentage of homework in the first week, a lower percentage the second week, and a higher

**Figure 6.5 •** Variability (o) and No Variability (•) in Within-Condition Patterns of Completed Homework Assignments.

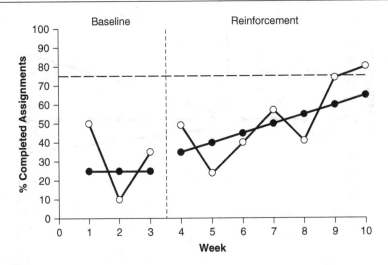

percentage again in the third week. Perhaps Stephen's parents are divorced, and he spends alternating weeks with his mom and dad, and mom places more emphasis on homework than dad. Discovering the causes of cyclical patterns, and variability over time in general, can lead to insights that can be incorporated into case conceptualization and intervention planning. For example, it might be especially important to work with Stephen's dad regarding homework. This is another way that graphing informs and improves your intervention planning and ultimately your clients' outcomes.

## Change Between Adjacent Conditions

Clients hope their problems will change for the better while receiving your help. You hope that your helping efforts will leave the client better off after your intervention than before. Change for the better in a client's problem might not be the only goal; there might also be more specific objectives, such as Stephen's goal of 75% completed homework assignments, but change for the better certainly is one important goal for most helping efforts.

### Baselines Revisited

The best (but not only) way to determine if a client is better off after receiving your help than before is to collect pre-intervention baseline data on the client's outcome and to compare those data to intervention data. A *baseline* is a period of time during which an outcome is measured repeatedly in the absence of an intervention. Of course this isn't to say that nothing is going on during baseline; for example, you are developing a case conceptualization and building an alliance with your client. Some kind of other intervention may even be happening, such as a school-wide push to encourage students to do their homework. During baseline, however, the specific intervention you will implement with your client is not yet in place.

Baselines usually, but not always, occur before interventions. Pre-intervention baseline data can be used as a reference point to determine client change, an issue we'll turn to later, but they also can be used to:

- confirm or disconfirm that the problem actually exists: for example, maybe to Stephen's harried teacher, it just seems like he doesn't do his homework, or perhaps Stephen just had a bad week or two. This provides another important argument for incorporating as much objectivity as you can into your data. Conversely, baseline data might provide the client with a sense of "validation that things are not right" (Barkham, Mellor-Clark, et al., 2010, p. 214);
- establish the extent of the problem: for example, to contrast the percentage of Stephen's homework completed to the desired level;
- determine whether the problem is getting better or worse and the pace of change if it is occurring; and
- develop and explore hypotheses useful for case conceptualization and intervention planning: for example, you might find that there are times when Stephen does complete his homework and discover the reasons for this, and you could use this information to plan an intervention.

The client's performance during baseline is the reference point for determining change, so sometimes change from baseline through intervention is referred to as *self-referenced change* (Parker & Hagan-Burke, 2007). It provides an estimate of what would happen to the client's outcome without intervention. For example, Keisha hypothesizes that her evidence-based intervention, appropriate to the problem and implemented with fidelity, will help Stephen complete more of his homework and that the objective will be reached in a reasonable amount of time. The intervention has helped many other students and other individuals increase desired behavior, so Keisha hypothesizes that it also will help Stephen.

On the other hand, Keisha recognizes that Stephen is an individual with unique characteristics and circumstances, so she will keep a close eye on what is happening during the intervention so she can make a change if things aren't working out as desired. To test her practice hypothesis, Keisha first collects baseline data and uses it to predict what would happen without intervention, as illustrated in Figure 6.6. Now, as she collects intervention data, she will test her hypothesis by comparing what actually unfolds during intervention to her baseline prediction. During intervention, Stephen completes more of his homework, relative to what she would expect from the baseline. More specifically, there is an immediate change for the better in level and trend and the objective is achieved and maintained for 2 weeks. Stephen has made progress, and Keisha can see how much progress he has made and how quickly the progress took place.

The evidence supports Keisha's practice hypothesis, but is the only explanation for the observed change that the intervention caused it? That's one good possibility, but there may be other reasonable explanations, too. For example, perhaps something else happened about the same time as the intervention, such as a change in Stephen's living situation. It would take a different type of design to answer this question with any degree of certainty, and we have more to say about this in Chapter 7. However, that doesn't mean that Keisha can't or shouldn't think critically about the reasons for this change, given the totality of the information she has about Stephen. Indeed, in all cases you should work collaboratively with your clients, and, as appropriate, others with knowledge of your clients, to understand and interpret your clients' progress.

**Figure 6.6** • Stable Baseline: Predicted (○) and Actual (●) Intervention Outcome Data.

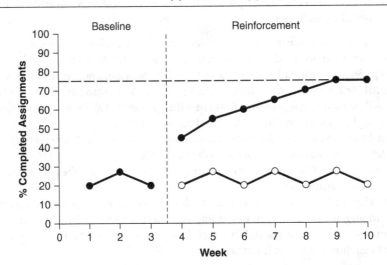

As you move from a pre-intervention baseline to intervention, you need to decide if there is a change relative to what you would predict from baseline. In general, the larger the change, the easier it is to detect accurately, and the more convincing the evidence is for change. For example, imagine that Stephen never completes his homework during baseline and then completes it every day during intervention; in this case, such a large change is easy to detect and the evidence is convincing. (We don't usually expect to see such dramatic change!) With any change, you also need to decide whether it is a change for the better or worse, whether the change is occurring at a satisfactory pace, and whether it is sufficient. You also need to consider how immediate the change is and whether the data in adjacent conditions overlap. We discuss these issues in more detail later, after first discussing changes in level, trend, and variability. These are not just technical issues; they require critical thinking and judgment.

## Level

In Figures 6.7 through 6.10, we see a baseline level of homework completion well below the desired level, suggesting a problem warranting intervention. We also see a stable baseline, that is not much variability and no discernable trend toward improvement or deterioration; this suggests that this problem probably won't get better or worse without intervention.

A change in level, sometimes called a *shift* in level, refers to an increase or decrease in the outcome from the end of one condition to the beginning of the next, for example, the last data point at the end of baseline and the first data point at the beginning of intervention or the median of the last three data points at the end of baseline and the first three data points at the beginning of intervention. Figure 6.7 shows no change in level, trend, or variability, suggesting that the intervention did not have an effect. In contrast, in Figures 6.8 and 6.9, you can see an immediate change for the better in level, but the change in Figure 6.8 is smaller and insufficient. Figure 6.10 shows an immediate change for the worse in level. Finally, all of the changes, or lack of change in the case of Figure 6.7, seem stable, in that the patterns last for 7 weeks.

**Figure 6.7** • Stable Baseline: No Change in Trend or Level From Baseline to Intervention.

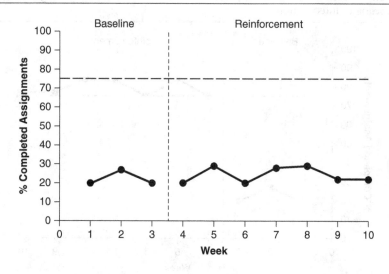

**Figure 6.8** • Stable Baseline: Change for the Better in Level (albeit insufficient) but No Change in Trend From Baseline to Intervention.

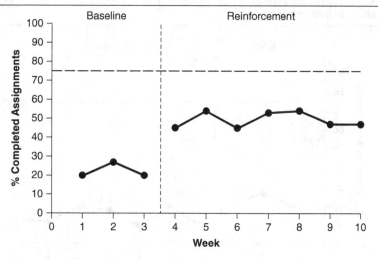

One plausible explanation for the results shown in Figures 6.8 through 6.10 is that the intervention had an effect on the percentage of homework assignments completed, albeit an insufficient effect in Figure 6.8 and an adverse effect in Figure 6.10. However, don't forget that there might be other reasonable explanations, and Keisha needs to think critically about the reasons for any change, given all that she knows about Stephen's situation.

Whether you change conditions and how and when you change conditions depend on the emerging outcome data. So, what would you do if you were measuring, monitoring, graphing, and analyzing data from Figures 6.7 through 6.10 in real time? In practice, you probably wouldn't continue down the same path week after week for 7 weeks, given the emerging

**Figure 6.9** • Stable Baseline: Change for the Better in Level but No Change in Trend From Baseline to Intervention.

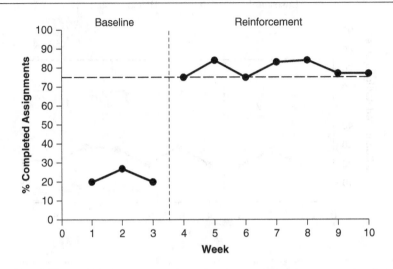

**Figure 6.10** • Stable Baseline: Change for the Worse in Level but No Change in Trend From Baseline to Intervention.

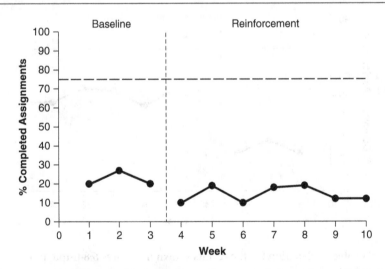

unwelcome patterns of data shown in Figures 6.7, 6.8, and 6.10. Given the data shown in Figures 6.7 and 6.10, you might want to implement an entirely new intervention—making this an A-B-C design. Given the data shown in Figure 6.8, you might want to add an additional element to your intervention—making this an A-B-BC design. Given the data shown in Figure 6.9, you might want to implement a plan for consolidating and maintaining the gains, and you probably wouldn't need to wait until week 10 to do this. Or you might want to refocus on another problem, such as Stephen's poor study skills.

# Trend

Figures 6.11 through 6.16 show baseline levels of homework completion well below the desired level—we clearly see a problem needing intervention. We see no discernable trend toward improvement or deterioration during baseline in Figure 6.11, 6.15, or 6.16, so this problem probably won't get better or worse without intervention. Figure 6.12 shows a deteriorating baseline, suggesting that this problem might get worse without intervention. Figures 6.13 and 6.14 (even more so) show improving baselines, suggesting that the problem might get better without intervention, although the pace of change illustrated in Figure 6.13 might be too slow. Each of these different baseline patterns would lead to different decisions about the intervention.

**Figure 6.11 •** Stable Baseline: No Change in Level and Change for the Better in Trend From Baseline to Intervention.

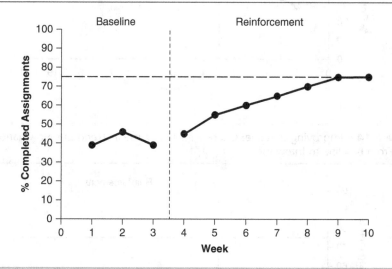

**Figure 6.12 •** Deteriorating (decreasing) Baseline: No Change in Level and Change for the Better in Trend From Baseline to Intervention.

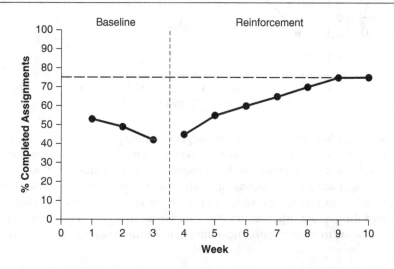

**Figure 6.13** • Improving (increasing) Baseline: No Change in Level or Trend From Baseline to Intervention.

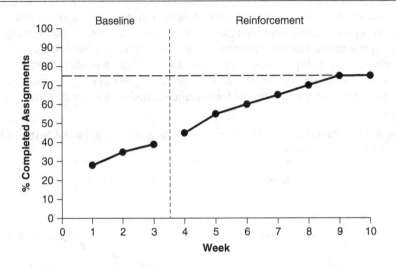

**Figure 6.14** • Improving Baseline: Change for the Worse in Trend but No Change in Level From Baseline to Intervention.

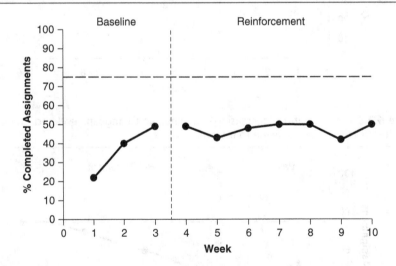

If Stephen's homework completion improves during intervention after a stable or deteriorating baseline, it's easy to conclude that Stephen is better off with the intervention than it would be if the baseline had been improving. For example, contrast Figures 6.11 (stable baseline) and 6.12 (deteriorating baseline) with Figure 6.13 (improving baseline).

Now examine Figure 6.13, which illustrates an improving baseline that continues unchanged throughout intervention. Here we see no change in level, trend, or variability from baseline to intervention, suggesting that the intervention has no effect. Imagine

**Figure 6.15** • Stable Baseline: Change for the Better in Level and Trend From Baseline to Intervention.

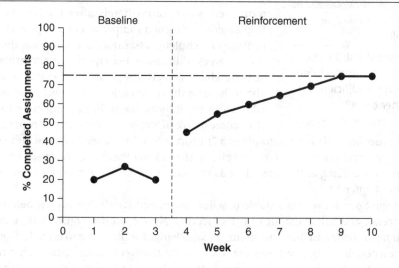

**Figure 6.16** • Stable Baseline: Change for the Better in Level and Change for the Worse in Trend From Baseline to Intervention.

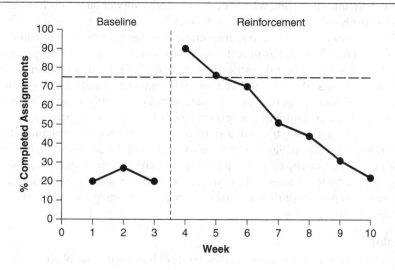

this figure without the condition change line and with the week 3 and 4 data points connected, and this becomes even more obvious; it's like nothing is happening. So, even though Stephen's problem improves over the course of the intervention and the objective is achieved, in the end it's possible that this would have happened anyway without the costs involved in providing the intervention. Perhaps Stephen is improving in response to repeated feedback about his performance. This is an example of a "testing effect," a change in an outcome that could be misinterpreted as an intervention effect, when in

## Engage, Assess, Intervene, Evaluate

***Practice Behavior Example:*** *Critically analyze, monitor, and evaluate interventions*

**Critical Thinking Question:** What questions would you need to consider when deciding whether the pace of change is sufficient in Stephen's case and in other cases?

fact the change is caused by repeated measurement of the outcome. (We'll have more to say about this in Chapter 7.)

Figure 6.14 also has an improving baseline but it tells a different story. Immediately after the intervention is implemented, Stephen's improvement stops and the percentage of completed assignments stabilizes at the level of the last week of baseline. Perhaps the intervention has an adverse effect, or perhaps some other event(s) occurs at about the time the intervention is implemented and that's what stops the improvement. For example, perhaps relatives come to live in Stephen's home and disrupt his homework schedule. This is an example of a "history effect," a change in an outcome that can be misinterpreted as an intervention effect, when in fact the change is caused by an external event occurring at the same time as the intervention. (We'll have more to say about this in Chapter 7.)

Figure 6.15 illustrates a stable baseline, an immediate change for the better in level and trend, and achievement of the objective. Now examine Figure 6.16, which also illustrates a stable baseline, and an immediate change for the better in level. In Figure 6.16, we see a deteriorating trend over the course of the intervention and ultimately a return to the baseline level—an immediate change for the better in level that is temporary. Again, it might be that these changes are caused by the intervention, extraneous factors, or some combination of these things. As always, you should use your knowledge of the client and his or her circumstances and relevant others to try to answer questions like these. Doing so will certainly enhance your client's outcomes.

What would you do if you were measuring, monitoring, graphing, and analyzing data from Figures 6.11 through 6.15 in real time in order to make needed changes as you went along? Of course in real-world practice, you're not likely to continue an intervention in the same way for 7 weeks if you see the data shown in Figures 6.14 and 6.16. Given the improving baselines shown in Figures 6.13 and 6.14 (especially), you might just monitor Stephen's progress as long as it continues to improve at a satisfactory pace. Figures 6.11, 6.12, and 6.15 show a steadily improving trend that starts immediately after the implementation of the intervention. In addition, Figure 6.12 shows a reversal of the deteriorating baseline trend, which provides especially convincing evidence for change, and Figure 6.15 shows a large change for the better in level and trend. So, for the data shown in Figures 6.11, 6.12, and 6.15, you would probably just want to stay on course. Graphing Stephen's progress allows you to do so with confidence.

### Variability

Figures 6.17 and 6.18 again show baseline levels of homework completion well below the desired level, suggesting a problem that needs attention. However, in Figure 6.17, we see a completely stable baseline and, in Figure 6.18, we see a baseline with considerable variability. In fact, in Figure 6.18, it's difficult to characterize the exact overall baseline level or to determine whether there is a trend. This makes it difficult to predict what might happen without intervention, so it will be difficult to detect change from baseline to intervention unless the change is large. In the face of the data in Figure 6.18, Keisha might choose to collect more information about Stephen's circumstances during baseline to try to explain the variability, and use that information for planning the intervention.

**Figure 6.17** • Stable Baseline: Change for the Better in Level From Baseline to Intervention.

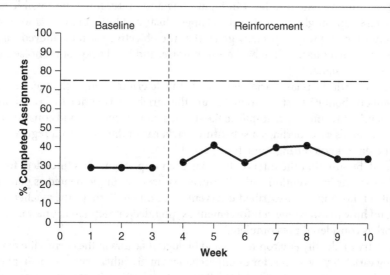

**Figure 6.18** • Variable Baseline: Ambiguous Change in Level (insufficient in any case) and Change for the Better in Variability From Baseline to Intervention.

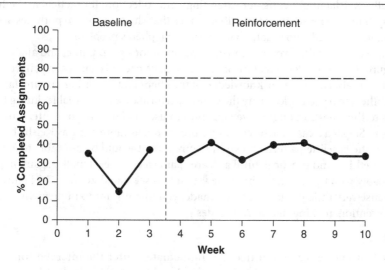

As you can see, the more stable the baseline, the easier it is to accurately detect change from one condition to the next. For example, imagine if a behavior or other outcome never occurred during baseline (e.g., Stephen never completed his homework), and picture how easy it would be to detect even the smallest change in this pattern during intervention. On the other hand, the less stable the baseline, the harder it is to accurately detect change from one condition to the next; this is especially true for relatively small changes. This is illustrated in Figures 6.17 and 6.18. In both figures, the intervention pattern and the overall baseline level (i.e., mean) are the same, but it's easier to see the small overall improvement in level in Figure 6.17 and pretty much impossible to see it in Figure 6.18. One might argue that the change illustrated in Figure 6.18 is so small that it isn't important anyway, especially given that the objective wasn't achieved. In a way, variability within a phase is like background noise, and less background noise makes it easier to hear the signal.

Given that within-phase variability clouds the determination of change, what can or should you do about it? First, try to make sure the variability isn't due to flaws in measuring the client's outcome; for example, make sure it's done accurately and consistently over time. In Stephen's case, perhaps a substitute teacher is in the classroom regularly and is using different criteria during some time periods.

Second, be sure that the intervention has been implemented as intended; for example, make sure the intervention with all critical features was implemented as planned and the client is following the prescribed intervention regimen. Perhaps the teacher does not understand how to award the reinforcement as intended or Stephen is unaware that late homework is considered not completed.

Third, try to identify environmental and biological factors in the client's life that might be causing variability over time, for example changes in his father's support or Stephen's anger at Keisha for "getting him in trouble." If possible, use this information for case conceptualization and intervention planning. Perhaps Keisha needs to speak with Stephen's father again or spend some time in their sessions discussing her role as Stephen's social worker.

Finally, Keisha might consider extending data collection, if practical and ethical, to see if variability decreases over time. Remember that she is testing hypotheses about the case; perhaps she needs more data to understand Stephen's problem.

What would you do if you were measuring, monitoring, graphing, and analyzing data from Figures 6.17 and 6.18 in real time in order to make needed changes as you went along? In practice, as always, use your knowledge of the client and his or her circumstances and relevant others to try to explore why the client's performance is so variable during baseline. Answers to this question might give you clues to use in planning your intervention. For example, in Stephen's case maybe computer time is not as motivating as Keisha believed.

Given the baseline pattern shown in Figure 6.18, it would be desirable to extend the baseline, if ethical and practical, until a clearer pattern emerges. Finally, again, in practice you probably won't proceed in the same way if you see data like those in Figure 6.17 or 6.18, because very little progress is being made; you might want to implement an entirely new intervention, making this an A-B-C design.

### Immediacy

Look back at Figure 6.2 and notice that immediately after the intervention is implemented, there is a change for the better in level and trend. Now, look at Figure 6.19 and notice that there is a change for the better in level and trend, but the change doesn't take place until the third week of the intervention—the change is delayed.

Immediacy refers to the amount of time it takes for a change in level, trend, or variability to occur after a change in condition. In general, the more immediate the change, the easier it is to attribute change in an outcome to the change in conditions, especially when the change is large, as shown in Figures 6.9 and 6.15. When the change is delayed, sometimes called a *lagged effect*, it is possible that the intervention did not cause the change. Rather, something happened between the intervention and the change that caused the change.

**Figure 6.19** • Stable Baseline: Delayed Change for the Better in Level and Trend Upon Implementation of Intervention.

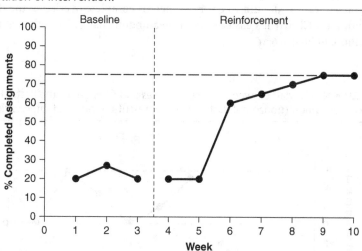

Not all intervention effects are immediate. In some cases, a delay is expected after a condition change. For example, some antidepressant medications require 2 or 3 weeks to take effect, and you wouldn't expect a large immediate weight loss in response to a diet and exercise program. When there's reason to expect a delayed intervention effect, and one occurs, it shouldn't necessarily give you pause in attributing the observed change to the intervention. So, for one problem, one intervention, or one client with a particular configuration of attributes, the expected response to intervention might be an immediate change for the better, and this would define satisfactory progress. For another problem, intervention, or client, the expected treatment response might be a delayed or gradual response, and that would define satisfactory progress. Careful case conceptualization often will allow you to predict such patterns.

To determine if there is an immediate change, compare the last data point at the end of a condition (e.g., baseline) to the first data point in the next condition (e.g., intervention). Then subtract the smaller value from the larger one (Cooper et al., 2007; Gast & Spriggs, 2010). For example, in Figure 6.2, the last baseline data point is 25%; the first intervention data point is 45%; the change in level equals 20% and is in the direction of improvement.

## Overlap

Overlap is the degree to which data in adjacent conditions share similar quantitative values. The less overlap, the more convincing the evidence that there is a change from one condition to the next—less is more. The more overlap, the less convincing the evidence that change has occurred from one condition to the next.

Look at Figure 6.20. Clearly there is a change for the better from baseline to intervention. Notice that all baseline data points fall outside the range of values for all intervention data points, and vice versa. The highest baseline value (50) is lower than the lowest intervention value (60)—there is no overlap in data points across conditions.

Now, look at Figure 6.21. Clearly there is no change from baseline to intervention. Notice that the highest (50) and lowest (35) baseline values are within the range of the intervention values (23–58) and vice versa—there is complete overlap in the data points across conditions. Clearly it's easier to infer meaningful change from the data in Figure 6.20 than those in Figure 6.21.

**Figure 6.20** • No Overlap Between Adjacent Phases and Change for the Better From Baseline to Intervention (horizontal dashed lines represent the range of intervention values).

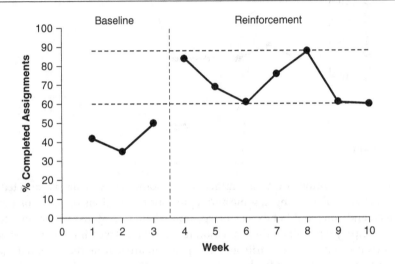

**Figure 6.21** • Complete Overlap Between Adjacent Phases and No Change From Baseline to Intervention (horizontal dashed lines represent the range of intervention values, which is the same for both phases).

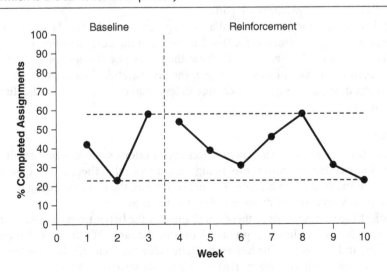

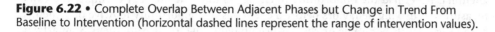

**Figure 6.22** • Complete Overlap Between Adjacent Phases but Change in Trend From Baseline to Intervention (horizontal dashed lines represent the range of intervention values).

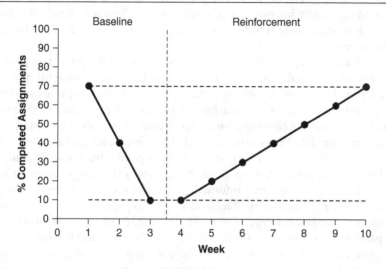

On the other hand, sometimes trend can override the importance of overlap in determining whether there is a change during intervention relative to the pattern predicted from baseline (Kennedy, 2005). For example, look back at Figure 6.13. There is no overlap, yet the intervention data are just what would be predicted from baseline. Or, look at Figure 6.22. There is complete overlap, yet clearly there is a change for the better in trend. So, don't use overlap alone to determine change.

The degree to which data in adjacent conditions share similar quantitative values can and is quantified in different ways, although consensus does not exist on the best way to do this (Manolov, Solanas, & Leiva, 2010; Wolery, Busick, Reichow, & Barton, 2010). The Improvement Rate Difference (Parker, Vannest, & Brown, 2009; Vannest, Harrison, Temple-Harvey, Ramsey, & Parker, 2010) is a promising and practical approach that you might consider if you want to quantify the degree of overlap in adjacent conditions, but watch for future developments in this area.

## Number of Observations

In general, the more often an outcome is measured over time, the more confident you can be in the pattern of outcome data collected during a phase, and the easier it will be to accurately determine whether change has occurred from one condition to the next, and the extent of the change. Basically, if you have more information, you'll have a better chance of making a good decision. Think about it this way: Suppose that you take a quiz in a class every week for 15 weeks and your professor averages your quiz grades to calculate your final grade. In contrast, suppose that your final grade is based on one quiz given during the semester. Chances are that the 15-quiz average would provide a better picture of your overall class performance.

How many times should you measure an outcome? It depends. During baseline, you don't need many (if any) data points to demonstrate that a behavior doesn't occur if the client has never had the opportunity to engage in the behavior. For example, you can't measure safe driving behaviors before a client has the opportunity to drive or a client's blood sugar levels before he or she has been taught how to measure them. Similarly, it isn't ethical to repeatedly measure certain outcomes, such as self-injurious behaviors, under conditions where there is little or no reason to think the problem will improve or might even worsen.

Let's think about Stephen. We have shown a baseline with three data points, but is 3 weeks long enough to determine that he has a problem completing his homework? Perhaps not, especially if we are looking at the first 3 weeks of school when students are becoming accustomed to their new teachers' demands and expectations. (Remember: Use all you know about the client and his or her circumstances when you interpret your quantitative outcome data.) On the other hand, if we observe long enough to be certain that this is a real problem, Stephen's grades may be beyond salvation and he may be so far behind that he can never catch up. So in this case, we will incorporate other sources of information such as the teacher's informal observations, records from the last school year, and Stephen's own declaration that homework is his problem.

The number of observations necessary to draw accurate conclusions also depends on the emerging pattern of outcome data. Ideally, during a pre-intervention baseline, you should monitor a client's outcome until you're able to establish the presence and extent of the problem and perhaps identify environmental influences on the problem to use in case conceptualization and intervention planning. If practical and ethical, you also should collect baseline data until the baseline is stable or, if baseline data are improving, continue monitoring the outcome until intervention seems needed. During intervention, you should collect enough observations to make sure that the problem is resolved sufficiently. After intervention, if possible, you should monitor the client's outcome long enough to ensure that the change is lasting. In Stephen's case, this might be done easily by staying in touch with his teacher.

Within-phase variability is another consideration involved in deciding on the number of observations needed. In general, the less within-phase variability, the fewer the number of data points you need to get an accurate picture of the pattern of outcome data within a phase and to compare one condition to the next. For example, a stable baseline requires fewer observations than a variable baseline (e.g., Figures 6.3 and 6.5), and the same is true of intervention conditions. To go back to our quiz example, imagine a situation in which you got the same quiz grade each week—a few weeks of this would give a good picture of your pattern of quiz grades. In contrast, if your quiz grades were all over the map, it would take longer to get an accurate picture of your typical quiz grade.

The number of observations you need also depends on the strength of the evidence about the effectiveness of the intervention. You might need fewer observations if the intervention is well established with clients similar to yours and if your client's results are similar to those from existing research. Similarly, in general you need fewer observations in subsequent replications of a condition if the pattern of data is similar to earlier implementations of the condition. For example, if you use an A-B-A-B design (discussed in more detail in Chapter 7) and the pattern of data during the second baseline or intervention phase is similar to the earlier baseline or intervention phase, you would need fewer observations in the second baseline or intervention phase.

Our final advice about the number of observations you need is this: When in doubt, if practical and ethical, continue to collect information. Yes, in practice, this might be easier said than done, and in some cases, it might not be practical or ethical—so don't do it. However, keep in mind the fact that you are testing a hypothesis that this intervention shown by research to be beneficial to some clients will also be beneficial with your client. More information puts you and your client in a better position to make accurate decisions about his well-being.

## Change Without a Pre-intervention Baseline

It's probably fair to say that most social workers don't see the need for collecting baseline data and they find it impractical or even harmful. After all, the client probably wouldn't be seeking your help or wouldn't have been referred for help unless there was a problem. In other cases, there are circumstances that ethically require immediate intervention, such as a client who is in imminent danger of self-harm. So, in a way the B-only design might be the default design used in practice, whether it's called this or not. (See Taylor, 2010, for examples of the use of the B-only design in psychiatry.) On the other hand, Rubin's (2008) cleverly named "B+" design, which employs a single baseline observation, might be used even more frequently, so it's important to understand this design and the conclusions that you can and can't draw from it.

There are circumstances where you might know with a high degree of certainty what your pre-intervention baseline data look like without having to collect them prospectively. For example, Keisha may be certain that Stephen has never attended the school's evening tutoring program, or Stephen's teacher has already documented the percentage of homework he has completed since school began. However, if you really don't know what's going on with the client's problem before you implement your intervention, be careful about assuming that you do, and seriously consider collecting baseline information if practical and ethical. Let's look at Figures 6.23 through 6.26 and explore the potential importance of pre-intervention baseline data.

Suppose that Keisha implements her intervention with Stephen without collecting baseline data, as shown in Figure 6.23. The percentage of homework completed is below the desired level from the beginning, the problem steadily improves over the course of your

**Figure 6.23** • B-Only Design Data.

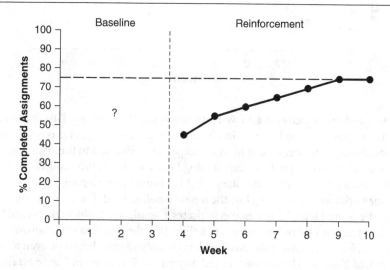

**Figure 6.24** • B-Only Design Data With Three Possible Levels of Baseline Data.

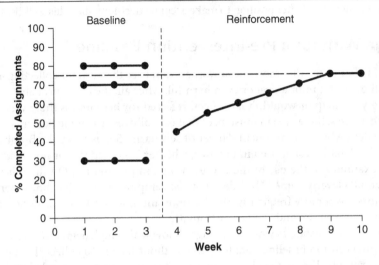

**Figure 6.25** • B-Only Design Data With Two Possible Baseline Trends.

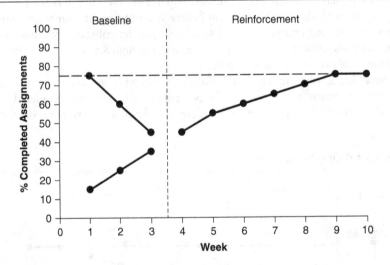

intervention, and the objective is achieved and maintained for 2 weeks. This might even be the expected response to the intervention based on experience or previous research. Mission accomplished, so to speak, or is it? What might a baseline add to this, if anything?

Let's consider three possible scenarios using Figure 6.24. If Keisha collects no baseline data before starting her intervention, she probably assumes that Stephen's pattern of completed homework looks something like the lowest baseline level illustrated in Figure 6.24: well below the desired level. This scenario indicates a significant problem that could benefit from intervention, and there is no reason to believe that the problem will improve without intervention. However, what if the baseline level is only slightly below or even above the desired level, as illustrated by the middle and highest baseline levels in Figure 6.24? Maybe

**Figure 6.26** • B-Only Design Data With Variable Baseline Data.

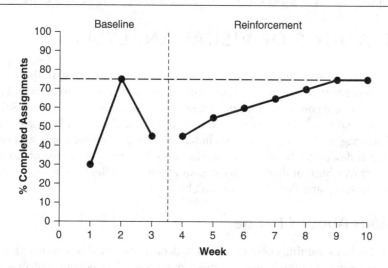

to a harried parent or teacher, it just seems like Stephen doesn't do his homework. The baseline level slightly below the desired level suggests that it might be more efficient to use a less potent and perhaps less expensive intervention, or maybe no intervention is worth the costs. In contrast, the baseline level slightly above the desired level, particularly with the trend you see during intervention, raises the possibility that Keisha's intervention has an adverse effect and that she continues doing harm for several weeks. Remember the old adage, "First, do no harm." In some cases, it may be better to do nothing.

Now, look at Figure 6.25. The improving baseline in this scenario suggests that Keisha's intervention has no effect, assuming it is implemented with fidelity, and the outcome is measured accurately. Therefore, in hindsight, Keisha might have been better off just monitoring the outcome and avoiding the costs involved in providing the intervention. In contrast, what if there is a deteriorating baseline, as illustrated in Figure 6.25? This suggests that the intervention reverses the deteriorating trend and has a beneficial effect on the percentage of homework completed.

What if there is an unstable baseline, as illustrated in Figure 6.26? This indicates that there might or might not be a problem before Keisha implements her intervention—maybe Stephen just had a couple of bad weeks. It also suggests that before implementing the intervention, she missed the opportunity to explore environmental factors associated with the changing levels of the problem, for example changes in the work schedule of Stephen's father, and this might have helped her develop a more effective intervention.

To make a long story short, we're not arguing that you should always collect pre-intervention baseline data. Sometimes it's not ethical, practical, or otherwise appropriate. Also, you can learn a lot from a B-only design. It's possible to determine over the course of an intervention whether the problem is improving, deteriorating, or remaining the same; whether the pace and pattern of change are satisfactory, based on previous research, theory, or experience; and whether the objective is achieved and maintained. However, as illustrated by the examples we just discussed, it can be hard to tell after an intervention if a client's problem is better, worse, or no different than if you had not intervened at all. After all, you don't know what would have happened if you hadn't intervened.

In addition, you can't determine the extent to which your intervention is responsible for any change, and hence whether the costs involved in using the intervention are warranted.

# LIMITATIONS OF VISUAL ANALYSIS

Visual analysis has its limitations, like any type of analysis. In particular, there's considerable evidence that under some circumstances, different people, experts and novices alike, draw different conclusions from the same data. (See Ximenes, Manolov, Solanas, & Quera, 2009, and Kahng et al., 2010, for recent research in this area.) Why is this a problem? Well, imagine that two professors independently grade your paper and one concludes that it deserves a B, whereas the other says it deserves a C. One or the other is wrong, or maybe both of them are wrong, and your paper deserves an A. In any case, something is wrong and their decisions can't be trusted.

## Decisions About Change

The first step in examining client change is to decide whether it has occurred. Either of these decisions might or might not be correct, so there are four possible outcomes.

First, suppose you decide that change has occurred and it really has; this is called a *true positive*. From this you might conclude that your intervention caused the change and move ahead based on this conclusion, for example continuing the intervention if there is improvement or trying a different intervention if there is deterioration. However, remember that all or some of the change might have been caused by your intervention or by something else, and you always need to consider this in deciding how to continue.

Second, suppose you decide that change has occurred when it really hasn't; this is called a *false positive*, *false alarm*, or *Type I error*. From this you might mistakenly conclude that your intervention (or something else) caused the change, and make a bad decision about how to move ahead, for example, continuing the intervention when you shouldn't.

Third, suppose you decide that change has not occurred and it really hasn't; this is called a *true negative*. From this you might conclude that your intervention didn't work and move ahead based on this conclusion, for example trying a new intervention. However, again remember to consider other possible explanations for the apparent failure; perhaps you didn't implement your intervention or measure your client's outcome adequately. Lack of progress does not necessarily mean that the intervention is not effective; it may mean you need to help the client obtain more support or resources from the environment to facilitate the intervention.

Finally, suppose you decide that change has not occurred when it really has; this is called a *false negative* or *Type II error*. From this you might mistakenly conclude that your intervention didn't cause any change and make a bad decision about how to move ahead, for example trying a new intervention when you shouldn't.

In practice, decisions are often fraught with ambiguity. Consider every decision to be a hypothesis in need of support, and recognize that sometimes you just won't have enough information to make a decision with certainty. To borrow Scriven's (2009) legal analogy, the "preponderance of the evidence" (i.e., enough evidence to indicate that it is more likely to be true than not) might allow you to decide that change has occurred, but it may be difficult in practice to conclude "beyond a reasonable doubt" (i.e., enough evidence to lead to no reasonable doubt in the mind of a reasonable person) that it has occurred.

## Increasing the Validity of Decisions

Sometimes you won't know beyond a reasonable doubt if your client has changed. However, under some circumstances, you can be more confident than others, and there are some things that you can do to increase the chances that you'll make valid decisions about change. We've already discussed some of these options, such as increasing the number of observations and reducing variability within phases, but we want to make a few more suggestions.

**Engage, Assess, Intervene, Evaluate**

***Practice Behavior Example:*** *Critically analyze, monitor, and evaluate interventions*

**Critical Thinking Question:** What questions would you need to consider when deciding whether the preponderance of evidence allows you to conclude that change occurred in Stephen's case and in other cases?

Larger changes are easier to detect accurately, and in general larger changes are more meaningful and important, so many authors argue that you should conclude that change occurred only when it's large and unmistakable (e.g., Figures 6.2 and 6.9) (e.g., Parsonson & Baer, 1986; Thyer & Myers, 2007). This argument certainly isn't accepted by everyone, but it seems reasonable to us when a small change isn't important to your client's well-being. However, although this strategy decreases the risk that you'll identify changes that aren't genuine, it also increases the risk that you'll miss genuine but small changes.

And of course sometimes small changes are very important; small weight loss can improve health, and the addition of even a small amount of social interaction can be very meaningful to a lonely client. (Kazdin, 2011, presents a good discussion of the importance of small effects under some circumstances.) When small changes are important, we suggest you try to identify them, but do it cautiously and keep in mind the added risk of identifying changes that don't really exist or that aren't important or meaningful. When small changes are important, we also suggest you collect as many observations as ethical and practical, because this makes it easier to detect small changes accurately.

Finally, at the beginning of this chapter we noted that visual analysis presumes that you measured your outcome accurately and that your intervention is appropriate to the problem and was implemented with fidelity. These features of your single-case design can influence the validity of your decisions and they are things that you can control to a degree. More specifically, the more accurate your outcome measure, the more likely it is that you'll detect change if it occurs. So, it's important to use outcome measures that are accurate, yet practical and efficient. Using several different measures can also help you make these decisions, when that is practical, although it introduces the issue of what to do when measures contradict one another. Perhaps even more important, the more appropriate your intervention to the problem and the better the job you do implementing it, the stronger its effect, and stronger effects are easier to detect accurately. Stronger effects also mean greater benefits to clients.

# CONCLUSIONS

You wouldn't fly an airplane without the appropriate tools: gauges and airspeed indicators, altimeters, maps or a GPS, and all the other modern marvels that allow pilots to know where they are and where they're heading. Working with a client may not carry quite the same urgent need for timely, accurate data (a crash is clearly more tragic than pursuing an ineffective intervention another week), but the basic rule applies: timely, accurate data are needed to go in the right direction. But it isn't enough to just have the tools. In this chapter, we've tried to demonstrate how critical it is to analyze the data provided by your tools and to interpret your findings accurately.

**PRACTICE TEST** The following questions will test your knowledge of the content found within this chapter and help you prepare for the licensing exam by applying chapter content to practice. For more questions styled like the licensing exam, visit **MySocialWorkLab.com**

1. Visual analysis assumes which of the following:
   a. Evidence-based interventions
   b. Outcome represented on the horizontal axis
   c. Time represented on the vertical axis
   d. Outcomes measured accurately

2. Which pre-intervention baseline pattern makes it easier to detect change from baseline to intervention:
   a. Stable baseline
   b. Variable baseline
   c. Improving baseline
   d. Deteriorating baseline

3. Which of the following makes it easier to detect change from one condition to the next:
   a. Greater variability within conditions
   b. Less overlap between conditions
   c. Smaller differences in level between conditions
   d. Fewer observations

4. A pre-intervention baseline is unnecessary for determining if:
   a. A client's problem is better than if you had not intervened
   b. A client's problem is worse than if you had not intervened
   c. An objective is achieved and maintained
   d. A client's problem is no different than if you had not intervened

5. A social worker is working with Trang, a 15-year-old student of Vietnamese descent. Trang and his parents argue continuously about how he spends his time. The social worker doesn't collect pre-intervention baseline data, but she does measure and monitor the frequency and intensity of Trang's arguments with his parents during intervention. What conclusions can the social worker make in the absence of a pre-intervention baseline?

6. A social worker is working with Trang, the client described in question 5. The social worker decides to collect pre-intervention baseline data on the frequency and intensity of Trang's arguments with his parents. The baseline data are highly variable, some days indicating clear problems and other days suggesting only minor problems. How should the social worker proceed?

## SUCCEED WITH

Visit **MySocialWorkLab** for more licensing exam test questions, and to access case studies, videos, and much more.

# 7

# Single-Case Designs

| | | Advancing Core Competencies in This Chapter | | |
|---|---|---|---|---|
| ■ Professional Identity | ☒ Ethical Practice | ☒ Critical Thinking | ■ Diversity in Practice | ■ Human Rights & Justice |
| ☒ Research-Based Practice | ■ Human Behavior | ■ Policy Practice | ■ Practice Contexts | ☒ Engage, Assess, Intervene, Evaluate |

Imagine that you're the director of a food bank. For the last 2 years, you have placed containers in a grocery store in town where shoppers can leave donations of food as they leave the store, but your agency has never tracked the donations there. Now, though, as the economy worsens and unemployment rises in your community, your agency is unable to keep up with the need for food, so you resolve to increase the donations you receive at this grocery store. Your objective is to get $1,500 a week in donations from this grocery store. With the cooperation of the grocery store, you implement an intervention designed to achieve this objective. The intervention involves prompts using point-of-sale reminders (signs located on the shelves urging shoppers to buy nearby items for donation), and it was inspired by research reported by Farrimond and Leland (2006).

An evaluation or research design is a plan that describes elements of an evaluation or research study and that ideally allows the evaluator or researcher to reach well-founded, valid conclusions. This overall plan usually includes questions or hypotheses to be addressed, the number and types of participants or clients to be included, the number and types of variables to be studied, and the collection and analysis of data. As Royse, Thyer, and Padgett (2010) noted, "Evaluation designs are roughly analogous to blueprints in that they suggest a plan or model to be followed. Even though you may know nothing about building a new house, you can appreciate the carpenter's frustration if the only instructions [he or she was] given were 'Build a house' " (p. 210).

Single-case designs are one family of evaluation and research designs characterized by the systematic repeated measurement of a client's outcome(s) at regular, frequent, predesignated intervals under different conditions, for example baseline and intervention. They allow you to monitor client progress, identify intervention effects, and, more generally, learn when, why, how, and the extent to which client change occurs.

In this chapter, we discuss the different arrangements of single-case design conditions (A-B, A-B-A, etc.) and the logic underlying these different arrangements. Rather than cover all possibilities, we limit our discussion to the designs we think you will find useful and practical in practice. (See Barlow, Nock, & Hersen, 2009, Bloom et al., 2009, Cooper et al., 2007, Gast, 2010, Johnston & Pennypacker, 2009, or Kazdin, 2011, for recent comprehensive discussions of single-case designs.) After you understand the basic logic of these designs, though, you won't have much trouble understanding or using the many other single-case designs.

## DID YOUR CLIENT CHANGE?

Building a single-case design is like buying options for a car—more options add to the value of the car (well, sometimes), but there's a cost (pretty much always). The A-B design is the basic single-case design. It's simple and highly versatile even without adding options, though as we'll discuss later, you can add options as you go along in response to ongoing, unfolding client change (e.g., the A-B-C design). You can use the baseline phase of the A-B design to confirm or disconfirm that the problem actually exists, establish the extent of the problem, and develop and explore hypotheses that might prove useful for case conceptualization and intervention planning. More generally, you can use the A-B design to determine whether your client is changing over time, whether changes are for the better or worse, whether the pace of change is satisfactory, and whether the amount of change is sufficient. Finally, you can use the A-B design to determine the extent to which your intervention is related to client change.

The A-B design does have limitations. You can't use it to determine the extent to which your intervention *causes* client change. Also, you can't use it to determine the extent to which client change is lasting, or whether your intervention will have the same effect with different clients, with different problems, or under different circumstances. However, you can extend the basic A-B design to do all these things, and the A-B design is the starting point for other more sophisticated designs.

## A-B Design

The A-B design is a two-phase single-case design consisting of a pre-intervention baseline phase (A) followed by an intervention phase (B). Ideally, the intervention is not implemented until the baseline is stable or perhaps deteriorating. However, as we discussed in previous chapters, sometimes in practice it's not ethical or practical to wait for a stable baseline, and a deteriorating baseline can pose problems of its own.

For example, suppose you record the value of donated food for 4 weeks before you implement your intervention. As you see in Figure 7.1, the baseline level of donations is 50% below the desired level [100(1,000 − 1,500) / 1,000) = −50%)]. This baseline pattern indicates a significant problem that could benefit from intervention, and there is no reason to believe the problem will improve without intervention; that is, we see no trend toward improvement during baseline. However, when you implement your intervention, donations immediately increase to the desired level and remain at that level throughout the intervention. We don't see any overlapping data points in the two conditions.

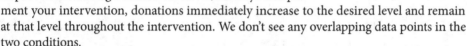

**Critical Thinking**

***Practice Behavior Example:*** *Distinguish, appraise, and integrate multiple sources of knowledge, including research-based knowledge, and practice wisdom*

**Critical Thinking Question:** What can you conclude from the pattern of results illustrated in Figure 7.1 and what different explanations can you offer for this pattern of results?

Clearly, your intervention is related to the level of donations, but is it the *cause* of this practical and immediate beneficial increase in donations? There are some signs that it is, but can you be sure? Let's consider these possibilities and discuss the issue of causality more generally.

# DID YOUR INTERVENTION CAUSE CLIENT CHANGE?

What do we mean when we say that the intervention *caused* donations to increase? Let's start with basic terms. A *cause* is a variable (e.g., an intervention) that produces an effect or is responsible for events or results (e.g., an outcome). An *effect* is a change in a variable (e.g., an outcome) that occurs at least in part as the result of another variable (e.g., an intervention). More specifically, an *intervention effect* is that portion of change in an outcome that can be attributed uniquely to an intervention, rather than to other influences.

Causation is a complicated topic (e.g., Donaldson et al., 2009; Shadish, Cook, & Campbell, 2002), to say the least, and you need both evidence and reasoning to attribute client change to your intervention. However, many would agree with Shadish et al. that in a causal relationship, the cause must *precede* the effect, the cause must *covary* with the effect, alternative explanations must be *ruled out*, and knowledge must be available of *what would have happened* in the absence of the cause. (See different points of view expressed in Donaldson et al., 2009.) Let's explore these requirements with our example illustrated in Figure 7.1.

First, without intervention you would expect donations to remain stable at $1,000 per week, the pattern observed during 4 weeks of baseline. This is analogous to information from a nontreatment control group in group comparison research. However, as you see, during intervention the value of donations increases relative to what you would expect without intervention.

Second, donations covary with condition—as conditions change, donations change and they change in the expected way, a change in level in this case, but covariation also can involve a change in level, trend, and/or variability. This is the same as saying that condition is *correlated with* or *related to* donations, terms that might be more familiar

**Figure 7.1** • A-B Design With Immediate Improvement to the Desired Level of Food Donations Upon Implementation of Intervention.

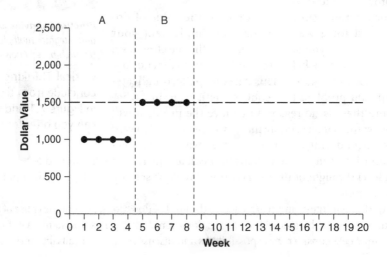

to you. This is a relatively strong relationship as evidenced by the fact that we don't see any overlapping data points between the two conditions, and there is a 50% increase in donations. In general, the accuracy of conclusions about the presence and strength of covariation is referred to as *statistical conclusion validity* (Shadish et al., 2002) because statistics usually are used to establish the presence, direction, and strength of relationships in research, for example correlations, other measures of effect size, and tests of statistical significance. However, with single-case designs, we typically use visual analysis for this purpose. The general idea still applies—that is, we are concerned about the validity of our conclusions about change—but we employ visual analysis instead of statistics to reach these conclusions.

Third, results show that donations don't increase until after intervention, and the increase is immediate. To attribute a change to an intervention, you must establish that the intervention occurred first. If you see an increase in donations before you intervene, as we see in Figure 7.2, it's unlikely that the intervention is the cause. Or, if change is delayed or gradual as we see in Figures 7.3 and 7.4, it might be that something other than the intervention occurred during the interim and caused the change. On the other hand, the gradual increase illustrated in Figure 7.4 might be what you expect from this intervention based on knowledge and critical thinking, and then it wouldn't be a problem.

Finally, you might wonder if events or processes other than the intervention caused the increase in donations. For example, perhaps intervention started the week before Thanksgiving and you're not sure if it's the beginning of the holiday season or your intervention that increased donations, or some part of the increase. You need to rule out *plausible* alternative explanations before you attribute the increase to your intervention, and this is where the A-B design comes up short. This is the heart of "internal validity," the accuracy with which you can attribute client change to your intervention, as opposed to other events or processes. This is the most difficult causal requirement because real or apparent changes in your client's outcomes can be caused by a variety of things other

**Figure 7.2** • A-B Design With Premature Change (increase in food donations) During Baseline.

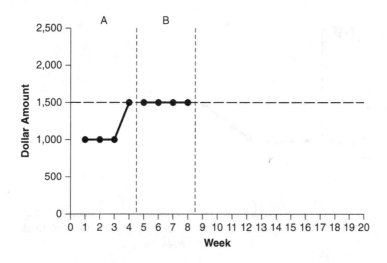

**Figure 7.3** • A-B Design With Delayed Change (increase in food donations) During Intervention.

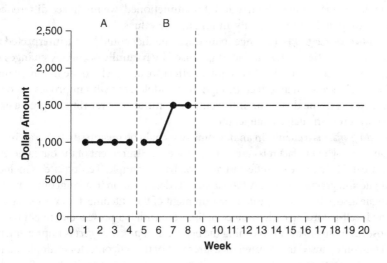

than your intervention. (Shadish et al., 2002, provide a comprehensive discussion of this topic.) These include the following:

- A *history effect* is a change in an outcome that could be misinterpreted as an intervention effect, when in fact it is caused by some other event that occurs at the same time as the intervention. For example, a national television network might run a series about food insecurity in America, raising awareness and sensitivity to the issue.

**Figure 7.4** • A-B Design With Gradual Change (increase in food donations) Upon Implementation of Intervention.

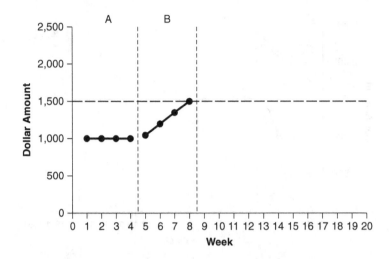

- An *instrumentation effect* is an *apparent* change in an outcome that could be misinterpreted as an intervention effect, when in fact it is caused by a change in how the outcome is measured. For example, if we were measuring the value of donated items using a scanner and it malfunctioned, we might see differences when we switched to manually adding up the values.
- A *maturation effect* is a change in an outcome that could be misinterpreted as an intervention effect, when in fact it is caused by naturally occurring changes in clients over time. Logically, this is not an effect we are likely to see in our example. You might see such an effect, though, in an adolescent who improves his or her behavior at home during an intervention; maturation over time might be expected to play a role in such a change, too.
- A *testing effect* is a change in an outcome that could be misinterpreted as an intervention effect, when in fact it is caused by repeated measurement of the outcome. Again, we are unlikely to see this effect in our food bank example. Testing effects include both fatigue and practice effects. A *fatigue effect* is deterioration in an outcome caused by fatigue associated with repeated measurement of the outcome; for example, a mother who is self-recording each instance of time-out with her preschooler might reduce those time-outs to avoid recording the behavior. A *practice effect* is improvement in an outcome caused by repeated measurement of the outcome; for example, taking multiple practice exams may improve a student's score on the Graduate Record Exam simply because he or she becomes familiar with the format of the exam.
- A *regression effect* is a change in an outcome that could be misinterpreted as an intervention effect, when in fact it is caused by the tendency of an individual with unusually high or low scores on a measure to subsequently have scores closer to the mean. For example, depressed clients frequently seek help when they have "hit bottom," and their scores are likely to improve somewhat in the following weeks, even without intervention. This is also known as *regression toward the mean*. We might

see a regression effect in our example if we initiated the intervention after only 1 week of very low donations, but this is not likely with 4 weeks of baseline data showing similar low levels.

These effects can masquerade as intervention effects, and they can occur individually or in combination. They make it difficult to determine the extent to which your intervention, as opposed to something else, is causing client change. These effects are known as *threats to internal validity*: reasons it might be partly or completely wrong (i.e., invalid) to attribute client change to your intervention. (See Shadish et al., 2002, for additional threats to internal validity that we don't find very relevant to single-case designs, at least in the context of outcome-informed practice.)

The designs we turn to next help you rule out threats to internal validity. However, to borrow again from Scriven's (2009) legal analogy, the "preponderance of the evidence" might allow you to rule out some threats to internal validity, but in practice it might be difficult to rule them out "beyond a reasonable doubt." In any case, it's important to remember that the ability to rule out threats to internal validity is an issue of design, but not just an issue of design. You need to use all available quantitative and qualitative evidence and information about your client, and good critical thinking skills, to decide what's plausible in any given case. As we have illustrated and argued throughout this book, collaborate with your client and others involved with your client to understand and interpret your quantitative results.

Why should you care if it was your intervention or something else that increased donations, as long as they increase to the desired level in a reasonable amount of time? Isn't this question important only to researchers, not to clients and practitioners? It depends on the costs of making a wrong decision about causality, as well as the benefits of making a correct decision. In some cases, causal knowledge might be important, and in other cases not so much.

Let's consider our example. If donations increase because of the holiday season (a history effect), or some other transitory process or event, such as a national campaign about

---

**A** number of events may happen during your intervention that require critical thought and reasoning to assess the specific impact of your intervention on food donations. Suppose a manufacturing plant nearby announces that it is laying off a large number of workers next month: This announcement might sensitize shoppers to food insecurity and lead to increased donations now, or it might scare them into buying and donating less, lest they be next to be laid off. Data alone cannot resolve the ambiguity; if you have the data, you might look to what happened to donations the last time the community experienced such a calamity. Also, how many employees of the plant shop in this store, as opposed to another one on the other side of town? What is happening to donations to other social service agencies in town?

Perhaps another social agency in town starts a new food bank during your intervention. You see your donations increase; perhaps the new agency's publicity appeals to shoppers' compassion and leads to general increases, or maybe shoppers make no distinctions among different agencies providing this service and think they are donating to this new agency. Maybe you see your donations go down, though; perhaps there is a finite amount your community can give, so more donations to other agencies mean fewer for your agency. Do you need to tweak your intervention to make your agency stand out more from others? Maybe your agency even needs to collaborate with this new food bank, in the interest of the entire community.

food insecurity, you wouldn't expect donations to remain at the desired level, and this would be detrimental to your clients. You would notice the drop if you were continuing to monitor donations, but there would be a deficit in donations before you could act to intervene. Also, if donations decrease later, or if you want to use the intervention in other stores, you won't be able to suggest a course of action with confidence. That is, you would know that donations increased for some reason, but you wouldn't know why. Or, if a seeming increase in donations is due to a change in how the value of donations is measured (an instrumentation effect), the "increase" wouldn't benefit your clients because it isn't real.

Finally, suppose you want to use this intervention in other grocery stores in town but you and the grocery store managers don't want to go to the expense and trouble of doing it unless you're relatively sure that it works. This might not be an issue if the intervention has few costs, but the greater the costs in materials and time, the more important it might be. If cost is an issue, you might not be able to get donations from other stores without evidence of effectiveness, and your clients would suffer. Unless there's already a convincing body of evidence concerning the effectiveness of your intervention, you'll have to provide the evidence. So, let's turn to designs that might help you do just that.

## A-B-A Design

If you remove your intervention and donations return to the baseline pattern, you can be more confident that your intervention is responsible for the increase in donations during intervention. You can't be certain, just more confident, because the pattern of baseline donations has been replicated twice and donations have covaried with baseline and intervention conditions both times, as expected. This brings us to our next design, the A-B-A design. This is a three-phase design consisting of a pre-intervention baseline phase (A1); an intervention phase (B); and a second baseline phase (A2) in which the intervention is withdrawn to determine if the outcome reverses to the initial baseline pattern. Ideally, the intervention is not withdrawn until the objective is achieved, or at least until a stable pattern is obtained.

Let's continue our example. You remove your intervention (the signs) and monitor donations for another 4 weeks. A shorter time might be better if the resulting pattern is clear, as it is in this example. In general, though, keep this phase short if the outcome deteriorates as expected. Maybe you want to determine the extent to which your intervention is responsible for the change illustrated in Figure 7.1; possibly you aren't able to keep the intervention in place, for example due to lack of resources or unwillingness of the store to continue. Or perhaps you want to see if the intervention has a durable effect. Results of this A-B-A design are shown in Figure 7.5. As you can see, when the intervention ends, the value of donations immediately falls to the baseline level. It seems increasingly likely that your intervention increased donations. However, you wonder if the reduction in donations could be due to the end of the holiday season, or something else that coincided with withdrawal of your intervention. It's possible, but less and less likely. Also, and more importantly for your clients, donations have now declined, and you want them back to the desired level—in this respect, the A-B-A design ends on a sour note when it works as designed.

What if after withdrawing the intervention (A2) the pattern of outcome data does not return to the initial baseline pattern (A1), as illustrated in Figure 7.6? It might be that the intervention did cause the increase in donations, and this effect was long-lasting; for example, perhaps shoppers got in the habit of making donations, and cashiers

**Figure 7.5** • A-B-A Design With Immediate Improvement to the Desired Level of Food Donations Upon Implementation of Intervention and Replication of Baseline.

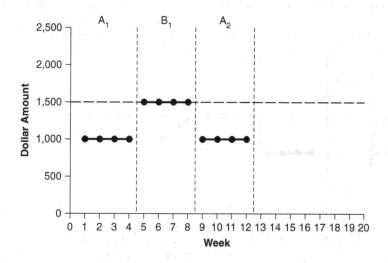

**Figure 7.6** • A-B-A Design With Immediate Improvement to the Desired Level of Food Donations Upon Implementation of Intervention and Failure to Replicate Baseline.

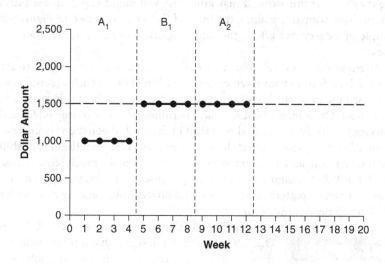

thanked them for making the donations, reinforcing and sustaining the behavior. We expect some interventions to have a long-lasting if not permanent effect, for example interventions designed to increase knowledge or skills, or changes in behavior such as social skills that then have their own rewards. In these cases, this design and variations of it (e.g., A-B-A-B) aren't appropriate. However, it doesn't seem likely that our intervention would fall into this category. Nevertheless, our intervention might have a lingering

**Figure 7.7 •** A-B-A Design With Immediate Improvement to the Desired Level of Food Donations Upon Implementation of Intervention and Gradual Deterioration During the Second Baseline.

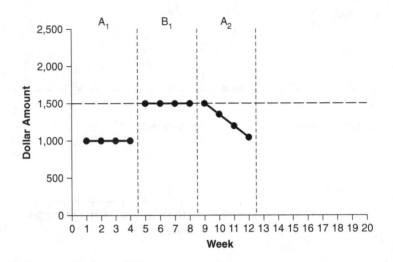

effect, perhaps by causing shoppers to think of the food bank and the community need every time they shop at this store. If that's the case, you might expect to see a decline in donations, perhaps something along the lines of the pattern shown in Figure 7.7. This is an example of a carryover effect, the lingering effect of one intervention phase on later phases.

The pattern of outcome data illustrated in Figure 7.6 makes it difficult to attribute the increase in donations to your intervention. You don't know which of several events or processes caused the increase. For example, this pattern might be due in part or entirely to a history effect. Or, it might be due to an instrumentation or testing effect, although the latter seems less likely given the abrupt shift in the level of donations from baseline to intervention. Also, a regression effect doesn't seem plausible given the abrupt shift from baseline to intervention, and a maturation effect wouldn't make much sense in this situation. So, with the A-B-A design and similar designs discussed later, the opportunity exists to replicate the baseline pattern, and verify if and how the outcome covaries with condition, but this won't necessarily occur.

**Engage, Assess, Intervene, Evaluate**

***Practice Behavior Example:*** *Critically analyze, monitor, and evaluate interventions*

**Critical Thinking Question:** What questions would you have about the pattern of results illustrated in Figure 7.6 and, if you were the social worker, what would you do next?

The B-A-B design is a variation of the A-B-A design. One advantage of this design is that it begins with intervention. Another advantage is that it ends with intervention—we hope with the desired outcome in place. The disadvantage of this design is that it doesn't provide a good estimate of what would happen without intervention. That is, a post-intervention baseline isn't a substitute for a pre-intervention baseline because it might be compromised by virtue of occurring after the intervention (i.e., there might be a carryover effect).

# A-B-A-B Design

Suppose you did obtain the pattern of results obtained in Figure 7.5, or even Figure 7.7. Would that be sufficient to attribute the increase in donations to your intervention? Maybe. However, if you reinstitute your intervention a second time and donations increase, you can be even more confident that your intervention is responsible for the increase in donations. The reason for this is that the pattern of donations during baseline and intervention is replicated twice and donations covary with condition as expected.

This brings us to our next design, the A-B-A-B design. This is a four-phase design consisting of a pre-intervention baseline phase (A1); an intervention phase (B1); a second baseline phase (A2) in which the intervention is withdrawn to determine if the outcome reverses to the initial baseline pattern; and a reintroduction of the intervention (B2) to see whether the initial intervention effects are replicated. Sometimes this is called a *reversal* or *withdrawal* design. Ideally, the intervention is not implemented until the baseline is stable or perhaps deteriorating, and the intervention is not withdrawn until the objective is achieved or a stable pattern is obtained.

Results of this A-B-A-B design are shown in Figure 7.8. As you see, when you implement your intervention the second time, donations immediately increase again to the desired level. The repeated increase and decrease in the level of donations associated with implementation and removal of your intervention provide relatively convincing evidence that it is your intervention, and not other factors, that is increasing donations. It's possible that something else coincided with implementation and withdrawal of the baseline and intervention twice, but it's unlikely.

What if after withdrawing the intervention (A2) the pattern of outcome data does not return to the initial baseline pattern (A1), as illustrated in Figure 7.6? This raises the same issues discussed with the A-B-A design. In addition, if this occurs, it wouldn't make

**Figure 7.8 •** A-B-A-B Design With Immediate Improvement to the Desired Level of Food Donations Upon Implementation of Intervention and Replication of Baseline and Intervention.

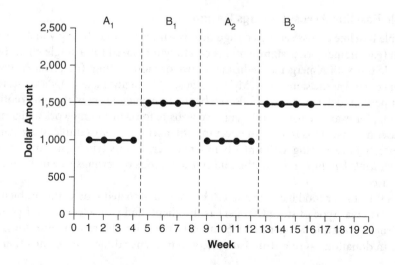

sense to reintroduce the intervention in an attempt to replicate the intervention effect. Remember, whether you change conditions, and how and when you change conditions, depend on your client's emerging pattern of outcome data; this pattern doesn't argue for reintroducing the baseline condition. However, it might be useful to continue monitoring donations to determine whether they remain at the desired level in case the increase is transitory; the change might be due to a history, instrumentation, or testing effect. Then, if donations start to decrease, you could intervene again.

The B-A-B-A design is a variation of the A-B-A-B design. This design has the same advantages and disadvantages as the B-A-B design. It also has the disadvantage of ending with a baseline phase, and possible deterioration of the outcome. The additional advantage of this design, in comparison to the B-A-B design, is that it provides the opportunity to determine if the baseline pattern is replicated.

## Multiple Baseline Designs

Suppose you can't reverse an outcome to baseline levels or it's unethical or impractical to do so. In these situations, the A-B-A design and variations of it aren't appropriate. For example, maybe you don't want to risk a decline in donations, viewing it as unethical, or possibly you're worried that the store won't reintroduce the intervention after you withdraw it. Perhaps your agency board is opposed to withdrawing the intervention.

Multiple baseline designs let you examine intervention effects without a withdrawal phase. In addition, they let you examine the extent to which you can replicate your intervention effect in different settings (multiple baseline design across settings), with different clients (multiple baseline design across clients), or with different problems (multiple baseline design across problems). Multiple baseline designs also let you examine the effect of your intervention in one setting, with one client, or with a particular problem before trying it in other settings, with other clients, or with other problems. Of course, before considering this design, you should have reason to believe that your intervention will be effective in the different settings, with the different clients, or with the different problems you have in mind. This is where evidence-based practice comes in, informed by critical thinking and your experience with the first setting, client, or problem.

### Multiple Baseline Across Settings Design

A multiple baseline across settings design begins with a baseline during which the same problem (e.g., homework assignments) is carefully measured for a single client (e.g., a 17-year-old boy with Asperger's syndrome) in two or more settings (e.g., history, English, and science class) at the same time (Myles, Ferguson, & Hagiwara, 2007). Baseline, ideally stable or perhaps deteriorating, is followed by the implementation of the intervention in one setting, for example using an interactive website to record homework assignments, while baseline conditions remain in effect for other settings, for example using standard school policy of recording assignments in a planner. In this type of multiple baseline design, *multiple baselines* refer to the multiple situations or settings in which outcomes are measured.

Let's turn to our food bank example. The value of donated food is the problem; you select a particular type of store (Kroger) as the client; and you select two different settings (Kroger West and Kroger East). You select stores on different sides of town so an increase in donations at one store isn't likely to influence donations at the other store due to shopping by the same people at both stores; that is, you want the outcome in one store to be independent of the outcome in the other store.

You start collecting baseline information at both stores at the same time, as illustrated in Figure 7.9. Initially the value of donations is well below the desired level in both stores—there is a problem needing intervention. Furthermore, there is no reason to believe that donations will improve without intervention; that is, you see no trend toward improvement during baseline. After 4 weeks of baseline at Kroger West, you implement your intervention there, and donations immediately increase to the desired level while donations at Kroger East don't change. You continue collecting baseline data at Kroger East for another 4 weeks, and you keep your intervention in place at Kroger West. Finally, you implement your intervention at Kroger East after an 8-week baseline, long enough

**Figure 7.9** • Multiple Baseline Across Settings (grocery store locations) With Immediate Improvement to the Desired Level of Food Donations Only Upon Implementation of Intervention.

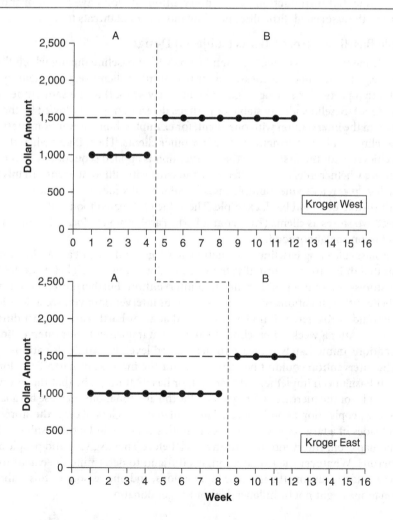

in your judgment to detect threats to internal validity in this setting, if they occur. For example, you would be able to detect if donations increase in both stores at the same time because of some external event.

Did your intervention cause the increase in donations? There are signs that it did: When you implemented your intervention at Kroger West, donations immediately increased to the desired level, but not until after you implemented your intervention, and the desired level of donations was maintained throughout. Donations from Kroger East did not increase until after you implemented your intervention in that store, and then donations immediately increased to the desired level. Is it likely that something other than your intervention caused the increase? It might be at one store, but it's less likely given that we see the same pattern of results at another store at a later time. It would be even less likely if you include a third or even fourth store with the same effect, but the baseline becomes longer with each successive store; this is a potential disadvantage of staggering the introduction of the intervention. However, staggering the introduction of the intervention across settings is essential to ruling out potential threats to internal validity, because without sequential introduction of the intervention, all you have is two or more A-B designs and the associated difficulties in ruling out potential threats to internal validity.

## Multiple Baseline Across Clients (subjects) Design

A multiple baseline across clients design begins with a baseline during which the same problem (e.g., being bullied) is measured for two or more clients (e.g., elementary school students) in a particular setting (e.g., an elementary school) at the same time (Ross & Horner, 2009). Baseline, ideally stable or perhaps deteriorating, is followed by the implementation of the intervention with one client, for example a bully prevention intervention, while baseline conditions remain in effect for other clients. Then, if and when the objective is achieved with the first client, the intervention is applied sequentially to remaining clients to see whether intervention effects are the same with different clients. In this design, *multiple baselines* refer to the multiple cases for which outcomes are measured.

Let's turn to our food bank example. The value of donated food is the problem, and you select two stores as clients (Kroger and Earth Fare). Both are located in the same setting, that is, one neighborhood.

You start collecting baseline information at Kroger and Earth Fare at the same time, as illustrated in Figure 7.10. Initially, the value of donations is well below desired levels in both stores—there is a problem needing intervention. Furthermore, there is no reason to believe that donations will improve without intervention; you see a deteriorating baseline trend at Kroger, and no baseline trend at all at Earth Fare, at least during the first 4 weeks. After 4 weeks of baseline at Kroger, you implement your intervention there and donations immediately increase to the desired level, but so do donations at Earth Fare. The intervention couldn't be responsible for the increase in Earth Fare donations because it hasn't been implemented there yet, or has it? It might be that the intervention is responsible for the increase at Kroger, and Earth Fare donations increase because many of the same people shop at both stores. This explanation is less likely if the stores are on different sides of a large city. Or, changes in both stores might be the result of a history effect; perhaps your intervention starts the week before Thanksgiving and people are feeling generous. Whatever the explanation, it's difficult to determine the extent to which the intervention is causing the increase in donations, and one reason for this is that Earth Fare donations might not be independent of Kroger donations.

**Figure 7.10** • Multiple Baseline Across Clients (grocery stores) With Immediate Improvement to the Desired Level of Food Donations in Both Stores Upon Implementation of Intervention at Kroger.

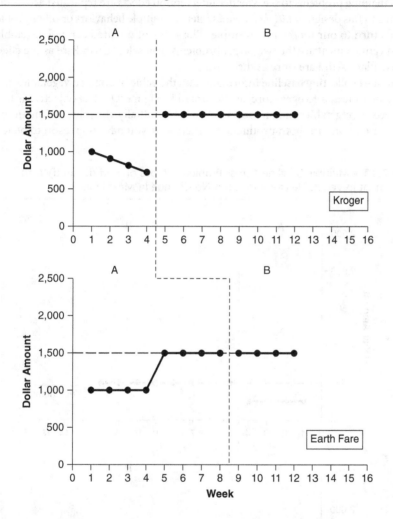

There is a way to handle this ambiguous result. You could discontinue the intervention briefly in both stores, determine if donations returned to baseline levels, and, if they do, reintroduce the intervention and determine if the intervention effect is replicated. This result would increase your confidence in the intervention effect, but of course it raises issues concerning withdrawal of the intervention.

## Multiple Baseline Across Problems (behaviors) Design

A multiple baseline across problems design begins with a baseline during which two or more problems (e.g., anger and anxiety) are measured for a single client (e.g., an adult male who experienced childhood sexual abuse) in a particular setting (e.g., a clinic) at the same time (Romano & De Luca, 2006). Baseline, ideally stable or perhaps deteriorating, is followed by the application of an intervention, for example cognitive behavior therapy, to one problem, while baseline conditions remain in effect for other problems. Then, if and when the objective is achieved for the first problem, the intervention is applied sequentially to the remaining problems to see whether intervention effects are replicated across different problems. In this design, *multiple baselines* refer to multiple behaviors or other problems.

Let's turn to our food bank example. The value of donated canned vegetables and donated canned meat are the two target problems; you select Earth Fare as the client, and one particular Earth Fare store as the setting.

You start collecting baseline information on the value of donated vegetables and meat at the same time at a Kroger store, as illustrated in Figure 7.11. The objective is to obtain $500 a week in vegetables and $1,000 a week in meat. Initially, the value of donations is well below desired levels for both products. Furthermore, you have no reason to believe that

**Figure 7.11** • Multiple Baseline Across Problems (types of food donated) With Improvement in Vegetable Donations but No Change in Meat Donations.

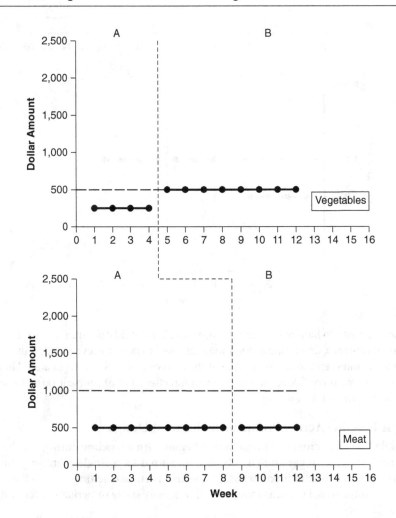

donations will improve without intervention; you see no trend toward improvement during baseline. After 4 weeks of baseline, you target donations of vegetables with your intervention and donations immediately increase to the desired level; donations of meat don't change. This fact clearly suggests that donations of meat are independent of donations of vegetables. You continue collecting baseline data on donations of meat for another 4 weeks, and you keep your intervention targeted at vegetables in place. Finally, you target donations of meat with your intervention after an 8-week baseline, long enough in your judgment to detect threats to internal validity that might influence donations of meat if they occur, for example, a drop in meat prices.

## Critical Thinking

***Practice Behavior Example:*** *Analyze models of assessment, prevention, intervention, and evaluation*

**Critical Thinking Question:** What single-case design would you select from among the designs discussed in this chapter if you were the director of this food bank, and how and why would you modify this design depending on the emerging pattern of outcome data?

What if donations of meat don't increase after intervention, as illustrated in Figure 7.11? Was the increase in the value of donated vegetables caused by the intervention or something else such as a seasonal overabundance of vegetables that leads to more donations? Or was the intervention effective in increasing donations of vegetables but not meat? Whatever the explanation, it's difficult to determine the extent to which the intervention caused the increase in vegetable donations. You could drop the intervention altogether and search for another intervention to improve donations of both vegetables and meat. Or you could discontinue the intervention targeted at donations of vegetables briefly, determine if donations of vegetables return to baseline levels, and, if so, reintroduce the intervention to determine if the intervention effect is replicated. This result would increase your confidence in the effect of the intervention on vegetable donations. Then you could search for another intervention to increase donations of meat.

# VARIATIONS ON A THEME

In this section, we discuss several additional single-case designs that can be useful for outcome-informed practice. These designs are built using the basic building materials and logic of the A-B design. In discussing these designs, we want to reinforce the idea that you should decide whether to change conditions and how and when to change conditions based on your client's emerging pattern of outcome data.

## Should You Go From A to B?

Let's go back to where we started (baseline) to review why and when you would implement an intervention. Baseline information can be used to corroborate or refute the presence and magnitude of perceived problems, among other purposes discussed in Chapter 6. For example, Figure 7.12 shows two different baseline patterns. In one pattern, the baseline value of donations is at the desired level. There's no problem, so an intervention is not warranted. However, you might want to continue monitoring donations to make sure they remain at the desired level, and intervene when and if donations start to decrease. In the second pattern, the value of donations is below your desired level. However, although there is a problem,

**Figure 7.12** • Baseline Pattern of Food Donations at (•) and Slightly Below (○) the Desired Level.

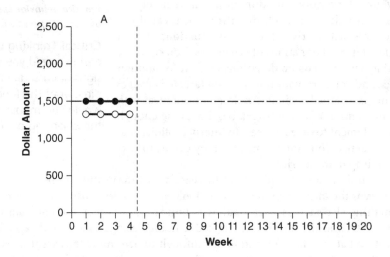

the baseline level is only slightly below the desired level ($150 below, or about 11%). Therefore, you might try a less powerful and perhaps less expensive intervention than suggested by the Figure 7.1 baseline pattern. Or, it may be that the Figure 7.12 baseline data are so close to the desired level that no intervention is worth the cost and effort, although you might want to continue monitoring donations and intervene when and if donations start to decrease. Clearly, these are decisions you cannot make rationally without baseline data.

Figure 7.13 shows two additional baseline patterns. One pattern shows an improving baseline, and at the end of baseline the objective is almost achieved. There's no problem

**Figure 7.13** • Improving (•) and Deteriorating (○) Baseline Patterns of Food Donations.

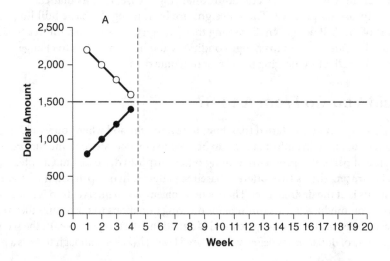

and so intervention is not warranted, although you may continue monitoring donations and intervene when and if donations start to decrease. Again, imagine the possible waste of starting your intervention in this circumstance without the benefit of pre-intervention baseline data. The other pattern shows a deteriorating baseline, and, if this trend continues, donations will be below the desired level in a week. So, an intervention is warranted to stop the decline and make sure the objective is achieved.

## Where Do You Go After B?

What do you do if you start with a basic A-B design and find that your intervention is only partially effective, completely ineffective, or even harmful? Figure 7.14 shows two different patterns of intervention data. In one pattern, no change occurs from baseline through intervention. This pattern suggests that your intervention is having no effect, assuming it is implemented with fidelity, and the outcome is measured accurately. In this situation, you might want to implement an entirely new intervention, and you might not want to wait for 4 weeks to do it. The addition of a new intervention would make your design into an A-B-C design. This is a three-phase design consisting of a pre-intervention baseline (A); an intervention phase (B); and a second intervention phase (C) in which a new intervention is introduced in response to the failure of the first intervention to produce sufficient improvement in the outcome. This is illustrated in Figure 7.15.

The A-B-C-B design is a variation of the A-B-C design. The advantage of this design is that it lets you explore the relative effects of two different interventions (B and C). The disadvantage is that results might be due at least in part to the order in which the interventions are implemented, for example, A-B-C-B instead of A-C-B-C; this is known as an *order effect*. That is, the effect of C may be different if it doesn't follow B.

In the second pattern illustrated in Figure 7.14, there is improvement from baseline to intervention, but the objective isn't achieved. In this situation, you might want to discontinue

**Figure 7.14 •** A-B Design Showing No Change (•) in Food Donations and Insufficient Improvement (○) During Intervention.

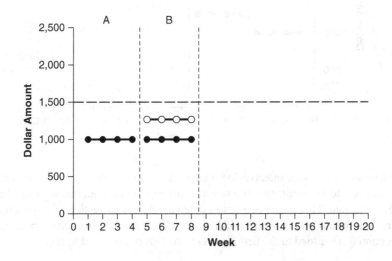

**Figure 7.15** • A-B-C Design Showing No Improvement in Food Donations Upon Implementation of the First Intervention, Followed by Immediate Improvement to the Desired Level Upon Implementation of the Second Intervention.

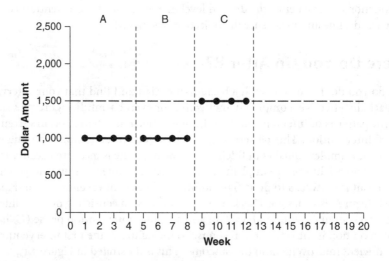

**Figure 7.16** • A-B-BC Design Showing Insufficient Improvement in Food Donations Upon Implementation of the First Intervention, Followed by the Desired Level of Improvement After Adding an Additional Component to the First Intervention.

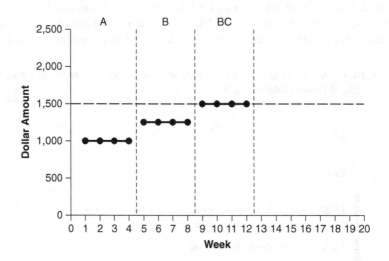

B and start an entirely new intervention, making your design into an A-B-C design. Or, you might want to add a new intervention to your existing intervention, making your design into an A-B-BC design. This is a three-phase single-case design consisting of a pre-intervention baseline (A); an intervention phase (B); and a second intervention phase in which a new intervention (C) is added to the first intervention. This is illustrated in Figure 7.16.

# FOLLOW-UP

A follow-up phase is a period of time after an intervention has ended during which outcome data are collected to determine the extent to which a client's progress is maintained. Even if a client's objective is achieved during intervention, in most cases true success requires permanent change for the better in a client's outcome. Consequently, a follow-up phase is a useful addition to any design, with a few exceptions (e.g., A-B-A design when the outcome reverses to the initial baseline pattern). Having said this, though, we recognize that it's not always possible to include a follow-up phase.

To illustrate the use of a follow-up phase, let's continue our example. Suppose the desired level of donations is achieved using an A-B design (e.g., Figure 7.1), A-B-A-B design (e.g., Figure 7.8), multiple baseline design (e.g., Figure 7.9), A-B-C design (e.g., Figure 7.14), or A-B-BC design (e.g., Figure 7.16). Now you wonder whether the effect of this intervention will be sustained when you turn your intervention over to the grocery store to manage so that you can move on to other efforts to stock your food bank. So, suppose that 2 weeks after intervention you start collecting follow-up data every other week.

Figure 7.17 shows two different patterns of follow-up data. Note that during follow-up data points aren't connected because donations are collected every other week—they're not contiguous. In one pattern, the progress attained during intervention is sustained during the 8-week follow-up period. In the second pattern, you see that a deteriorating trend during follow-up that starts immediately after the completion of the intervention—the client's outcome is drifting back toward the pre-intervention baseline level. In the latter situation, you very well might want to take action to reverse this deteriorating trend before 8 weeks are up.

**Figure 7.17** • A-B-Follow-up Design Showing Immediate Improvement to the Desired Level of Food Donations Upon Implementation of the Intervention, and Follow-up Data Showing Two Different Patterns: Sustained Improvement (•) and Deterioration (o).

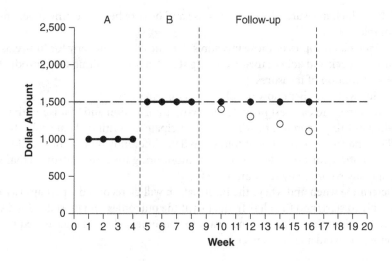

In a perfect world, limited resources would not inhibit our desires to conduct follow-up with any client for whom it seems like it would be helpful. In the real world, when a client terminates services, a new one probably appears immediately to fill your time. In the real world, managed care organizations cover a limited number of visits and probably make no provisions at all for reimbursing the cost of follow-up data collection with clients. So if you do check back with clients about whether they are maintaining their progress, you probably do it on your own time—in-between conducting evidence-based practice literature reviews. We don't see any signs that this situation is going to change.

Di Noia and Tripodi (2008) provide elaborate details for setting up plans for follow-up with single-case designs, but given the real-world conditions we discussed earlier, we don't believe most social workers will be able to implement those plans. We can suggest a compromise that might be useful in situations where you think follow-up is especially important. This might include cases where the length of intervention was especially short, perhaps due to insurance limitations, the client does not seem confident about maintaining progress, or where you can reasonably anticipate future challenges and stresses in the client's life. The compromise involves using your final session(s) with clients to teach them how to continue to monitor their targets and to plan for maintenance problems. This process might also have the added benefit of teaching and reinforcing problem-solving skills that are likely to be useful to the client in other situations.

The final phase of intervention (which we will not discuss in detail here, but see Hepworth et al., 2006) usually involves a summary of the progress a client has made and some attention to maintenance of the improvements that have been made. In addition, you usually will help your client plan for new situations that might arise to threaten his or her progress: new crises, stresses, or loss of resources, for example. This would be an appropriate time to look at the client's data and to emphasize the role the charts have played in his or her progress. (The discussion of Watson & Tharp, 2007, about self-directed interventions provides details that might be helpful for some clients.) If the client expresses interest, you might work with him or her to construct a follow-up plan that resembles the measurement plan you constructed at the beginning of the case, as discussed in Chapter 8:

- Select which measures the client can use and be sure he or she remembers how to complete them.
- Provide blank copies of those measures that the client can copy for future use. Be sure to check and adhere to any copyright restrictions limiting the reproduction or distribution of measures.
- Decide with the client how to collect this information.
- Determine who can best provide follow-up information and, if it is not the client, whether this person will be willing to participate in continued data collection. The client may want to document follow-up data differently than he or she did during intervention, for example by using self-monitoring for some outcomes that were originally recorded by relevant others.
- Determine when and where the information will be recorded—perhaps twice weekly to start, and then less frequently if the outcomes remain stable for a specified length of time. You may not want to continue collecting data as frequently as before, to avoid a fatigue effect.

- Finally—and this is key—discuss with the client how to use the follow-up data. It may be useful to set specific criteria for the client's either reinstituting part of the intervention by himself or herself or scheduling an appointment, or the client may not want to be this specific. In any case, having a plan for monitoring may provide added confidence that progress can be maintained.

## CONCLUSIONS

We hope that the earlier chapters in this book have prepared you to consider the various design options outlined in this chapter. You can see the considerable amount of critical thinking that goes into the selection of an appropriate design and the ramifications of the design you select. All of these designs are only as useful as the critical thinking that goes along with them.

**PRACTICE TEST** The following questions will test your knowledge of the content found within this chapter and help you prepare for the licensing exam by applying chapter content to practice. For more questions styled like the licensing exam, visit **MySocialWorkLab.com**

1. In outcome-informed practice, how and when you change conditions depends first and foremost on your
   a. Need to demonstrate a causal relationship between intervention and outcome
   b. Ability to collect pre-intervention baseline data
   c. Client's emerging pattern of outcome data
   d. Need to demonstrate accountability to funders and other stakeholders

2. The A-B design can be used to determine the extent to which
   a. Your intervention causes client change
   b. Your client is changing over time, and whether changes are for the better or worse
   c. Client change is lasting
   d. Your intervention is implemented with fidelity

3. Which of the following is the most difficult criterion for determining a causal relationship:
   a. Alternative explanations must be ruled out
   b. Cause must covary with the effect

   c. Effect must follow the cause
   d. Knowledge must be available of what would have happened in the absence of the cause

4. A history effect is a/an
   a. Apparent change in an outcome that could be misinterpreted as an intervention effect, when in fact it is caused by a change in how the outcome is measured
   b. Change in an outcome that could be misinterpreted as an intervention effect, when in fact it is caused by naturally occurring changes in clients over time
   c. Change in an outcome that could be misinterpreted as an intervention effect, when in fact it is caused by repeated measurement of the outcome
   d. Change in an outcome that could be misinterpreted as an intervention effect, when in fact it is caused by some other event that occurs at the same time as the intervention

5. A social worker is working with a 17-year-old student, Joel, with Asperger's syndrome. One problem is that Joel forgets to record his homework assignments. Baseline data indicate that the percentage of homework assignments Joel records each day is steadily improving. Why do you think Joel is making progress without intervention, and what should the social worker do next?

6. A social worker is working with Joel, the client described in question 5. Pre-intervention baseline data indicate that Joel's problem is getting worse. So, the social worker develops and implements an intervention, and after 2 weeks Joel achieves his objective. What can you conclude from these results, and what different explanations can you offer for these results?

# SUCCEED WITH

Visit **MySocialWorkLab** for more licensing exam test questions, and to access case studies, videos, and much more.

# 8

# Foundations of Evidence-Based Outcome Measurement

| Advancing Core Competencies in This Chapter | | | | |
|---|---|---|---|---|
| Professional Identity | Ethical Practice | ✖ Critical Thinking | ✖ Diversity in Practice | Human Rights & Justice |
| ✖ Research-Based Practice | Human Behavior | Policy Practice | ✖ Practice Contexts | ✖ Engage, Assess, Intervene, Evaluate |

Andrew is a 15-year-old with multiple problems. His grades and behavior at school have been declining for about a year, and he has now failed the tenth grade, although at one time he was a good student and athlete. His parents have discovered marijuana in his room, and he also has been binge-drinking with older friends when he slips out at night. Andrew comes, under pressure, with his parents to a mental health clinic for an appointment with Sarah, an LCSW (licensed clinical social worker). The family also has a 6-year-old daughter who is not present.

Andrew is about 5 feet 10 inches tall and thin. His hair is long and unwashed, and he slumps over and does not make eye contact with anyone. Sarah notes that his clothes are dirty and wrinkled in contrast to his parents' neat professional appearance. He answers Sarah's questions in a sullen, disinterested tone. *Does he think he has a problem?* "Yeah. Everyone is on my case all the time." *Is he using drugs and alcohol?* "That's my business." *Is he distressed about his problems at school?* "Who cares? School's a waste of time anyway." After a painful hour of talking with the family, Sarah does not feel that she has made a connection with Andrew at all. His demeanor suggests to her that he is an unhappy young man, and she makes a note to explore the possibility of depression.

Andrew's parents seem concerned about him, and until the past year, they have been very involved in his life. His father, a draftsman, coached Andrew's

*(continued)*

soccer and softball teams when he was younger, and they collected stamps together until Andrew lost interest. His mother, a nurse, volunteered in Andrew's classrooms and helped out with Cub Scouts throughout elementary school. The entire family never missed one of his games or school events. The family is active in a church, although they have not been able to get Andrew to go for some time. Extended family lives about 50 miles away, and they get together about once a month.

Ideally, Sarah would like to work with this entire family, but Andrew makes clear that he will not participate in any kind of intervention with his parents.

He agrees without enthusiasm to meet with Sarah alone at least once to determine whether he wants to work with her further, although he says, "You're wasting your time."

Sarah understands that this will be a complex case with a great deal of data to be collected before she and Andrew can construct an intervention plan (if Andrew is willing to go ahead). She will need accurate information from Andrew about personal and complicated issues, as well as information from other sources such as his parents and teachers. The quality and success of her work with Andrew will depend in large part on good measurement and monitoring.

# MEASUREMENT

Suppose a teacher based your course grade on her informal impression of your learning. Would that be reasonable and fair? Would you expect different teachers using the same method to give you equivalent grades? How might your grade be biased—in your favor or not? Can you think of ways that decisions made about you based on this method might be misinformed or harmful to you?

Measurement is a formalized way of collecting information that you use every day in practice. Before intervention, you must decide whether a problem exists. During intervention, you must decide whether the problem is improving and, if so, whether the pace of change is sufficient. Before terminating your intervention, you must decide whether the goal has been achieved. All of these decisions are based on measurement of some kind, and *the quality of your decisions is directly related to the quality of your measurements.*

Measurement is a systematic process that uses rules to assign labels to characteristics of people, objects, or events. Measurement rules describe steps for assigning labels in an explicit and consistent manner so the labels accurately represent the characteristic measured. For example, you might ask a client to rate the degree to which she and her husband agree about family finances:

| 1 | 2 | 3 | 4 | 5 | 6 | 7 |
|---|---|---|---|---|---|---|
| Do not agree at all | Agree very little | Agree a little | Moderately agree | Agree a lot | Mostly agree | Totally agree |

Numbers like these are the most common labels assigned by measurement. However, numbers can mean different things. Sometimes they indicate qualitative differences; for example, a DSM (*Diagnostic and Statistical Manual of Mental Disorders*) diagnosis can indicate a psychotic or mood disorder; a person has a full- or part-time job; or a person is divorced or separated. Most often they indicate quantitative differences: differences in amount or quantity. For example, on the scale for rating the degree to which a husband

and wife agree about family finances, 2 indicates more agreement than 1, 3 indicates more than 2, and so on.

As we discussed in Chapter 2, an outcome measure is a tool used to measure the status of a client's problem along some dimension. For example, standardized scales are often used to measure the severity of depressive symptoms. The overall strategy used to measure the status of each problem is known as a *measurement plan*. A good measurement plan starts with selecting from among different types of measurement methods such as standardized scales or behavioral observation. It involves selecting specific measurement instruments, such as the Quick Inventory of Depressive Symptomatology (QIDS; Rush et al., 2003, 2006; Trivedi et al., 2004), based on the evidence about those instruments. The measurement plan also specifies how to obtain this information: whether by computer-administered or self-administered paper-and-pencil questionnaire, in person or by mail, email, or telephone. It specifies who can best provide this information, for example the client, the practitioner, or a collateral source, and when, such as before your weekly session with the client. It also delineates where, such as in the waiting room or your office, and how often, for example weekly or monthly, this information should be collected.

# MEASUREMENT ERROR

Ideally, an outcome measure would provide a perfect picture of the status of a client's problem. In an ideal world, changes over time in an outcome measure also would correspond perfectly to actual changes in the outcome. In the real world, there will always be measurement error, discrepancies between measured and actual (true) values of an outcome.

Good practice decisions depend on good outcome measurement. For example, imagine if your physician employed a broken sphygmomanometer (blood pressure cuff) to measure your blood pressure and then used this information to recommend whether or not you should take medication to reduce your blood pressure. Your confidence in this physician would plummet. Both physicians and social workers should do what they can to minimize measurement error in the measures used in practice with clients; this is one of the main reasons for using a systematic process with explicit and consistent rules to determine client outcomes.

There are two types of measurement error: random and systematic. Both result from flaws in the measurement process. You can and should try to prevent or minimize both kinds of measurement error, although this won't always be possible. When it isn't possible, you must interpret your results with due consideration of the likely flaws in the measurement process and the possible effects of those flaws on your results. Remember: Formalized measurement isn't perfect, but it's a lot better than the alternatives (e.g., haphazard guesstimates).

Most of the time there is some random error in the measurement process. *Random* means unsystematic or chance occurrence, such as rolling dice or flipping a coin. Random measurement error can be caused by:

- respondent or observer fatigue, such as when a tired observer takes her eyes off a child in the classroom;
- misunderstandings or carelessness in reading or following instructions, such as when a cell phone call interrupts Andrew while he is completing a depression questionnaire and he skips over a word or two on an item;

- boredom, such as Andrew's becoming bored by the repeated structure of multiple test items and failing to read a question closely;
- memory lapses, such as when detailed instructions are forgotten after a time;
- lack of motivation, such as Andrew's not paying attention to questionnaires that may not be appropriate to him.

Random measurement error also can result from the conditions under which outcome data are collected, such as a room that is noisy, chaotic, or stressful. We can see a problem with measurement error in situations where clients complete measures in a waiting room, where they are distracted by cell phone conversations and televisions. Finally, random measurement error can result from properties of the methods used to collect outcome data, such as poorly worded questions or instructions; vague, incomplete, or overly complex definitions of behaviors; or observers who are poorly trained or supervised. Each of these situations can easily lead to different interpretations of wording by those completing the items or making observations, and thus to random error.

Random measurement errors tend to cancel each other out and average to zero, so unlike systematic errors, they will not bias your results, that is, cause them to lean in a particular direction. However, they do increase the variability of measured values, and increased variability makes it more difficult to detect genuine change, as we discussed in Chapter 6. For example, Andrew's depression might appear to get better or worse from week to week due simply to chance errors in measuring his symptoms due to some or all of the situations described earlier, when in fact his mood is staying about the same. Sarah's decision-making about the appropriateness of the intervention and whether it should be changed or tweaked is likely to be faulty in such a case.

On the other hand, systematic measurement error is a tendency to err in a particular direction, for example rolling loaded dice or flipping a loaded coin. It can be caused by flaws in the measurement process such as tendencies of some clients or other respondents to answer questions or behave in ways that appear socially desirable, perhaps in an effort to look better, or in ways that exaggerate or minimize problems, in order to qualify for services. It can also result from the tendency of some social workers or other respondents to be consistently too lenient or severe in rating clients, or to rate clients favorably or unfavorably in a specific area due to an overall favorable or unfavorable impression of the client. For example, Sarah might sympathize with Andrew and interpret some of his behaviors more positively than she would those of another person because he reminds her of her little brother.

In addition, systematic measurement error can result from the conditions under which outcome data are collected, such as perceptions about how the information will be used. For example, Andrew is likely to answer differently on some measures if he believes the data will be shared with his parents or school authorities. Finally, systematic measurement error can result from properties of the methods used to collect outcome data, including poorly worded questions or instructions or inadequately defined behaviors. For example, Sarah will search for well-tested measures for Andrew with clearly worded questions and instructions—if possible, measures that have been tested for these issues with adolescents.

The type of measurement method used, for example self-reports or behavioral observation, the specific measurement instrument used, and the source of the information also can result in systematic errors. Self-reports of illegal drug use, for example, may result in systematic underreporting, as may reports by parents or teachers, because the behavior is

After two more sessions in private with Andrew, Sarah believes that she has a fairly clear picture of what is going on with him, though she holds her conclusions lightly and continues to search for confirming—and especially disconfirming—evidence.

As he recounts the history of his problems to Sarah, they both realize that his problems started about 15 months ago when he broke his elbow in a baseball game. The recovery was slow and painful and benched him from both baseball and soccer, and Andrew became depressed about this change in his life. He missed the excitement and camaraderie of practices and games and felt so isolated from his teammates, who were also his best friends, that he drifted away from them. Now he was socially isolated and cut off from the most positive aspects of his life.

After this realization, Andrew was willing to take the QIDS-SR, which, while not necessarily the single best method for measuring and monitoring the severity of depressive symptoms with adolescents, has a number of advantages (Elmquist, Melton, Croarkin, & McClintock, 2010). Andrew's score indicated a moderate to severe depression. So in this first part of her case conceptualization, Sarah was able to pinpoint the cause of Andrew's problems. But what has maintained the problems in the last 15 months? This part of her case conceptualization will be key to constructing an intervention plan with Andrew, and she must figure out a measurement plan to first determine the seriousness of the other problems (alcohol and drug use, failing grades and poor behavior at school, and behavior problems at home).

hidden. In Andrew's case, we also would be aware of the possibility of errors in reports from his parents and teachers about drug use because Andrew probably hides his use from them.

In such cases, systematic measurement errors lead to over- or underestimates of the actual values of a variable, creating a distorted picture of the status of a client's problem at any given time or over time. For example, Andrew might initially underreport the amount of alcohol he drinks each week. Later, after he trusts Sarah, he may report this information accurately, and it will appear that his alcohol use has increased.

The most dangerous aspect of measurement error is that it can give us distorted impressions of client progress. Imagine rolling dice each week to measure Andrew's depression. Even if Andrew's depression changed for better or worse, Sarah wouldn't be able to detect it with this measure, and she wouldn't want to use this information to decide whether her intervention should be implemented, continued, changed, or terminated. Before we turn to the specifics of measurement error, though, we need to discuss the correlation coefficient, an important statistic that you'll see in the rest of the chapter and run across as you read the professional literature.

# CORRELATION

A correlation tells us whether and how two variables are related. For example, if parents' knowledge of child development increases with the number of children they have, then child development knowledge and number of children are correlated positively. A *positive correlation* means that people with higher values on one variable (e.g., number of children) tend to have higher values on another variable (e.g., child development knowledge); this fact does not imply that there is any kind of causal relationship involved. (Think back to our discussion of causality in Chapter 7.)

Two variables also can be negatively correlated. For example, if parent–child conflicts decrease as parents' knowledge increases, then parent–child conflicts and child development knowledge are correlated negatively. A *negative correlation* means that people with lower values on one variable tend to have higher values on another variable. Finally, two variables might be uncorrelated. If two variables are uncorrelated, values on one variable are not related to values on another variable. For example, if parents with few children are as knowledgeable about child development as parents with many children, then number of children tells us nothing about how knowledgeable parents will be about child development.

A correlation can range from −1.0 to +1.0. The sign of a correlation indicates whether variables are correlated positively or negatively, and a correlation of 0 means there's no linear relationship. (Remember our discussion of linear and curvilinear patterns in Chapter 6.) The absolute value of a correlation (i.e., the actual number, ignoring the sign) indicates the strength of the relationship—the larger the absolute value, the stronger the relationship. So, a correlation of −.80 indicates a stronger relationship than a correlation of +.50.

# RELIABILITY

Random measurement error causes inconsistencies in measurement. For example, two people observing the same event might report that different things occurred. The same question asked of the same person on two occasions might elicit two different answers. Phrasing two questions about the same thing in different ways might result in different answers from the same person.

*Reliability* is a general term for the consistency of measurements, and *unreliability* means inconsistency caused by random measurement errors. We find out if a measurement is consistent by repeatedly and independently measuring the same phenomenon under the same circumstances. The same event might be observed by two observers; the same question might be asked of the same person on two occasions; or the same question might be asked of a person in two different ways. To the extent that results are the same, the measurements are reliable.

A test of reliability requires observations to be independent and made under the same circumstances. *Independence* means that one measurement doesn't influence another measurement. For example, if Andrew's parents talk about his behavior before they

---

Sarah wants to use a measure of Andrew's alcohol consumption that is highly reliable so that she can determine the severity of Andrew's drinking and whether it is changing over time as they work together. Could she just ask him every week, "How much did you drink last week, Andrew?" There are at least two ways that asking this question is likely to result in unreliable data:

- "How much" is imprecise. Andrew may answer "not much"; what does this mean? He and Sarah (and persons in general) may disagree about what is "not much." Is drinking six cans of beer in an evening "not much" or is it "too much"?

- What is a "drink"? The alcohol content is equivalent in 12 ounces of beer, 5 ounces of wine, or 1.5 ounces of 80-proof distilled spirits. What if Andrew chugs 16 ounces of beer or 4 ounces of vodka? He may consider each of these to be "one drink."

complete measures of it for Sarah, the measurements will not be independent. *Under the same circumstances* means that the measurement is made under the same conditions. For example, if Andrew completes a questionnaire about his drug use in private on one occasion, and with his parents present on the next occasion, the circumstances would be different and we would probably expect variation in his responses based on that difference.

Just as there are different types of measurement inconsistencies (e.g., between observers, times, questions), there are different types of reliability. In addition, measurements might be consistent in one way but not another. Therefore, think of the reliabilities of measurements. Finally, notice that reliability refers to measurements (e.g., scores on a measure), not to a measure. This is an important distinction because reliability is a function of the properties of a measure, the conditions under which the measure is used, the characteristics of the population with which the measure is used, and the interaction among these different elements (Streiner & Norman, 2008).

## Test–Retest Reliability

Test–retest reliability indicates the degree to which measurements are consistent over time. It is determined by independently measuring the same group of people, under the same circumstances, with the same measure, on two occasions. The correlation between scores on the first and second administration indicates the degree of test–retest reliability if the interval is short enough that we can assume that the measured characteristic didn't change, but long enough that the measurements are independent (oftentimes 1 or 2 weeks). A high positive correlation indicates consistent measurements over the time period studied; that is, those with high scores the first time have high scores the second time.

Test–retest reliability is important for monitoring progress over time. With a stable measure (i.e., one that doesn't vary just due to chance), you can be more confident that observed changes in the problem indicate real changes, not changes caused by random errors over time. Consider values less than .70 as suspect, from .70 to .79 as adequate, from .80 to .89 as good, and .90 or greater as excellent.

Figures 8.1 and 8.2 illustrate the effects of unreliability on monitoring Andrew's progress. Both figures were based on the same data indicating significant improvement in depression from baseline through intervention. However, Figure 8.1 illustrates how the underlying data would appear with perfect reliability (1.0), and Figure 8.2 shows the same underlying data with poor reliability (.5). Notice how difficult it is to discern patterns in Andrew's scores in Figure 8.2, both at baseline and during intervention. Planning and monitoring the effectiveness of the intervention would be virtually impossible for Sarah.

Sometimes you can get a rough idea of the test–retest reliability of measurements for a client. Plot and visually examine the pattern of results over time during baseline; a baseline with relatively little variability over time and little or no trend (i.e., a stable baseline) provides some evidence of test–retest reliability. However, if you do not find a stable baseline, don't automatically fault the measure, because genuine change might be occurring. For example, Sarah will collect baseline data about Andrew's binge drinking for a couple of weeks to get a clear picture of how much he drinks, in what circumstances, and the consequences of his drinking. If he drinks only on the weekends when he can slip out with his buddies, we might have 4 separate days to collect data. If Andrew's self-report data for those 4 days are wildly disparate (e.g., no drinking at all on one weekend,

**Figure 8.1** • Reliability Equals 1.0.

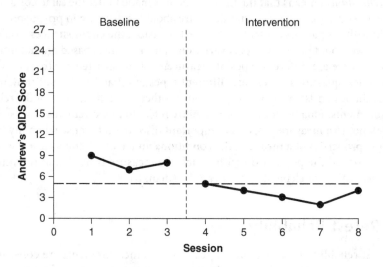

**Figure 8.2** • Reliability Equals .5.

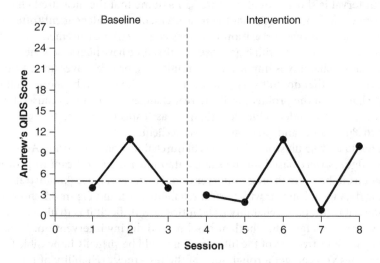

six beers in 3 hours the next Saturday, and one beer on Sunday), Sarah may need to proceed without a stable baseline and/or look at the reliability of Andrew's data.

## Internal-Consistency Reliability

A *construct* is a complex concept such as anxiety, depression, social support, interpersonal functioning, or quality of life. It is inferred or derived from a set of interrelated attributes such as behaviors, experiences, subjective states, or attitudes of people, objects, or events.

Typically, it's embedded in a theory. Usually, you can't measure it directly; rather, you measure it using multiple indicators, such as questionnaire items.

Depression is a construct. It isn't observable directly, but rather it is inferred or derived from a set of interrelated attributes that include behaviors, experiences, and subjective states. For example, the Quick Inventory of Depressive Symptomatology—Self-Report (QIDS-SR), which is reproduced in Appendix A, is a 16-item standardized self-report scale that measures severity of depressive symptoms (Rush et al., 2003, 2006; Trivedi et al., 2004). Theories of depression and research suggest that behaviors, experiences, and subjective states such as those represented by the QIDS-SR items go together (i.e., they are positively correlated) because they are all indicators of the same construct (i.e., depression). Streiner and Norman (2008) aptly observed that a construct such as depression "can be thought of as a 'mini-theory' to explain the relationships among various behaviors or attitudes" (p. 257).

Internal-consistency reliability indicates the degree to which responses to a set of items on a standardized scale are measuring the same construct (e.g., depression) consistently and answers this question: *Does having any particular item in the scale add to the coherence of the scale?* (Kane, Kane, & Eells, 2004). Internal consistency reliability is determined by administering a standardized scale such as the QIDS-SR to a group of people and determining the extent to which they respond consistently, that is with similar patterns, to different items. (If depression is well measured by the scale, we would expect to see depressed people have similar patterns of responses to the questions.) Typically, coefficient alpha (also known as *Cronbach's alpha*) is the statistic used to quantify internal-consistency reliability. Sometimes a method known as *split-half* reliability is used to quantify internal-consistency reliability, but this method isn't used much anymore.

Why is it important that the measures you use have internal consistency? Most measures like the QIDS-SR (Rush et al., 2003, 2006; Trivedi et al., 2004), discussed earlier, are designed to measure one construct, in this case the severity of depressive symptoms. If, for example, QIDS-SR items measured more than one construct, it wouldn't make sense to combine responses across items to get a total score because we wouldn't be sure what the score means. (It would be like calculating the percentage of questions you answered correctly on a test that contained questions about math, science, history, etc.; what body of knowledge would you say was being measured by the test?) Internal-consistency reliability provides an indication of the extent to which all of the items measure the same construct.

Internal-consistency reliability is important for multi-item questionnaires designed to measure a single underlying construct, for example for standardized scales such as the QIDS-SR and other multi-item scales discussed in Chapter 9. Poor internal-consistency reliability suggests that the scale items don't measure the construct reliably, either because the items measure several different constructs or because there are too few items to measure the construct. In Andrew's case, as Sarah looks for standardized measures to use with him, she should consider values of less than .70 as suspect, from .70 to .79 as adequate, from .80 to .89 as good, and .90 or greater as excellent.

## Inter-rater Reliability

Inter-rater reliability, also known as *interobserver* or *interjudge* reliability or agreement, indicates the degree of consistency in ratings or observations between or across raters, observers, or judges. It is determined by having two or more observers independently

**S**arah may consider behavioral observation to measure Andrew's behavior at home. For example, his parents might independently record the number of pleasant exchanges between Andrew and his little sister, the number of family meals per week where Andrew is present, or Andrew's compliance with a list of chores. If they independently record vastly different numbers while observing the same behaviors, Sarah will be forced to find another means of measuring Andrew's behavior unless she can determine and correct the origins of this inter-rater unreliability. Otherwise, the data will not be useful for observing changes in Andrew's behavior during the intervention, or even for discovering the extent of the problem.

observe the phenomenon in which you're interested under the same circumstances, with the same measure or other criteria or standards for making judgments or observations, and comparing their reports. Inter-rater reliability is measured in several ways: the correlation between scores for different observers, the percentage/proportion agreement between or among raters, or other coefficients, such as Cohen's kappa (Cooper et al., 2007; Stemler & Tsai, 2008).

When scores are consistent across observers, you can be more confident that observed changes indicate real changes, rather than changes due to random errors. Consider values less than 70% (or .70) as suspect, from 70 to 79% (or .70 to .79) as adequate, from 80 to 89% (or .80 to .89) as good, and 90% (or .90) or greater as excellent. Standards for some inter-rater reliability coefficients, such as Cohen's kappa or intraclass correlations, may be different (Stemler & Tsai, 2008).

You can test inter-rater reliability yourself. For example, suppose that you are a school social worker and each day for a week you ask a teacher and a teacher's aide to independently record the number of times a student gets out of his seat without permission. You could then check the degree of agreement between the teacher and the aide using methods we discuss in Chapter 11.

A less precise but still useful way to examine inter-rater reliability is to graph the information. For example, suppose that one of Andrew's parents' major complaints is that Andrew does not spend enough time with the family. They agree that they want Andrew to spend at least 60 minutes of positive time with the family each day. You ask them to independently record the amount of positive time spent together each day for the next week. This baseline information is shown in Figure 8.3. Inter-rater reliability clearly is good, except for Sunday when there was a 15-minute disagreement that you should explore with the clients. (Also, but this doesn't have anything to do with reliability, it is interesting to note that on Saturday and Sunday the 60-minute goal was achieved, a fact that you would want to explore with the clients before developing your intervention.) What's more, as you can see from Figure 8.3, an advantage of a graph like this is that you can see whether the extent of agreement is such that your conclusions would be the same regardless of who provides the information (Kazdin, 2011).

### Research-Based Practice

***Practice Behavior Example:*** *Use research evidence to inform practice*

**Critical Thinking Question:** What type(s) of reliability evidence would you want to have, at least minimally, before using the QIDS-SR with Andrew?

**Figure 8.3** • Baseline Report of the Daily Amount of Andrew's Positive Time Spent With Family by Father (●) and Mother (○).

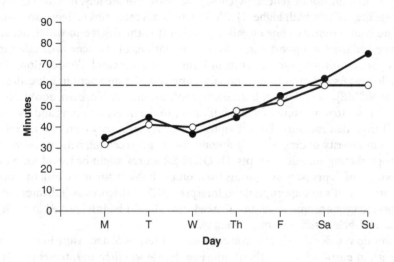

## What Type of Reliability Should You Consider?

In some cases, you can examine inter-rater reliability with your clients, but usually you won't be able to compute other types of reliability. Do consider these different types of reliability when you select and interpret results from existing measures, though, and be consistent in how you use measures. When you evaluate the reliability of results obtained with existing measures, weigh the quality of evidence available for competing measures of the same problem and draw conclusions based on the relative weight of the favorable and unfavorable evidence. Consider whether the population studied was similar to your client. For example, Sarah will prefer measures that have been used successfully with adolescents, whose skills and habits might differ from those of adults enough to affect the quality of the data obtained. Determine whether results were obtained under conditions similar to yours. Look for evidence of short-term test–retest reliability, inter-rater reliability for observational measures, and coefficient alpha for standardized scales.

# VALIDITY

Reliability indicates whether something is measured consistently, but that "something" may still not be what you're trying to measure. Validity involves interpreting the meaning of that something. It relates to *what* we are measuring, and the extent to which we can make valid statements about a person based on his or her scores on a measure. For example, can you interpret QIDS-SR scores as an indicator of the severity of depressive symptoms in general, or just a particular type of depressive symptoms, such as depressed mood? Do these interpretations hold across different populations, such as both men and women? Do they hold when the QIDS-SR is used for different purposes, such as monitoring the progress of clients in a mental health clinic, screening job applicants for depression, and predicting suicide attempts? Or, should you interpret QIDS-SR scores simply as an indicator of general psychological distress or anxiety, in which case you can't conclude that a client with higher QIDS-SR scores has more severe depressive symptoms?

The contemporary view of validity is that it is the degree to which accumulated evidence and theory support particular interpretations of test scores, or other measurements, *for certain purposes* (American Educational Research Association, American Psychological Association, and National Council on Measurement in Education [AERA, APA, & NCME], 1999; Furr & Bacharach, 2008; Streiner & Norman, 2008). Notice that we don't refer to a measure as valid, but rather to the interpretations and uses of scores derived from that measure. For example, QIDS-SR scores may be useful for monitoring changes in severity of depressive symptoms for clients receiving help for depression, but not for predicting suicide attempts. Or QIDS-SR scores might be useful for monitoring the severity of depressive symptoms for women, but not for men. Finally, maybe evidence suggests it's not appropriate to interpret QIDS-SR scores as indicators of severity of depressive symptoms at all, but instead they should be interpreted as indicators of general well-being, self-esteem, or anxiety.

How do you decide whether you can interpret results of a measure in a particular way for a certain purpose? Think about how you decide whether an intervention is best for your client: You consider the accumulated body of knowledge, not just a single piece of research, and you make critical and informed judgments about the quality of the evidence and the relevance and suitability of the information for your particular client. You use the same process for interpreting the evidence about a measure. Let's review some of the ways you might evaluate and ensure validity when you select, construct, and use measures.

## Face Validity

Face validity indicates the degree to which a measure of a construct or other variable appears to measure a given construct in the opinion of clients, other respondents, or other users. Look at the QIDS-SR items. On the face of it, do they look like they measure depressive symptoms? If so, you would say the QIDS-SR has face validity, sometimes called *test appeal*.

There's no standard method to determine face validity, no way to quantify it, and no standard against which to determine how much of it is necessary. It is the weakest form of validity evidence. However, it cannot be dismissed entirely because if a measure doesn't make sense as a measure of his or her problems, a client might not be willing and

---

**S**arah wants to measure Andrew's behavior at home because this is an important issue to his parents and sister. She would like to construct an individualized rating scale (see Chapter 10) to be completed by both Andrew and each of his parents. To do so, she will have to work with both Andrew and his parents to come up with items that make sense to all of them as important measures of behavior; that is, the method must have face validity. Given Andrew's unwillingness to work with his parents, at least early in the intervention, it may be difficult to construct a measure that has face validity for all of them. For example, Andrew does not consider his failure to answer his sister's questions and comments in a loving tone to be a problem, so he may be unwilling to self-report such instances.

motivated to use it. You might not even be willing to use it. So, face validity evidence might be important, but it's not sufficient.

## Content Validity

Content validity indicates the degree to which questions, behaviors, or other types of content represent a given construct, for example how comprehensively the full range of relevant content is represented and irrelevant content is not. For example, the QIDS-SR questions are a sample of many possible questions that could be asked to measure the severity of depressive symptoms, as illustrated by the three depression measures reproduced in Appendix A. Content validity refers to the extent to which this sample is representative of the larger universe of questions, typically as judged by experts in an area.

As another example, consider the following questions designed to measure child neglect (Combs-Orme & Orme, 1986):

- Have you sometimes left young children under 6 years old home alone while you were out shopping or doing anything else?
- Have there been times when a neighbor fed a child (of yours/you were caring for) because you didn't get around to shopping for food or cooking, or kept your child overnight because no one was taking care of him or her at home?
- Has a nurse or social worker or teacher ever said that any child (of yours/you were caring for) wasn't being given enough to eat or wasn't being kept clean enough or wasn't getting medical care when it was needed?

Suppose you used these questions to measure child maltreatment (i.e., child neglect and abuse). Although the questions might provide a fair representation of child neglect questions, they are not representative of the broader construct of child maltreatment because they don't include questions about physical and sexual abuse. Therefore, you wouldn't be able to interpret the results of this measure as a valid indicator of child maltreatment, though it might be quite appropriate for measuring child neglect only.

Content validity is especially important in the development of a measure, but content validity evidence is also important when you select and interpret scores derived from measures. Content validity evidence is much more systematic than face validity evidence. Typically, content validity is based on theory, previous research, and judgments of experts in the area of interest. Ultimately, however, support for interpretations of test scores or other measurements must be determined using other methods.

## Criterion Validity

Criterion validity indicates the degree to which scores on a measure can predict performance or status on another measure that serves as a standard, sometimes called a *gold standard*. The standard is called a *criterion*. The validity of the criterion must already be established because it is the yardstick against which the measure is validated.

Usually, criterion validity evidence is obtained by administering both measures to the same sample. The higher the correlation between scores on the two measures, the better the criterion validity. However, there are two types of criterion validity evidence: concurrent and predictive.

Concurrent validity indicates the degree to which scores on a measure correlate with a contemporaneous criterion. Usually, concurrent validity evidence is collected when we want to replace an existing measure with a simpler, cheaper, or less invasive one (Streiner & Norman, 2008). For example, the QIDS-SR was designed as a shorter, time-efficient version of the 30-item Inventory of Depressive Symptomatology—Self-Report (IDS-SR). To determine the criterion validity of the QIDS-SR, both measures were administered at about the same time to the same group of people, and the correlation between scores on the two measures was calculated to quantify the criterion validity of the QIDS-SR (Rush et al., 2003, 2006; Trivedi et al., 2004). Or, as another example, suppose that a self-report measure of the quantity of marijuana use is constructed. Results of a urine toxicology analysis for marijuana use might be used as the criterion. Both measures would be administered at about the same time to the same group of people, and the correlation between scores on the two measures would be determined. Since the toxicology test is regarded as the gold standard, the concurrent validity of the new measure must be demonstrated by a high correlation with the toxicology test.

Sometimes you can collect concurrent validity evidence with a particular client. For example, one reason Andrew is doing poorly in school is that he doesn't complete his homework. Sarah may ask Andrew to keep a record of his school assignments and when he completes them. She is not sure that his self-reports are valid, so she checks with his teachers on randomly selected days (it would be too hard to do it every day). Teacher reports are the criterion. As shown in Table 8.1, there is perfect agreement between self-reports and teacher reports for four of five checks ($4/5 \times 100 = 80\%$ agreement), and this provides support for the concurrent validity of the self-reports. Thus, Sarah feels confident using Andrew's self-reports, rather than troubling the teacher for those data.

Predictive validity indicates the degree to which scores on a measure can predict a criterion measured in the future. Usually, predictive validity evidence is collected when we want to use results from a measure (e.g., ACT or SAT scores), to find out what might happen in the future (e.g., successful graduation from college), in order to take some course of action in the present (e.g., admit a student to college). In Andrew's case, Sarah might want to be sure that her measure of alcohol abuse has predictive validity, for example that scores predict future health or social problems with alcohol. In this way, she can be sure that the scores represent urgent issues for her intervention with Andrew.

**Table 8.1** **Homework Completion Reported by Andrew and Teacher.**

| Day | M | T | W | Th | F | M | T | W | Th | F |
|---|---|---|---|---|---|---|---|---|---|---|
| Student | Yes | No | Yes | Yes | Yes | No | Yes | Yes | Yes | Yes |
| Teacher | Yes | No | | No | | | | Yes | | Yes |

# Construct Validity

Construct validity indicates the degree to which scores on a measure can be interpreted to represent a given construct, as evidenced by theoretically predicted patterns of associations with measures of related and unrelated variables, group differences, and changes over time. So, for example, you would expect a measure of anxiety to correlate with other measures in certain ways: depression (positively), happiness (negatively), and optimism (negatively, perhaps). At the same time, you might not expect a measure of anxiety to correlate with measures of height, intelligence, and literacy.

Different people interpret the saying "All roads lead to Rome" differently (naturally), but one interpretation is that there are many different ways of doing something. This certainly applies to construct validity. Indeed, the contemporary view of construct validity is that it encompasses all other kinds of validity evidence (Furr & Bacharach, 2008; Streiner & Norman, 2008). That is, face, content, and criterion validity evidence provide evidence of construct validity. There are also a number of other ways of generating construct validity evidence (AERA, APA, & NCME, 1999; Furr & Bacharach, 2008; Streiner & Norman, 2008). However, convergent and discriminant validity evidence are especially important, and sensitivity to change is especially important when you want to monitor progress and inform practice with individual clients. In any case, construct validity evidence is not something that is decided from a single study, or even a small number of studies, just like the effectiveness of an intervention is not settled from a single study. Construct validity is comprised of the ongoing cumulative collection of evidence about interpretation(s) of scores derived from a measure when the measure is used for different purposes, under different circumstances, and with different populations.

Convergent validity indicates the degree to which scores derived from a measure of a construct are correlated in the predicted way with other measures of the same or related constructs or variables. Convergent and other forms of construct validity take the form of testing predefined hypotheses based on a theory of the construct (e.g., attachment theory or the diathesis-stress model of depression). For example, based on theory you might hypothesize that scores on a new measure of depression should correlate positively with existing measures of depression, anxiety, number of environmental stressors, and number of lost workdays; should correlate negatively with social support, self-efficacy, and self-esteem; and should be higher for those diagnosed with depression than for those who are not. This last issue is sometimes referred to as *known-groups validity*. If scores on the new depression measure do not correlate with these other measures in expected ways, something is wrong.

Discriminant validity indicates the degree to which scores derived from a measure of a construct are uncorrelated with, or otherwise distinct from, theoretically dissimilar or unrelated constructs or other variables. For example, if a new measure of depression were as highly correlated with another measure of depression as with measures of distinct but related constructs such as anxiety, well-being, stress, post-traumatic stress disorder, and overall physical health, it would be unreasonable to interpret scores on the new measure as indicators of severity of depression.

Sensitivity to change, also called *responsiveness*, indicates the degree to which a measure detects genuine change in the variable measured. In particular, for an outcome measure to be useful with a client, it should detect important change in the status of a client's problem over time. Sensitivity to short- and long-term changes is especially important when you use a measure to monitor a client's progress (Meier, 2008). You can do the following to increase sensitivity to change:

- *Use direct measures.* When the measured problem is the same as the given problem, the measure is direct. When the measured problem is a substitute for the given problem, the measure is indirect. For example, if Sarah is interested in Andrew's satisfaction with the social support he receives from his friends, she won't use parental observations of the number of times he goes out with them per week; the same behaviors are evaluated differently by different people, and behaviors are not necessarily indicators of satisfaction.
- *Review available evidence.* Evidence concerning the sensitivity of existing measures is increasingly available (e.g., Albers et al., 2010; Hunsley & Mash, 2008). Weigh the quality of evidence when selecting an existing measure. In particular, look for measures that have demonstrated sensitivity to change in response to interventions similar to yours.
- *Use measures that can detect relatively small changes.* Consider the previously mentioned scale for rating the degree to which a husband and wife agree about family finances. It would be much more difficult to detect small changes if you used a 2-point scale such as 0 (do not agree at all) and 1 (totally agree). Or, imagine that you're trying to lose weight at a healthy 1 pound per week, but your scale

---

As Sarah continues her case conceptualization, she turns her attention to the factors that are maintaining Andrew's depression. She hypothesizes these factors to be:

- loss of satisfaction from participation in and success at sports;
- loss of the friendships and social support that he received from his teammates;
- loss of satisfaction and self-esteem he once derived from good grades and participation in extracurricular activities;
- loss of positive regard from his teachers and fellow students;
- loss of the structure imposed by his previously busy schedule.

Sarah constructs a measurement plan to document the extent of these losses and so she can monitor changes over the course of intervention. She notes:

- It is important to measure not Andrew's participation and success at sports, but rather the satisfaction he experiences. He may return to sports but not be as successful at first as he once was, or he may take up other enjoyable activities, but the issue of importance will be the satisfaction his participation provides. Sarah will search for measures that have shown good construct validity as indicators of satisfaction.
- Similarly, Sarah will seek a good measure of satisfaction with social relationships. A measure of the number of times he goes out per week would not have construct validity as an indicator of his satisfaction with his social relationships; neither would a measure of the number of friends he has.
- Measures of self-esteem may be useful for monitoring Andrew over the course of intervention, but Sarah will be sure to select a measure that is responsive to change. Self-esteem is a big issue that is complicated and related to many aspects of life. A general measure of self-esteem may not be valid for monitoring how well Andrew's intervention is working over time.

shows only changes in 10-pound increments—the scale is not sensitive to meaningful changes in weight. In Andrew's case, even small improvements in his depression might be meaningful and important to him and his family, so Sarah must be careful to employ measures that can document small changes.

- *Select informants carefully.* Measures of some things can be more or less sensitive, depending on the informant. For example, youth self-report measures of depression are more sensitive than parent reports of their children's depression (Dougherty, Klein, Olino, & Laptook, 2008).
- *Consider the time frame.* For example, a measure that requests information about the past 6 months probably will be less sensitive to ongoing change brought about by an intervention than one that requests information about the past week.

**Research-Based Practice**

*Practice Behavior Example:* Use research evidence to inform practice

**Critical Thinking Question:** What type(s) of validity evidence would you want to have, at least minimally, before using the QIDS-SR with Andrew?

## What Type of Validity Should You Consider?

When you evaluate validity evidence for existing measures, weigh the quality of evidence available for competing measures of the same problem and draw conclusions based on the relative weight of favorable and unfavorable evidence. Look for evidence of construct validity, including convergent and discriminant validity, and especially sensitivity to change, but content and criterion validity evidence also provide important information. Remember that scores on a measure are not valid or invalid, but rather *valid or invalid for a particular purpose.* So, consider your purpose in deciding what type of validity evidence is relevant; for example, are you monitoring client progress or trying to determine whether a client has a problem? Finally, when you construct a measure, give careful attention to its content validity before you use it; define the problem and make sure that the questions or behaviors are representative of what you intend to measure. For example, if Andrew's school problems include poor attendance, tardiness, failure to complete his homework, and disrespectful behavior, his grades may not have content validity as an overall indicator of his school performance.

# RELATIONSHIP BETWEEN RELIABILITY AND VALIDITY

Random errors (unreliability) reduce validity. So, if scores derived from a measure aren't reliable, there's no point in examining whether they're valid. For example, if you flipped a coin to measure whether a client had a problem, you wouldn't expect the measurements to give you any kind of true picture. However, there is a continuum of reliability—most measures are not completely reliable or unreliable.

Even if scores derived from a measure are reliable, it is possible that they are not valid. Think back to the child neglect questions. A father being investigated for child neglect might answer "no" to these questions when the true answer is "yes," and he might

**Figure 8.4** • Relationship Between Reliability and Validity.

continue to answer "no" on repeated occasions; his responses would be reliable (consistent), but still not valid.

Figure 8.4 illustrates reliability and validity. In both clusters, the problem is hit consistently in about the same spot (reliable). However, in one case it is the correct spot, the center (reliable and valid), and in the other case it is not (reliable but not valid).

## CLIENT CHARACTERISTICS

"What is the best way to measure a client's problems so his or her progress can be monitored over time in a way that will result in the most favorable outcomes for this client?" Reliability and validity of measurements are influenced by client characteristics, just like the effectiveness of an intervention is influenced by client characteristics. For example, measures of couple distress constructed and tested with White, middle-class married couples might or might not be useful for measuring distress in couples from different ethnic or socioeconomic groups, or for gay and lesbian couples (Snyder, Heyman, & Haynes, 2008). And, some measures of depression may not be appropriate for use with geriatric populations, because sleep difficulties and decreased energy, common symptoms of depression, are also common in nondepressed older persons (Yesavage & Brink, 2008). (Compare the Geriatric Depression Scale to the more generally applicable Center for Epidemiologic Studies Depression Scale, both reproduced in Appendix A.)

Numerous characteristics of clients can influence validity (Suzuki & Ponterotto, 2008). For example, the content or language of items on a scale may be well understood by some groups but not others. Or, items developed and written in English may be poorly translated into another language (Padilla & Borsato, 2008). Some formats, such as multiple-choice, may be unfamiliar or offensive to individuals from some cultures

(Okawa, 2008). Methods used to administer measures may disadvantage one group compared to another, for example computer-based assessment for those with little experience using computers (Ahluwalia, 2008). The construct measured also may have different meanings for different groups. For example, quality of life, marital discord, depression, and other constructs can mean something different in different cultures (Okawa, 2008; Utsey & Bolden, 2008).

These issues require you to be sensitive. First, you must find measures specific to your client's concerns or that have been used successfully with people from your client's group. This is not always possible, though, and indeed the lack of culturally appropriate measures for clients of various population groups is recognized as an important problem (Suzuki & Ponterotto, 2008; Tran, 2009). However, in some cases you may have to go ahead and use measures in which you have less confidence, interpreting them with sensitivity and due caution.

# DECIDE WHERE, WHEN, AND HOW OFTEN TO COLLECT DATA, AND FROM WHOM

The accuracy of your measurements also depends on who provides information, the circumstances under which information is collected, when information is collected, and how frequently information is collected. Accuracy also depends on your using a consistent process for collecting, scoring, interpreting, and reporting results of the measure. These are important considerations in your overall measurement plan.

## Who Should Provide Outcome Data?

Client outcomes can be viewed through different lenses. Information might be provided by the client (directly, without interpretation from the practitioner or anyone else, or more indirectly, through interpretation by the practitioner or someone else), the practitioner, another professional such as a colleague, someone else in the client's environment, or some combination of these. Each type of informant has potential advantages and limitations. That's why, as we discussed in Chapter 4, it's important to triangulate.

### Client

Clients are often called upon to assess their own behaviors, feelings, thoughts, or other experiences or attributes. These are known as *client self-reports*, or sometimes these are called *patient-reported outcomes* (PROs). Clients are present when the problem is occurring, so they are in a uniquely favorable position to self-report what happens. Indeed, for some problems clients are the *only* direct source of information, for example thoughts or feelings or other internal states. Also, the client may be highly motivated to change the problem and therefore willing to monitor progress. In addition, oftentimes self-reports are convenient and relatively easy to acquire, and can provide a wealth of information. Finally, except for illegal behaviors, the client typically defines the problem, so his or her perspective is important.

Client reports also have potential limitations. Sometimes they are not feasible or can't be trusted for one reason or another. For example, clients may not be able to provide needed information because they are too young or otherwise limited. Other times the client may not want to provide information, or may provide inaccurate information; for example, clients might tell you what they think you want to hear, especially when you can make important decisions about their lives based on this information. Finally, sometimes self-reports in and of themselves change the problem, and this makes it difficult to determine why changes occur.

## Practitioner

By virtue of your professional training, experience, and familiarity with the client, you are in a unique position to observe and understand your clients. However, the validity of practitioner reports may vary with how practitioners think information will be used, for example for a review of job performance versus an insurance audit. Data may be biased because of the practitioner's desire to succeed. Or, the practitioner might not be present when the problem occurs, since most problems obviously don't occur only or mainly during office or home visits. Finally, evidence shows that in the area of mental health, practitioners tend to overestimate improvement and underestimate deterioration in relation to client reports (Worthen & Lambert, 2007). In fact, generally speaking, practitioners are just not good at judging subjectively how well their clients are responding to intervention. See the discussion of this issue in Chapter 3.

## Relevant Others

Numerous people interact with your clients daily and might be able to provide valuable information about them: *in homes*—parents, spouse, children, or siblings; *in schools*—teachers, aides, volunteers, cafeteria workers, or social workers; *in institutions and hospitals*—house parents, physicians, psychologists, nurses, aides, secretaries, occupational therapists, volunteers, social workers, or other residents of the institution.

There are advantages to having relevant others provide information about a client. First, the ultimate goal of your intervention efforts is to improve the way clients function in their day-to-day environments, and these individuals are in a unique position to provide this information. Second, since some interventions are interpersonally-based, for example treatment of couples and families, multiple perspectives are needed to monitor progress. Third, sometimes relevant others may be able to observe the problem unobtrusively and reduce the chances that the client will behave differently simply by virtue of being observed. Fourth, sometimes clients can't self-report information accurately, so it's necessary to get information from a proxy, for example caregiver reports of the ability of an older person with dementia to perform self-care activities such as feeding, bathing, dressing, and grooming. Finally, in some cases collaterals may be extremely motivated to monitor progress because the problem is especially distressing to them (e.g., Andrew's parents).

There also are potential limitations to information from relevant others. First, some clients do not have relationships with others who can provide information. Second, relevant others may be unwilling to cooperate, or may fudge information, depending on how they think it might be used. Third, the reason collateral sources are so useful—their day-to-day relationships with clients—also might bias their responses. Fourth, collateral sources might not know enough about a particular client's problem to provide adequate

Four weeks after his family's first visit to the mental health center, Andrew and Sarah agree on an intervention plan. They will tackle Andrew's depression by dealing with the factors that are maintaining his depression, beginning with the loss of satisfaction and friendships resulting from his sports injury. Andrew will return to baseball, and his parents have agreed to pay for any physical therapy or other extra training he needs. Both Andrew and Sarah believe that taking this step first may reduce his depression and that improvements in his mood will reduce his disrespectful and discourteous behavior at home and at school. In a few weeks, Andrew also will meet with each of his teachers about improving his grades, and he and Sarah will plan and rehearse for these conversations to improve the odds of their success.

Andrew's case involves consistent monitoring of data from multiple sources. Andrew will complete individualized rating scales of his satisfaction with his social life and participation in sports and, later, other school activities. Sarah will observe and record his demeanor in each session and go over the QIDS-SR that he will complete each week before the session alone in a private testing room. Andrew's parents will provide observational data of his behavior at home. Finally, Andrew's teachers will provide valuable observational data of his behavior in the classroom and extracurricular activities, his completion of assigned work, and improvements in the quality of his work. Sarah believes that triangulating data from all of these data will provide valid information for monitoring the success of Andrew's intervention, and she is prepared to make changes quickly if the data do not show progress.

information. Fifth, sometimes it can be time-consuming and otherwise expensive to collect information from collaterals. Finally, if a client has access to information provided by collateral sources, it can prove embarrassing or harmful to the client's relationship with those persons, for example when a collateral provides information about a neighbor's child neglect.

### Independent Evaluators

Sometimes other professionals, such as your colleagues or supervisor, can provide valuable observations of your clients. For example, a supervisor may review a random sample of audiotapes of your sessions with a client or even conduct an interview with your client. Independent evaluators have the advantage of being less personally invested in a client, so they might be able to give more objective assessments. On the flip side, independent evaluators are less involved with clients and so less familiar with them. In addition, in busy agencies your colleagues might not have time to provide independent assessments.

You must weigh the pros and cons of all the factors for a particular client, use whoever is available, able, and willing to record, and try to minimize the disadvantages and maximize the advantages of different informants. Also, typically, no individual is a perfect source of information, so it's best to collect information from various informed sources. If the bulk of information from different sources is consistent, you can have greater confidence in the information, and if it isn't consistent, at least you'll know that you need to proceed with caution.

## When and Where to Collect Data?

Urie Bronfenbrenner (1977) characterized developmental psychology as "the science of the strange behavior of children in strange situations with strange adults for the briefest possible periods of time" (p. 513). Much the same can be said of human service professionals in the sense that at times what we know about clients is obtained in situations that are unfamiliar to the client—artificial, short-lived, and calling for unusual behaviors that don't necessarily generalize to real-life situations. For example, typically you will observe your client only in your office or maybe in the client's home. Or, a teacher observes a student only in school at certain times of the day. Or, you will ask your client some questions but not others, or focus on one aspect of your client to the exclusion of others.

When a client's problem is observed only sometimes or under some circumstances, try to make sure that your observations are representative of the problem. That is, make sure that the observations are similar to or typical of observations made at other times and under different circumstances. If it isn't possible to select representative times or circumstances, consider what errors might be introduced into your measurements. For example, think about making observations of your client once a week in your office. How and why might a client's behavior be different under these circumstances than in his or her natural environment? Or, consider a homeroom teacher's morning classroom observations of a child and ask how and why the child's behavior might be different at different times, for example late afternoon, or under different circumstances, for example at home. Factor these considerations into your interpretations of the information you collect.

Whatever the measurement circumstances, make them as conducive as possible to accurate measurement. For example, a questionnaire designed to elicit information about alcohol consumption might be valid when administered under some conditions such as individually with guarantees of confidentiality, but not others such as in the presence of family members. Or, a client might be able to self-monitor behaviors or other experiences accurately if you tailor the task to the client's abilities, clearly explain what needs to be done and why it's important to do it carefully, and give the client easy-to-use tools to do it. Whatever setting is used to collect outcome data, make sure that it is conducive to collecting accurate information. For example, you would prefer a quiet setting with adequate room, lighting, and ventilation for the completion of standardized scales.

Finally, once you select the times and circumstances for measuring the client's problem, stick to your decisions unless there's a good reason to do otherwise. For example, suppose you ask Andrew to rate the intensity of his feelings of loneliness each day. For the first few weeks, he does it in the evening, the time he feels most lonely, and then when the intervention begins, he does it during the morning, the time he feels least lonely. This apparent decrease in loneliness might then be misinterpreted as an intervention effect, when in fact it is caused by a change in how loneliness is measured, that is, an instrumentation effect, as discussed in Chapter 7. More generally, changes over time might be due to real progress or to changes in when data are collected; this situation makes it difficult to decide whether your intervention should be implemented to begin with, continued, changed, or terminated.

## How Often Should Data Be Collected?

Think about a professor basing your entire course grade on one pop quiz. Would that give a good picture of your performance? Or think about a professor who bases grades on one final exam. Would she know what students knew about the subject to begin with? Would she know how students were doing throughout the semester so she could change her teaching methods if necessary? Could she assign grades that accurately portrayed what students knew about the course content from a single quiz or test?

Client outcomes should be measured at regular, frequent, predesignated intervals to monitor clients' progress, before, during, and after intervention (if possible). This lets you know in a timely manner if your client is making satisfactory progress, so if he or she is off track, you can do something about it sooner, rather than later.

As a general rule, a problem should be measured often enough to detect significant changes in the problem, but not so often that it becomes burdensome to those collecting data or intrudes on intervention efforts. We will have more to say about this in following chapters.

**Critical Thinking**

*Practice Behavior Example:* Distinguish, appraise, and integrate multiple sources of knowledge, including research-based knowledge, and practice wisdom

**Critical Thinking Question:** What questions would you consider in deciding when, where, and how often you would administer the QIDS-SR to Andrew?

# ENGAGE AND PREPARE CLIENTS

It's important to engage clients in the development and implementation of measurement plans and to prepare them well. Careful attention to these issues will enhance the quality of the information you collect. Most of the following applies to clients as well as other types of informants:

- *Be certain the client understands and accepts the value and purpose of monitoring progress.* Explain that the information will be used to monitor client progress so needed changes can be made quickly to achieve a successful outcome. Emphasize the importance of providing accurate information, and motivate the client to provide accurate information. For example, Sarah might say the following to Andrew, taking advantage of the fact that most people have experience with physicians:

  *Your physician needs accurate information about you to help understand your particular needs before prescribing treatment, and she also needs some way of finding out whether treatment is working. I also need ongoing information about your concerns to ensure that I thoroughly understand these concerns and that we're making progress in resolving them. You're in a unique position to provide information that's important to the success of our helping effort, so it's important that you give me the most accurate information you can, although I know that some of this information might be embarrassing. Even if the problem seems to be getting worse after we start working on it, it's important that I know this if I'm going to be of help to you.*

- *Discuss confidentiality.* Clients might be reluctant to provide accurate information if they don't know who has access to the potentially embarrassing information they're asked to provide. Therefore, discuss what information you can and can't keep confidential (e.g., Polowy, Morgan, Bailey, & Gorenberg, 2008; Reamer, 2009). Your agency should provide you with updated information on this issue. If you practice social work independently, consult the relevant laws in your state and NASW (National Association of Social Workers) to be sure that you have timely information.

- *Present measures with confidence.* Present the measures you select to your clients with confidence. Sometimes practitioners with little experience using outcome measures present them to clients apologetically; this is likely to undermine the client's confidence in the process or its importance.
- *Don't ask for information the client can't provide.* Reported information is limited by what a client is willing and *able* to tell you. For example, Andrew might be willing to report, but unable to remember, the frequency and amount of his marijuana use in the previous year. Andrew's parents are certainly not able to report how depressed or unhappy he is, though they may be able to describe and document behaviors that indicate depression.
- *Be sure the client is prepared.* Explain the task and be sure the client understands what to do and that he or she is able to do it. Encourage clients to ask questions, and make it clear that you have time to answer them. Make sure the proper measurement tools are available, such as questionnaires and administrative forms, and that they are simple, inexpensive, and easy to use. Provide encouragement and support for the client's efforts within a context of rapport and trust, and do whatever possible to remove obstacles the client might face in these efforts. You might complete a measure together during the session to be sure the client knows what to do.
- *Be careful how you respond to information.* Your reaction to information can distort the information. For example, Sarah won't show surprise or disapproval in response to Andrew's reports of his alcohol and marijuana use, and she will carefully avoid seeming pleased by his reports in order to avoid encouraging him to reply in any specific way.
- *Use the information that is collected.* Measurement information should be used to improve client outcomes, and it should be clear to the client how the information is being used for the client's benefit. If not, your client might not take data collection seriously. It won't take Andrew long to realize that it doesn't matter how accurate and consistent his self-report data are if Sarah and he never discuss them.

# IS THE MEASURE PRACTICAL AND DOES IT CONTRIBUTE TO FAVORABLE OUTCOMES?

Suppose you identify the most reliable and valid measure of depression. It contains 100 items, takes an hour to complete, requires extensive training to administer, score, and interpret, is available only to practitioners with special training, is administered by computer, is expensive, and isn't acceptable to your client. No matter how reliable or valid, we can be pretty sure that this measure won't be useful or used to monitor progress and contribute to beneficial outcomes with individual cases. Or, as Yogi Berra said, "In theory there is no difference between theory and practice. In practice there is." Reliability and validity are necessary, but not sufficient characteristics of outcome measures. Cost, benefit, efficiency, and acceptability also are important.

A measure must be relatively easy to use if you want to use it to monitor progress and make practice decisions with individual cases. Ease of use involves several considerations, including the time it takes to administer, score, and interpret the measure, and the characteristics of the client. For example, a client who lives in a chaotic environment might be overwhelmed by keeping a structured diary, and another client with poor reading skills might not be able to complete a self-report questionnaire accurately. Observers might get tired of making observations, or a standardized scale might be too time-consuming for a practitioner to use. More generally, some measures just might not be acceptable to some clients or others who are asked to provide information.

When measures are used to monitor progress and inform practice with individual cases, it's especially important that scores derived from those measures are relatively simple to understand and explain. As Lyons (2009) observed, the information "should be clear, unambiguous, relevant, easy to translate into intervention planning recommendations, and accessible to providers, consumers, and policy makers" (p. 29). For example, what does a particular QIDS-SR score mean: mild depression, moderate depression, or severe depression? Or, what is the smallest change in a QIDS-SR score that would be considered clinically meaningful or otherwise important by the client, or that would justify a change in the intervention? These questions have to do with the interpretability of scores, the degree to which qualitative meaning can be assigned to quantitative scores (Terwee et al., 2007).

Finally, accessibility of a measure is an important practical consideration. Some measures are difficult to acquire; for example, they might be expensive. Some professionals might not have access to other measures; for example, some measures are available only to professionals with special training.

# CONCLUSIONS

The decisions we make in practice are only as good as the information on which they are based, and in outcome-informed practice, we strive to use the best available information about how the client is doing to guide our actions. We try to employ the best measures and to use them in the best ways to maximize the quality of our information, but we also recognize the many ways information can be compromised. Once again, critical thinking is key to using the principles in this chapter to maximize your clients' chances of achieving their goals.

**PRACTICE TEST** The following questions will test your knowledge of the content found within this chapter and help you prepare for the licensing exam by applying chapter content to practice. For more questions styled like the licensing exam, visit **MySocialWorkLab.com**

1. A social worker decides to develop a strategy to measure and monitor his client's progress in reducing unrealistic, maladaptive modes of thinking. The overall strategy used to measure and monitor his client's progress is known as a/an:

   **a.** Outcome measure

   **b.** Measurement plan

   **c.** Measurement method

   **d.** Screening measure

2. A social worker decides to use the Parent Daily Report (PDR, reproduced in Appendix A) to measure and monitor progress in reducing a 12-year-old foster child's behavioral problems. The PDR is a 30-item checklist of child behavior problems as reported by parents, typically during a brief telephone interview. Suppose that the internal-consistency reliability of this measure is .88. Should the social worker consider this level of reliability as

   **a.** Suspect

   **b.** Adequate

   **c.** Good

   **d.** Excellent

3. A social worker considers using the QIDS-SR (reproduced in Appendix A) to measure and monitor progress in reducing the severity of a young woman's depressive symptoms. Which of the following is the most important and overarching type of validity evidence the social worker should look for before using this measure for this purpose:

   **a.** Face validity

   **b.** Content validity

   **c.** Criterion validity

   **d.** Construct validity

4. A social worker meets with a 19-year-old male with a social phobia. The social worker and client develop a mutually agreed-upon intervention and goals and objectives. Which of the following should the social worker do next:

   **a.** Select outcome measures

   **b.** Decide who should provide the outcome data

   **c.** Engage the client in the development of the measurement plan

   **d.** Decide when, where, and how often data should be collected

5. A social worker meets with a 70-year-old Hispanic man referred to him for depression. A colleague suggests that he use the 15-item Geriatric Depression Scale (GDS-15) to measure and monitor his client's progress. What would the social worker want to know about the GDS-15 before using it with his client, and what information would be most important?

6. A social worker decides to use the GDS-15 with the client described in question 5. What things should the social worker do to ensure and check the accuracy of the GDS-15 data he gets from this client?

## SUCCEED WITH

# 9

# Standardized Scales

| Advancing Core Competencies in This Chapter | | | | |
|---|---|---|---|---|
| Professional Identity | ☒ Ethical Practice | ☒ Critical Thinking | ☒ Diversity in Practice | Human Rights & Justice |
| ☒ Research-Based Practice | Human Behavior | Policy Practice | ☒ Practice Contexts | ☒ Engage, Assess, Intervene, Evaluate |

Marie Kasper is a frail 92-year-old European-American woman who lived in her own home (two blocks from her daughter and granddaughter) until a month ago. Her health has been declining since her husband of 68 years died a year ago, and in the last month she has had difficulty recovering from a bladder infection. Only 2 months ago, she could bathe and dress herself and prepare simple meals during the day, though she had been eating dinner and spending most evenings with her daughter and granddaughter since her husband died. Her physician has scheduled an appointment for an evaluation by a neurologist, as she has begun having great difficulty walking and speaking, although she seems to understand what is going on around her. In addition, she now has occasional problems with incontinence.

Mrs. Kasper's daughter Barbara and her granddaughter Amanda, age 17, provide care for her, with the help of a neighbor who checks on her once in the middle of the morning while Amanda is at school. Amanda has just begun as a full-time student in a nearby junior college, and she attends classes each morning until about 1:00 p.m., when her grandmother is mostly alone and sleeping. Barbara works nearby as a teacher and gets home about 4:00 in the afternoon. Barbara is an only child and a classic member of the "sandwich generation" as she struggles to care for her mother while still parenting her daughter.

*(continued)*

The family was referred to social worker Eileen Jefferson by Mrs. Kasper's geriatrician, who is worried about Barbara's stress. Barbara is overworked and fatigued, but determined to care for her mother at home. Amanda also frequently misses school events she would like to attend and occasional classes when her grandmother needs her. Eileen will conduct an assessment of Mrs. Kasper's condition and the family's resources to advise Barbara and the physician about possible services.

From reading the records, Eileen is concerned about Barbara and Amanda, noting that the physician mentions that both seem exhausted. Eileen is especially concerned about Barbara, who has told the physician that she does not sleep much. Barbara was in some pain when she last took her mother to the doctor, citing difficulty helping Mrs. Kasper on and off the toilet and into and out of the bathtub.

Standardized scales measure constructs of relevance to a wide range of clients, for example clients with depression or substance abuse. Rather than developing standardized scales yourself, you select them from the many standardized scales already available. The focus of this chapter is on how to select and use standardized scales to monitor client progress over time in a way that will result in the most favorable outcomes for your clients. We also recommend and describe some exemplars of standardized scales; Appendix A contains examples of standardized scales, and Appendix B contains a current list of online and published resources for standardized scales.

## OVERVIEW OF STANDARDIZED SCALES

*Standardization* refers to the use of identical procedures to collect, score, interpret, and report the results of a measure. Standardization is important to assure that differences over time or among different people are due to what is measured, not to the use of different measurement procedures.

Standardized scales usually contain multiple statements, questions, or other types of items rated along some dimension (e.g., a 7-point scale ranging from "strongly disagree" to "strongly agree"), items that require the selection of one option from several available (e.g., multiple choice), or items that require some form of a "yes" or "no" response. Responses to these items are combined into a single score to measure a construct such as self-esteem or interpersonal functioning. Uniform procedures are used to collect, score, interpret, and report the numerical results of standardized scales. Standardized scales usually have norms (a topic we discuss later) and empirical evidence of reliability and validity.

Standardized scales measure problems in terms of constructs relevant to a wide range of clients. They are like a common yardstick that can be used with different people and against which different people can be compared. This is in contrast to individualized rating scales (Chapter 10), behavioral observations (Chapter 11), and self-monitoring (Chapter 12), which most often are developed on a client-by-client basis and are designed to measure relatively unique aspects of an individual's experience.

# EXAMPLES OF STANDARDIZED SCALES

There are far too many standardized scales to discuss them all here. For example, two recent books by Fischer and Corcoran (2007a, 2007b) describe and reproduce hundreds of standardized self-report scales. Appendix B contains a list of online resources for outcome measures and a list of books published since 2000 that reference, describe, evaluate, and, in many cases, include copies of standardized scales. In addition, journals such as *Research on Social Work Practice*, *Social Work Research*, *Psychological Assessment*, *Applied Psychological Measurement*, *Quality of Life Research*, *Educational and Psychological Measurement*, and *Assessment* feature newly developed standardized scales and research on existing standardized scales.

In this chapter, we will give you a sample of standardized scales that meet many of the guidelines we discuss later for selecting standardized scales. Table 9.1 provides examples of self-report scales, Table 9.2 of standardized scales that can be completed by practitioners, and Table 9.3 of scales that can be completed by collateral sources or relevant others. (See Hunsley & Mash, 2008, and Rush, First, & Blacker, 2008, for more information about many of these measures.) Also, many of the scales listed in Table 9.2 can be used by independent observers. Finally, systematic reviews of standardized scales in particular areas are increasingly available (Albers et al., 2010; Eigenmann, Colagiuri, Skinner, & Trevena, 2009; Elmquist et al., 2010; Furukawa, 2010; Kamper, Maher, & Mackay, 2009; Sikkes, de Klerk, Pijnenburg, Scheltens, & Uitdehaag, 2009; Stinson, Kavanagh, Yamada, Gill, & Stevens, 2006), as are criteria for judging the quality of such reviews (Mokkink et al., 2009; Terwee et al., 2007). (See also Standards for the Reporting of Diagnostic accuracy studies at http://www.stard-statement.org.)

**Table 9.1**  **Examples of Standardized Self-Report Scales.**

- *Alcohol Use Disorders Identification Test (AUDIT):* The AUDIT is a 10-item self-report measure of the quantity and frequency of alcohol use. It provides indicators of hazardous alcohol use, dependence, and adverse consequences suggesting harmful use of alcohol. The AUDIT also can be completed by a collateral source. The AUDIT is copyrighted but can be reproduced without permission. It can be obtained from http://www.who.int/publications, and it is reviewed and reproduced in Rush et al. (2008).
  Primary reference: Babor, T. F., Biddle-Higgins, J. C., Saunders, J. B., & Montiero, M. G. (2001). *The Alcohol Use Disorders Identification Test (AUDIT): Guidelines for use in primary health care.* Geneva, Switzerland: World Health Organization.

- *Drinker Inventory of Consequences (DrInC):* The DrInC is a 50-item measure of five alcohol-related problem areas: physical, intrapersonal, social responsibility, interpersonal, and impulse control over the respondent's lifetime (DrInC-2L) and since the last interview (DrInC-2R). The DrInC is in the public domain and it is available online or from:
  Center on Alcoholism, Substance Abuse, and Addictions (CASAA)
  The University of New Mexico
  2650 Yale SE MSC11-6280
  Albuquerque, NM 87106
  Tel: (505) 925-2300

*(continued)*

Fax: (505) 925-2301
Website: http://casaa.unm.edu/inst.html
Primary reference: Miller, W. R., Tonigan, J. S., & Longabaugh, R. (1995). *The Drinker Inventory of Consequences (DrInC): An instrument for assessing adverse consequences of alcohol abuse* (Project MATCH Monograph Series, Vol. 4) (NIH Publication No. 95-3911). Rockville, MD: National Institutes of Mental Health.

- *Stages of Change Readiness and Treatment Eagerness Scale (SOCRATES):* The SOCRATES is a 19-item measure of readiness for change in alcohol and illicit drug users. It is in the public domain and may be used without permission. The alcohol and drug use versions, scoring templates, and guidelines for interpretation are available free of charge from:
  Center on Alcoholism, Substance Abuse, and Addictions (CASAA)
  The University of New Mexico
  2650 Yale SE MSC11-6280
  Albuquerque, NM 87106
  Tel: (505) 925-2300
  Fax: (505) 925-2301
  Website: http://casaa.unm.edu/inst.html
  Primary reference: Miller, W. R., & Tonigan, J. S. (1996). Assessing drinkers' motivation for change: The Stages of Change Readiness and Treatment Eagerness Scale (SOCRATES). *Psychology of Addictive Behaviors, 10*, 81–89.

- *Children's Depression Inventory (CDI):* The CDI is a 27-item measure of depressive symptoms in youth and it can be used with children ages 7–17. Self-report, parent, and teacher versions are available. The CDI is copyrighted and can be obtained from:
  Multi-Health Systems
  P.O. Box 950
  North Tonawanda, NY 14120-0950
  Tel: (800) 456-3003
  Fax: (888)-540-4484
  Website: http://www.mhs.com
  Primary reference: Kovacs, M. (2003). *Children's Depression Inventory manual.* North Tonawanda, NY: Multi-Health Systems.

- *Beck Depression Inventory Second Edition (BDI-II):* The BDI-II is a 21-item measure of depression. It is copyrighted and can be obtained from:
  Pearson
  19500 Bulverde RD
  San Antonio, TX 78259
  Tel: (800) 211-8378
  Fax: (800) 232-1223
  Website: http://pearsonassess.com
  Primary reference: Beck, A. T., Steer, R. A., & Brown, G. K. (1996). *Beck Depression Inventory-II manual.* San Antonio, TX: Psychological Corporation.

- *Center for Epidemiologic Studies Depression Scale (CES-D):* The CES-D is a 20-item measure of depressive symptoms (see Appendix A). It is in the public domain, and the companion website for this book contains an Excel file, CESD.xls, that contains the CES-D items and scores the CES-D. Primary reference: Radloff, L. S. (1977). The CES-D Scale: A self-report depression scale for research in the general population. *Applied Psychological Measurement, 1*, 385–401.

- *Inventory of Depressive Symptomatology (IDS) and Quick Inventory of Depressive Symptomatology (QIDS):* The 30-item IDS and the 16-item QIDS measure the severity of depressive symptoms (see Appendix A). Both are available in clinician and self-report versions, and both are available free for download from http://www.ids-qids.org/.

- **Geriatric Depression Scale (GDS):** The 30-item and the 15-item GDS measure depressive symptoms in geriatric populations (see Appendix A). Both versions are in the public domain and are available free for download from http://www.stanford.edu/~yesavage/GDS.html.
  Primary reference: Yesavage, J. A., & Brink, T. L. (1983). Development and validation of a geriatric depression screening scale: A preliminary report. *Journal of Psychiatric Research, 17,* 37–49.

- **Clinical Outcomes in Routine Evaluation—Outcome Measure (CORE-OM):** The central measure within the CORE-OM family of measures is a 34-item global measure of distress, including subscales measuring subjective well-being, problems/symptoms, and life/social functioning, and it also includes items on risk to self and to others. Also, there are two 18-item parallel short forms that can be administered at alternate sessions, a 10-item version (CORE-10) that can be used for screening and progress monitoring, and another 5-item version (CORE-5) that also can be used for monitoring ongoing progress. In addition, there is a 10-item measure designed for use with clients in the 11–16 age range (Young Person's CORE [YP-CORE]). The CORE-OM and related measures and materials are copyrighted but are available free by placing a request at http://www.coreims.co.uk/forms_mailer.php. It also can be obtained from:
  CORE IMS Ltd
  47 Windsor Street,
  Rugby
  CV21 3NZ
  Tel: 01788 546019
  Fax: 01788 331407
  Email: admin@coreims.co.uk
  Website: http://www.coreims.co.uk/
  CORE Net Website: http://www.coreims-online.co.uk
  A CORE decade: http://www.coreims.co.uk/CORE-A-Decade-of-Development.pdf
  CORE News Issue 1: http://www.coreims-online.co.uk/newsletterissue1.pdf

- **Peabody Treatment Progress Battery (PTPB):** The PTPB is a battery of 10 instruments designed for use with youth aged 11–18 years old to monitor treatment outcomes and processes, in varied service settings, including outpatient care, in-home treatment, and foster care. The 10 measures include the Symptoms and Functioning Severity Scale (33 items, clinician, youth, and adult caregiver forms, and two parallel forms of 17 and 16 items); Brief Multidimensional Students' Life Satisfaction Scale-Center for Evaluation and Program Improvement Version (6-item youth form); Children's Hope Scale (6-item youth form); Treatment Outcome Expectations Scale (10-item youth and adult caregiver forms); Therapeutic Alliance Quality Scale and Therapeutic Alliance Quality Rating (13- and 10-item forms of the Therapeutic Alliance Quality Scale for youths and caregivers, respectively, and 4-item clinician form of the Therapeutic Alliance Quality Rating); Youth Counseling Impact Scale (11-item youth form); Motivation for Youth's Treatment Scale (10-item youth form and 9-item caregiver form); Satisfaction With Life Scale (5-item caregiver form); Caregiver Strain Questionnaire—Short Form (10-item caregiver form); and Service Satisfaction Scale (5-item youth and caregiver forms). These measures are available for free use and can be obtained from http://peabody.vanderbilt.edu/ptpb.
  Primary reference: Bickman, L., Riemer, M., Lambert, E. W., Kellwy, S. D., Breda, C., Dew, S. E., et al. (Eds.) (2010). *Manual of the Peabody Treatment Progress Battery* (2nd ed.). [Electronic version]. Nashville, TN: Vanderbilt University. Retrieved from http://peabody.vanderbilt.edu/ptpb/

*(continued)*

- *Outcome Questionnaire (OQ) System:* The central measure within the OQ family of measures is the OQ-45, a 45-item measure of subjective discomfort, interpersonal relations, social role performance, and positive aspects of satisfaction and functioning. Also, there is a 30-item version of the OQ-45, and a 10-item version designed for use as a screening measure in primary care medical settings. Finally, there is a 45-item Severe Outcome Questionnaire (SOQ) designed for patients who have severe psychopathology, and several versions of the Youth Outcome Questionnaire (YOQ) suitable for parental/guardian report as well as self-report for children. The software system for use with these measures is called the OQ-A. The OQ measures and associated software are copyrighted and can be obtained from:
  OQ Measures
  P.O. Box 521047
  Salt Lake City, UT 84152-1047
  Tel: (888) 647-2673
  Fax: (801) 747-6900
  Website: http://www.OQMeasures.com
  Primary reference: Lambert, M. J., Burlingame, G. M., Umphress, V., Hansen, N. B., Vermeersch, D. A., Clouse, G. C., et al. (1996). The reliability and validity of the Outcome Questionnaire. *Clinical Psychology and Psychotherapy, 3,* 106–116.

- *Partners for Change Outcome Management System (PCOMS):* The PCOMS is made up of two 4-item scales, one focusing on client outcome, the Outcome Rating Scale (ORS), and the other focusing on the therapeutic alliance, the Session Rating Scale (SRS). More specifically, the ORS measures four areas of client functioning, each with one item: individual (personal well-being), interpersonal (family, close relationships), social (work, school, friendships), and overall (general sense of well-being) functioning. The SRS measures four areas of the quality of the therapeutic alliance: quality of the relational bond ("I felt heard, understood, and respected"), goals and topics ("We worked on and talked about what I wanted to work on and talk about"), approach or method ("The therapist's approach is a good fit for me"), and overall ("Overall, today's session was right for me"). Comparable 4-item scales are available for children and young children. The PCOMS forms are copyrighted but they are provided free of charge to individual mental health practitioners, and they can be downloaded from http://heartandsoulofchange. com/measures/. Information about the commercially available web-based version of PCOMS can be obtained from:
  Primary reference: Duncan, B. L. (2011). *The Partners for Change Outcome Management System (PCOMS): Admini*stration, *scoring, and interpretation manual update for the Outcome and Session Rating Scales.* Chicago, IL: The Heart and Soul of Change Project.
  (See the "Resources" link on this webpage for more information about PCOMS in general.)

- *Treatment Outcome Package (TOP):* The TOP is a 58-item measure of the level of severity in 11 domains (depression, panic, mania, psychosis, sleep, sex, work, quality of life, substance abuse, suicide, violence). Also, 48-item child and 58-item adolescent versions are available. The TOP is copyrighted and can be obtained from:
  Behavioral Health Laboratories (BHL)
  293 Boston Post Road West, Suite 330
  Marlborough, MA 01752
  Tel: (800) 329-0949
  Fax: (508) 281-6416
  Website: http://www.bhealthlabs.com/
  Primary reference: Kraus, D. R., Seligman, D., & Jordan, J. R. (2005). Validation of a behavioral health treatment outcome measure and assessment tool designed for naturalistic settings: The Treatment Outcome Package. *Journal of Clinical Psychology, 61,* 285–314.

- *Penn State Worry Questionnaire—Past Week (PSWQ-PW):* The PSWQ-PW is a 15-item measure of pathological worry during the past week (see Appendix A). It is in the public domain and can be found in:
  Primary reference: Stöber, J., & Bittencourt, J. (1998). Weekly assessment of worry: An adaptation of the Penn State Worry Questionnaire for monitoring changes during treatment. *Behavior Research and Therapy, 36,* 645–656.

- *Rosenberg Self-Esteem Scale (RSES):* The RSES is a 10-item measure of self-esteem. It may be used without explicit permission. The author's family, however, would like to be kept informed of its use. Send information about how you have used the scale, or send published research resulting from its use, to:
  The Morris Rosenberg Foundation
  c/o Department of Sociology
  University of Maryland
  2112 Art/Soc Building
  College Park, MD 20742-1315
  Information about the RSES, and a copy of the RSES, can be obtained from http://www.bsos. umd.edu/socy/Research/rosenberg.htm.
  Primary reference: Rosenberg, M. (1989). *Society and the adolescent self-image* (Rev. ed.). Middletown, CT: Wesleyan University Press.

- *Faces Pain Scale—Revised (FPS-R):* The FPS-R is a self-report scale for the measurement of pain intensity in children and adults. It consists of six gender-neutral faces depicting "no pain" (neutral face) to "most pain possible" expressions, placed at equal intervals horizontally. The FPS-R (and related measures) is reviewed in Stinson et al. (2006). It is copyrighted but it may be photocopied and used for noncommercial clinical and research use free of charge. Information about the FPS-R and a copy of the FPS-R can be obtained from http://painsourcebook.ca/docs/ pps92.html.
  Primary reference: Hicks, C. L., von Baeyer, C. L., Spafford, P., van Korlaar, I., & Goodenough, B. (2001). The Faces Pain Scale—Revised: Toward a common metric in pediatric pain measurement. *Pain, 93,* 173–183.

- *Working Alliance Inventory (WAI):* The WAI has separate forms for clients and therapists, and each of these is available in full length (36 items) and short form (12 items). Also, observer and couples' versions are available. The WAI is reviewed and reproduced in Rush et al. (2008) and Fischer and Corcoran (2007b), and it is copyrighted but can be used with permission from:
  Adam O. Horvath, EdD
  Department of Education
  Simon Fraser University
  8888 University Dr., 8556edb
  Burnaby, BC
  Canada V5A 1S6
  Tel: (778) 782-2160
  Email: horvath@sfu.ca
  Website: http://www.educ.sfu.ca/alliance/allianceA/
  Primary reference: Horvath, A. O., & Greenberg, L. S. (1989). Development and validation of the Working Alliance Inventory. *Journal of Consulting and Clinical Psychology, 36,* 223–233.

- *Columbia Impairment Scale (CIS):* The CIS is a 13-item global measure of impairment in children and adolescents, and it measures four dimensions: interpersonal relations, psychopathology, job or schoolwork, and use of leisure time. There are two versions of the CIS, one administered

*(continued)*

to the child and another to the parent. The CIS can be used without permission, and it can be obtained from:
Hector R. Bird, MD
Department of Child Psychiatry
New York State Psychiatric Institute
1051 Riverside Dr.
New York, NY 10032
Tel: (212) 543-2591
Fax: (212) 543-5730
Primary reference: Bird, H., Andrews, H., Schwab-Stone, M., Goodman, S., Dulcan, M., Richters, J., et al. (1996). Global measures of impairment for epidemiologic and clinical use with children and adolescents. *International Journal of Methods in Psychiatric Research, 6,* 295–307.

- *Panic Disorder Severity Scale (PDSS):* See Table 9.2.

---

**Table 9.2**

## Examples of Standardized Scales for Practitioners.

- *Brief Psychiatric Rating Scale (BPRS):* The BPRS is an 18-item measure of global psychiatric symptom severity. It was developed for use by an appropriately trained mental health professional upon completion of a clinical interview with a client. It is reviewed and reproduced in Rush et al. (2008), and it is in the public domain and available without cost.
Primary reference: Overall, J. E., & Gorham, D. R. (1988). The Brief Psychiatric Rating Scale (BPRS): Recent developments in ascertainment and scaling. *Psychopharmacological Bulletin, 24,* 97–99.

- *Children's Depression Rating Scale—Revised (CDRS-R):* The CDRS-R is a 17-item measure of depressive symptoms based on a semistructured interview with a child (or an adult informant who knows the child well). The interviewer rates 17 symptom areas (including those that serve as *DSM-IV* criteria for a diagnosis of depression). The CDRS-R is copyrighted and can be obtained from:
Western Psychological Services
12031 Wilshire Blvd.
Los Angeles, CA 90025-1251
Tel: (800) 648-8857
Fax: (310) 478-7838
Website: http://portal.wpspublish.com/
Primary reference: Poznanski, E. O., & Mokros, H. G. (1999). *Children's Depression Rating Scale-Revised (CDRS-R).* Los Angeles, CA: Western Psychological Services.

- *Group Engagement Measure (GEM):* The GEM was developed to measure the engagement of individual members of treatment groups along seven dimensions: (1) attendance, (2) contributing, (3) relating to worker, (4) relating with members, (5) contracting, (6) working on own problems, and (7) working on other members' problems. The original 37-item GEM is a leader-report measure of engagement for each group member, but it has been adapted successfully for use as a self-report measure. In addition, there is a 27-item version of the GEM (see Appendix A), and there is a 21-item version of the GEM that measures all but two of the seven dimensions (attendance and contracting). The GEM is copyrighted, and for permission to use it contact:

Mark J. Macgowan, PhD, LCSW
Robert Stempel College of Public Health & Social Work
Florida International University
11200 SW 8th Street, GL 485
Miami, FL 33199
Tel: 305-348-5883
Email: Macgowan@fiu.edu
Academic Website: http://swjpa.fiu.edu/faculty/macgowan/
http://www.EvidenceBasedGroupWork.com
Primary references (GEM-37): Macgowan, M. J. (1997). A measure of engagement for social group work: The Groupwork Engagement Measure (GEM). *Journal of Social Service Research, 23*(2), 17–37. Macgowan, M. J. (2006). The Group Engagement Measure: A review of its conceptual and empirical properties. *Journal of Groups in Addiction and Recovery, 1*(2), 33–52.
Primary reference (GEM-27): Macgowan, M. J., & Newman, F. L. (2005). The factor structure of the Group Engagement Measure. *Social Work Research, 29*(2), 107–118.

- *Panic Disorder Severity Scale (PDSS):* The PDSS was developed to measure the overall severity of panic disorder. It is a 7-item questionnaire completed by the clinician, although a client self-report version is also available. The PDSS is copyrighted, although use is freely permitted without further permission for clinical use in not-for-profit institutions and in research approved by an institutional review board. It is available from:
M. Katherine Shear, MD
Columbia University School of Social Work
1255 Amsterdam Ave.
New York, NY 10027
Email: ks2394@columbia.edu
Primary reference: Shear, M. K., Brown, T. A., Barlow, D. H., Money, R., Sholomskas, D. E., Woods, S. W., et al. (1997). Multicenter collaborative Panic Disorder Severity Scale. *American Journal of Psychiatry, 154,* 1571–1575.

- *Children's Depression Inventory (CDI):* See Table 9.1.

- *Inventory of Depressive Symptomatology (IDS) and Quick Inventory of Depressive Symptomatology (QIDS):* See Table 9.1.

- *Treatment Outcome Package (TOP):* See Table 9.1.

- *Working Alliance Inventory (WAI):* See Table 9.1

**Table 9.3**

**Examples of Standardized Scales for Relevant Others.**

- *Eyberg Child Behavior Inventory (ECBI) and Sutter-Eyberg Student Behavior Inventory—Revised (SESBI-R):* The 36-item ECBI and 38-item SESBI-R measure conduct problems in children ages 2–16, as observed by parents and teachers, respectively. The ECBI is reproduced in Fischer and Corcoran (2007a), and the ECBI and SESBI-R are copyrighted and can be obtained from:
Psychological Assessment Resources
16204 N. Florida Ave.
Lutz, FL 33549
Tel: (800) 331-8378
Fax: (800) 727-9329
Website: http://www.parinc.com

*(continued)*

Primary reference: Eyberg, S. M., & Pincus, D. (1999). *The Eyberg Child Behavior Inventory and Sutter-Eyberg Student Behavior Inventory*. Professional manual. Lutz, FL: Psychological Assessment Resources (PAR).

- **Parent Daily Report (PDR):** The current version of the PDR is a 30-item checklist of child behavior problems as reported by parents, typically during a brief telephone interview (see Appendix A). At each assessment, parents are asked to report on the occurrence or nonoccurrence of 30 specific behaviors within the past 24 hours.
Primary reference: Chamberlain, P., Price, J. M., Reid, J. B., Landsverk, J., Fisher, P. A., & Stoolmiller, M. (2006). Who disrupts from placement in foster and kinship care? *Child Abuse & Neglect, 30*, 409–424.
- **Children's Depression Inventory (CDI):** See Table 9.1.
- **Treatment Outcome Package (TOP):** See Table 9.1.
- **Alcohol Use Disorders Identification Test (AUDIT):** See Table 9.1.
- **Columbia Impairment Scale (CIS):** See Table 9.1.

# EVALUATING AND SELECTING STANDARDIZED SCALES

Given the large number of standardized scales available, how do you select the best ones for your particular clients? Here, we provide guidelines for selecting standardized scales. These guidelines are based on the more general material described in Chapter 8 regarding basic measurement principles.

Few scales meet all the following criteria, and you need to know the limitations of a scale before using it. When you select and use a scale, be clear about which criteria are not met, and estimate how that might affect your use of the scale. For example, you might find that a standardized scale measure of alcohol abuse has been tested with men but not women. If your client is a woman and you suspect that women are more likely to underreport alcohol-related problems, you might take very seriously any hint of alcohol problems from a woman's responses.

## Purpose

Standardized scales can be used for different purposes. They can be used to identify whether a client has a significant problem in a particular area, and they also can be used to measure and monitor your client's outcomes to determine if your client is making

---

During their first visit, conducted in the home, Eileen meets Mrs. Kasper and assesses her condition. She has already studied the medical records but wants to see how Mrs. Kasper functions in her home. Eileen has investigated a number of measures for this purpose, consulting Kane et al. (2004), an excellent reference about assessment of older persons. She selects one of the measures that Kane et al. recommend for measuring activities of daily living.

Barbara acts as a proxy to help Eileen complete the Rapid Disability Rating Scale-2 (RDRS-2; Linn, 1988), which has subscales that measure the constructs of most interest to Eileen: amount of assistance with daily living required, degree of disability, and degree of special problems. Scores range from 18 to 72, and Mrs. Kasper's score is 30. Linn and Linn (1982) report average scores of 21–22 for elders living in the community, 32 for hospitalized older adults, and 36 for elders in nursing homes.

satisfactory progress, which is the primary focus in this chapter. McMurtry, Rose, and Cisler (2008) discuss the use of standardized scales for screening, that is scanning many potential problem areas and identifying problems that require further assessment to determine if services might be needed.

The first consideration in selecting a standardized scale is to determine what you want to measure. Standardized scales are available for measuring behaviors, feelings, cognitions, attitudes, and almost every conceivable specific problem area—ranging from alcoholism and anxiety to sexual satisfaction and suicide potential. It's important to be as precise as possible, so if you want to measure marital conflict, don't select a measure of marital satisfaction, for example.

In addition, in the selection of any measurement method, there should be reason to believe that its use will benefit your client in some way. Will it help determine whether a client is in need of intervention in a particular area? Will it help determine whether a problem is improving or deteriorating, so any necessary modifications in the intervention plan can be undertaken? Will it help determine what may be causing or maintaining the client's problem? In most cases, a single standardized scale won't help answer all of these questions, but if the answer to most or all of these questions is *no*, rethink the use of that particular scale.

## Reference Populations and Normative Groups

Standardized scales typically are designed for use with particular populations, such as older persons or children (ages 4–18), known as *reference populations*. Samples used to develop and test standardized scales are known as *normative groups*, although sometimes they're called *standardization groups* or *standardization samples*, and the process used to establish norms or uniform procedures for a measure is referred to as *standardization*. Ideally, a normative group is representative of the reference population. Also, ideally the reference population and associated normative group are similar in important ways to the client with whom you hope to use a particular standardized scale.

An important issue in the selection of evidence-based interventions is the extent to which the evidence is based on samples from populations of people who are similar in important respects to your particular client. The same issue is important in the evaluation and selection of standardized scales. For example, Eileen will select measures that have been tested with elders in the community, rather than in assisted living or nursing care, since she would expect substantial differences in functioning by elders in these settings.

Eileen will also consider cultural issues as she selects measures to use with the family. Mental health and illness are embedded in culture (Crockett, Randall, Shen, Russell, & Driscoll, 2005), and the expression of psychopathology or poor well-being arises from the joint effects of culture, gender, and socioeconomic status (Mano, Davies, Klein-Tasman, & Adesso, 2009). Therefore, we cannot expect a measure of depression or self-esteem—or perhaps especially stress from caring for an aged loved one in the home—that is developed and tested with European-Americans, as most such measures are, to mean the same thing when used with people of other cultures. (See Gupta, 1999, for a discussion of these issues in relation to the development of a measure of caregiver strain for use with Indian/ Pakistani caregivers.)

**A**s Eileen learns more about Mrs. Kasper's family, she discovers that even though Barbara is an only child, she has extended family living in little towns all around within 200 miles, and they are very close. Although they are too far away to help with daily care, at least one of them visits monthly, and there are frequent telephone calls. In an emergency, Barbara knows that she can call on them and receive help, and this has happened several times. The extended family identifies as Polish-American, and they clearly operate from a position of familism that values caregiving of one another (Greene & Jones, 2007). There is a history and several current examples of multigenerational families living together to care for one

another, and this is expected and honored. Eileen is not able to find measures designed and tested for this specific culture, but she will certainly consider these issues as she selects and employs measures, particularly those related to caregiver burden and social support, and she will interpret the data cautiously.

Eileen selects the Family Strain Questionnaire—Short Form (FSQ-SF; Vidotto, Ferrario, Bond, & Zotti, 2010) to measure Barbara and Amanda's caregiving stress. The FSQ-SF has only 30 items and takes 5–10 minutes to complete. The measure was designed to be used by busy physicians and nurses with caregivers of persons with any condition, so special training is not required, and reliability exceeds .85.

How does culture affect the use of standardized measures? Crockett et al. (2005) explain four issues:

- *Construct validity:* A construct, such as *depression* or *anxiety*, may differ in meaning between two groups, so a measure developed for one group may not capture all the dimensions of the construct as understood by another group. Thus, the measure may not be measuring the same thing in both groups.
- *Functional equivalence:* Behaviors may be expressed in different situations by different groups, serve different purposes, have different antecedents, correlate with different measures and behaviors, and have different consequents.
- *Item equivalence:* Different items may measure a different construct in different cultures.
- *Scalar equivalence:* A construct may be measured on different metrics by different cultures. That is, a given value may represent different degrees, intensity, and magnitude in two cultures.

### Ethical Practice

***Practice Behavior Example:*** *Apply strategies of ethical reasoning to arrive at principled decisions*

**Critical Thinking Question:** What problems, including ethical problems, might you encounter if you used a standardized scale to measure and monitor marital conflict with gay or lesbian couples if the scale was developed for and standardized with heterosexual couples?

Assessing *measurement equivalence*, as it is called, is an ongoing process of data collection. Recognizing the use of culturally appropriate standardized measures as a critical part of evidence-based practice (Gilgun, 2005), however, you must take the best evidence you can find, evaluate that evidence, and, as Gilgun says, "hold it lightly" as you engage in assessment, intervention, and monitoring of client outcomes.

Sometimes the evidence for a standardized scale is based on normative groups from reference populations who are different from your client in important respects, and this can raise problems. For example, measures of couple distress constructed and tested with White, middle-class married couples might or might not be useful for measuring distress in couples from different ethnic or socioeconomic

> **S**earching for measures of depression to use with Mrs. Kasper, Eileen is aware that some may not be appropriate for use with geriatric populations for a variety of reasons. She compares the Geriatric Depression Scale (GDS) to the Center for Epidemiologic Studies Depression Scale (CES-D), both reproduced in Appendix A. She knows that sleep difficulties and decreased energy, which are common symptoms of depression in younger persons and are included on the CES-D, are also common in nondepressed older persons. She also knows that thoughts of death and hopelessness, symptoms of depression on the CES-D, may mean something different later in life (Yesavage & Brink, 2008). She is also aware that the CES-D fails to include some items needed to fully measure depression in older clients. In thinking about these issues, Eileen is assessing the content validity of the CES-D for use with older clients such as Mrs. Kasper.
>
> Eileen also wants to gauge Barbara's depression. Barbara's demeanor suggests that there may be a problem. Eileen will not use the same measure she has selected for Mrs. Kasper, of course, because it was designed for elders. For Barbara, she selects the Quick Inventory of Depressive Symptomatology—Self-Report (QIDS-SR; Rush et al., 2003, 2006; Trivedi et al., 2004), which is described in detail later.

groups, or for gay and lesbian couples (Snyder et al., 2008). Similarly, constructs measured by standardized scales such as quality of life or depression can mean something quite different in different cultures (Okawa, 2008; Utsey & Bolden, 2008).

## Reliability and Validity

Use the guidelines discussed in Chapter 8 to evaluate the reliability and validity of standardized scales, weigh the quality of evidence available for competing measures of the same problem, and draw conclusions based on the relative weight of favorable and unfavorable evidence.

At a minimum, there should be evidence of adequate internal-consistency reliability (i.e., coefficient alpha of .70 or greater). Also, look for evidence of short-term test–retest reliability and interobserver reliability for observational measures. In each case, the higher the reliability, the better the reliability; as a general rule, reliability of .80 or greater indicates reasonably good reliability.

Look for evidence of construct validity, especially sensitivity to change, but content and criterion validity evidence also provide important information. Remember that scores derived from a measure are not valid or invalid, but valid for a particular purpose. So, consider your purpose in deciding what type of validity is relevant. At a minimum, there should be evidence of construct validity and, as with all measurement methods, reason to believe that the scale can be used to decide whether your intervention should be implemented, continued, changed, or terminated.

## Practical Considerations

Standardized scales differ considerably in terms of time, effort, and training needed to administer, score, and interpret them, as well as the cost and ability to acquire them. Be realistic, as discussed in Chapter 8. Make sure the scale is efficient, cost-effective, and acceptable to clients, practitioners, and other involved parties. Find scales that are reasonably brief and don't take more than 15 minutes to complete. Make sure the person asked to complete the scale is willing and able to do it. For example, consider the reading level and ability, something you can check with, for example, Microsoft Word; sixth-grade reading

**Research-Based Practice**

***Practice Behavior Example:*** *Use research evidence to inform practice*

**Critical Thinking Question:** What standardized scale(s) would be most appropriate for measuring and monitoring anxiety in clients seeking mental health services according to reviews of outcome measures compiled by the National Institute for Mental Health in England (http://www.dh.gov.uk/en/Publicationsandstatistics/Publications/PublicationsPolicyAndGuidance/DH_093316)?

level is about right in most cases. Check for and adhere to copyright restrictions. Ensure that the cost of the scale is reasonable. Be sure that you have the necessary training to acquire, administer, score, and interpret the scale.

There has been increasing recognition of the importance of the ease with which measures can be used in practice. This has led to the development of a large number of standardized scales that can be used relatively easily on a repeated basis because they are relatively brief; can be administered, scored, and interpreted without much time and effort; and can be used by diverse professionals without extensive training in their use (e.g., Fischer & Corcoran, 2007a, 2007b).

For example, Hudson and his colleagues have been in the forefront of developing practical standardized scales that can be used to measure and monitor client progress (Hudson, 1997; Hudson & Faul, 1998). Over 35 scales have been developed based on an assessment of the types of personal, interpersonal, and social dysfunctions that appear to take up a large portion of social workers' time. You can view these scales, order them, and get additional information about them from http://www.walmyr.com.

## DECIDE WHERE, WHEN, HOW OFTEN, AND FROM WHOM TO COLLECT DATA

The considerations involved in deciding where, when, how often, and from whom to collect data are much like those discussed in Chapter 8. There are a few additional points we want to make in regard to standardized scales, especially self-report scales.

As a general rule, a problem should be measured often enough to detect significant changes in the problem, but not so often that it becomes burdensome to those collecting data or intrudes on intervention efforts. We generally recommend that scales be completed about once a week unless they are very brief (e.g., 10 items), in which case they might be completed more often.

Make sure that the client has a private, quiet, physically comfortable place to complete the scale. For example, you might ask the client to complete it at home so he or she will not feel the potential pressure of feeling rushed or watched. Or, if the scale is relatively brief, you may ask the client to complete it just before you meet or during the first few minutes of your meeting. Then, you can be sure it will be completed at about the same time and under the same conditions on a regular basis, and you will be available to answer questions and provide immediate feedback. However, except for intake interviews, don't have clients complete scales right after you meet because results might be distorted by what happens during your meeting.

## ENGAGE AND PREPARE THE CLIENT

Use the guidelines discussed in Chapter 8 to engage and prepare clients (or other informants) to use standardized scales. This is as important as selecting the right scale. In addition to guidelines discussed in Chapter 8, there are a few special considerations that arise

> **A**s she sat down with Mrs. Kasper, Barbara, and Amanda to complete a set of measures at their first appointment, Eileen says:
>
> *I always ask my clients to fill out some question-naires at the beginning and during the course of our work together to monitor how you are doing. This helps us evaluate what is going on in your situation, and this will help us to stay focused on YOUR goals.*
>
> *You'll see that some of the questions on these questionnaires are quite personal. However, just like what you say to me, your answers are confidential and I'll only use them to help you reach your goals. Complete and accurate answers to these questions will give us the best chance to reach those goals, and I'll ask you to interpret the results to me so I can better understand what you are trying to tell me. If at any point you have any questions about any of this, please don't hesitate to ask.*

in using standardized scales. For example, a client might respond to each item in the same or a patterned way—for example, all 2's on a 5-point scale. In other cases, a person might tend to agree or disagree in response to items regardless of the content of the items. In addition, sometimes people exaggerate problems, minimize problems, or provide what they view as socially acceptable instead of genuine responses in order to give a certain impression.

One of the most effective ways to control such problems lies in how you present scales to informants, urging the informant to be completely honest because that is the only way you can plan the optimal intervention program. In addition, encourage the informant to respond to each item independently—not in a pattern. If you do find a patterned response, use the resulting data cautiously, if at all, and talk with the informant to determine the reason for the responses and to increase the accuracy of the responses to the scale.

# SCORING AND INTERPRETING STANDARDIZED SCALE SCORES

As we discussed in Chapter 8, a score is a number derived from a measure that represents the quantity or amount of an attribute or observation such as the severity of depressive symptoms. For example, for a multi-item standardized scale, the score might be computed by adding up the item scores, or by adding up the item scores and then dividing by the number of items to get the mean item score. That is, the scale score is computed by combining the results from two or more related items using a specified formula or procedure. Oftentimes, such a score is called a *total score* or *composite score*, and the formula used to compute it is called the *scoring formula*. Different standardized scales are scored differently, so check the relevant article or manual for a scale to find out how to score it, follow the directions carefully, and check and double-check your work.

## Scoring the QIDS-SR

The Quick Inventory of Depressive Symptomatology—Self-Report (QIDS-SR; Rush et al., 2003, 2006; Trivedi et al., 2004), a 16-item standardized self-report scale that measures the severity of depressive symptoms, QIDS-SR, is reproduced in Appendix A, and the

**Table 9.4**     **Steps for Scoring the QIDS-SR.**

Enter the highest score on any one of the four sleep items (1–4)
Enter score on item 5
Enter the highest score on any one of the appetite/weight items (6–9)
Enter score on item 10
Enter score on item 11
Enter score on item 12
Enter score on item 13
Enter score on item 14
Enter the highest score on either of the two psychomotor items (15 and 16)
Total score range 0–27

procedures for scoring it are shown in Table 9.4. Each of the nine scores that go into the total score corresponds to the nine symptom domains used in the *DSM-IV-TR* (*Diagnostic and Statistical Manual of Mental Disorders*, fourth edition, text revision; American Psychiatric Association, 2000) to define major depressive disorder. Other information about the QIDS-SR and related versions of the QIDS-SR can be obtained at http://www.ids-qids.org/.

The QIDS-SR measures one construct, severity of depressive symptoms, and it is an example of a *unidimensional* scale that measures a single attribute or construct. Other standardized scales measure more than one construct by combining responses from different subsets of items into separate measures of distinct but related constructs. For example, the OQ-45 (Outcome Questionnaire-45), described in Table 9.1, has subscales that measure subjective discomfort, interpersonal relations, social role performance, and positive aspects of satisfaction and functioning. These are called *multidimensional* scales, and the measures of different constructs are called *subscales*.

Multidimensional scales often provide measures of distinct but related constructs, and a measure of an overall construct thought to unify the distinct constructs. For example, the Clinical Outcomes in Routine Evaluation—Outcome Measure (CORE-OM), described in Table 9.1, provides a global measure of distress, and it also has subscales that measure subjective well-being, problems/symptoms, and life/social functioning.

## Interpreting the QIDS-SR Total Score

Scores from different standardized scales are interpreted differently and you should check the relevant article or manual for a scale to find out how to interpret scores. In addition, scores from standardized scales should be interpreted with regard to evidence concerning the scale such as reliability and validity. The QIDS-SR provides a typical example of how a total score is interpreted.

The QIDS-SR total scale score has a potential range of values from 0 through 27, and higher scores indicate greater severity of depressive symptoms. Table 9.5 provides

| Table 9.5 | Interpreting QIDS-SR Scores. | |
|---|---|---|
| **QIDS-SR Interpretation** | | **QIDS-SR Score** |
| No depression | | ≤5 |
| Mild depression | | 6–10 |
| Moderate depression | | 11–15 |
| Severe depression | | 16–20 |
| Very severe depression | | ≥21 |

numerical values for the QIDS-SR that are used to separate people into categories with distinct substantive interpretations, as you might use percentage correct on a test to assign grades of A, B, C, and so on. These scores can be used to make treatment decisions, for example to determine the status of a client's problem before intervention and as a benchmark for success during and upon completion of intervention. Such scores are known as *cut scores, cutting scores, cutoff scores,* and *clinical cutting scores* (Kellow & Willson, 2008).

The standard error of measurement (SEM) is an estimate of the degree of random measurement error (i.e., unreliability) in scores derived from a measure. The SEM quantifies the degree of uncertainty in a score, and it can be used to determine the range of values within which an individual's true score is likely to fall. For example, the standard deviation for the QIDS-SR in the normative sample is 5.57, coefficient alpha is .87 (Rush et al., 2006), and the SEM is 2.0:

$$SEM = SD\sqrt{1 - \alpha}$$

$$SEM = 5.57\sqrt{1 - .87} = 2.0$$

If a client scores a 6 on the QIDS-SR, there are two out of three chances (68% to be exact) that the client's true score falls between 4 and 8 (i.e., 6 ± 2). Therefore, the client's true score falls somewhere between "mild depression" and "no depression" (see Table 9.5), and you should wait for more information before you decide whether the client falls in the clinical range.

Cut scores are only as good as the normative samples on which they are based. The validity of a cut score for a specific client depends on the extent to which the normative sample is representative of the population of which the client is a member. For example, cut scores developed on majority group populations may not be appropriate for individuals who differ from those reference populations (Malgady & Colon-Malgady, 2008; Okawa, 2008). So, if your client differs substantially from the normative group (e.g., on ethnicity or income), the norms may not be applicable and you should use the cut scores with caution.

After three sessions, Eileen sits down to review her assessment data and consider her recommendations. The neurologist's report finds no evidence of stroke or brain disease, but Mrs. Kasper's medical records and RDRS-2 scores show her to be frail and unable to perform most activities of daily living without significant assistance. Cognitive testing demonstrates that her information processing has slowed considerably, but severe hearing loss appears to be related to some of her communication difficulties, and a referral has already been made to an audiologist. She has difficulty speaking, but her physicians believe most of this is due to her low levels of energy. Her score of 3 on the QIDS-SR indicates that she is not clinically depressed.

Barbara, on the other hand, scores very high on the FSQ-SF, falling into the highest category of concern, which suggests that she is at high risk of depression and possibly physical health problems. Her score of 16 on the QIDS-SR indicates that she is severely depressed. Amanda's FSQ-SF scores are normal, although in their conversations Eileen notes some indications that she is developing some resentment against her mother and grandmother, and Eileen would like to follow up on this.

Eileen's current case conceptualization is based on her understanding of the stresses of caregiving for an older relative and the physical and emotional effects of those stresses on caregivers. Her model of practice with elders, the functional-age model of intergenerational therapy (FAM; Greene & Jones, 2007), integrates the functioning of the elder and the adaptive capacity of the caregiver to seek solutions for the entire family. Based on her assessment, Eileen believes that the family urgently needs supportive services.

Eileen makes a referral to an agency for a daily 2-hour caregiver who will bathe Mrs. Kasper and manage her medications during the morning when both Barbara and Amanda must be gone, and she is investigating other services that might relieve some of Barbara's stress and allow Amanda to participate more fully in college. Eileen also suggests that Barbara inquire whether extended family might rotate coming to care for Mrs. Kasper one weekend a month so that she and Amanda can go to a family member's lake house for some relaxation.

Eileen offers to meet with Barbara and Amanda every other week in their home to monitor Mrs. Kasper's functioning and Barbara and Amanda's stress. She suggests that each week Barbara complete the QIDS-SR, and that both she and Amanda complete the FSQ-SF, and the caregiver also will complete the RDRS-2 for Mrs. Kasper. They will review the data together when they meet to monitor the family's situation. If these minimal services do not improve Barbara's stress, or if Barbara's depression worsens, and especially if Mrs. Kasper's functioning declines beyond Barbara and Amanda's capacity to cope, they will discuss more intensive services or even assisted living.

## Reverse-Worded Items

Many scales include reverse-worded items. For example, the CES-D, a standardized self-report scale that measures depressive symptoms (Radloff, 1977; Radloff & Lock, 2008), is reproduced in Appendix A. Notice that except for items 4, 8, 12, and 16, higher values indicate greater depression. These four items are known as *reverse-worded items*.

Lower values for reverse-worded items indicate more of what is measured by the scale (e.g., depression). Reverse-worded items are included to reduce or detect the tendency of some respondents to agree more than disagree with items regardless of item content, or to respond according to their general beliefs and feelings about the topic rather than the specific content of the items. They also are included to alert inattentive respondents that the content of the items varies. However, sometimes reverse-worded items can be confusing and you should watch out for responses to them that are inconsistent with responses to other items.

One of the first steps in scoring the CES-D, and any scale with reverse-scored items, is to reverse the scores on these items. For the CES-D, a score of 0 is rescored as a 3, a score of 1 is rescored as a 2, a score of 2 is rescored as a 1, and a score of 3 is rescored as a 0. The following is a simple way to rescore reverse-worded items (Hudson, 1997):

$$Y = K + 1 - X$$

where $Y$ is the value for the rescored item, $K$ is the largest possible score value for the item (e.g., 3 for CES-D items), and $X$ is the original value for the item.

## USING STANDARDIZED SCALES TO DETERMINE CLINICALLY SIGNIFICANT IMPROVEMENT

Standardized scales can be used to determine whether clinically significant improvement occurs for a particular client. In this context, *clinically significant improvement* means that a client's measured functioning on a standardized scale is in the dysfunctional range before intervention (e.g., 6 or more on the QIDS-SR) and in the functional range after intervention (e.g., less than or equal to 5 on the QIDS-SR), and that the change is reliable (e.g., a change of 5.7 or more on the QIDS-SR).

The most widely used procedure for determining clinically significant improvement was developed by Jacobson, Follette, and Revenstorf (1984) and Jacobson, Roberts, Berns, and McGlinchey (1999). This procedure has been tested under a number of different conditions, compares favorably to alternative methods, is the most widely used method, and is easy to compute. (See Kellett, 2007, for an example of the use of this procedure with a single-case design, and Lambert & Ogles, 2009, for a recent review of this method.) The procedure involves determining whether a reliable change has occurred, if the change is in the direction of improvement or deterioration, and whether the change is *clinically significant*.

*Reliable change* means that change in a client's scale score from one time to another is more than you would expect just from measurement error. To compute reliable change, you need two things from previous research: (1) the internal-consistency reliability (coefficient alpha) of the scale from the normative sample used to test the scale and (2) the standard deviation from the normative sample used to test the scale. Usually, these two pieces of information can be found in articles about or the manual for the scale. The standard deviation for the QIDS-SR is 5.7 and coefficient alpha is .87 (Rush et al., 2006).

Reliable change is simple to compute, but we won't detail the computations here (Bauer, Lambert, & Nielsen, 2004). Instead, on the companion website, you will find an Excel workbook that calculates reliable change automatically after you enter the needed information, and it tells you whether reliable change has occurred or not. The reliable change for the QIDS-SR is 5.70, meaning that a change this large (or larger) is probably not just due to measurement error, but rather due to systematic change.

Reliable change can be in the direction of improvement or deterioration, and you determine which based on whether higher scale scores indicate improvement or deterioration, and whether the pretest score was higher or lower than the posttest score. For example, Eileen administers the QIDS-SR to measure Barbara's depression. Higher scores indicate greater depression, and Eileen is alarmed to see that Barbara's pretest score at their first appointment is 16, a score indicating severe depression. Her posttest score, a month after the conclusion of services is 4, a decrease of 12 points, so reliable change has occurred (i.e., 12 is greater than the reliable change of 5.70). More specifically, *reliable improvement* has occurred, because higher scores indicate greater depression, and the posttest score is lower than the pretest score.

If reliable change has occurred in the direction of improvement, the next step is to determine whether the improvement is clinically significant. If the client has moved from being in a dysfunctional score range to a functional score range, clinically significant improvement has occurred. (If a scale does not have a clinical cutting score, see "Determining a Clinical Cutoff" on our companion website for a discussion of how to determine one.)

Let's continue our example. We determined that Barbara has experienced reliable change and, more specifically, reliable improvement. Since the QIDS-SR has a clinical cutoff of 5 or less (no depression), we also can say that clinically significant improvement occurred because Barbara's pretest score (16) was in the dysfunctional range and the posttest score (4) in the functional range.

To summarize, *clinically significant improvement* occurs if the client's score shows reliable change in the direction of improvement and the score moves from the dysfunctional to the functional range. *Reliable improvement*, but not necessarily clinically significant improvement, occurs if the client's score shows reliable change in the direction of improvement, but does not move from the dysfunctional to the functional range. *No change* occurs if the client's score does not show reliable change and does not move from the dysfunctional to the functional range. (Change from dysfunctional to functional that is not reliable is, well, not reliable.) Finally, reliable deterioration occurs if the client's score shows reliable change in the direction of deterioration. (We are assuming that the client began in the dysfunctional range; otherwise, why would you intervene? Therefore, we do not discuss change from the dysfunctional to the functional range.)

Remember this is just one more piece of information that Eileen will use in the context of all of the other quantitative and qualitative information that she has about this family, and she will use and interpret this information about clinically significant improvement on the depression measure only in this broader context. When you use standardized scales or other measures, work together with your client to understand and interpret his or her progress. Clinically significant improvement as defined earlier does not automatically guarantee a meaningful change in a client's real-world functioning or quality of life, and it might or might not be meaningful to the client, relevant others, or society at large. These are issues that you and the client must determine in the course of your work together.

Remember, too, that this procedure is only as good as the available normative group(s), and in some cases, the information from representative normative groups will not be available. In addition, remember that this method allows you to rule out measurement error as a plausible explanation for change, and to determine whether the change was clinically significant, but it does not speak to the question of whether it was your intervention or something else that caused the change—this is an issue of design, as we

**M**rs. Kasper dies peacefully in her bed 10 months after Eileen began her work with the family. Meeting one more time to review their work together, Eileen points out to Barbara and Amanda that they should be proud of the good care they provided for Mrs. Kasper right up to the end. At the same time, she congratulates them for being able to ask for and receive the help they needed on their difficult journey. First, they were able to access Eileen's help; she points out that many people wrongly feel that they are failing when they seek professional help. Second, they accepted Eileen's suggestion for a daily helper, finding that this help greatly relieved their worries about Mrs. Kasper's being alone all morning and allowing them to focus on their work when it was required. In addition, Barbara's back pain was relieved so she was able to continue to work and care for her family. Finally, they asked extended family for coverage so that they could get away from the home one weekend a month. This weekend became a valuable resource for them and also provided opportunities for other family to say their good-byes to Mrs. Kasper.

Barbara and Amanda agree with what Eileen can observe from the measures they used: Amanda's caregiving stress, which was somewhat mild, was reduced slightly, even as her grandmother's functioning scores and health deteriorated over the last 10 months, and she was able to participate in school activities more fully. Barbara's stress and depression scores were reduced in clinically significant ways and remained fairly low as her mother's health failed. Both Barbara and Amanda acknowledge that the reduction of stress enabled them to be fully with Mrs. Kasper as she died and to feel satisfied with their caregiving for her. They have no regrets and feel that their family has been strengthened by this experience.

discussed in Chapter 7. Also, as with any method for determining change, the method is only as good as the measurement instrument used and how you use it.

Finally, traditionally clinical significance involves comparing pretest and posttest scores. This provides some indication of change from start to finish, and certainly provides a benchmark for evaluating the success of an intervention. However, don't misunderstand us here; we are not suggesting that you collect only pretest and posttest scores. It's critical to monitor outcomes on an ongoing basis (practice-based evidence) from baseline through intervention and beyond, if possible, so that you can use this information to modify your intervention plan as needed to help your clients achieve their goals.

**Engage, Assess, Intervene, Evaluate**

***Practice Behavior Example:*** *Help clients resolve problems*

**Critical Thinking Question:** What questions would you have and what decisions would you make if your client evidenced clinically significant improvement on a standardized scale, but she did not believe that a meaningful change had occurred in her real-world functioning or her quality of life?

# USING STANDARDIZED SCALES TO EVALUATE EXPECTED TREATMENT RESPONSE

In the past 15 years or so, several standardized self-report scales have been developed in combination with computerized feedback systems that let you monitor your client's progress and, even better, give you session-by-session feedback about whether your client is making satisfactory progress. More specifically, session-by-session progress for an individual client is determined in comparison to normative data from ongoing responses to treatment of thousands of different clients with different mental health problems, who have been treated in different settings with different interventions by professionals from different disciplines. Feedback from these systems is available soon after the measure is completed so it can be used in real time to monitor client progress and modify services as needed to reduce treatment failures and increase overall treatment effectiveness.

Several such systems are available and are described in Table 9.1. These include the Outcome Questionnaire (OQ) measures (e.g., Lambert, 2010b), the Clinical Outcomes in Routine Evaluation (CORE) measures (e.g., Barkham et al., 2010), the Partners for Change Outcome Management System (PCOMS) (e.g., Anker et al., 2009; Miller, Duncan, Sorrell, & Brown, 2005; Reese et al., 2009), and the Treatment Outcome Package (TOP) (e.g., Kraus & Castonguay, 2010). The OQ measures, for example, work as follows (Lambert, 2010b):

- clients complete the questionnaire using a computer, a kiosk, a personal digital assistant, or paper and pencil;
- responses are fed directly into the Outcome Questionnaire—Analyst (OQ-A) software and a report is instantly created using statistical algorithms drawn from over a decade of research;
- clinicians use the report to tailor the client's treatment; and
- administrators can use this information to track trends and report on treatment successes.

The OQ-A received near-perfect ratings as an evidence-based practice from the Substance Abuse and Mental Health Services Administration's National Registry of Evidence-Based Programs and Practices (http://www.nrepp.samhsa.gov/programfull-details.asp?PROGRAM_ID=191). As noted in this review, hundreds of sites across the United States (and in Australia, Germany, and Norway) have used the OQ-A with more than 100,000 clients.

What's especially exciting about these systems is the fact that there is an increasing body of methodologically rigorous research demonstrating that this feedback process reduces treatment failures (including dropout) and improves overall client outcomes, especially for clients who aren't making satisfactory progress (e.g., Anker et al., 2009; Harmon et al., 2007; Hawkins, Lambert, Vermeersch, Slade, & Turtle, 2004; Lambert et al., 2001, 2002; Whipple et al., 2003). Indeed, in some respects the effect of this process is comparable to the effect found for evidence-based interventions.

This approach to outcome-informed practice has been implemented in a number of large managed behavioral health care organizations in the United States (Bohanske & Franczak, 2010; Brown & Minami, 2010), including United Behavioral Health (http://www.unitedbehavioralhealth.com/products/core.htm) and ValueOptions (http://www.valueoptions.com/providers/News/ontrack/OnTrackOutcomesUpdateNewsletter.pdf?SUBMIT=submit), and in other countries. In particular, the CORE measures are widely used throughout the United Kingdom and are being used in other European Union countries such as the Netherlands and Denmark.

This is an emerging area of research and practice that shows great promise for improving client outcomes in mental health settings. We believe that you should take a careful look at one or more of these systems if you work in the field of mental health.

# SINGLE-ITEM GLOBAL
# STANDARDIZED SCALES

Most standardized scales contain multiple items. However, there are single-item standardized scales developed for practitioners or independent observers that are useful for
the overall assessment of client functioning. These include, for example, the (1) Children's
Global Assessment Schedule (Bird, Canino, Rubio-Stipec, & Ribera, 1987; Shaffer et al.,
1983); (2) Global Assessment of Functioning Scale, based on Axis V of the *DSM-IV-TR*
(American Psychiatric Association, 2000); (3) Social and Occupational Functioning
Assessment Scale (Goldman, Skodol, & Lave, 1992), presented in Appendix B of *DSM-IV-TR*
(American Psychiatric Association, 2000); and (4) Global Assessment of Relational Func-
tioning Scale (Dausch, Miklowitz, & Richards, 1996). All of these measures are discussed
in Rush et al. (2008).

Global ratings of client functioning have advantages (e.g., Dougherty et al., 2008).
They allow practitioners to use professional judgment to measure client functioning in
a holistic fashion; the practitioner can take all of the known relevant information into
account, weigh it, and make a judgment about client functioning in its entirety. They are
also easy to use, accessible, and relevant for use with a wide range of clients. Finally, they
can provide an overall measure of the degree of impairment associated with a particular
problem, such as substance use disorders or depression.

Global ratings of client functioning also have potential disadvantages (e.g., Dougherty
et al., 2008). Measures of global functioning don't provide a basis for determining the degree of change in specific areas targeted for intervention. Also, professional judgment and
discretion in the measurement of global constructs allows room for the introduction of
idiosyncratic biases, although detailed anchors help reduce this problem.

Single-item global measures of client functioning completed by practitioners can be
efficient and useful in the repeated measurement of client functioning. However, they
should not be used as the sole basis for monitoring progress because of their potential for
bias and the fact that they often do not provide information about specific areas targeted
for intervention.

# SPECIAL CONSIDERATIONS
# OF CULTURE AND ETHNICITY

As we discussed earlier in relation to Mrs. Kasper's Polish-American family, notions of
well-being, illness, family, and just about every other construct are embedded in culture.
Culture encompasses the distinctive values, customs, beliefs, knowledge, art, history, institutions, and language shared by a particular social group at a particular time and place.
In the United States, in addition to what we call the *mainstream culture*, numerous other
cultures thrive, and many individuals live in more than one culture. Social workers' collaboration with their clients must exist within their cultures; the use of standardized measures is no exception. Next, we discuss three specific cultures as exemplars of how you
might go about incorporating your clients' cultural identities into this process. Clearly,
there are many cultures in this country and in many nations; because we cannot cover all

the cultures you may encounter in your practice, we hope these exemplars demonstrate a process you may use with any culture.

## African-Americans

Although African-Americans make up 12.8% of the U.S. population (U.S. Census), they constitute a distinct cultural group based on their African ancestry, centuries of oppression and discrimination, and other characteristics. Even within the African-American culture, there are subcultures based on ancestry and geography. Although many of the standardized measures that were normed on European-Americans may be appropriate for use with African-Americans, practitioners should not automatically assume a specific measure to be applicable to African-American clients.

How would you decide what measure to use with an African-American couple whose problem centers around their young child's disruptive behavior? This chapter details the procedures for locating and selecting appropriate measures generally, but you also need evidence that the measure you select is appropriate for monitoring outcomes with African-American parents and children specifically. Child-rearing is particularly embedded in cultural expectations of role behavior and competence (Keller, 2003).

You might begin by looking at one of the compendia of measures listed in Appendix B, applying this chapter's recommendations for judging the measures you find. Looking across those resources, you will see two well-validated measures commonly used to measure disruptive child behavior: the Achenbach rating forms (Child Behavior Checklist/1.5-5, Child Behavior Checklist/6-18, Teacher Report Form, and Youth Self-Report Form) (Achenbach & Rescorla, 2000, 2001) and the Eyberg Child Behavior Inventory (ECBI) (Eyberg & Pincus, 1999). Each of these measures is consistent with your purpose of measuring child problem behaviors, but the Achenbach rating forms contain over 100 items each and are somewhat expensive (http://www.aseba.org/). The ECBI is short, involves no cost, and sounds like a good candidate. Therefore, you take the next step to examine the measure's use with African-American clients.

A quick PsycInfo search using the name of the measure with "African-American" reveals only six research articles. (More might be found with extensive searches, but we recognize that most practitioners cannot expend a lot of time on these activities.) Sivan, Ridge, Gross, Richardson, and Cowell (2008) report on a focus group in which African-American parents found the measure to be acceptable. Gross et al. (2007) found evidence for the appropriateness of the measure with both African-American and Hispanic 2- to 4-year-old children. In many cases, you might pursue more information, but this process at least provides you some assurance that the measures you select have not been found to be problematic for your client's specific demographic group. You should use the most specific information about your clients' target problem (e.g., specific problem behaviors, child age, context of the problem behaviors) to find the best match for your clients—and then be appropriately cautious in interpreting the data.

## American Indians

American Indians (Native Americans) represent unique cultures in American society because of a history of colonial subjugation that has taken their lands, much of their culture, and even their children. Yet it is erroneous to refer to "Native American culture," for there is tremendous heterogeneity among the more than 500 tribes in America, encompassing religious and spiritual traditions, language, customs, family structure, and other aspects of culture. (For a discussion of cultural issues and assessment, see Allen, 2010.) Indeed, probably the most striking commonality among these disparate groups is their horrific historical treatment by the majority culture.

The nonnative social worker who encounters a Native American or Alaska Native client is faced with a considerable challenge, not only in selecting appropriate interventions (Jackson & Hodge, 2010), but in selecting appropriate standardized instruments for monitoring client outcomes. The less experience you have interacting with the culture, the more caution you should exercise in interpreting your data.

In this chapter, we discuss two common measures of depression: the CES-D (Radloff, 1977; Radloff & Lock, 2008) and the QIDS-SR (Rush et al., 2003, 2006; Trivedi et al., 2004). Both measures have demonstrated good reliability and validity in the general population and are inexpensive and easy to administer. Which measure, if either, would you use with a Native American or Alaska Native client? We cannot address all the practice issues you would confront in such a situation, but let's think about how you would select a standardized measure for monitoring your client's outcome.

We did a quick search on the PubMed database for both measures, along with the terms *American Indian* or *Native American* or *Alaska Native*. There were no hits for the QIDS-SR, although it is possible that the measure has been used with this population, of course. In many studies, there are diverse groups of participants, but small numbers do not permit analysis by ethnicity (Lau, 2006). We found a number of reports of the use of the CES-D, which has been used with Native adults (e.g., Whitbeck, McMorris, Hoyt, Stubben, & LaFromboise, 2002), adolescents (e.g., Dick, Beals, Keane, & Manson, 1994; Ginsburg et al., 2008), and elders (e.g., Chapleski, Lamphere, Kaczynski, Lichtenberg, & Dwyer, 1997). Many of the studies do not identify the participants' tribal affiliations, and certainly none have a broad representation of tribes.

Nevertheless, on the whole the research suggests that the CES-D may be a useful tool to monitor American Indian clients' outcomes. The social worker needs to be aware that many Native American cultures do not distinguish between mind and body as the majority culture does (Chapleski et al., 1997), so mood and physical complaints may be thought of as more equivalent than is the case with European-Americans. It is important that the practitioner use the CES-D or any standardized scale or measure as just one piece of information in monitoring the client's outcome, and this may be especially true when you are working with American Indian or Alaska Native clients. Critical thinking and caution are called for when interpreting data in this situation; for example, you might be sure to collect the most important data in multiple ways and compare your results. Agreement in your data would enhance your confidence, whereas discrepancies would signal the need for more information and/or extreme caution in applying the data when making critical decisions about intervention.

## Hispanics

Hispanics are this country's largest minority group (13.3% according to the 2010 U.S. Census) and continuing to grow. In many parts of the country, especially along the border with Mexico and in large cities, a substantial proportion of social work clients may be Hispanic, and the proportion of citizens from Hispanic cultures is growing. Social workers whose practices include specific cultural groups such as Mexican-Americans, groups from

Central and South America, and islands such as Cuba and Puerto Rico should be familiar with the cultures of those specific groups (while remembering that each client is an individual) in order to be prepared to deliver high-quality, culturally-sensitive services. General information about Hispanic music or art, stereotypes about machismo or the "Latin temper," and even fluency in one dialect of Spanish may be of limited use with your clients.

There are two major issues to consider when you are looking for an appropriate standardized measure for your Hispanic clients. First, the designation *Hispanic* includes individuals from many distinct cultures; know your client's background. Some research shows subtle differences in how measures perform with different Hispanic groups (Crockett et al., 2005). When possible, select measures that have been tested with your client's specific cultural group.

Second, in many cases you may wish to have your client complete a measure in Spanish. Although many of the most popular measures have been translated into Spanish, this does not guarantee measurement equivalence—or even that your client understands the items in the same way as another Hispanic client. Translation does not guarantee functional equivalence (discussed earlier in this chapter), and in fact presents the opportunity to confound the effects of language and culture (Cortes et al., 2007). In many cases, items cannot be directly translated; words may have no direct translation or may have different functional meanings in different cultures. Equivalent scores on different language versions of the same scale may not indicate the same level or magnitude of the construct being measured. Yet often these measures are used without the support of evidence about their psychometric properties (Fernandez, Boccaccini, & Noland, 2007).

Varela, Sanchez-Sosa, Biggs, and Luis (2008) examined the cultural equivalence of three widely used measures of fear and anxiety in children (Revised Children's Manifest Anxiety Scale, Multidimensional Anxiety Scale for Children, and the Fear Survey Schedule for Children Revised). Their work suggests that the measures they tested were equivalent across European American, Hispanic-American of both Central American and Mexican origins, and Mexican youth. However, results also suggested that somatic symptoms may be more normative for Hispanic youth than for the majority culture. Thus, social workers delivering services to Hispanic youth might want to keep this in mind as they measure client outcomes. Level of acculturation may also be relevant (Montalvo, 2009); you might select one measure for a first-generation immigrant and another for a client whose family has been in the United States for several generations.

Even these three relatively superficial examples with fairly prominent subcultures in the United States illustrate the complexity of culture considerations in administering standardized measures; the issues become even more complex when we think about adapting and delivering evidence-based interventions to individuals from cultures not represented in the research base. We can only advise that social workers thoroughly search the literature for all available information on their own clients' cultural groups, while also treating their clients as individuals.

## USING STANDARDIZED SCALES IN GROUPS

Standardized scales can be used with group interventions to monitor the progress of individual group participants in much the way they can be used with individuals. Standardized scales also can be used to measure problems focused on group-centered functioning (Macgowan, 2008; Strauss, Burlingame, & Bormann, 2008; Toseland & Rivas, 2009).

One excellent example is the work done by Macgowan, who developed the Group Engagement Measure (GEM). The GEM was developed to measure the engagement of individual members of treatment groups along seven dimensions: (1) attendance, (2) contributing, (3) relating to worker, (4) relating with members, (5) contracting, (6) working on own problems, and (7) working on other members' problems (Macgowan, 1997, 2006). The original 37-item GEM is a leader-report measure of engagement for each group member, but it has been adapted successfully for use as a self-report measure. In addition, there is a 27-item version of the GEM that is reproduced in Appendix A, and there is a 21-item version of the GEM that measures all but two of the seven dimensions (attendance and contracting) (Macgowan & Newman, 2005).

# COMPUTER MANAGEMENT OF STANDARDIZED SCALES

Personal computers are being used increasingly in the administration, scoring, interpretation, storage, analysis, and general management of standardized scales. However, just as there are too many standardized scales to describe here, it's also impossible to detail the many different computer programs for the management of standardized scales. (For good examples of how computers can be used in outcome-informed practice, explore the websites for the OQ-45, the CORE, the TOP, and the Outcome Rating Scales/Session Rating Scales presented in Table 9.1.) This is a rapidly growing area, so look for current developments in journals such as *Journal of Technology in Human Services*, *Social Science Computer Review*, *Behavior and Information Technology*, and *Computers in Psychiatry/Psychology*; in software and book review sections of professional journals; and in *The Eighteenth Mental Measurements Yearbook* (Spies, Plake, Geisinger, & Carlson, 2010).

# ADVANTAGES AND PRECAUTIONS FOR USING STANDARDIZED SCALES

Standardized scales have important advantages. First, they are usually pretested for reliability and validity. Second, in contrast to unstructured interviews, for example, standardized scales are structured to systematically and comprehensively elicit information, and this can increase the likelihood that the necessary information will be obtained. Third, many standardized scales can be used to compare the functioning of a client to the functioning of a normative population; you can use this information as one element for deciding whether your intervention should be implemented, continued, changed, or terminated. Finally, many standardized scales are simple to use; they frequently are inexpensive, readily available, generally take very little time or energy on the part of either practitioner or client, and can be easy to administer and score.

Despite their advantages, standardized scales should not be used to measure every problem; nor should their results be accepted uncritically. One area for caution is that the name given to a standardized scale indicates the construct the author *intended* to measure. Just because a measure is called a measure of *depression* doesn't necessarily mean that that's what it measures. Also, just because two or more standardized scales claim to measure the same construct doesn't necessarily mean that they're interchangeable. Evidence of reliability, and especially validity, is necessary.

Another issue is the fact that in many, if not most, cases you won't know all that you'd like to know about the reliability and validity of a particular standardized scale. In such cases, be cautious in your interpretation of the results in proportion to the amount of information available.

Even if you find a standardized scale with comprehensive evidence of reliability and validity, remember that the research conducted on such scales is always done with large groups, under circumstances that are different in important ways from practice, and sometimes with people who are different from your clients in important ways. Typically, research participants don't have an ongoing relationship with the researcher; they don't complete the scale more than once or twice at most; and their scores don't have a bearing on their receipt of services.

Another thing you should be cautious of is the fact that standardized scales measure problems in terms of general constructs assumed to be relevant to different clients, but they might not correspond to the unique realities of a particular client. One apparent solution to this problem is for you to add or delete items in an attempt to tailor it to a particular client. However, such *ad hoc* modifications might compromise the reliability and validity of the scale in unknown ways and might undermine your ability to compare the results of the scale with results from previous research. Also, typically standardized scales are copyrighted and can't be changed without violating copyright law. Therefore, we don't recommend tailoring standardized scales to particular clients.

Related to the fact that standardized scales measure problems in terms of constructs is the fact that some of these constructs are relatively general, and are thus relatively indirect measures of problems. For example, measures of global impairment might be useful for providing overall pictures of changes, but such overall scores might be relatively insensitive to client change in delimited areas of social functioning targeted for intervention.

If you can't find a standardized scale suited to a particular client problem, consider the construction and use of individualized rating scales (Chapter 10), the direct observation of client-specific behaviors (Chapter 11), and self-monitoring (Chapter 12). Or, you could use one of these alternative individualized measurement methods along with a standardized scale to get at client-specific aspects of the problem, such as idiosyncratic aspects of a child's conduct problems (Weisz et al., in press). Remember: *The goal is to fit the measurement method to the client's problem, not to fit the client's problem to a convenient measurement method.* Finally, as with all measures, remember that the score from a standardized scale is just one more piece of information that you can use in the context of all of the other quantitative and qualitative information that you have about your client; you should use and interpret this information only in this broader context and you should work collaboratively with your client to understand and interpret this information.

## CONCLUSIONS

If you use them judiciously, standardized scales are invaluable tools for making important practice decisions, and particularly for monitoring your client's response to intervention. Knowledge of the strengths and limitations of standardized measures, as well as how to use them appropriately, adds to your ability to use them in the pursuit of your clients' goals.

**PRACTICE TEST** The following questions will test your knowledge of the content found within this chapter and help you prepare for the licensing exam by applying chapter content to practice. For more questions styled like the licensing exam, visit **MySocialWorkLab.com**

1. Which of the following is the least important information needed to select a standardized scale:
   a. Measures the intended construct in the opinion of clients, other respondents, or other users
   b. Correlates in predicted ways with other measures of the same or related constructs or variables
   c. Does not correlate with theoretically dissimilar or unrelated constructs or other variables
   d. Detects genuine change in the measured construct

2. Clinically significant improvement occurs if a client's score on a standardized scale
   a. Shows reliable change in the direction of improvement, but does not move from the dysfunctional to the functional range
   b. Does not show reliable change and does not move from the dysfunctional to the functional range
   c. Shows reliable change in the direction of deterioration
   d. Shows reliable change in the direction of improvement and the score moves from the dysfunctional to the functional range

3. Which of the following is an advantage of global ratings of client functioning:
   a. Provide a basis for determining the degree of change in specific areas targeted for intervention
   b. Allow practitioners to use professional judgment to measure client functioning in a holistic fashion
   c. Can be used as the sole basis for monitoring client progress
   d. Minimize the effect of idiosyncratic practitioner biases

4. Which of the following is an advantage of standardized scales:
   a. Research conducted on standardized scales is done on large groups, under circumstances different from practice
   b. Usually pretested for reliability and validity
   c. Can be used to measure client-specific behaviors
   d. Applicable with clients from different racial and ethnic backgrounds

5. A social worker in an assisted living facility is working with a depressed client, Ruford. The social worker uses the CES-D to measure and monitor his depression. On one occasion, Ruford has the following scores for items 1 through 20: 2, 3, 3, 0, 3, 2, 2, 0, 3, 2, 2, 1, 3, 2, 3, 1, 2, 3, 2, 3. Use the information in Appendix A to compute and interpret the CES-D total score.

6. A social worker is working with Ruford, the client described in question 5. Ruford scored 25 on the CES-D at first, and after 6 weeks of intervention, he scored 10. Did reliable improvement occur? Did clinically significant improvement occur? (Use the information in Appendix A to answer these questions.)

## SUCCEED WITH

Visit **MySocialWorkLab** for more licensing exam test questions, and to access case studies, videos, and much more.

# 10

# Individualized Rating Scales

| Advancing Core Competencies In This Chapter | | | | |
|---|---|---|---|---|
| ■ Professional Identity | ■ Ethical Practice | ✖ Critical Thinking | ✖ Diversity in Practice | ■ Human Rights & Justice |
| ✖ Research-Based Practice | ■ Human Behavior | ■ Policy Practice | ■ Practice Contexts | ✖ Engage, Assess, Intervene, Evaluate |

Audrey Silva is 81 years old. She is relatively healthy, though she takes a number of medications to control high blood pressure, osteoporosis, and arthritis. She lives alone in the apartment where she has lived for 40 years, having lost her husband to cancer 6 years ago. She has a good social network, including her church, several neighbors with whom she is friendly, and a niece (Elaine) who lives about 30 minutes away. Mrs. Silva's son Aaron lives on the other side of the city, approximately an hour's drive. He is single and an attorney with a good income. Aaron, Elaine, and Mrs. Silva meet with a social worker (Michael) at the Senior Center, where Mrs. Silva attends some activities, to talk about assisted living. Aaron is urging his mother to move to a nice facility near him and

offering to help with expenses, but she loves her home and neighborhood and does not want to move.

Mrs. Silva has always been an active, involved woman with many interests. Recently, her son, who calls her daily, has noticed some confusion when they speak, and on his frequent visits he has noticed that her housekeeping seems to have deteriorated. (The apartment is not unhygienic; it's just not as immaculate as it once was.) He says his mother is not as cheerful as she once was, often sounding sad and discouraged. He has the impression that she is not getting out as much as she always has—at least once a day for a church event, shopping, or meeting with friends.

Elaine, who calls a couple of times a week, reports that her aunt sometimes seems confused about what day it is; she recently went to take her aunt to lunch for an event they had planned, and Mrs. Silva had forgotten about it. Elaine thinks her aunt seems much frailer lately, as well, often stopping to get her balance by holding onto something. Finally, she fears that Mrs. Silva is depressed, often sitting in silence and staring into space, rather than chattering as she always has.

Mrs. Silva admits that she is physically frailer and not as "quick on the uptake" as she once was, saying "I'm 81 years old, for Pete's sake!" She is more reflective these days, she says, but she adamantly insists

that she is not depressed and is happy to complete a screening measure "to prove it." She completes the 15-item Geriatric Depression Scale (GDS-15; Sheikh & Yesavage, 1986; Yesavage & Brink, 1983, 2008), which is reproduced in Appendix A. Michael selects this measure because he knows that other measures of depression may not be appropriate for use with geriatric populations for a variety of reasons (e.g., sleep difficulties and decreased energy are common in nondepressed older persons, and thoughts of death and hopelessness may mean something different later in life).

In many cases, no standardized measure exists to measure your client's specific problem or circumstances. In many other instances, you will want to use both standardized and individualized measures. How can you do that in a way that enhances the objectivity with which you monitor your client's progress? Certainly, there is always a measure of subjectivity involved, but the more objectivity you can add, the more confident you can be that positive outcomes are not due solely to wishful thinking (yours *and* your client's).

This chapter describes how to develop scales for rating the degree, magnitude, or intensity of problems identified for individual clients. Often this type of measure is called a *target complaint scale* (e.g., Battle et al., 1966; Mintz & Kiesler, 1982; Ogles, Lambert, & Fields, 2002). However, following Bloom et al. (2009), we call it an *individualized rating scale* (IRS) because it is developed on a client-by-client basis and is designed to measure unique aspects of each client's experience. IRSs are easy to develop and use with a wide range of clients to identify and quantify individualized client problems, and they allow you to monitor client progress in a way that is especially sensitive to the unique perceptions of individual clients. IRSs are important sources of practice-based evidence for monitoring and improving outcomes for your specific client.

# CONSTRUCTING IRSs

All IRSs are constructed in a similar way: the client's problems are identified, and then a scale is developed to measure the degree, magnitude, or intensity of each problem.

## Identify and Define Problems

In Chapter 4, we discussed the assessment process. The quality of your individualized measure depends directly on the quality of your assessment. Operationalizing each problem and goal explicitly is key to identifying the targets to be monitored with any kind of measure, including an IRS. In particular, recall our discussion of content validity in Chapter 8, and make sure when you construct an IRS that it includes the full range of identified problems and does not contain irrelevant problems.

The assessment process is difficult. Mrs. Silva is not angry, but she is adamant that she has no problem living independently and will not move to assisted living. Michael tends to agree that she does not evidence any confusion or disorientation in the meeting; however, it is clear that Aaron and Elaine are extremely concerned about her. "*That* is the problem," she says, "not me. I don't even know what they're worried about." Further discussion operationalizes the substance of Aaron and Elaine's worries:

- Diet (Is she eating three nutritious meals each day? Is her kitchen well stocked with fresh, nutritious food?)
- Medication (Does she take all of her medications as directed and on time?)
- Social activities (Does she have enough pleasant interaction each day with other people? Is she getting out enough? Is she lonely?)
- Physical safety in the home (Is her home safe? What would she do in an emergency, such as a fire?)
- Mood (Is she depressed?)
- Cognitive functioning (Is she confused? Is she able to solve normal daily problems?)

At the end of the first session, all parties are able to agree to the problem stated as: *Mrs. Silva's son and niece are worried that she is not safe continuing to live alone in her apartment.* They agree on one goal: *Aaron and Elaine will be confident that Mrs. Silva is able to live at home alone safely.*

Although the statements of the problem and goal focus on her son and niece, Mrs. Silva is willing to make some changes in her behavior to achieve the goal. She agrees to do two things immediately: First, she will have a complete physical exam, including assessment of her cognitive abilities and mental health. Second, she agrees reluctantly that it is now difficult for her to keep her apartment as clean as she would like. She agrees to a housekeeper to come for a few hours twice a week to do the heavy cleaning and some light shopping.

Michael and his clients also agree that a prospective baseline is critical to moving ahead with any intervention in this case, so they focus on setting up a measurement plan. Mrs. Silva rightly points out that since the problem they have agreed on is her loved ones' anxiety about her—rather than anything she is doing—that is what should be monitored. Therefore, they agree to a week of monitoring Aaron and Elaine's worries about Mrs. Silva, with no other changes except moving ahead with hiring a housekeeper.

The target is not general anxiety, of course, as might be measured by any of several standardized measures (e.g., the Penn State Worry Questionnaire—Past Week, reproduced in Appendix A). Rather, it is Michael and Elaine's specific worries about Mrs. Silva's safety and well-being. After much discussion, they construct a rating scale from 1 (no worry) to 3 (some worry, but mild and transitory) to 5 (frequent or moderate worry that sometimes interfered with my usual activities) to 7 (frequent extreme worry that disrupted my day), and it's agreed that Aaron and Elaine will complete it each evening.

## Engage, Assess, Intervene, Evaluate

***Practice Behavior Example:*** *Collect, organize, and interpret client data*

**Critical Thinking Question:** What questions would you consider and what decisions would you make when identifying and defining Mrs. Silva's problems, goals, and objectives?

# Selecting Rating Dimensions

A *dimension* is a quantitative quality or property of a person, object, or event much like height, length, and width are dimensions of an object. A *rating* is a systematic estimation of some characteristic of a person, object, or event along some dimension using a numerical scale that results in a numerical score. A *rating scale* is a measurement instrument used to elicit ratings on those dimensions.

Numerous problems can be rated, including quality of time spent with family; expressions of warmth and empathy between spouses; positive coping responses; class participation; exercise; panic attacks; suicidal ideation; aggression; drug or alcohol cravings; tension or migraine headaches; self-injurious thoughts and behaviors; anger; fear; sadness; guilt; or shame.

## Selecting the Number of Response Categories

A *response category* is a point on a rating scale that represents the degree, magnitude, or intensity of a problem. If you use too few response categories, a scale will be insensitive to important changes over time. For example, a lot of information would be lost if Aaron and Elaine simply indicated they were either worried or not worried—there's a lot

To prepare Elaine to rate her worry about her aunt each day, Michael goes through the values of the scale and asks Elaine to recall when she has felt that way about her aunt, and her responses are shown in Table 10.1.

Michael will go through a similar process with Aaron to make sure that each value indicates the same amount of worry and that the distances between the points are equivalent for both.

**Table 10.1**

**Rating Scale of Elaine's Worry About Her Aunt.**

| | Worry About Mrs. Silva's Safety and Well-Being |
|---|---|
| 1 | Not at all worried ("Well, a 1 is a day when I don't worry about her at all. I might think of her, but I don't worry. So one day last week I saw a blooming azalea and I just thought, 'Oh, Aunt Audrey would love that azalea!'") |
| 2 | |
| 3 | Minimally worried, did not interfere with my activities ("I think yesterday was a 3. It was raining hard when I left for work, and I thought 'I hope Aunt Audrey doesn't go out until this rain lets up.' That's probably pretty typical for me.") |
| 4 | |
| 5 | Moderately worried, interfered with some activities ("Last Sunday was a 5. I tried to call Aunt Audrey three times to see if she wanted to go out to dinner with me that evening, and I could never get her on the phone. I was very concerned and kept thinking about it until late in the afternoon when she called me back. She'd been at a church retreat all day.") |
| 6 | |
| 7 | Very worried, disrupted my work or activities much of the day ("I guess the day I went to get Aunt Audrey for lunch downtown and she had no memory of our date was a 7. Not only had she forgotten, but it was 11:00 and she was still in her bathrobe. That's just not like her! I was so concerned that I dropped my afternoon plans and insisted she get ready right then and spend the entire day with me so I could watch her.") |

of ground between these two extremes. Conversely, too many response categories make it difficult to distinguish accurately among different categories. For example, it's hard to see how a rater could make accurate distinctions on a 100-point scale.

We recommend 7-point scales (Streiner & Norman, 2008). However, within a certain range (e.g., 5–9), the number depends in part on the ability of the rater to distinguish accurately among different categories. If a client can't distinguish among seven categories, try five. However, fewer than five categories (and perhaps even five categories) may not be sensitive enough to detect meaningful client progress. Conversely, raters may find it difficult to use a scale with more than nine categories, and even nine categories may be difficult for some people.

## Selecting Rating Scale Anchors

Ratings are represented by numbers, which represent gradations that are similar to gradations on a ruler. However, although everyone knows from experience what an inch or a foot is, the numbers on rating scales require definition. These numbers are defined by providing brief explicit labels, descriptions, or examples as shown in our example; these are called *anchors*. Without adequate anchors, it's difficult for a rater to provide reliable and valid ratings, and it's difficult to interpret ratings. Ideally, all of the points on a rating scale should be labeled with clear, precise, and explicit anchors, but at least try to anchor every other number, as in our example. Raters may then use the unanchored values to express "a little more" or "a little less."

Anchors can be tailored to individual clients and problems, as we illustrate in our case example. You might help your client come up with word pictures, thoughts, and behaviors to use as anchors, as Michael did. Begin by asking your client to anchor one end of the scale and then the other. Then, you and the client can anchor all or most of the gradations in between, and practice using the scale. If the client has trouble providing anchors, you might offer suggestions, such as "When you're very worried about your aunt or mother, how does that show?" Be sure to check the accuracy of such anchors with the client.

In some situations, for example working with clients who have serious mental illnesses, clients may be unable to participate fully in the construction of the IRS. We recommend involving the client as much as possible and keeping the scale as simple as you can, for example using no more than five response categories. Be certain that the client understands the importance of completing the IRS and the instructions, and practice completing it together in the session. It is especially important in these cases to have data from other sources, and other types of data from your client when possible, and to conduct frequent checks of the reliability and validity of the data. For example, you might ask questions such as this: *On Tuesday, your bad feelings score was the worst for the whole week. What made that day so much worse than the rest of the week?* In addition, look for inconsistencies among your various data sources; if the client's day treatment supervisor says your client appeared happy on the day he scored himself as feeling very bad, your measure may not be reliable or valid.

You also can use generic anchors to rate a number of different client problems, such as the following, and Table 10.2 illustrates one possible format for doing this:

- Quality of social support or of time spent with a spouse, children, or friends: (1) poor, (2) fair, (3) good, (4) very good, (5) excellent.

| Table 10.2 | **Rating Scale With Brief Generic Anchors.** | | | | | | |
|:---:|:---:|:---:|:---:|:---:|:---:|:---:|:---:|
| | **Agreement Between You and Your Spouse About Finances** | | | | | | |
| 1 | 2 | 3 | 4 | 5 | 6 | 7 |
| Do not agree at all | Agree very little | Agree a little | Moderately agree | Agree a lot | Mostly agree | Totally agree |

- Degree of impairment caused by migraine headaches, asthma attacks, self-injurious thoughts, panic attacks, alcohol consumption, illegal drug use, or diabetes: (1) no impairment, (2) minimal impairment, (3) mild impairment, (4) moderate impairment, (5) marked impairment, (6) severe impairment, (7) unable to function.
- Satisfaction with marriage, job, spouse, child, or relationship with social worker: (1) extremely dissatisfied, (2) very dissatisfied, (3) somewhat dissatisfied, (4) mixed, (5) somewhat satisfied, (6) very satisfied, (7) extremely satisfied.
- Frequency of enuresis, compliance with a diabetes regimen, adherence to an exercise program, or medication adherence: (1) less than 1 day a week, (2) 1 day a week, (3) 2 or 3 days a week, (4) 4 or 5 days a week, (5) nearly every day.
- Frequency of self-injurious thoughts, anger, fear, sadness, guilt, anxiety, or shame: (1) never, (2) rarely, (3) occasionally, (4) frequently, (5) always. You could also use (1) none of the time, (2) very rarely, (3) a little of the time, (4) some of the time, (5) a good part of the time, (6) most of the time, (7) all of the time.
- Severity of drug or alcohol cravings, stress, self-deprecating or intrusive thoughts, or tension or migraine headaches: (1) not at all, (2) slight, (3) moderate, (4) severe, (5) very severe.
- Degree of distress with social life, financial situation, or physical health: (1) no distress, (2) very little distress, (3) somewhat distressed, (4) moderately distressed, (5) very distressed, (6) extremely distressed, (7) most distressed I've ever felt.
- Feelings about spouse, children, job situation, or future: (1) extremely negative, (2) quite negative, (3) slightly negative, (4) neutral, (5) slightly positive, (6) quite positive, (7) extremely positive.
- Degree of agreement between you and your spouse concerning finances, child-rearing, or sex: (1) do not agree at all, (2) agree very little, (3) agree a little, (4) moderately agree, (5) agree a lot, (6) mostly agree, (7) totally agree.
- Importance of close relationships, social support, financial security, or change from one time to the next: (1) not at all important, (2) quite unimportant, (3) somewhat unimportant, (4) mixed, (5) somewhat important, (6) quite important, (7) extremely important.

Generic anchors are easy to use because they can be applied to different problems and clients and they make it easier to compare across problems. On the other hand, individually-tailored anchors have some advantages over generic anchors. They probably are more relevant and meaningful to a particular client, and so they are more easily interpreted. Also, they generally are less ambiguous and more precise because they're developed by and for a particular client and problem.

Whatever anchors you select, arrange the anchors and numbers on a rating scale so that higher numbers represent more of the attribute you're measuring. This makes the ratings easier to interpret. For example, in rating the severity of a problem, higher numbers should indicate greater severity. Also make sure that the anchors are congruent with the problem being rated; for example, it wouldn't make much sense to rate the degree of satisfaction with migraine headaches, or the degree of impairment brought about by social support.

## Creating Equidistant Response Categories

To the extent possible, construct response categories so the intervals between them are equal. For example, view the scale as a thermometer with equal intervals, and ask the client to think of the words anchoring the scale as representing equal intervals.

Equal intervals make it easier to evaluate change. For example, suppose you used the following categories: (5) very serious, (4) somewhat serious, (3) quite serious, and so on, and suppose the distance between "very serious" and "somewhat serious" is greater than that between "somewhat serious" and "quite serious." When change in the problem over time is graphed, a change from 5 to 4 will appear the same as a change from 4 to 3, despite the difference in the actual amount of the change.

## Selecting Time Period, Event, or Situation

Problem ratings can refer to different time periods, events, or situations. For example, you might ask your client to rate problems at a certain time at the end of each day or week. Or you might ask your client to provide ratings in response to a certain event or situation such as after an interaction with a particular person. In any case, the selected time periods, events, or situations should be specified clearly. (We will have more to say about this in Chapter 12.)

As a general rule, problems should be rated often enough to detect significant changes, but not so often that rating becomes burdensome to the rater or intrudes on intervention efforts. Fortunately, IRSs are easy to complete, administer, score, and interpret, so you can use them frequently to monitor client progress.

## Setting Goals

One way to set a goal using an IRS is to select the point on the scale that represents the goal the client, you, or a relevant other hopes to achieve. For example, Elaine and Aaron probably recognize that they can never be completely unconcerned about Mrs. Silva, but they would like to reduce their worries to a level that does not interfere with work and other activities the great majority of the time. They also realize that as Mrs. Silva gets older there will be medical emergencies and other crises and that it isn't realistic to think they won't worry in those situations. Each sets a goal of two, which corresponds to a low level of worry that doesn't interfere with daily activities. Selecting the point on the scale that represents goal achievement clearly defines the goal so that Michael and his clients know when it has been reached.

fter a week of collecting data, Michael meets again with Mrs. Silva, Aaron, and Elaine. Michael reports that Mrs. Silva's scores on the GDS do not indicate that she is clinically depressed, so they turn to the IRS.

After much discussion, Aaron and Elaine's data suggest some patterns in their worrying. Aaron is most worried on days when he doesn't speak with his mother until late in the day, when she has no social activities for the day, and when he detects any suspicious sound in her voice (Figure 10.1, days 1–7). Elaine is most worried when her aunt behaves in ways that are very uncharacteristic of her (Figure 10.2, days 1–7). They realize that they

**Figure 10.1** • Aaron's Ratings of Worry About Mrs. Silva's Safety and Well-Being.

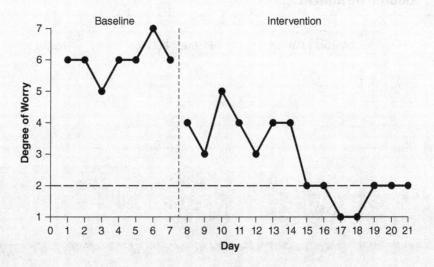

**Figure 10.2** • Elaine's Ratings of Worry About Mrs. Silva's Safety and Well-Being.

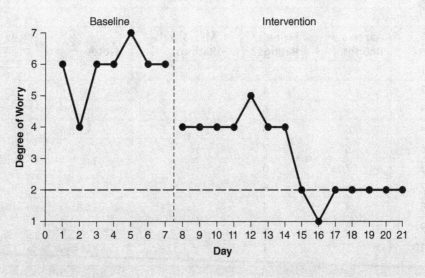

(continued)

both worry most consistently about her safety and least about her mood, and they both worry less when they know the other will be calling or visiting Mrs. Silva.

Mrs. Silva is surprised by the data and concerned about the worry she is causing her son and niece, especially when they discuss the disruption of work and other activities. She wants to know what she can do to alleviate their concerns.

As a first step, Michael suggests that they consider two brief calls a day: one in the morning after Mrs. Silva has breakfast and her medication and another after dinner and her evening medication. That way they can reassure themselves specifically

**Table 10.3**  **Google Document.**

| Date | Aaron's Ratings | Elaine's Ratings | Notes |
|------|-----------------|------------------|-------|
| 3/1  |                 |                  |       |
| 3/2  |                 |                  |       |
|      |                 |                  |       |
|      |                 |                  |       |
|      |                 |                  |       |
|      |                 |                  |       |
| 3/21 |                 |                  |       |

**Table 10.4**  **Completed Google Document.**

| Date | Aaron's Ratings | Elaine's Ratings | Mrs. Silva's Ratings | Notes |
|------|-----------------|------------------|----------------------|-------|
| 3/1  | 6 | 6 | | |
| 3/2  | 6 | 4 | | |
| 3/3  | 5 | 6 | | |
| 3/4  | 6 | 6 | | |
| 3/5  | 6 | 7 | | |
| 3/6  | 7 | 6 | | |
| 3/7  | 6 | 6 | | |
| 3/8  | 4 | 4 | | Church ladies' auxiliary meeting |
| 3/9  | 3 | 4 | | Lunch with Doris |
| 3/10 | 5 | 4 | | Tai chi at Senior Center |

| Date | Aaron's Ratings | Elaine's Ratings | Mrs. Silva's Ratings | Notes |
|------|-----------------|------------------|----------------------|-------|
| 3/11 | 4 | 4 |   | Pink Lady duty at hospital |
| 3/12 | 3 | 5 |   | Art deco exhibit at gallery |
| 3/13 | 4 | 4 |   | Nephew from New York called—nice, long-talk! |
| 3/14 | 4 | 4 |   | Church meeting |
| 3/15 | 2 | 2 | 4 | Coffee with neighbor downstairs |
| 3/16 | 2 | 1 | 3 | Read all day, wonderful novel |
| 3/17 | 1 | 2 | 5 | Art museum with Elaine |
| 3/18 | 1 | 2 | 3 | Minister called, brief conversation |
| 3/19 | 2 | 2 | 4 | Church meeting |
| 3/20 | 2 | 2 | 2 | Rained all day, stuck at home |
| 3/21 | 2 | 2 | 5 | Walked to library, stopped at Starbucks |

on two issues of concern: diet and medications. They will split up the call schedule. Second, Michael suggests that Aaron and Elaine complete the individualized measure using Google Docs, a free file-sharing program that allows writing and editing by anyone in a group. (A free Google account is required. Go to Google.com, click on *More*, and select *Documents* for details.) In this way, either one can check or update the data online at any time. Mrs. Silva agrees with this plan and also asks to be a user, "so I can keep an eye on what these two are saying about me," she says with a smile.

Another way to set a goal using an IRS (and other measures) is to decide on percentage change in the rating from one time to another. Research investigating the efficacy of chronic pain treatments illustrates this. For example, pain intensity often is measured on a scale from 0 to 10, with 0 indicating "no pain," higher scores indicating "greater pain," and 10 indicating "pain as bad as you can imagine" (McDowell, 2006). Provisional benchmarks have been developed for evaluating the magnitude of changes in pain intensity (Dworkin et al., 2008). Reductions of 30–49% represent *moderate* improvement, and reductions of 50% or more represent *substantial* improvement. However, benchmarks that apply to changes in pain intensity won't necessarily apply to reductions in other problems.

Suppose that you had Mrs. Silva rate the degree of pain caused by her arthritis using the Faces Pain Scale—Revised (Hicks, von Baeyer, Spafford, van Korlaar, & Goodenough, 2001) (see http://painsourcebook.ca/docs/pps92.html

## Research-Based Practice

***Practice Behavior Example:*** *Use research evidence to inform practice*

**Critical Thinking Question:** What questions would you consider and what decisions would you make when constructing scales to measure and monitor the degree, magnitude, or intensity of each of Mrs. Silva's problems?

**M**ichael, Aaron, Elaine, and Mrs. Silva meet for the third time. The data seem to indicate that both Aaron and Elaine are feeling less worried about Mrs. Silva (Figures 10.1 and 10.2, days 8–14, respectively). They also are happy to see Mrs. Silva add a few comments to the Google document on her own, noting some social activities for the day (data not shown here). She enjoys doing this, saying it makes her feel quite modern and independent. Michael suggests that perhaps Aaron and Elaine can continue charting in the mornings after breakfast, whereas Mrs. Silva could enter the evening data. Moreover, they construct a new chart for Mrs. Silva. She will list her social engagements or any comments she has about her day, and a rating of the day, to be completed each evening. She prefers a 5-point scale, and she will rate her day from 1 (not a good day) to 3 (a satisfactory day) to 5 (a wonderful day). Mrs. Silva describes what these anchor points mean to her, as shown in Table 10.5.

**Table 10.5    Mrs. Silva's Ratings.**

| | Daily Well-Being |
|---|---|
| 1 | A lonely day where I don't get out of the apartment or have any nice telephone calls that I enjoy. I would feel kind of lonely. Fortunately, these days don't happen often! |
| 2 | |
| 3 | A day when I have at least one positive event; the day is just fine. |
| 4 | |
| 5 | A great day when I have a really nice time. I might have lunch with a good friend or see an exhibit at the museum or spend the day at our church's community garden. I would probably feel a little tired but very happy with my day. |

for a reproduction of this scale), and the goal is to reduce pain by 50%. If her mean baseline rating is 5 (pretreatment rating) and the mean rating for the last week of intervention is 2 (posttreatment rating), there is a reduction of 60%. So, the goal has been achieved and exceeded.

Use this formula to calculate percentage change:

$$100 \left[ \frac{\text{Posttreatment} - \text{Pretreatment}}{\text{Pretreatment}} \right] = \% \text{ Change}$$

In our example, degree of arthritis pain changed from an average of 5 during baseline to an average of 2 during the last week of intervention, a 60% reduction in pain:

$$100 \left[ \frac{2 - 5}{5} \right] = -60\%$$

# DECIDE WHERE, WHEN, HOW OFTEN, AND FROM WHOM TO COLLECT DATA

As we discussed in Chapter 8, a good measurement plan specifies how to obtain the measurement information (e.g., paper-and-pencil IRS form), who can best provide this information (e.g., the client), when (e.g., before going to sleep at night), where (e.g., at home), and how often (e.g., daily) this information should be collected. The considerations involved in making these decisions are no different than those discussed in Chapters 8 and 9. For example, you see those illustrated in Michael's attention to these details, as well as how he makes changes in the plan as his clients' circumstances warrant. In addition, you see Michael's use of new technology with Google Docs, which can be especially useful when several people are collecting data and need to be able to access and share the data easily. We expect technology to open up many such new alternatives for data collection in the near future.

# ENGAGING AND PREPARING THE CLIENT

Use the guidelines discussed in Chapter 8 to engage and prepare clients (or other informants) to use IRSs. This is as important as carefully constructing IRSs. For example, Michael discusses the IRS with each of the individuals in the client system, working with them to provide personalized anchors and being sure that all of them have the same understanding of how to complete the measures. He also will log in to Google in a session to actually create the document they will use, and all of them will practice completing the measure there. (Michael obviously would suggest another method of collecting data if his clients did not own and use computers or were not comfortable collecting the data this way.)

# ADVANTAGES AND PRECAUTIONS IN USING IRSs

As illustrated in the case example, IRSs are tailor-made for each client and situation as the need arises, to measure important problems along whatever dimension seems most appropriate. You can use IRSs with many of your clients, and IRSs have numerous advantages. Note that Michael uses the data collected using the IRS to guide the next step in the intervention, for example by having Mrs. Silva take over charting the data in the evenings. The collection of ongoing data is not "busy work"; it's Michael's guide to next steps in the intervention.

The first advantage of IRSs is that they allow considerable flexibility in the types of problems that can be measured. Therefore, they can be used with many different types of clients; this is an especially important consideration for social workers and other human service professionals who work with diverse client populations in many different settings.

**Engage, Assess, Intervene, Evaluate**

***Practice Behavior Example:*** *Assess client strengths and limitations*

**Critical Thinking Question:** What questions would you consider and what decisions would you make when determining how to obtain IRS data in Mrs. Silva's case, who can best provide this information, and when, where, and how often this information should be collected?

**A**t their fourth and final meeting, Mrs. Silva, Aaron, and Elaine agree that enormous progress has been made (Figures 10.1 and 10.2, days 15–21). Mrs. Silva has a better understanding of her son and niece's concerns about her and also finds that she likes recording her meals and medications herself. She has begun to do her own entries most of the time and to list her doctors' appointments and other events to help her remember, though her son and niece still call frequently. Aaron and Elaine are reassured that Mrs. Silva is competent to live alone safely and spend much less time worrying about her. They often leave her notes on Google Docs, and they often use the entries as taking-off points for chatting about her activities.

Second, IRSs can be used to measure the degree, magnitude, or intensity of problems, attributes that are important for many problems, such as feelings of worry, depression, guilt, or pain. Since IRSs are designed for each unique client, these attributes can be tied to the client's own perspectives.

Third, IRSs require little time to administer, score, and interpret; this makes them especially easy to administer repeatedly over time. In a way, they require little more than the systematic collection of information routinely collected in a less formal way in practice. The availability of an archive of information provides an excellent tool for discussions in intervention sessions, charting progress over time and placing progress in context.

Fourth, depending on the situation and type of problem, IRSs can be used to obtain information from the four perspectives discussed in Chapter 8: client, practitioner, relevant other, and independent evaluator.

Fifth, scores derived from IRSs are easy to understand and really don't require much if anything in the way of interpretation or special skills or training; however, as always, you work collaboratively with your clients to understand and interpret these ratings. Sixth, IRSs are free, unlike many standardized scales discussed in Chapter 9. Finally, there's good reason to believe that IRSs have good test–retest reliability, interobserver reliability, internal-consistency reliability, and different types of validity, including sensitivity to change (e.g., Arnold et al., 2003; Bachar, Canetti, Yonah, & Bonne, 2004; Busseri & Tyler, 2004; Buxton, Rodger, Cummings, & Leschied, 2006; Kaye, 2001; Kivlighan, Multon, & Patton, 2000; Schaefer, Koeter, Wouters, Emmelkamp, & Schene, 2003; Weisz et al., in press).

There are times when IRSs might not be the measure of choice. If your goal is to increase or decrease the frequency or duration of a behavior, such as excessive alcohol consumption, getting to appointments on time, exercising, or self-injurious thoughts and behaviors, use behavioral observation (Chapters 11 and 12). If the problem of interest is a construct with general relevance to different clients, or a construct that requires multiple indicators (i.e., items) to measure accurately, such as social functioning, and you want to compare your client to a normative group, use standardized scales (Chapter 9).

## CONCLUSIONS

Although we present many different options for collecting client data, there is no substitute for the kind of perspective you get from IRSs. If you are thoughtful about how you construct and use IRSs, and you combine these data with data from other sources (and thus with different strengths and weaknesses), these measures are invaluable tools for monitoring your client's progress.

**PRACTICE TEST** The following questions will test your knowledge of the content found within this chapter and help you prepare for the licensing exam by applying chapter content to practice. For more questions styled like the licensing exam, visit **MySocialWorkLab.com**

1. A rating is a
   a. Quantitative quality or property of a person, object, or event
   b. Brief explicit label, description, or example
   c. Point on a rating scale that represents the degree, magnitude, or intensity of a problem
   d. Systematic estimation of some characteristic of a person, object, or event along some dimension using a numerical scale that results in a numerical score

2. Ideally, a rating scale should have which of the following characteristics:
   a. 9 to 13 response categories
   b. Generic anchors
   c. Clear, precise, and explicit anchors
   d. Unequal intervals between response categories

3. If a client's pretreatment rating is 8 and his posttreatment rating is 4, his percentage change is:
   a. 50
   b. −50
   c. −25
   d. 100

4. An advantage of IRSs is that they can be used to
   a. Measure the degree, magnitude, or intensity of problems
   b. Compare your client to a normative group
   c. Measure an increase or decrease in the frequency or duration of a behavior
   d. Measure complex constructs

5. A social worker in a residential treatment center for emotionally disturbed adolescent boys is working with Bob and other adolescent boys in a conflict–resolution group. Develop an IRS for Bob.

6. A social worker is working with Bob, the client described in question 5, and decides to use an IRS to measure and monitor Bob's ability to resolve conflicts. Discuss how to obtain the measurement information, who can best provide this information, and when, where, and how often this information should be collected.

## SUCCEED WITH

Visit **MySocialWorkLab** for more licensing exam test questions, and to access case studies, videos, and much more.

# 11

# Behavioral Observation

| Advancing Core Competencies in This Chapter | | | | |
|---|---|---|---|---|
| ■ Professional Identity | ■ Ethical Practice | ✖ Critical Thinking | ✖ Diversity in Practice | ■ Human Rights & Justice |
| ✖ Research-Based Practice | ■ Human Behavior | ■ Policy Practice | ✖ Practice Contexts | ✖ Engage, Assess, Intervene, Evaluate |

Juan Moreno is a 33-year-old single father of 4-year-old Chico. He meets with social worker Clara Soto because recently Chico bit another child at Head Start. Chico has other problems at school: not paying attention to his teachers, disrupting class, and bothering other children by grabbing toys, teasing, and being overly physical. This is the first biting incident, and Chico has not been aggressive in other ways.

The first session is a meeting of Mr. Moreno, Clara, Chico's two classroom teachers, and the teacher's aide. Clara explains that the purpose of the session is to discuss Chico's problems and to try to help him change his behaviors in the classroom and with the other children. They believe that the biting was a one-time case of extreme frustration and hope that dealing with Chico's other problem behaviors will reduce the probability of repeating this more serious problem.

The group first operationalizes Chico's targeted disruptive behaviors. After much discussion, the teachers agree on the following problem behaviors:

- Talking to, tapping, or poking other children when they are supposed to be engaged in directed activities
- Speaking out in class without raising his hand
- Leaving his seat to wander the classroom when he is supposed to be engaged in directed activities

The teachers provide wildly disparate estimates of the frequencies of these behaviors, so Clara suggests a week of baseline data collection. She works with the teachers to construct a form to record these problem behaviors. Graciela, the teacher's aide, will observe Chico for 30 minutes each day in four contexts (free play, different directed activities, lunch, and story time). Clara spends some extra time with Graciela operationalizing each of the target behaviors to ensure the reliability and validity of the data.

Our favorite philosopher, Yogi Berra, allegedly once opined that "you can observe a lot just by watching." This chapter will teach you how to do that: to observe and record behaviors using direct observation by practitioners, relevant others, or independent observers. The next chapter will add to this knowledge by discussing how to use self-monitoring with your clients. In both chapters, we discuss dimensions along which behavior can be measured, the collection of contextual information, and when and where to observe behavior. We also discuss practical methods for recording behavior and for ensuring and confirming the reliability and validity of observations.

Behavior refers to what people *do* (e.g., expressions of criticism and contempt), in contrast to what people *have* (e.g., depression). It includes how people move and what they say, think, and feel (Cooper et al., 2007; Friman, 2009; Yoder & Symons, 2010).

The range of behaviors practitioners attempt to change is immense (e.g., Luyben, 2009), for example, creating and following a schedule; giving constructive feedback; bullying, fighting, and other forms of physical aggression; exercising; binge eating and purging; cigarette smoking; and driving while intoxicated. Others include expressions of warmth or empathy; enuresis; migraine headaches; asthma attacks; self-injurious thoughts and behaviors; panic attacks; problematic avoidance of situations; difficulty sleeping or sleeping too much; expressions of criticism, contempt, and praise; truancy; homework completion; property destruction; theft; excessive alcohol consumption; and illegal drug use.

Many practitioners also deal with spousal, sexual, or animal abuse, and other forms of violence. In addition, in many contexts, compliance with interventions is an important issue; compliance behaviors include medication adherence, compliance with a diabetes regimen, adherence to an exercise program, attendance at AA (Alcoholics Anonymous) meetings, and attendance at parenting classes mandated for parents with children in foster care, to name just a few examples.

Behavior includes overt events—events that can be observed by others (at least theoretically)—such as amount of time a client spends with his or her spouse or children; number of times a client has sexual intercourse; number of completed intervention tasks; amount of time nursing home residents spend interacting with one another; number of times a parent compliments his or her child; or number of office, home, or telephone contacts with clients. It also includes covert events—events that occur within the individual and therefore cannot be observed directly by others—such as number of suicidal, self-deprecating, or intrusive thoughts; nightmares; feeling anxious, under stress, or overwhelmed; craving of alcohol or drugs; or ruminating about concerns.

People can observe their own behavior whether it's overt or covert. When a person systematically observes and records his or her own behavior (or, as we will discuss in

**Engage, Assess, Intervene, Evaluate**

***Practice Behavior Example:*** *Collect, organize, and interpret client data*

**Critical Thinking Question:** What questions would you consider and what decisions would you make when identifying and defining Chico's behavioral problems, goals, and objectives?

Chapter 12, other experiences), it's called *self-monitoring*. Outside observers (e.g., independent observers, relevant others, practitioners) can only observe overt behaviors directly; this is called *direct observation*, the subject of this chapter. Many principles and practices of behavioral observation apply to both direct observation and self-monitoring, but some don't, and we'll draw distinctions between these two methods where applicable.

Behavioral observation ideally is conducted in real time (as the behavior is occurring), not retrospectively (e.g., at the end of a day), in order to avoid recall biases. We may believe we can remember every instance of anger or inappropriate behavior to write down later, but this is not likely, especially given the need for accuracy if we are to monitor progress closely. Behavioral observation ideally occurs in the natural environment, not under contrived circumstances, so the observations will apply to the real-life environment of the client. In addition, they ideally are made repeatedly over time to examine the flow of behavior and conditions influencing behavior. Exceptions to these ideals are necessary for practical reasons, and we will have more to say about these circumstances later.

## PURPOSES

Behavioral observation can be used for different purposes: First, it can help pinpoint and define behaviors targeted for intervention. Second, it can provide a way to explore and clarify the dynamic contexts in which targeted behaviors occur; this can help you and the client generate working hypotheses about the mechanisms causing and maintaining targeted behaviors, and develop interventions based on these hypotheses. Finally, and the main focus of this chapter, it can be used to monitor client progress on targeted behaviors and provide guidance for intervention planning. In other words, it provides important practice-based evidence that you can use in concert with evidence-based practice to improve outcomes for your clients.

The group convenes for the second time to go over the baseline data recorded by Graciela (see Figure 11.1).

Immediately the group notices that Chico's problems are most apparent during times when the class is engaged in specific directed activities such as work sheets and art projects and during lunch. There are no infractions during free play (Graciela says he tends to engage appropriately and happily with other children) and few during story time (Graciela reports that Chico is usually engrossed in the story). Clara notes that Chico is only 4 years old and hypothesizes that his normal short attention span may make it difficult for him to stay with directed activities, including lunch, whereas free play and stories hold his attention well. Graciela states that Chico's behavior is consistent with Clara's point; Chico's behavior at lunch and in directed activities is fine for a while, but deteriorates with time. Moreover, Graciela also notes that her observations demonstrate to her that other children (especially boys) have similar issues. Chico's usual behavior

**Figure 11.1** • Form for Recording Chico's Problematic Target Behaviors.

| Class activity | Date/time | Tap, poke, talk | Talk out of turn | Wander |
|---|---|---|---|---|
| Directed activities | Monday | √√√ | √√√ | √√ |
| | Tuesday | √√√ | | √ |
| | Wednesday | √√ | √√ | √√ |
| | Thursday | √√√√ | √√√ | √√ |
| | Friday | √√ | √√√ | √ |
| Free play | Monday | | | |
| | Tuesday | | | |
| | Wednesday | | | |
| | Thursday | | | |
| | Friday | | | |
| Lunch | Monday | √√√ | | √√ |
| | Tuesday | √√√√ | | √√ |
| | Wednesday | √√ | | √√ |
| | Thursday | √√√√√√ | | √ |
| | Friday | √ | | √√√ |
| Story time | Monday | √ | | |
| | Tuesday | | | |
| | Wednesday | √ | | |
| | Thursday | | √ | |
| | Friday | √ | | |

is not that far off the behavior of his peers who are functioning normally.

Clara suggests a minimal intervention based on differential reinforcement of other behaviors, a relatively unintrusive intervention that is shown by research to be effective in preschool settings (Cooper et al., 2007). Chico's appropriate behaviors (staying in his seat, working on task, raising his hand to speak, etc.) will receive positive reinforcement. (Positive reinforcement is any consequence of a behavior that results in a subsequent increase in the behavior.) Inappropriate behaviors will be ignored as much as possible, and those behaviors should decrease.

Graciela, who normally circulates throughout the classroom, will observe Chico again this week, 30 minutes each in only the two troubling situations. When he is on task and behaving appropriately, she will praise Chico with a pat or short comment such as "I like how you're staying in your seat, Chico." Selection of the reinforcer is not difficult; most children like to be praised, and Chico is no exception.

They will observe the outcomes of these actions to determine if more intense intervention is needed.

# DECIDING WHAT DIMENSIONS OF BEHAVIOR TO MEASURE

Suppose you are buying a new desk for your small home office. What would you want to know about the dimensions of the desk? You probably would want to know its height, length, and width. How would you quantify these dimensions? You probably would use inches, or feet and inches. Or, if you were almost anywhere else in the world other than the United States, you probably would use units of measurement based on the International System of Units, the modern form of the metric system. In any case, you would use certain standardized units of measurement to quantify different dimensions of the desk. Using a standardized system ensures that when you get your new desk home, it will fit just right in the space where you want it.

Typically, behavior is quantified along two primary dimensions. First, you can measure the number of times a behavior occurs: a count. Second, you can measure how long a behavior lasts: its duration.

## Counts

A *count* is simply the number of times a behavior occurs within some time period, for example an hour or day, irrespective of the duration of the behavior. Counts are used when a behavior occurs too frequently and needs to be decreased (e.g., binge eating or interrupting others), or doesn't occur often enough and needs to be increased (e.g., getting to appointments on time or praising a child for appropriate behavior). If the intervention goal is to change the frequency of a behavior, count the number of times it occurs. For example, Clara and Chico's teachers want to reduce the frequency of his disruptive behaviors.

A count requires an observed behavior to have two characteristics: First, it should have a clear beginning and ending so separate occurrences of the behavior can be distinguished. For example, it might be difficult to accurately observe the number of times Chico is cranky since a clear beginning and ending of the behavior would be hard to identify. Second, the length of time each behavior occurs should be about the same each time it occurs so the units counted are roughly equal. If you are targeting a behavior that lasts 2 minutes one time and 30 minutes the next time, a count probably won't tell you what you need to know.

Once the behavior is clearly defined, the observer records how many times the behavior occurs (see Figure 11.2). A period of time is designated in advance. If the behavior occurs frequently, the time period would be shorter, whereas longer observation periods are necessary for infrequently occurring behaviors to be sure you have an accurate picture of their occurrence. At the end of each observation period or at the end of the day, you tally the total occurrences of the behavior.

Counts can be expressed as rates. A rate is a count per unit of time, such as a minute, hour, or day. If the length of the observation period is the same each time, and this is preferable if practical, use a count and report the length of the observation time. If the observation time varies from session to session, use rates. Otherwise, observed changes over time might be due to changes in the opportunity for the behavior to occur. You'll also have difficulty interpreting any changes you see.

**Figure 11.2** • Sample Form for Recording Frequency of Occurrence of Behavior.

| Observer: | | Client: | |
|---|---|---|---|
| Behaviors: | | Time period (hours/day): | |
| Date | Number of times behavior occurred | | Additional comments |
| | | | |
| | | | |
| | | | |
| | | | |
| | | | |
| | | | |
| | | | |
| | | | |
| | | | |
| | | | |

Rates are computed by dividing the number of times a behavior occurs by the observation time; that is, rates are proportions. For example, if Graciela observes Chico at lunch for 10 minutes and observes three inappropriate behaviors, the rate of occurrence per minute would be 3/10, or .33. You also could multiply .33 by 60, the number of minutes in an hour, to get the rate per hour, which would be 19.8, although you need to be careful about how you interpret this number. (That is, you might not observe this rate if you actually observe Chico for a full hour.)

A count also can be expressed as a percentage of the time it occurs in response to an event or stimulus. For example, Graciela might record each instance of Chico's wandering from his seat during instructions for a task. However, percentages based on fewer than 30 response opportunities can be misleading because they can be unduly affected by small changes in behavior—in the same way that getting an additional question correct on a 10-item quiz is different than on a 100-item test, for example (Cooper et al., 2007).

## Duration

For some behaviors, the major concern is that the behavior lasts too long or not long enough. In this case, measure the duration of the behavior. For example, a father and mother might record the amount of time they spend reading to their children; spouses might record the amount of enjoyable time they spend together; a client with a sleep disorder might record the number of hours per day he or she sleeps; or a parent might record the amount of time per day a child spends crying. Graciela might record the duration of time that Chico is appropriately on task while completing his work sheets. This would provide the inverse of

In the third session, Graciela reports that Chico seems to be responding well to the differential reinforcement, and the data seem to support her hypothesis (completed data form not shown). Figure 11.3 shows the data chart in which we added up the number of different problematic behaviors in the interest of saving space. (You also might want to construct separate graphs for each of the four problematic behaviors.) Note the comparison between baseline (A) and the first week of intervention (B). Although there is still some misbehavior and variability in the data, the frequencies of all problem behaviors are less than you would expect from baseline. (Note that in this figure we excluded infractions that occurred during free play and story time from the baseline count.)

**Figure 11.3** • Number of Chico's Problematic Target Behaviors During Baseline (A), Differential Reinforcement of Other Behaviors (B), and Token Economy Conditions (C).

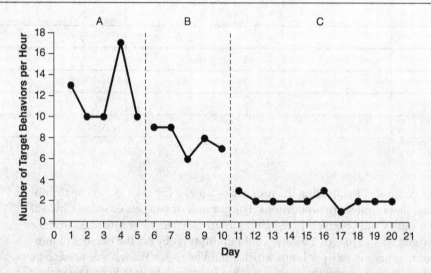

Clara asks Graciela to describe her experiences with Chico this week. Graciela reports that it is difficult to reinforce Chico's positive behavior during directed class activities because it is distracting to Chico and the children around him. He appears to like the positive attention, but sometimes he has difficulty returning his attention to the task.

How can Graciela reinforce Chico during directed activities without disrupting class activities and distracting Chico? They discuss a number of possibilities and decide to switch to a token economy (Cooper et al., 2007) during both lunch and directed activities. A *token economy* is a behavior change system with three components: a specific list of target behaviors, tokens or points that an individual earns for performing those behaviors, and backup reinforcer items for

which the individual may exchange his or her tokens. Graciela will still be offering positive reinforcement to increase Chico's appropriate behaviors, hoping to reduce the inappropriate ones, but the intervention should be less intrusive.

Graciela will explain to Chico that she will watch him during class sometimes and if he is staying in his seat and doing what he has been asked to do, she will place a star on a chart. She will hang the chart by his cubby hole where he can check it whenever he wants. Chico will earn a reward (a selection from the class surprise box used for rewards) when he accumulates 20 stars. Graciela also will show him his chart after each observation period, during breaks from class activities, and praise his performance to provide immediate positive reinforcement.

information about his time off task, but it might be less helpful in this case for suggesting appropriate interventions. That is, it may be easier to target specific off-task behaviors to reduce than to come up with specific ways to increase on-task behavior.

Duration is simple to measure, though it does require time. The observer just records the time the behavior begins and ends (see Figure 11.4). Stopwatches or runners' chronographs are useful and practical because they're relatively precise, but a wristwatch will do.

If observation periods are equal in length, and this is preferable if practical, duration can be expressed in terms of amount of time a behavior lasts and the observation time noted. When observation periods are not equal, duration should be expressed as the proportion or percentage of time a behavior occurs during an observation period. This is similar to a rate for counts. For example, a teacher's aide might observe Chico for 1 hour one day and 30 minutes the next. The aide records that Chico plays happily with other children without incident for 40 minutes the first day and 20 minutes the second. The time in play per hour is the same both days ([40/60] × 60 = 40 minutes per hour and [20/30] × 60 = 40 minutes per hour).

Measuring the number of times a behavior occurs or the length of time it occurs requires that the beginning and ending of the behavior be defined clearly. For example, imagine trying to record the duration of a tantrum in which a child cries continuously for several minutes, whimpers for short periods, stops all noise for a few seconds, and begins intense crying again.

---

**Figure 11.4** • Form for Recording Duration of Behavior.

---

| Observer: | | Client: | |
|---|---|---|---|
| **Behaviors:** | | **Time period (hours/day):** | |
| **Date** | **Length of time behavior occurred (e.g., minutes)** | **Total time (e.g., minutes)** | **Additional comments** |
| | | | |
| | | | |
| | | | |
| | | | |
| | | | |
| | | | |
| | | | |
| | | | |
| | | | |
| | | | |
| | | | |
| | | | |

## Additional Dimensions of Behavior

Sometimes it's useful to measure how long it takes for a behavior to occur in relation to a stimulus, such as the amount of elapsed time between the teacher's telling Chico to return to his seat and when he sits. This dimension of behavior is referred to as *response latency*, or just *latency*. Latency is useful when the goal is to increase or decrease the amount of time between the opportunity for a behavior to occur and the occurrence of the behavior.

In other circumstances, it can be useful to measure the amount of elapsed time between occurrences of two successive instances of a behavior, such as the time between completing two tasks or between two thoughts. This is known as *interresponse time* and it's useful when the goal is to increase or decrease the amount of time between instances of the same behavior. (Increasing interresponse time also reduces the number of such behaviors, of course, so a person might gradually stop smoking by increasing the interresponse time between cigarettes.)

When you measure latency or interresponse time, compute the average time, that is the mean or median, for an episode of behavior. For example, suppose the goal is to reduce the amount of time Chico takes to move from one activity in class to another. This often happens when the teacher moves the class from one activity to the other. On the first day, there are five transitions from one activity to the next, and Chico takes 5, 10, 3, 5, and 2 minutes, respectively, to join the class. Average latency for that day is computed by adding these times together and dividing by number of episodes of behavior, in this case the number of transitions (i.e., $5 + 10 + 3 + 5 + 2 = 25/5 = 5$ minutes).

Finally, behavior can be measured in terms of magnitude, strength, intensity, or force (Cooper et al., 2007). Sometimes magnitude is evaluated by psychophysiological devices (Friman, 2009), many of which are not practical for most practitioners. However, individualized rating scales (Chapter 10) are also a practical way to measure magnitude.

# BEHAVIOR PRODUCTS

*Behavior products* refer to the effects or results of behaviors, not the behaviors themselves. That is, rather than monitoring behavior in real time, you measure a temporary or permanent effect of the behavior after it occurs.

A number of behaviors can be measured by changes they make in the environment. For example, the number of cigarette butts in an ashtray indicates the number of cigarettes smoked. The number of uncovered electrical outlets, accessible medicines, and dangerous cleaning products indicates home safety risks for toddlers. Results of a urine toxicology analysis for drug abuse indicate drug abuse. Results of a pregnancy test indicate—well, you know.

---

In session 4, it is clear that Chico's behavior is much improved (see days 11 to 15 on Figure 11.3), and the teachers even state that an outside observer would probably consider his behavior to be as good or better than that of the average boy in the class. Does this mean that the token economy intervention is the cause of Chico's behavior change? Not necessarily. The group discusses other possible explanations: Have there been any changes at home? Changes in classroom activities? No obvious alternative explanations emerge. They decide to continue the intervention as is for another week to be sure that Chico's behavior is stable.

For example, Chico has had difficulty completing work at school due to his disruptive behaviors, including daily art projects, short work sheets, and other activities. These are sent home each day with a list of activities assigned, so Mr. Moreno could use them to monitor Chico's completion of activities, testing the hypothesis that improvements in his behavior will correlate with improvements in his academic performance.

There are advantages to using behavior products. First, a product lends itself to precise quantification; for example, you can tell exactly how many cigarettes your client smokes by counting cigarette butts left in an ashtray (at least in that location). Second, the observer doesn't have to be present when a behavior is performed. For example, instead of watching a child litter his or her room, the observer can count how many articles weren't put away after the play period. Third, using behavior products generally doesn't interrupt the flow of behavior. For example, even when the client is recording, he or she can carry out daily activities in an uninterrupted fashion, recording the information only at certain predefined times, such as before going to bed. Finally, behavior products are relatively easy to record.

Behavior products have some potential problems, too. First, information is generally limited to "how many" or "how much," and controlling conditions cannot be evaluated easily. Second, many important behaviors, such as feelings and thoughts, don't leave products. Third, you have to be sure that the product really is a direct product of the behavior of concern, and not the result of other factors. For example, just because Chico doesn't finish his finger painting doesn't mean he was being disruptive; perhaps the little girl next to him took his paints. Finally, some behavior products may not be sensitive to changes in actual behavior, so these changes may not be noticed when only behavioral products are monitored.

# DECIDING WHETHER TO COLLECT CONTEXTUAL INFORMATION

Sometimes the conditions controlling or maintaining a targeted behavior are not clear. For example, while working with an aggressive adolescent, you might want to know when and where the aggressive behavior occurs and what follows it (Feindler & Gerber, 2008). Contextual information can help you and the client generate working practice hypotheses about the environmental factors that cause and maintain targeted behaviors, and it can help you develop interventions based on these hypotheses. For example, Graciela's observations demonstrating that Chico behaved appropriately during free play and story time allowed Clara to hypothesize about specific challenging situations for Chico. If Chico continues to be disruptive at preschool at inconsistent times, we may want to collect data on and pay special attention to whether there are certain circumstances that appear to be related to that disruptive behavior. Perhaps it occurs when bad weather prevents getting outside to burn off physical energy, or when the music teacher is there (we might want to look at this teacher's disciplinary skills), or even right after a sugary snack.

We will have more to say about this in Chapter 12. Figures 11.5 and 11.6 are examples of forms you can use for collecting contextual information.

## Research-Based Practice

***Practice Behavior Example:*** *Use research evidence to inform practice*

**Critical Thinking Question:** What questions would you consider and what decisions would you make when determining how to measure and monitor Chico's behavior using direct observation?

**Figure 11.5** • Form for Recording Behaviors, Antecedents, and Consequences.

| Observer: | | Client: | |
|---|---|---|---|
| Behavior to be observed: | | | |
| Date/time/location | What happened before | Behavior | What happened after |
| | | | |
| | | | |
| | | | |
| | | | |
| | | | |
| | | | |
| | | | |
| | | | |
| | | | |
| | | | |
| | | | |

**Figure 11.6** • Form for Recording Behaviors, Antecedents, Consequences, Settings, and Activities.

| Observer: | | | Client: | | | |
|---|---|---|---|---|---|---|
| Behavior to be observed: | | | | | | |
| Date/time | Setting | Activity | Antecedent | Behavior | Consequence | Comments |
| | | | | | | |
| | | | | | | |
| | | | | | | |
| | | | | | | |
| | | | | | | |
| | | | | | | |
| | | | | | | |
| | | | | | | |
| | | | | | | |
| | | | | | | |
| | | | | | | |
| | | | | | | |

# DECIDING WHEN AND WHERE TO OBSERVE BEHAVIOR

Sometimes it isn't practical to observe a behavior each time it occurs. This is especially true with direct observation, but it also can be a problem with self-monitoring. An observer might not be available or willing to make direct observations. Or, the behavior might occur so frequently (e.g., tic behaviors) or over such a long period of time (e.g., being sedentary) that it would be difficult to record every occurrence.

When it's not possible to observe each occasion of a behavior, sampling can be used to estimate frequency, duration, or other dimensions of a behavior. Accuracy of these estimates depends on the representativeness of the samples, that is, how similar the sampled observations are to observations made at other times and under different circumstances.

## Time Samples

*Time sampling* is observing behavior during certain selected fixed or random times believed to be representative of the behavior (Cooper et al., 2007). It is useful when the target occurs so frequently that it is not possible to record all occasions or when the observer is available only during selected periods. In the beginning, when Chico is extremely disruptive at school, for example, we may be able to get a good picture of his behavior with short morning and afternoon samples only.

If the behavior occurs often and regularly, you need fewer periods during the day to be reasonably certain that observations are representative. Of course, if the target occurs in more than one situation, for example during both recess and during directed activities, it's important to include all those situations in the sampled time periods.

## Situation Samples

*Situation sampling* typically involves observing behavior only in situations where it's likely to occur. For example, it would be inefficient for a client to record how much time he spends with his children at his workplace, unless he works at home. You also wouldn't try to observe how a child interacts with classmates at home unless they visit her at home. A key challenge in situation sampling is to include all situations in which the behavior is likely to occur. If you don't, the sample may provide a distorted picture of behavior. Chico's case illustrates how observing in different situations can alert us to those on which we need to focus. Graciela saves time and labor by abandoning monitoring Chico during free play and story time, because it is clear that his behavior is appropriate in those situations.

---

**D**ata for the fourth week of observation (see days 16 to 20 on Figure 11.3) again show a stable pattern of appropriate behavior for Chico, and everyone agrees that it is time to gradually wean Chico from the token economy. This will be done over several weeks as Chico is reinforced more by social praise and less by tokens (stars) and backup reinforcers (prizes from the surprise box). Graciela will continue to observe Chico, reducing the schedule eventually to 1 day per week and then none as it is clear that Chico's behavior is stable.

## Analogue Situations

Ideally, behavior should be observed in the environment where it naturally occurs, that is where you want behavior change to occur. Sometimes this isn't practical, though, especially with direct observation. In these situations, consider using *analogue* situations.

Analogue situations are contrived circumstances designed to elicit a sample of behavior that is representative of behavior that occurs in the natural environment (Gold & Marx, 2006; Rosqvist et al., 2006). Behaviors are observed in a simulated situation designed to approximate the real-life situation. For example, you might observe parents and children playing together in home-like play rooms with comfortable chairs and a variety of available toys. This type of analogue situation provides a relatively natural setting to observe parent-child interaction.

There are several other types of analogues: paper-and-pencil, audiotape/videotape (not described here because we don't think you'll have occasion to use it in practice), role-playing, and enactment (Gold, & Marx, 2006; Rosqvist et al., 2006). Clients are asked to respond to these analogues as they ordinarily would in the natural environment. A basic assumption underlying the use of analogue situations is that the closer the analogue situation resembles the natural environment, the more likely the behavior is to be representative of the natural environment.

With paper-and-pencil analogues, a client responds orally or in writing to a situation presented in written form. For example, Rhodes et al. (2006) developed vignettes designed to assess foster parent applicants' skills for managing the unique challenges of fostering. Foster parents were asked what they would do if faced with each of a set of common foster parenting dilemmas, and then trained raters rated the appropriateness of the responses.

In a role-playing analogue, clients visualize situations in the natural environment and their responses, or act out situations with the practitioner or others (e.g., in group therapy) role-playing relevant people. For example, Van Camp et al. (2008) presented foster parents with nine role-play situations, one for each parenting skill taught in their intervention. The practitioner introduced each situation and acted out the role of the child. Then, the percentage of steps performed correctly by foster parents was measured.

In the enactment analogue, the client interacts in the agency or clinical setting with people he or she has difficulty interacting with in the natural environment. For example, husbands and wives are asked to discuss problems of their own choosing, such as finances, children, household tasks, or sexual intimacy, and different dimensions of their communication behavior are observed, for example expressions of criticism and contempt, as well as appreciation or respect. (Snyder et al., 2008, summarize observational methods in this area.)

Analogues sound appealing. The problem is that behaviors elicited in analogue situations may or may not predict behaviors in the natural environment and, in fact, the research in this area is somewhat mixed, if not discouraging (Gold & Marx, 2006; Rosqvist et al., 2006). Therefore, when you use analogues, it's a good idea whenever possible to collect information concerning concurrent validity of those data. This might involve having the client, a relevant other, or even an independent observer make periodic observations in the natural environment. In some cases, you might be able to use collateral information to verify the data from an analogue.

### Research-Based Practice

***Practice Behavior Example:*** *Use research evidence to inform practice*

**Critical Thinking Question:** What questions would you consider and what decisions would you make when determining how to observe Chico's behavior, who can best observe Chico's behavior, and when, where, and how often Chico's behavior should be observed?

# USING PRACTICAL INSTRUMENTS FOR RECORDING OBSERVATIONS

Practicality is essential with any measure for recording client behaviors. The instruments should be as easy as possible for the observer to use. Keep it simple.

## Principles for Selecting Instruments

Selection depends on the nature of the behavior, the capabilities and motivation of the observer, and the complexity of the situation. Consider these questions when choosing instruments:

- Is the method portable enough to be used easily where the behavior occurs? (Many times, a small 3" × 5" card will suffice, rather than a clipboard or pad of paper.)
- Is the method unobtrusive enough that it won't be distracting or embarrassing to those whose behavior is being recorded? Chico may be distracted from his school-work or embarrassed in front of his peers if the teacher's aide follows him around with a stopwatch and a notebook, making notations every time he does something. On the other hand, the students may be accustomed to her clipboard and pencil.
- Is the method *likely* to be used? No recording method is of much value if it won't be used.
- Is the method pleasant or enjoyable to use? It's worth the time to sit down with the observer and come up with imaginative or pleasant ways of recording data.

## Some Instruments for Your Use

Figures 11.1, 11.2, 11.4, 11.5, and 11.6 illustrate simple forms for recording behavioral observations. Chapter 12 illustrates additional forms for self-monitoring. However, sometimes it isn't practical to record observations directly on forms. Imagine having a client use one of these at work to self-monitor. There are less obtrusive, but simple and effective instruments for these situations. Each has been used successfully to record behaviors. Most focus on counting behavior. If you record duration, you'll also need a timepiece.

- Pedometers can be used to measure activity levels.
- Coins or poker chips can be moved from one pocket to another or from one compartment in a purse to another every time a specified behavior occurs. Golf score counters also can be used to count behaviors.
- Knitting stitch counters can be used to count behaviors.
- Small cards kept in a pocket or purse can be used to record observations.
- Mr. Moreno might put a penny in a saucer every time Chico does as he's told the first time at home. Both father and child could monitor the saucer frequently as a reminder of how well Chico is doing.

As you can see, you're limited in your use of recording devices only by your imagination; most instruments are accessible, inexpensive, and easy to use. In addition to the simple instruments described earlier, there also is an increasing array of powerful computer technology available for direct observation and analysis of behavior. Typically, this technology includes a specially designed hand-held keyboard or a small laptop computer

**S**ometimes a standardized list of behaviors is used to record whether a behavior occurred during a certain time period. The Parent Daily Report (PDR) Checklist (Chamberlain et al., 2006; Chamberlain & Reid, 1987), which is reproduced in Appendix A, is an excellent example of a widely used checklist of this kind. The PDR is a 30-item checklist of child behavior problems as reported by parents, typically during a brief telephone interview. At each assessment, parents are asked to report on the occurrence or nonoccurrence (not the frequency) of 30 specific behaviors within the past 24 hours. The PDR was developed as an inexpensive, easy-to-administer, and relatively unobtrusive alternative to direct behavioral observation by outside observers, at the same time avoiding the need for aggregate recall over a number of days. It also does not require estimates of the frequency with which specific behaviors occur (Chamberlain & Reid, 1987).

and the observer simply presses different keys to record observations of different behaviors. Time of the behavior is usually recorded automatically, making it possible to examine the sequence of events, and often it's also possible to record duration and frequency of the same behavior. The raw observational data can be printed or transferred to a personal computer to be charted and analyzed (e.g., MOOSES™ [Multi-Option Observation System for Experimental Studies] software program described at http://mooses.vueinnovations.com/; and Behavioral Assessment System for Children, Portable Observation Program [BASC-2, POP] described at http://www.pearsonpsychcorp.com.au/home).

We suspect that smartphones such as the BlackBerry and iPhone and similar devices such as the iTouch and iPad will be used increasingly for behavioral observation. Google *behavioral observation* and *smartphone* to see what's new.

# ENSURING AND VERIFYING THE ACCURACY OF OBSERVATIONS

As with any measurement method, there are a number of ways that the reliability and validity of behavioral observations can be enhanced or compromised (e.g., Baer, Harrison, Fradenburg, Petersen, & Milla, 2005; Yoder & Symons, 2010). The definition of the behavior might be vague, incomplete, or too complex. The behavior might be difficult to observe because of problems or distractions in the observational situation. A client's behavior might change as a result of self-monitoring or being observed by someone else. The observer might be biased, perhaps expecting certain behaviors from the person being observed because of assumptions regarding how he or she "should" behave; this is especially likely when observers are asked to make global or subjective evaluations of behavior. The instruments for collecting data might be cumbersome or poorly designed. The observer might unintentionally change how he or she measures a behavior due, for example, to changes in how he or she interprets the original definitions of the behavior; this situation is known as *observer drift*, a form of instrumentation error.

When the reliability or validity of your observations is compromised, it's difficult to know whether any recorded change in behavior results from genuine change. The following guidelines will help you maximize the reliability and validity of behavioral observations.

# Maximizing Reliability and Validity of Observations

There's no fool-proof method for ensuring reliability and validity, but the following strategies will go a long way toward maximizing both (Baer et al., 2005; Cooper et al., 2007; Kennedy, 2005; Yoder & Symons, 2010):

- Define target behaviors clearly and specifically. Think about each target in terms of who is doing what, to what extent, and under what conditions. Make sure observers understand what behaviors to record and how to recognize them when they occur. Provide examples and nonexamples of the target behaviors. For example, is Chico "leaving his seat" when he scoots his chair over by another student's? Is he distracting another student from work if the other student initiates an interaction? Extensive discussion and practice can avoid errors.
- Select representative times and situations if samples are used, and see that the behavior is recorded immediately after its occurrence—delays can lead to incomplete or distorted data. For example, you might avoid recording instances of Chico's leaving his seat while there is a guest clown from the circus in the classroom and all of the children are having trouble staying seated.
- Train and retrain observers. Make sure observers know whose behavior to record, how to record it, and when and where to record it. Select recording instruments that are practical and easy to use, and familiarize observers with instruments before they start using them. Role-play or practice making observations until the observer is comfortable and accurate. Use one or two trial observation sessions and then discuss them and make necessary revisions. Give observers continued training, especially if the intervention is a long one, to avoid drift in understanding what should be observed.
- Monitor observers. Make sure observers don't become fatigued. Be encouraging and supportive, and offer a good deal of praise for recording efforts. Check data as soon as possible after they are recorded, and correct problems as soon as possible. Conduct unannounced reliability checks on a random basis, if possible; such checks increase the reliability of observations by making observers more vigilant. For instance, it might be useful for one of the classroom teachers to be trained and to record Chico's behaviors along with Graciela occasionally to check interobserver reliability (see next section).
- Make observers as inconspicuous as possible to minimize reactivity. A familiar teacher's aide is a less disruptive observer of Chico than a nurse in a white coat, for example.
- Don't inform relevant others or independent observers of expected changes in clients' behavior, if possible. This precaution will minimize the chances that observations will be distorted because of observers' expectations about change.

# Reliability

Check the interobserver reliability of publicly observable behaviors, if practical. The procedure for calculating reliability depends on whether you are measuring counts or duration (for other methods, see Cooper et al., 2007; Stemler & Tsai, 2008; Yoder & Symons, 2010).

## Counts

Observers should independently record observations during the same time period. Then, calculate percentage of agreement in the number of behaviors recorded. If both observers record the same number of behaviors, interobserver reliability is 100%. If one observer records more than the other, divide the smaller number by the larger and multiply by 100.

Suppose the teacher records 10 occurrences of Chico's disruptive behavior and Graciela records 12. Divide 10 by 12 and multiply by 100 ([10/12] × 100 = 83%). (Sometimes you might see reliability reported as .83, which means results weren't multiplied by 100.) As discussed in Chapter 8, interobserver reliability of 80% or greater agreement is good.

There's a potential problem with this method, though. The 83% means that the two observers agree on total frequency, not that they necessarily agree 83% of the time on the same behaviors. It may be that one observer recorded 12 occurrences of the behavior and the other observer recorded 10 entirely different occurrences. Thus, the reliability figure should be interpreted cautiously because the two observers might not be observing the same behaviors. However, this problem can be minimized by carefully using the strategies discussed earlier for maximizing reliability and validity of observations.

### Duration

Interobserver reliability is computed for duration in almost the same way as for counts. The smaller duration is divided by the larger duration, and the result is multiplied by 100. Suppose the first observer observed that Chico played cooperatively with his fellow students without incident for 20 minutes and the second observer for 25 minutes. Divide 20 by 25 and multiply by 100 ([20/25] × 100 = 80%). As with counts, interpret this type of reliability estimate cautiously, because even with high agreement you cannot be absolutely certain that the same behaviors were being observed. However, as with counts, this problem can be overcome by clear definitions of behaviors.

## Validity

You can use the methods in Chapter 8 to verify the validity of behavioral observations by comparing the observations to some standard (i.e., criterion validity) or to other measured variables (i.e., construct validity). For criterion validity, you might compare a student's reported frequency of completed homework assignments with the teacher's records. Or, for construct validity, you could compare a student's reported study time with changes in grades, assuming that study time and grades are positively related. To check construct validity, you also could compare changes in study time and grades in response to an evidence-based intervention designed to increase these outcomes.

### Minimizing Reactivity

Reactivity is the degree to which measurement procedures produce changes in what is being measured. Reactivity can compromise the validity with which a behavior is measured, although recent research suggests that this might not be as big a problem as once thought. (Yoder & Symons, 2010, provide a summary of recent research in this area.) Here we provide suggestions for minimizing reactivity in direct observation. None of these guarantees nonreactivity, of course; they merely minimize it. In Chapter 12, we discuss similar guidelines for self-monitoring.

- Observers should be as unobtrusive as possible. They should avoid interactions and eye contact with those they are observing. They should be positioned away from the ordinary flow of movement while still allowing an unobstructed view of the entire area. An observer's clothing and behavior should not create any unusual attention.

- Observers' presence should be explained to those being observed in simple, matter-of-fact language.
- Observers should follow all formal and informal rules of the observational setting.
- Observers should enter the setting during the least disruptive time, such as before, rather than during, a session.
- Observers should spend time in the setting before data collection, so that everyone is accustomed to their presence.

# SETTING GOALS AND OBJECTIVES

Some behavioral goals may be relatively straightforward, for example, completely eliminating self-injurious thoughts and behaviors; smoking; enuresis; panic attacks; binge eating or purging; bullying; migraine headaches; truancy; theft; spousal abuse, sexual abuse, animal abuse, or other forms of violence; illegal drug use; binge drinking or other forms of excessive alcohol consumption; or driving while intoxicated. Other such goals might include paying all bills on time; getting to work on time; using safe-sex practices; disciplining children without yelling; or attending all mandated parenting classes or AA meetings.

Other behavioral goals might be more a matter of degree and should be individualized according to the values and preferences of the particular client and others as appropriate. These goals might include time spent sleeping; exercising; reading or talking with children; doing homework or studying; interacting with family or friends; feeling anxious, under stress, or overwhelmed; or ruminating about some concern. Similarly, goals concerning caloric intake; number of negative self-statements; use of cognitive reframing; number of restrictive procedures at a group home; verbal abilities among Alzheimer's patients; number and value of food items donated to a food pantry; or on-task behaviors of students with disabilities need to be individualized.

We will not expect Chico to be perfectly behaved at school; rather, we hope to see behavior more like the average preschool student. Clara incorporates her understanding of child development when she notes that it is normal for 4-year-old boys to have relatively short attention spans, and the group does not seek to completely eliminate Chico's disruptive behaviors. Rather, the goal is to bring his behavior more in line with other students', a range where he can enjoy and benefit from class activities. Indeed, normative data from peers who are functioning normally or well and whose behavior doesn't warrant intervention could be collected and used to determine objectively the extent of Chico's problem and to set objectives for him. This is similar in many ways to using a clinical cutting score, as discussed in Chapter 9.

Finally, sometimes goals are the products of behavior change, not behavior change itself (Cooper et al., 2007). For example, maintaining a healthy blood glucose level or blood pressure, avoiding psychiatric hospitalization, losing or gaining weight, getting good grades, having more friends, and getting a full-time job may be goals. These are not behaviors, but rather goals that may be achieved by behavior changes. In such cases focus on the behavior change needed to achieve these goals, that is the *mechanisms* or process by which change occurs, and confirm that the goals were achieved.

# ADVANTAGES AND PRECAUTIONS IN USING BEHAVIORAL OBSERVATION

Direct observation of behavior has a number of potential advantages. First, in contrast to rating scales with a limited number of ordered categories, direct observation of behavior can provide a more sensitive measure of change because the number of times a behavior occurs or its duration provides a larger potential range of values and thus greater room for change. Second, direct observation of behavior can avoid some of the recall biases associated with the retrospective reports oftentimes involved in using standardized scales or individualized rating scales. Third, direct observation of behavior can be used to measure and monitor outcomes with young children and others with limited verbal ability; this obviously can be a problem with self-reports. Finally, direct observation of behavior may be less subject to irrelevant characteristics of raters.

Behavioral observation is not without potential problems, particularly when direct observation is used in the natural environment (Cooper et al., 2007; Friman, 2009). First, it's possible that an outside observer's presence may affect the situation, producing an unrepresentative sample of behavior. This is not a problem in Chico's case because he knows Graciela, but if an outsider needed to be brought in to observe, we might have her sit in for a while before she begins observing so that Chico is accustomed to seeing her in the classroom. Second, in a setting in which clients move about freely, it's often difficult to observe accurately. Third, observing behaviors in the natural environment may be costly and impractical. Finally, because the observer hypothetically has no control over the environment, the conditions under which data are collected might vary over time, making it difficult to interpret changes over time in the behavior.

Self-monitoring avoids some of the problems of direct observation (Cooper et al., 2007; Sigmon & LaMattina, 2006), but it's not without its own potential problems, as well as advantages. (We will have more to say about these issues in Chapter 12.)

# CONCLUSIONS

Most (if not all) problems that bring clients to us involve people's behavior. Even problematic interior states such as depression or anxiety involve behavior, some of it covert but much of it observable by others. Behavioral observation allows us to go right to the heart of the matter, rather than filtering information through various lenses. (Of course, even our observations are filtered through perceptions.) Whenever possible, we recommend including direct observation of clients' behavior in your tool box.

**PRACTICE TEST** The following questions will test your knowledge of the content found within this chapter and help you prepare for the licensing exam by applying chapter content to practice. For more questions styled like the licensing exam, visit **MySocialWorkLab.com**

1. Behavioral observation should be
   a. Carried out retrospectively
   b. Done in analogue situations
   c. Made under different circumstances over time
   d. Conducted in real time

2. Behavioral observation can be used for all but which of the following purposes:
   a. Pinpoint and define behaviors targeted for intervention
   b. Measure constructs relevant to a wide range of clients
   c. Generate working hypotheses about the mechanisms causing and maintaining targeted behaviors
   d. Measure and monitor client progress

3. A count is the
   a. Amount of time between occurrences of two successive instances of a behavior
   b. Amount of time it takes for a behavior to occur in relation to a stimulus
   c. Number of times a behavior occurs within some time period
   d. Amount of time that a specific behavior occurs

4. Which of the following would enhance the reliability and validity of behavioral observations:
   a. Define target behaviors clearly and specifically
   b. Inform observers of expected changes in clients' behavior
   c. Use different observers over time
   d. Make observers as conspicuous as possible

5. A social worker in an in-patient residential facility is working with an 10-year-old autistic girl, Susan, who has trouble interacting with her peers. Identify and define a behavior for intervention, dimensions along which the behavior should be quantified, and when, where, and how the behavior should be measured and monitored.

6. A social worker is working with Susan, the client described in question 5. Discuss how to ensure and check the reliability and validity of Susan's observed behavior.

# SUCCEED WITH

Visit **MySocialWorkLab** for more licensing exam test questions, and to access case studies, videos, and much more.

# 12

# Self-Monitoring

## Advancing Core Competencies in This Chapter

| Professional Identity | Ethical Practice | ✖ Critical Thinking | Diversity in Practice | Human Rights & Justice |
|---|---|---|---|---|
| ✖ Research-Based Practice | Human Behavior | Policy Practice | Practice Contexts | ✖ Engage, Assess, Intervene, Evaluate |

**K**evin is a 26-year-old who sees Chloe Austin, a social worker, for help with social anxiety and isolation. He has been diagnosed with Asperger's syndrome (AS), which he describes as "a disorder that makes it hard for me to get along with other people." AS is a pervasive developmental disorder that is part of the *autism spectrum* (Gaus, 2007). The condition is often called *high-functioning autism* because while individuals with this diagnosis have average or above-average intellectual functioning and verbal abilities, they suffer from a number of typical autism symptoms, including stereotypy and social deficits. Individuals with AS often present with symptoms of anxiety and depression because they yearn for the social connections that are so hard for them to form and maintain (Hofvander et al., 2009).

Kevin reports that he is unable to carry on normal social conversations. "People tell me I only talk about myself and my own interests," he says. "I guess I'm self-centered." He also is unable to read social cues that alert most people when they are boring or angering others, and people tend to avoid him after one encounter. Because he has experienced so much disappointment and rejection, Kevin is anxious in social situations and has become more and more isolated. Currently, he finds it difficult to spend any time at all in the presence of others and rarely leaves his apartment.

Kevin is an intelligent, attractive young man. He makes a living as a content writer on the Internet, mostly writing blogs and web content about his interests, which currently include Labrador retrievers, aviation history, and opera. Kevin has many online relationships but wants to have more of a social life in the real world.

When a person systematically observes and records his or her own behavior or other experiences, it's called *self-monitoring*. In its most basic form, self-monitoring consists simply of a person's identifying an experience such as an activity, thought, or feeling and recording its frequency, duration, magnitude, or other dimensions. Frequently, self-monitoring is expanded to include the collection of information about the conditions under which the experience occurs; this is called a *client log* or *structured diary*.

Self-monitoring is a form of self-report. It is distinct from standardized self-report scales in that, for the most part, standardized scales involve reports of experiences that occurred *at another time and in another place* (Sigmon & LaMattina, 2006, p. 146). Self-monitoring involves self-observations made over time in the client's normal environment when the observations occur, or close to the time they occur. This is important because reports about past experiences might not be recalled accurately, or they might be influenced by the immediate circumstances in which they are obtained. For example, level of depression reported for the past week might be influenced by the current level. Self-monitoring can be used to reduce these potential distortions and to better understand clients within the context of the normal environment over time (Hektner, Schmidt, & Csikszentmihalyi, 2007; Stone, Shiffman, Atienza, & Nebeling, 2007).

# PURPOSE

Self-monitoring is useful for several purposes. First, it can help pinpoint, define, and operationalize client problems in a way that reflects the unique perceptions and circumstances of individual clients. Although we can read about AS and the problems these individuals experience, we can help Kevin only by understanding his specific circumstances and issues as he experiences them. Second, self-monitoring can provide a way to explore and clarify the dynamic contexts in which problems occur; this can help you and the client generate working hypotheses about the mechanisms causing and maintaining problems (i.e., the case conceptualization), and develop and implement interventions based on these hypotheses. Third—and the main focus of this chapter—self-monitoring can be used to monitor client progress. Self-monitoring is an important way of gathering practice-based evidence that you can use in concert with evidence-based methods to improve outcomes for your clients.

Self-monitoring also can be used to teach the client to focus on his or her unique situation in an orderly way that can enhance and promote client functioning (Avina, 2008; Cooper et al., 2007; Watson & Tharp, 2007). For example, it is often used with cognitive behavior therapy (CBT) to teach clients to identify and change unrealistic, maladaptive modes of thinking in order to change negative moods and maladaptive behaviors (Persons, 2008). (Although self-monitoring can also be useful for prevention, we won't focus on this function here, because that is better left to books dedicated to that purpose.)

Thought records, sometimes called *automatic thought records* or *dysfunctional thought records*, are one tool for self-monitoring. They are systematic journals that are often used in CBT to help identify and change dysfunctional thought patterns and behaviors (Persons, 2008). Thought records take somewhat different forms, but typically they involve a record of behaviors, emotions, thoughts, and coping responses in particular situations at particular times (e.g., Persons, 2008). You can find good examples of thought records and similar forms that you can download and use in your practice without charge at http://www.getselfhelp.co.uk/freedownloads2.htm.

# DECIDING WHAT TO MEASURE

## Pinpointing and Defining the Problem

We've emphasized the importance of operationalizing clients' problems, goals, and outcomes. Self-monitoring is a useful tool for this purpose because it can clarify the unique circumstances of individual clients in a way that no other data collection method can. For example, clients can keep structured diaries of situations and whether they're dissatisfied or satisfied with their responses in order to identify problematic situations and client strengths. Such a record could be used to generate practice hypotheses about problems for intervention; for example, Chloe might realize that Kevin's negative thoughts are confined to interactions with young women, or that he is less uncomfortable in certain settings. Figures 12.1, 12.2, and 12.3 provide examples of client recording forms. See Watson and Tharp (2007) for others.

## Quantifying the Problem

The dimensions used to quantify problems are the same as discussed in previous chapters. The simple act of self-monitoring a problem gives a count. Duration also can be recorded. Individualized rating scales are useful for measuring the degree, magnitude, or intensity of problems.

---

**Figure 12.1** • General Format for Client Log.

---

| Client: | | Day and date: |
|---------|---|---------------|
| Time | Client records important event | Client records reaction to event |
| | | |
| | | |
| | | |
| | | |
| | | |
| | | |
| | | |
| | | |
| | | |
| | | |
| | | |
| | | |

**Figure 12.2** • Form for Collecting Contextual Information About a Problem.

| Client: | | | | Day and date: | | | | |
|---|---|---|---|---|---|---|---|---|
| Time | Place | Activity | Who was there? | Problem behavior (what happened?) | Events before problem | Events after problem | Other events during problem | Your reaction |
| | | | | | | | | |
| | | | | | | | | |
| | | | | | | | | |
| | | | | | | | | |
| | | | | | | | | |
| | | | | | | | | |
| | | | | | | | | |
| | | | | | | | | |
| | | | | | | | | |
| | | | | | | | | |
| | | | | | | | | |

**Figure 12.3** • Form for Collecting Contextual Information About Interactions.

| Client: | | | | Day and date: | | | |
|---|---|---|---|---|---|---|---|
| Time | Place | Who was there? | What I said? | What they said? | What I said? | Other events that followed | Your reaction |
| | | | | | | | |
| | | | | | | | |
| | | | | | | | |
| | | | | | | | |
| | | | | | | | |
| | | | | | | | |
| | | | | | | | |
| | | | | | | | |
| | | | | | | | |
| | | | | | | | |
| | | | | | | | |
| | | | | | | | |

**K**evin's ultimate goal is to interact comfortably with others on a regular basis, perhaps in a club or other kind of interest group. This is an ambitious goal for Kevin, who has not participated in a group since his high school choir, so Chloe suggests working on intermediate goals first. He and Chloe agree on an intermediate goal of spending time among other people every day without anxiety. They do not have a good idea right now about the severity of Kevin's problems, so in the first week Kevin will collect baseline data by self-monitoring his discomfort in the presence of other people.

Since Kevin has no social networks and is too intimidated yet to form any, they decide that he will visit a nearby coffee shop daily, stay as long as he is able to, and measure his anxiety each time. Chloe explains the reasons and procedures for self-monitoring.

Chloe and Kevin construct a simple form to record the time of each visit (Figure 12.4), how long he stays, and the intensity of his discomfort (from 1 to 10, with 10 being the most uncomfortable he has ever felt in a social situation). They spend several minutes constructing anchors for the individualized anxiety scale. For example, 1 indicates absolutely no anxiety, as he might feel alone at home, whereas 10 indicates the worst anxiety he has ever felt in

a social situation; he describes one occasion he recalls and the thoughts and physical sensations he experienced on that occasion.

Self-monitoring is ideal for Kevin; he is very detail-oriented, as are many individuals with AS. He will use his iPhone voice memo function, speaking into a Bluetooth microphone. Half the customers in the coffee shop are speaking into Bluetooth devices, he reports, so he will not feel self-conscious. Because his anxiety level is likely to fluctuate while he is in the coffee shop, he will record only the highest level of anxiety he experiences on each occasion.

**Figure 12.4 •** Kevin's Duration and Discomfort Log.

| Date and location | Duration | Discomfort |
|---|---|---|
|  |  |  |
|  |  |  |
|  |  |  |
|  |  |  |
|  |  |  |
|  |  |  |
|  |  |  |

## Contextualizing the Problem

Sometimes it's unclear what conditions are controlling or maintaining behaviors or other experiences. For example, when working with a depressed client, you might want to pin

**S**leep diaries, also known as *sleep logs*, are excellent tools for contextualizing sleep problems. They are often used in practice to determine the nature and extent of sleep disorders, to develop and explore hypotheses for case conceptualization and intervention planning for clients with sleep disorders, and to monitor client progress in reducing their sleep problems (Benca & Lichstein, 2008; Currie, 2008). Benca and Lichstein provide examples of sleep diaries, a discussion of practical issues in the use of sleep diaries, and common

characteristics of such diaries. Other good examples are available online from the National Institutes of Health (http://science.education.nih.gov/supplements/nih3/sleep/guide/nih_sleep_masters.pdf), the American Psychological Association (http://www.apa.org/pubs/videos/4310583-diary.pdf), the American Academy of Sleep Medicine (http://www.sleepeducation.com/pdf/sleepdiary.pdf), and the National Sleep Foundation (http://www.sleepapneacenter.com/files/SleepDiaryChart.pdf).

At their second meeting, Kevin is pleased that he has carried out his assignment but despairs of ever being normal. His data indicate that the longest he was able to stay in the coffee shop was 8 minutes, and his discomfort was high each time he was there (Figure 12.5).

Referring to Kevin's log, Kevin and Chloe discuss his experiences in the coffee shop, and Kevin recounts his discomfort mounting as he sat each day. Chloe asks for a moment-by-moment account: What was happening? What was he thinking? What physical sensations did he experience? Their discussion suggests that Kevin's dysfunctional thoughts may play a major role in his extreme discomfort.

Chloe explains how dysfunctional thoughts can result in anxiety and depression, and tells him that CBT has been used successfully to alleviate such problems with individuals on the autism spectrum (Gaus, 2007; Lang, Regester, Lauderdale, Ashbaugh, & Haring, 2010). Kevin agrees to try it. They make a list of many of the negative thoughts Kevin experienced this past week and come up with corrective thoughts for each.

Kevin will monitor again this next week, adding his negative and corrective positive thoughts to the duration of his stay in the coffee shop and his level of discomfort. Again Kevin will speak into his Bluetooth microphone and transfer the data to a form when he gets home. If he forgets to correct his negative thoughts in the coffee shop, Chloe instructs him to do that when he translates his data from his iPhone voice memo to his log.

**Figure 12.5** • Kevin's Daily Number of Minutes (●) and Discomfort (O) in the Coffee Shop During Baseline (A), Positive Thought Correction (B), and Conversation Rehearsal (C).

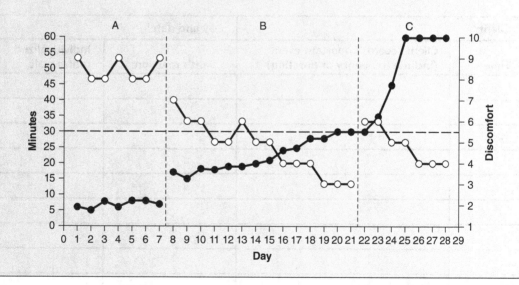

down the conditions under which the client's unrealistic, maladaptive modes of thinking occur (Persons, 2008). When working with an aggressive client, you might want to know when and where the aggressive behavior occurs and what follows it (Feindler & Gerber, 2008). If your client is a child with a sleep disorder, you might want to know his or her bedtime routine, caffeine consumption, and coping strategies (Benca & Lichstein, 2008; Currie, 2008).

## Research-Based Practice

***Practice Behavior Example:*** *Use research evidence to inform practice*

**Critical Thinking Question:** What questions would you consider and what decisions would you make when using self-monitoring to pinpoint and identify Kevin's problems, quantify his problems, contextualize his problems, and set goals and objectives?

Contextual information can help you and the client generate working hypotheses about the mechanisms causing and maintaining problems, and develop interventions based on these hypotheses. However, it is difficult to get accurate contextual information retrospectively, partly because we forget and partly because our memories are biased by subsequent events. Self-monitoring is an especially useful way to collect this important information with as little loss of information as possible. It would be particularly easy for Kevin to forget his negative thoughts since they are so frequent, so monitoring them in real time is the best way to get an accurate picture of those negative thoughts.

Figure 12.6 illustrates the types of information you might collect. You can modify these forms to be more explicit and to individualize for your particular client, possibly engaging the client more effectively.

**Figure 12.6** • Log Illustrating Open Time Categories With an Individualized Rating Scale.

| Client: | | Day and date: | |
|---|---|---|---|
| Time | Client records important event (include frequency or duration) | Client's reaction | Individualized rating scale |
| | | | |
| | | | |
| | | | |
| | | | |
| | | | |
| | | | |
| | | | |
| | | | |
| | | | |
| | | | |
| | | | |

At their third meeting, after the second week of data collection, Chloe and Kevin review his data (Figure 12.5) and note that he is spending more time in the coffee shop now with less discomfort. Kevin decides he would like to spend at least 30 minutes per day there eventually, keeping his discomfort level at or below 5.

Kevin's thought diary (Figure 12.7) provides much material for discussion. Each time he is in the coffee shop, Kevin's thoughts focus on evaluation of himself: How he looks to others and what they think of what he does and says, rather than on others and what they are doing and saying. Chloe points this out as an example of self-centeredness and suggests that Kevin consciously try to think about others during these times. They talk about the give and take of conversation and how that is difficult to do if one is thinking only about himself or herself.

Moreover, Kevin's corrective thoughts often are not as positive as they could be, and Chloe and he go through and think of more positive responses for several instances. Cognitive rigidity is a common problem with AS (Gaus, 2007), so Chloe spends more time on this discussion than she might with the neurotypical client.

**Figure 12.7 • Kevin's Thought Diary.**

| Day | Situation | Negative thoughts | Corrective thought |
|---|---|---|---|
| 1 | Waiting in line | This is hopeless. Why am I doing this? What a waste of time! | I can do better. This is important. |
|   | Walk over to ask a woman to take extra chair from her table | What an idiot I am. There are plenty of chairs around. | I'm not an idiot. I need a chair. |
| 2 | Order coffee, talk to barista | Talking to me is just part of her job. | She talks to everyone, but that's OK. |
|   | Return barista's good-bye when leaving | Why would she want to say good-bye to me? She has no interest in me. | She didn't have to say good-bye, so she must have wanted to. |
| 3 | Order, talk to barista | She remembers me from yesterday! She's just being nice because she's paid to be. | She might think I'm not so bad. |
|   | Ask a man if he likes the Mac he's using at the table next to me | He's busy and I'm just bothering him. | He didn't act like I'm bothering him. |
|   | Open door for lady, comment on how hot it is | Weather! How lame is that! | Everyone talks about the weather. |
| 4 | Order coffee | He must wonder why I'm in here alone every day. | Lots of people are here alone. |
|   | Tell the woman outside I like her dog, talk about labs for a few minutes | She's busy. Why am I bothering her? Other people don't look stupid when they do this stuff. | She acts like she likes talking about her dog. |
|   | Order lunch from cute girl at counter | She has lots more customers. I shouldn't be bothering her. I look like an idiot. | She talks to everyone. I'm not bothering her. |
| 5 | Ask girl in line how she likes her IPod | This is so obvious. She must know I'm nervous. | It doesn't matter if she knows I'm nervous. |

(continued)

**Figure 12.7 •** (Continued)

| Day | Situation | Negative thoughts | Corrective thought |
|-----|-----------|-------------------|--------------------|
|  | Answer her when barista calls out to tell me good-bye as I'm leaving | Maybe she notices me because I look like such an idiot. | I come in here a lot so she remembers my face. |
|  | Buy a newspaper, comment about headlines to clerk | I'm boring him to death. No one in here wants to talk to me. | He answered me, so it must be OK to talk. |
| 6 | Greet barista | She remembered me again—and told me her name is Karen! Why would she do that? | She is a friendly girl. |
| 7 | Pick up my order, talk to Karen about how nice the weather is today | I can't believe she's talking to me. She probably feels sorry for me. | She doesn't act like she feels sorry for me. |

# DECIDING WHEN AND WHERE TO MEASURE

Clients can record information in response to predefined events or situations, for example after an interaction with a particular person; this is called *event-contingent sampling*. Or, clients can record information at predefined times each day, such as just before leaving work for the day or every 2 hours; this is called *interval-contingent sampling*. (If Kevin spends lengthier periods of time outside his home, he might record his thoughts and discomfort every hour, rather than constantly.) Finally, clients can record information at random times, perhaps by using a smartphone as a cue; this is called *signal-contingent sampling*. Signal-contingent sampling can be impractical for practice (at least with current technologies), so we'll limit our discussion to interval- and event-contingent sampling (Hektner et al., 2007).

It can be hard for clients to remember to record information. There are relatively inexpensive technological solutions to this problem. For example, the WatchMinder is a programmable vibrating reminder watch that looks like a standard sports wristwatch, and it can be programmed to provide discreet reminders to do various things throughout the day (http://www.watchminder.com/).

## Event-Contingent Sampling

Event-contingent sampling is best used for self-monitoring experiences surrounding specific events that don't occur too frequently or that don't occur at regular intervals, such as unprotected sex or instances of road rage. The occurrence, duration, magnitude, or other dimensions of the event can be recorded, and should be recorded as soon as possible after the event. For this to work, the client must be able to recognize the event and make a timely record of it.

For example, a couple seeking help with their relationship could be asked to record events with each other that they find enjoyable and their responses to these

**O**ftentimes people who are depressed or anxious withdraw or become inactive, and this inactivity makes their mood even worse. Activity scheduling is a part of many cognitive behavior interventions and it is used to increase pleasurable activities or activities that create a sense of mastery in order to enhance feelings of enjoyment and a sense of accomplishment (e.g., Gaus, 2007; Persons, 2008; Wright, Turkington, Kingdon, & Basco, 2009).

As part of activity scheduling, clients are asked to record their activities and their pleasure in and/or mastery over specific activities. Forms used to record this information look much like daily planners with room for recording the degree of pleasure in and/or mastery over events. (See "Activity Diary" at http://www.getselfhelp.co.uk/freedownloads2.htm for examples.) You can then use this information for case conceptualization and to monitor client progress.

events, in order to accentuate the positive in a situation where there is conflict and distrust. This information then could be used to generate hypotheses about strategies to enhance the relationship. For example, the couple's data may help them realize that after mutually enjoyable leisure activities, they are less likely to argue for a while; perhaps they should schedule more such activities to do together regularly. Such a record also would indicate the frequency of enjoyable events (per day or week), and this could be charted to provide a quantitative basis for monitoring progress. It also would be simple to have each partner rate his or her degree of satisfaction with each interaction using an individualized rating scale. These ratings would indicate which of the enjoyable interactions were most satisfying, providing further clues about how to enhance the quality of the relationship, as well as information that could be used to monitor client progress.

## Interval-Contingent Sampling

When a behavior or other experience is ongoing (such as anxiety) or occurs frequently (such as obsessive thoughts), it's best to ask clients to record observations at fixed, predefined times during the day. Then, at each interval the client can record his or her experience at that particular moment. Or, the client can record information about the previous interval if there's good reason to believe he or she can recall the information accurately; for example, a client might be able to accurately record the number of cigarettes smoked or cups of coffee drunk in the last hour.

In general, information should be collected often enough to get an accurate picture of the experience, but not so often as to become burdensome for the client. For example, suppose a client rated her anxiety once during the day. This momentary snapshot might not give a good picture of her anxiety for the entire day. On the other hand, it wouldn't be practical for the client to rate her anxiety every 15 minutes. The number and length of intervals each day should be tailored to the experience you are asking the client to record and to the characteristics of the client.

### Research-Based Practice

***Practice Behavior Example:*** *Use research evidence to inform practice*

**Critical Thinking Question:** What questions would you consider and what decisions would you make when determining how to measure and monitor Kevin's behavior and other experiences using self-monitoring?

It is clear at the fourth session as Chloe and Kevin look at his data for the third week (Figure 12.5) that he has made important progress. He is spending much more time in the coffee shop, having reached his goal of 30 minutes, and experiencing much less discomfort. Moreover, his thought diary (not shown) demonstrates improvement in the number and content of his negative thoughts, as well as consistent positive corrections.

Chloe suggests that it might be time to extend the intervention a bit to include interacting with the people there. By now Kevin recognizes many of the baristas and regular customers, and they frequently speak to Kevin and engage him in short, superficial conversations. Perhaps Kevin should initiate conversations with them. The idea makes Kevin tense, but he agrees.

Chloe and Kevin make a list of short greetings and comments that Kevin can use in the coffee shop, such as comments about the weather, the local baseball team, upcoming holidays, and so on, rehearsing each. Chloe gives Kevin feedback about his tone of voice and eye contact, issues that can be problems for individuals with AS (Gaus, 2007). Kevin's goal for the coming week is to initiate at least three such short interactions each day. He will continue to monitor how long he stays in the shop (although he says he no longer feels the urge to flee as he did before) and his level of discomfort, and will keep a separate diary of the interactions he initiates in the coffee shop. Again he will use his iPhone voice memo application, leaving it running while he is in the coffee shop so it will record his interactions. He will copy his interactions onto his form when he gets home.

# SELECTING INSTRUMENTS FOR SELF-MONITORING

The forms illustrated throughout this chapter can be used for self-monitoring. Also, most of the forms and instruments described in Chapter 11 can be adapted for self-monitoring. Many other forms are available on the Internet (e.g., http://www.getself-help.co.uk/freedownloads2.htm).

# ENGAGING AND PREPARING THE CLIENT

Use the guidelines discussed in Chapter 8 to engage and prepare clients to self-monitor. There are also a few special considerations that arise in self-monitoring:

- Explain that self-monitoring provides a record of events that otherwise might be forgotten.
- Describe, demonstrate, and practice self-monitoring in advance, perhaps using hypothetical situations and role-playing. Ask the client to record events as succinctly as possible.
- Ensure that the client is willing and able to self-monitor. Self-monitoring assumes that clients are literate, capable of writing, and sufficiently motivated.
- Provide individualized self-monitoring forms. For some clients, a small pocket notebook might be best. For others, smartphones might be useful for self-monitoring. (Smartphones such as the BlackBerry and iPhone, and similar devices such as the iTouch and iPad, are being used increasingly for self-monitoring. Google *self-monitoring* and *smartphone* to see what's new.)

- Review self-monitored information with the client. Read it aloud or have the client read it aloud to reduce misunderstandings and to give the client the opportunity to add details.

Self-monitoring is not for everyone. Many people will tire of self-monitoring, especially if they are collecting extensive contextual information. One way to reduce the burden is to limit the collection of contextual information to baseline or the initial assessment period. However, do ask clients to continue self-monitoring the frequency, duration, or magnitude of problems for monitoring their progress. Of course many clients, such as Kevin, enjoy the reflection, details, and routine of self-monitoring. Often the client's attitude and ability to self-monitor will be evident when you first discuss it, but sometimes you will have to draw conclusions about this after a week or two of observing a client's records.

**Engage, Assess, Intervene, Evaluate**

***Practice Behavior Example:*** *Assess client strengths and limitations*

**Critical Thinking Question:** What questions would you consider and what decisions would you make when determining how to have Kevin self-monitor his behaviors and other experiences and when, where, and how often Kevin should self-monitor?

## ENSURING AND VERIFYING THE ACCURACY OF SELF-MONITORING

Self-monitoring captures a rich array of information about clients' perceptions of their problems and the unique circumstances under which these problems occur. However, the diversity and subjectivity of some of this information has the potential to reduce its reliability and validity. Use the strategies discussed in Chapters 8 and 11 to maximize reliability and validity.

Use the strategies described in previous chapters to verify the reliability and validity of information collected using self-monitoring by obtaining and comparing information from different sources and different measurement methods. However, *what* the client chooses to report and *how* it's reported are as important as objective reality. Thus, both what the client does and does not report are topics for discussion between you and the client. The two of you can decide on the meaning and utility of such information. Even if your client's data can't be checked objectively, this doesn't mean that the information automatically should be excluded from consideration. The decisions the client makes to include or exclude certain events can provide fruitful discussion topics for assessment and intervention.

Reactivity is the degree to which measurement procedures produce changes in what is being measured, as we discussed in Chapter 11. There are some distinct issues concerning the reactivity of self-monitoring that you should consider when designing a self-monitoring plan or interpreting information collected using self-monitoring. The following factors may reduce reactivity in self-monitoring:

- Passage of time
- Self-monitoring of more behaviors
- Intermittent recording, rather than continuous recording
- Verbal behavior, rather than motor behavior

**A**t the fifth session, Kevin's log of interactions (not shown) shows that he initiated at least three social interactions per day at the coffee shop. Although all were superficial interactions, Kevin indicates satisfaction with them and pride in his accomplishment. Many resulted in short conversations about computers, dogs, weather, and so on, and Kevin feels a sense of belonging as a result of these interactions.

Overall, Kevin's data (Figure 12.5) demonstrate slow (as would be expected with AS) but steady progress during his work with Chloe. Kevin is now consistently correcting his negative thoughts (*No, I'm not an idiot. I'm just nervous because this is kind of new for me.*) and is experiencing much less discomfort in the coffee shop. It is no longer necessary for him to monitor the duration of his stays in the coffee shop, as he frequently takes his laptop and stays there for an hour or two. He also regularly has conversations that are a bit longer and go beyond the weather. Kevin states that he looks forward to going to the coffee shop every day and has started timing his visits to talk to the two people he especially likes: a guy about his age who does web design and an older woman who brings her Labrador retriever and sits out on the patio. Kevin considers them friends. Chloe and Kevin discuss how he can avoid being too self-centered in these conversations. They role-play good questions he can ask and also discuss how he can avoid being too intrusive.

Chloe suggests that it's time to take stock. Kevin seems to have reached his goal of interacting socially with others at the coffee shop every day without intense discomfort. Would he like to move toward forming a more intimate social network, perhaps through an interest group or club? Kevin is not sure; he is quite comfortable with his social life now, limited as it is. Chloe feels that continued work might enable Kevin to improve his social life even more, perhaps by inviting others out or to his home, but Kevin declines, for now. He has reached his goal.

On the other hand, the following factors may increase reactivity in self-monitoring:

- Motivation to change
- Recording a behavior before it occurs (e.g., smoking, eating), rather than after
- More obtrusive recording devices

Sometimes self-monitoring is used as a means to teach the client to focus on his or her unique situation in an orderly way. In these situations, reactivity is desirable and is used as a method of self-directed change (Avina, 2008; Cooper et al., 2007; Watson & Tharp, 2007). For example, positive behaviors tend to increase and negative behaviors tend to decrease when self-monitored; this circumstance can be used to further such changes. Kevin probably initiates more interactions because he is recording the data than he might otherwise; this reactivity is not undesirable in this situation. Practitioner instructions that behaviors will or should change can promote change. Setting specific goals, being rewarded for progress, and receiving feedback on performance also can change performance.

## SETTING GOALS AND OBJECTIVES

Self-monitoring just consists of having a person identify an experience and record its frequency, duration, magnitude, or other dimensions in order to monitor progress, so there are no unique considerations involved in setting goals with self-monitoring other than those discussed in Chapters 10 and 11. However, self-monitoring can provide an important opportunity for you to discover what the client hopes to achieve, as well as a valuable way for you to accentuate the positive and gain client cooperation and motivation.

**W**e can legitimately ask what role self-monitoring played in Kevin's reaching his goal. Chloe might be able to help Kevin recognize the destructiveness of his negative thoughts by simply talking about them in their sessions, and Kevin might be able to extend his time in the coffee shop and reduce his discomfort without keeping daily records of those things. On the other hand, self-monitoring clearly demonstrates what is going on for Kevin. Writing down the time he spends in the shop, his negative thoughts, and his interactions with others helps him to focus in an organized way on the specifics of his problem and his efforts to change. We suggest that the simple act of writing these things down in an organized fashion can provide a focus that helps clients bring their resources to bear on problems more successfully than they could without that focus.

In this case, self-monitoring also allows Kevin and Chloe to track his progress as he improves. There is great value in seeing your success as you work on a problem. Moreover, if Kevin does not see the level of success we see here, perhaps because Chloe and he have misidentified the source of his problems or because the steps they try are too ambitious for his resources at the time, self-monitoring will allow them to recognize that failure quickly so they can try something else.

## ADVANTAGES AND PRECAUTIONS IN USING SELF-MONITORING

Self-monitoring can provide a rich source of quantitative and qualitative information about overt and covert experiences in a relatively inexpensive and efficient way. Since self-monitored information is collected in real time, ideally, and in the client's natural environment, self-monitoring has the potential to provide especially accurate and relevant information to guide practice. When self-monitoring is expanded to include the collection of contextual information, it can provide a useful basis for generating intervention and prevention hypotheses and connecting qualitative data to outcome-informed practice. Finally, self-monitoring has the added benefit of increasing clients' awareness of their behaviors and the circumstances in which behavior occurs, and this in itself can change behavior in a beneficial direction.

Self-monitoring is not without potential problems (Cooper et al., 2007; Sigmon & LaMattina, 2006). It can be reactive and, although the reactive effects of self-monitoring tend to be short-lived, they can still make it difficult to monitor client progress. Self-monitoring also places a relatively heavy burden on clients, especially compared to brief standardized self-report scales, and sometimes clients are unwilling or unable to self-monitor. Finally, it's difficult to verify the accuracy with which covert behaviors or private overt behaviors are self-monitored.

## CONCLUSIONS

In some cases, we are able to collect several types of data to provide multiple rich perspectives on clients' lives and their progress as they work with us. In many cases, however, the nature of clients' specific target problems make self-monitoring the only method of collecting data. And, of course, in outcome-informed practice, achievement of the client's goals is the single critical objective, so nothing can be more important than the client's unique perspective. When it is done competently, self-monitoring provides a very important indicator of the results of social work practice.

**PRACTICE TEST** The following questions will test your knowledge of the content found within this chapter and help you prepare for the licensing exam by applying chapter content to practice. For more questions styled like the licensing exam, visit **MySocialWorkLab.com**

---

**1.** Self-monitoring should be
   **a.** Conducted in real time
   **b.** Carried out retrospectively
   **c.** Done in analogue situations
   **d.** Made under different circumstances over time

**2.** Self-monitoring is uniquely suited to
   **a.** Measuring and monitoring client progress
   **b.** Setting client goals
   **c.** Enhancing and promoting client functioning
   **d.** Identifying conditions controlling or maintaining client behaviors or other experiences

**3.** Information is recorded in response to predefined events or situations is called
   **a.** Random sampling
   **b.** Interval-contingent sampling
   **c.** Event-contingent sampling
   **d.** Signal-contingent sampling

**4.** Which of the following may increase the reactivity of self-monitoring:
   **a.** Passage of time
   **b.** Obtrusive recording devices
   **c.** Intermittent recording
   **d.** Recording verbal behavior

**5.** A social worker is working with a 25-year-old single woman, Ava, who can't sleep through the night. How would you engage and prepare Ava to self-monitor her sleep patterns and associated contextual factors?

**6.** A social worker is working with Ava, the client described in question 5. What would you do to ensure and verify the accuracy with which Ava self-monitors her sleep patterns and associated contextual factors?

---

## SUCCEED WITH

Visit **MySocialWorkLab** for more licensing exam test questions, and to access case studies, videos, and much more.

# 13

# Summing Up

Social work practice is about helping your clients reach their goals. It is not about proving that any particular intervention method works. It is not about practicing the intervention that you know or like best. It is not even about pleasing your supervisor or your agency. When you become a social worker, you sign on to the National Association of Social Workers (NASW) Code of Ethics, and the Code makes it clear that your professional obligation is to place your clients' well-being as your top priority. It isn't complicated.

What is complicated is keeping your eyes on the prize, that is making each session and each practice decision contribute toward achieving your clients' goals. In this chapter, we return to the discussion of measure, monitor, and modify (if needed).

## MEASURE

You can't practice social work without measurement: Do you need to determine whether your client has a problem that would benefit from intervention and, if so, how severe that problem is? Do you need to know whether your client is changing over time, whether the change is for the better or worse, or whether the pace of change is sufficient? Do you want to find out if your client has achieved his or her goals and objectives? The question is not whether you're going to measure client outcomes. The question is whether you're going to do it in a haphazard or systematic (yet practical) way that gives you sound information you can use to help clients achieve their goals and objectives.

It's easy to imagine the objections to our assertion that systematic measurement is absolutely essential:

- *I am required to log seven client appointments per day. I don't have time.*
- *It's too complicated.*
- *That won't work with the kinds of clients I have.*

- *I have 25 years of practice experience. I can read my clients well enough without systematic measurement.*
- *When clients relate symptoms to me, I take them at their word. Who needs measurement?*

*I don't have time.* Measurement need not be intimidating or impractical. Nor does it require a great deal of time for the social worker or the client. Take, for example, Mark, from Chapter 1, who works with Dahlia, a Muslim university student struggling with depression. Completion and scoring of Dahlia and Mark's QIDS (Quick Inventory of Depressive Symptomatology) forms require about 10 minutes in each session and provide a jumping-off point for discussion.

Neither does measuring her problems require extensive time or effort for Dahlia or add to the burden her problems are causing her. Dahlia probably spends about 15 minutes on her daily collection of data about her sleeping, studying, and sadness. The discussions that result from those data allow Mark to recognize and open discussion about the ultimate cause of her depression, that is her religious doubts and adjustment to a new culture. The first mention of these issues comes at the end of the second session—as a direct result of reviewing Dahlia's daily logs. It's certainly possible that these issues might come to light eventually in the absence of monitoring, but perhaps Dahlia's grades would suffer irreparably before she could begin to deal with these issues effectively.

In fact, Mark's systematic approach to the measurement of Dahlia's problems probably takes no longer than an exclusively open-ended approach, whereby he would allow Dahlia to tell the entire story in her own words and in her own time. We believe that this will usually be the case, as systematic measurement of client problems leads to a focus on the client's goals that keeps the intervention on track.

*It's too complicated.* It's true that planning is required to collect systematic data from your clients. You need knowledge of the assessment process and of how to locate and evaluate existing measures, as well as how to develop sound measures of your own. You need to know how to collect data properly and to interpret the data you collect. But what is the alternative?

Suppose you measure your clients' problems the way one of this book's authors (Terri Combs-Orme) goes to the grocery store. *I have a list of what I need somewhere, but I usually forget to take it with me. I'll just wing it. I spend way too much time in the gourmet section—I don't really need anything from that section but I love the displays, and it smells so good in there. I buy lots of things I don't need and possibly can't afford, while forgetting the ingredients for dinner tonight and ingredients for the cookies I said I'd take to the church bake sale. When I get home, I realize I wasted an hour and still have nothing for dinner.*

An assessment that is not driven by systematic measurement can turn out similarly. For example, I begin by asking the client what brought him to see me today, and he spends the first half of the session telling me how miserable he has been in his marriage for years. I ask some pertinent questions—I do get some important details, though in a relatively unsystematic way. Then I allow him to talk for 15 minutes about how dominating his mother is because it's obviously important for him to vent, and besides it might be related to his marital problems. As we conclude the session, I may hastily ask him the requisite questions about feelings of hopelessness and thoughts of harming himself before we set up another meeting. Have we made any progress toward achieving the client's goals? Do I know what those goals are yet?

On the other hand, I may spend a good part of the session filling out an intake form. Most agencies have such forms for administrative purposes, and they must be completed. But frequently they provide little opportunity for learning the details of my client's problems. I will need to use the rest of the time in the first session as efficiently as I can, and I hope that I can send the client home knowing that I have at least a decent understanding of his problems and hope that he can achieve his goals.

Don't the benefits of systematic measurement seem worth the investment, both for you and for your client?

*That won't work with the kinds of clients I have.* Client characteristics vary vastly, and our measurement methods must also vary. Systematic measurement does not require the same kind of methods for every client, and indeed it requires flexibility and "starting where the client is."

In Chapter 1, Mark tailors the measurement process to his client's preferences and circumstances. Dahlia is a tech-savvy college student who used computers frequently, so she uses her new iPad to collect data about her sleeping, studying, and sadness. On the other hand, Mr. Jackson in Chapter 4 prefers a small spiral notebook carried in his pocket. Kevin in Chapter 12 likes electronics and gadgets and enjoys using his iPhone to monitor his comments to strangers in the coffee shop. In Chapter 10, Michael takes advantage of technology to help Mrs. Silva's son and niece solve the problem of staying in daily touch with each other and communicating about her situation.

In every case, social workers must assure themselves that their clients understand and agree with what is being asked of them, are able to provide the required information, and understand the importance of providing accurate information. Perhaps this is easy for Mark, who is working with a college student who is accustomed to taking notes and documenting her work carefully; in other cases, a social worker might need to put more effort and time into explaining the value of this part of the intervention. For example, Mr. Jackson may become impatient with the time required to log his experiences, or Andrew in Chapter 8 might feel like self-monitoring his depression or behaviors is simply one more instance of an adult telling him what to do. Part of a good measurement plan is making sure that the client is on board.

Moreover, in order to avoid bias that sometimes results from the collection of information from one source or a single measurement method, you should incorporate as many kinds of information as you can. That is, you should triangulate. Mark and Dahlia both complete a standardized scale, the QIDS, to measure the severity of Dahlia's depressive symptoms. Dahlia also self-monitors the number of hours she sleeps and studies, and she completes an individualized rating scale daily to monitor her sadness. Mark combines this quantitative information with qualitative observations based on his expertise and experience, and at each step he actively seeks and incorporates Dahlia's understanding and interpretations of the outcome data. When you triangulate like this and your various types of data all point in the same direction, you can have more confidence in your understanding of your client's problems and circumstances. If your data are inconsistent or appear to be contradictory, you need to collect more information and resolve the discrepancies, or in some cases to simply decide what is the most credible evidence. Would you prefer not to know that you do not have accurate or complete information?

We can certainly imagine situations where it is more challenging to collect relatively objective and varying types of information, such as with clients with severely limited literacy or numeracy. Social workers may need to administer questionnaires orally, enlist the help of family members, and find other creative ways to measure clients' problems. If a client with limited literacy has no family or friends, the challenge in collecting collateral information is especially great. However, it may be especially important to measure carefully in these cases because there is a high probability that such an isolated individual has a distorted or at least incomplete picture of things.

A more fundamental response to this objection is this: If your clients or those involved with your clients cannot provide accurate objective data about their problems and outcomes, how can you work with them at all? Effective social work practice with any model or type of intervention always relies upon accurate information about the client and his or her problems. We are simply advocating for a systematic approach to gathering that information.

*I can read my clients well enough without systematic measurement.* Research simply does not bear out this claim. We are all subject to bias, particularly confirmatory bias— the tendency to look for and pay attention to information that confirms our impressions and beliefs while paying less attention to information that disconfirms those beliefs. In fact, great expertise and years of experience may *increase* the tendency to trust our judgments too much and to see only confirming information.

Outcome-informed practice does not ignore the social worker's expertise, experience, and subjective judgments. Just as you integrate the best available research about the effectiveness of interventions you consider and select, you should use your personal resources toward the ultimate aim of achieving your clients' goals. Used as part of the scientific method, in which you consider your diagnoses and case conceptualizations as hypotheses (and indeed works in progress), your skills and personal experience are vital. They are simply not enough.

*When clients relate symptoms to me, I take them at their word. Who needs measurement?* It is vital to listen to your clients' narratives carefully. They deserve that respect, and we can learn a great deal from what they say. But this is only one, albeit the most important, source of information about your clients' problems. Systematic measurement through the use of standardized scales, individualized rating scales, and observations of behavior by the client and others contributes to a rich, deep database for understanding the problems and planning for intervention. Your physician doesn't stop with "My stomach hurts," and your mechanic doesn't stop with "My car sounds funny." It wouldn't get them very far toward fixing the problem. Every case in this book illustrates how systematic measurement brings you more material for understanding your clients' complex circumstances, engaging in productive discussion during your sessions, and moving more efficiently toward achievement of your clients' goals.

In Chapter 7, your agency has maintained a food bank for the hungry in your community for 2 years. This is a laudable pursuit, and it has taken on new importance as unemployment has risen and poverty rates have climbed to their highest levels since the 1960s. But in those 2 years, your agency has not measured the outcomes of your campaign, which has consisted simply of placing bins in the stores with signs asking for donations. Of course you have not invested a lot of time in this intervention, either: maybe a couple of hours a month to pick up food donations and stack them in the storage closet. Perhaps it doesn't matter too much that you have no idea how effective the intervention is, given this small investment. On the other hand, could you have used those 2 hours a month in a way that would have benefited the hungry in your community more? Who knows?

Of course, it isn't enough just to assemble a lot of information. The information needs to be reliable and valid and at the same time practical and efficient. Recall from Chapter 9 social worker Eileen Jefferson's desire to gauge Mrs. Kasper's ability to perform the important activities of daily living. You might believe that you know what those activities are and that it would be simple to inquire of her daughter Barbara using yes–no or open-ended questions: *Can your mother dress herself without help in the morning? Can she use the bathroom without help?* and so on. Then you just look at her answers, and they should provide a reasonable picture of the amount of assistance Mrs. Kasper needs. It sounds simple enough.

But the fact is that ad hoc open-ended questions do not yield the kind of information Eileen needs to plan for appropriate services for Mrs. Kasper. What does it mean to dress herself in the morning without help? Is she dressing without help when she asks her daughter to start the long zipper on the back of her dress, which is too low for her to reach? Perhaps she has stopped wearing clothes with buttons and zippers altogether because they require assistance; should this count in your calculations of how independent she is? Is being able to put her clothes on without help even a good indicator of how able she is to take care of herself? Should other tasks such as preparing her own meals or managing her medication be weighted more heavily? Fortunately, researchers have considered these issues for years, and Eileen is able to select from a variety of scales that have been tested with thousands of subjects in similar circumstances to Mrs. Kasper's. There are data to indicate the extent to which respondents understand the questions in the same way and that scores on the measure correlate with important outcomes. Standardized scales don't solve all your problems in understanding your clients' problems, but they remove a lot of the guesswork.

We doubt that many social workers would argue with the contention that it is critical to collect reliable, valid data for selecting and implementing interventions. There may not be as much consensus that the information you collect should be based on a combination of the social worker's subjective impressions, the client and his or her family's own words, and relatively objective data collected from different sources using different methods. You would never simply administer a collection of standardized scales to your client without integrating more subjective contextual information and critical thought into your assessment; neither should you neglect to include the most objective information you can obtain.

## MONITOR

Good measurement of your client's situation gets you off to a great start. Reliable and valid data from multiple sources and multiple methods allow you to form hypotheses about the origins and maintaining factors of your client's problems, his or her life circumstances, strengths, and resources for solving his or her problems. You may be able to state a tentative diagnosis for the record, although it remains open to change as you collect more information. Using the scientific method, you are able to propose several hypotheses about your client's problems, perhaps including the possible appropriateness of one or more interventions.

Solid measurement used with careful thought and discussion probably by itself already has been helpful to your client. Where appropriate, baseline data clarify the nature of the problem: how severe it is, in what circumstances it does and does not occur, the consequences of the problem, and so on. Of course sometimes it is not possible or ethical to delay intervention to collect baseline data; in those cases, however, it is often possible to work with the client to construct a retrospective baseline. If it is possible to graph those data, the graph may provide a focal point for further discussion and deeper understanding of the problem.

Recall from Chapter 1 that it isn't until Gayle collects and discusses the relatively objective baseline data about the specific circumstances causing such distress to Diane and Greg that Sandra finally understands what problems are being created by her behavior. These data, and the critical discussion about them in the session, encourage Sandra to accept and participate in the intervention. In other cases, baseline data may reveal that there is no problem or that the problem does not merit intervention, particularly if the intervention is costly in terms of time or labor. The shortage of resources in which we work today makes this information valuable.

But quality measurement does not end with assessment. You need to continue to monitor client progress during the intervention phase so you and your clients can continue to make informed decisions during intervention. Ongoing feedback about client progress is essential because even under the best circumstances evidence-based interventions don't come with a guarantee of success for each and every client. And of course circumstances usually aren't ideal. For example, you might not have the expertise to implement the best empirically supported intervention, or you might not have the time, agency support, or other required resources. Similarly, your client's culture, ethnicity, age, gender, sexual orientation, or social class may be different in important ways from the participants involved in testing the most promising intervention. In many cases, there may not even be an empirically supported intervention available for the complex problems faced by your client. In such cases, you may select and alter an intervention that has been used successfully for other, related problems, or you may have to combine two promising interventions. In all of these cases, monitoring during intervention takes on added importance.

In Chapter 3, as Gordon strives to help Eve improve her compliance with her medication regime, the research doesn't provide much guidance. His client is female, whereas most of the subjects in research studies on compliance with HIV-positive clients involve males. Moreover, she is poor, a mother, and suffering from the side-effects of her medication. The best evidence Gordon finds suggests that he proceed from an individualized case conceptualization and try to mitigate the specific barriers to Eve's compliance with her medication. He proceeds, and based on this approach, extreme stress appears to be behind Eve's noncompliance. She is most likely to miss her medication when she is worrying about not being able to pay her bills, not finding work, experiencing particularly bad side-effects, and feeling that she is not providing the parenting that her daughter needs. She has few coping skills when these circumstances occur and feels totally overwhelmed.

There are multiple interventions to improve coping and reduce stress, and the evidence shows them to be highly effective with many people. Deep breathing, yoga, systematic relaxation: all can reduce the physiological and emotional effects of stress. Moreover, social support is a key resource for reducing stress; Eve might benefit from bringing her partner to her sessions. But these techniques do not appear to be helping Eve remember her medication—or at least not often enough to satisfy her physician. And Eve doesn't want to involve her partner in her intervention.

Without monitoring Eve's compliance with her medication regimen, Gordon and Eve might not recognize the extent to which Gordon's intervention is not helping. She believes she is doing pretty well, and early in the intervention she believes her compliance is improving—maybe as a result of wishful thinking. Without monitoring Eve's medication and her viral load, Gordon might just assume that Eve is making good progress as she claims and continue as is. After all, there is good scientific evidence that the interventions they have implemented are effective for reducing stress, and it is clear that Eve's problems result from poor coping with excessive stress. The monitoring data show, though, that Eve is not benefiting sufficiently. It can be difficult to detect lack of progress without systematic monitoring because of our very human tendency to gather evidence that confirms our expectations of success, while dismissing or failing to seek contradictory evidence. Moreover, Gordon does not have time to tinker with the intervention; Eve's health might deteriorate to the point that she may die.

But monitoring is a lot more than just watching; without critical thinking, it is useless. In Chapter 6, Keisha's work with Stephen demonstrates that the usefulness of monitoring your clients' progress depends on your ability to interpret unfolding patterns of change over time. For this, we believe that graphing your clients' data is essential, because the visual cues provide information that is provided in no other way. Patterns emerge in ways that they simply don't without those visual cues.

You will compare what's happening before the intervention to the first week after the intervention and beyond. You may consider what happens with one intervention as compared to what happens with another, or what happens when you discontinue an intervention. And you'll be looking at several issues simultaneously. You will observe the levels of the data—are scores higher or lower over time and between conditions? Do you see an upward or downward trend within a phase? If you see an improving trend during baseline, should you delay the intervention for a while?

You'll be wary of variability, which is apparent as you examine a line graph. Perhaps the variability provides important clues to what is causing or maintaining the problem. Moreover, it might be unwise to start or change an intervention until you see a more stable pattern. And what if you see cycles in the client's outcomes, for example 3 days of reduced anxiety followed by 3 days of increased anxiety, and so on? What might account for those cycles, and can you exploit that information to help your client achieve his or her goals?

You'll consider whether you see overlapping data between baseline and intervention or between two different interventions. On the other hand, overlaps do not necessarily mean that real change is not occurring. You'll look at the overlaps within the context of the whole series of data.

And if you do see clear changes from baseline to intervention—is the change immediate, or is it gradual? You may feel in some cases that only an immediate change indicates success, whereas in others you are expecting gradual changes. How will you use this information to plan your continuing work with your client? How will you decide whether change is permanent or not? Graphing your client's outcomes and critically appraising those graphs give you the tools to help your client achieve his or her goals as quickly and efficiently as possible.

Finally, remember as you monitor that some single-case designs are better than others for drawing valid conclusions about causal relationships. With any design, you'll have to think critically as you use the data to make ongoing decisions. Consider Andrew in

Chapter 8. Suppose his behavior at home dramatically improves because of a transitory process or event, such as his hitting a home run in one of the first games he plays after he returns to the team. The change is likely due to a history effect, and Sarah, his social worker, won't necessarily expect his progress to be maintained over the following days. On the other hand, perhaps Andrew's joy at this success will work with the other things he is doing to solidify the changes, reduce his depression, and set him on a new path. Sarah will monitor carefully.

And if Andrew's grades improve when the school changes its grading scale, is this simply an instrumentation effect? If so, we might not expect this change to last. Or perhaps the implementation of the new grading scale coincides with Andrew's rising interest in keeping his grades up so he can remain on the baseball team. Different single-case designs provide differing degrees of confidence that an intervention is responsible for a client's progress, but all require the use of accurate data and critical thinking.

In some cases, monitoring during intervention takes on even more urgency. Although we may not like to think about it, our interventions can in fact cause harm; such negative effects caused by an intervention are called *iatrogenic effects*. Let's assume that Eve in Chapter 3 agrees to involve her partner Joe in her intervention; he agrees to remind her when it's time for her HIV medication when they are both at home. The reminders may even be effective when he is not at home. But what if Eve feels harassed by Joe? His involvement may increase her level of stress, and she may fail to take her medicine more frequently when he is not at home. This is a situation you would want to identify quickly, and consistent monitoring is your best tool for doing so.

Graphing and monitoring, by themselves, may not get you where you want to go. When implemented within the appropriate design and augmented with deliberate critical thinking and contextual information about your client, however, it can mean the difference between success and failure for your clients. If your intervention is not moving this client toward his or her goals, your obligation is toward the client—not the intervention that should be working. And if you do not monitor systematically and carefully, and with due caution against the bias that we all have toward seeing improvement, how can you meet this ethical obligation?

## MODIFY IF NEEDED

In the end, of course, you do not systematically and constantly monitor your client's progress out of idle curiosity. You do it to inform the decisions you make every time you meet with your client.

We can't overstress this fact: Even if you are not aware of it, you make several critical decisions every time you meet with your client. The most subtle decision you make—that is to continue as you have been—is a declaration that your intervention is proceeding as planned, the client is moving toward achieving his or her goals, and no changes are needed. You may not consciously think about it, but that's what you are saying.

In some cases, such as we see with Eve in Chapter 3, you may decide that your intervention is not effective, that your client is not moving toward achieving her goals, or that your client is not achieving her goals quickly enough. Then you need to make some changes. In Eve's case, the changes are a matter of life and death. In others, it may simply be a matter of not letting a case stagnate for weeks. Our own experience tells us that this happens easily. Clients may continue to come to see you because they derive satisfaction from talking with you every week, even if they are making no real progress toward achieving their goals. You may continue to see them out of hope that "things will kick in soon," and because you do not want to abandon them. But neither of you can really see anything happening.

We can imagine in Chapter 4 that Mr. Jackson's social worker, Susan, will work with him using cognitive behavior therapy. They cannot change his boss's appalling behavior and Mr. Jackson does not want to look for employment elsewhere, so they work on helping Mr. Jackson change his own responses to his boss's inappropriate racist talk. It is easy to imagine Mr. Jackson finding some relief in changing his automatic thoughts from *I am a powerless weakling and there is nothing I can do* to something more functional for him, such as *He is the one with the problem here. I am just going to do my job well and try to protect my guys from this as well as I can.* We would expect changing these thoughts to bring some relief to Mr. Jackson.

On the other hand, monitoring might show that Mr. Jackson is making progress in changing his negative thoughts and responding in a less unhealthy manner, but that progress is not sufficient. Perhaps his blood pressure remains high, or he still isn't sleeping as well as he once did. Possibly fatigue is making him short-tempered with his family and keeping him home from church. These data might suggest to Susan that they should amend the intervention by adding deep breathing, or involving his wife more actively in the treatment, or even including some behavior training to allow Mr. Jackson to voice his objections to his boss in a manner that is not risky to his employment. Systematic monitoring provides the data to allow us to both discontinue unsuccessful interventions and enhance those that are successful. Once again, the social worker keeps her eyes on the prize.

What else might Susan do to improve on Mr. Jackson's progress?

- She may assess the status of the helping alliance, client motivation to change, and environmental and biological factors in Mr. Jackson's life. Has Mr. Jackson lost faith in the intervention? Does he resent Susan for not being willing to try to make his boss change his behavior? Or perhaps Mr. Jackson's son is having trouble in school, and he feels powerless to help him. These are issues that can impede Mr. Jackson's achievement of his goals, and they should be handled sooner rather than later.
- Are they moving too fast? Perhaps Mr. Jackson needs more time to practice altering his cognitions or additional role-play in the sessions to master these skills. Maybe he needs to meet more frequently with Susan or to add group therapy to his intervention so that he can practice and receive feedback from more individuals, particularly other men.
- If Mr. Jackson shows excellent ability to change his thoughts to be more positive but continues to have physiological symptoms of high blood pressure and inability to sleep, perhaps a physical examination is in order. Does he need medication?
- Susan may need to collect more information. How is Mr. Jackson functioning in his other roles as husband, parent, community leader, and church member? If she observes his functioning beginning to slip in these other roles, they may need to return to the case conceptualization. Perhaps Mr. Jackson's problems at work are part of a larger picture.

Some situations might require immediate or intensive action (e.g., a client's depression is becoming severe and possibly dangerous), and other situations might allow more time, but the important principle is that monitoring allows you to make changes sooner, rather than later, when the client is not progressing as expected. In Mr. Jackson's case, if Susan doesn't make changes in a timely fashion, the physiological damage caused by his situation could lead to heart attack or stroke, deteriorated relationships with family and friends, or even the loss of his job.

This is a good time to think again about the scientific approach. Susan is not locked into her initial case conceptualization, and she continues to seek disconfirming information about that as well as the appropriateness of her diagnosis and intervention. Although cognitive behavior therapy has been shown to be effective in numerous rigorous studies with a variety of types of individuals and problems, she is not committed to this intervention. She is committed to the achievement of Mr. Jackson's goals.

There is a tendency to wait and see when things are not progressing as expected. Once, before the age of managed care, that might have been an acceptable strategy. Now, as clients are limited to a certain number of sessions by insurance policies, it may simply not be possible.

# CONCLUSIONS

Social work practice is complex—just like life. Although your professors strive to prepare you for independent practice with a range of clients in a range of circumstances, we cannot prepare you for every situation you may face. What we hope to do is to give you a framework that, when combined with critical thought, will be useful in any circumstance. We believe that outcome-informed evidence-based practice can be an important part of that framework.

We acknowledge again that the individual elements of this type of practice are not unique. Social work has been moving toward a more scientific way of practicing for many years. The current emphasis by the Council on Social Work Education on using methods that are supported by research on effectiveness is part of that evolution. So, too, are the calls for at least the last 30 or more years that we evaluate our own practice. In this book, we present easy-to-follow procedures for using both evidence-based practice and practice-based evidence to focus on achieving the best outcomes for *each individual client*.

We make no claims that this is easy to do. These are turbulent times, with poverty and unemployment at high levels and continuing declines in funding for social services; the fallout from these circumstances makes up the raw material that social workers deal with every day. We hope you will find that the material in this book provides you with the tools you need to do this difficult job.

# Appendix A

## SELECTED STANDARDIZED SCALES

This appendix contains a sample of standardized scales that have promising or well-established psychometric properties and are practical for use in monitoring client progress. We provide the primary reference and one or more recent reviews for each measure (in some cases, a discussion of the measure in the context of measures of the same or other related constructs). You can find information about the reliability and validity of these measures in these and related sources.

We report the procedure for scoring each measure, the clinical cutting score(s) (when available), and estimates of reliable change (RC) and the standard error of measurement (SEM). We computed the RC and SEM (both discussed in Chapter 9) using the standard deviation and coefficient alpha found in the primary reference for each measure (when available). However, because oftentimes there is not a single appropriate standard deviation and coefficient alpha, consider these to be approximations and, as always, try to locate normative information from reference populations relevant to your particular clients.

Again, we want to thank the authors of the measures presented in this appendix for allowing us to reproduce their measures, and for kindly answering our questions about their measures. In particular, we want to thank Jussara Bittencourt, Patricia Chamberlain, Mark J. Macgowan, A. John Rush, Joachim Stöber, and Jerome Yesavage.

### Quick Inventory of Depressive Symptomatology—Self-Report (QIDS-SR)

The 30-item Inventory of Depressive Symptomatology (IDS) and the 16-item QIDS both measure the severity of depressive symptoms. These measures are available in clinician (IDS-$C_{30}$ and QIDS-$C_{16}$) and self-rated versions (IDS-$SR_{30}$ and QIDS-$SR_{16}$).

The QIDS-SR is copyrighted (© UT Southwestern Medical Center at Dallas, 2007). However, copies of the QIDS and IDS may be downloaded from http://www.ids-qids.org/ and used without permission. References for these measures and a variety of other information about these measures also are available at this website.

**Scoring and interpretation:** See Chapter 9.

**Primary reference:**

Rush, A. J., Trivedi, M. H., Ibrahim, H. M., Carmody, T. J., Arnow, B., Klein, D. N., et al. (2003). The 16-item Quick Inventory of Depressive Symptomatology (QIDS), Clinician Rating (QIDS-C), and Self-Report (QIDS-SR): A psychometric evaluation in patients with chronic major depression. *Biological Psychiatry, 54*, 573–583.

**Recent reviews:**

Rush, A. J., Giles, D. E., Sclesser, M. A., & Fulton, M. L. (2008). Inventory of Depressive Symptomatology (IDS); Quick Inventory of Depressive Symptomatology (QIDS). In A. J. Rush Jr., M. B. First, & D. Blacker (Eds.), *Handbook of psychiatric measures* (2nd ed., pp. 511–513). Washington, DC: American Psychiatric Association.

Persons, J. B., & Fresco, D. M. (2008). Adult depression. In J. Hunsley & E. J. Mash (Eds.), *A guide to assessments that work* (pp. 96–120). New York: Oxford University Press.

**Figure A.1** • The Quick Inventory of Depressive Symptomatology (16-Item) (Self-Report) (QIDS-SR$_{16}$)

Name or ID: _____    Date: _____

CHECK THE ONE RESPONSE TO EACH ITEM THAT BEST DESCRIBES YOU FOR THE
PAST SEVEN DAYS.

**During the past seven days...**

**1. Falling Asleep:**

☐ 0   I never take longer than 30 minutes to fall asleep.

☐ 1   I take at least 30 minutes to fall asleep, less than half the time.

☐ 2   I take at least 30 minutes to fall asleep, more than half the time.

☐ 3   I take more than 60 minutes to fall asleep, more than half the time.

**2. Sleep During the Night**

☐ 0   I do not wake up at night.

☐ 1   I have a restless, light sleep with a few brief awakenings each night.

☐ 2   I wake up at least once a night, but I go back to sleep easily.

☐ 3   I awaken more than once a night and stay awake for 20 minutes or more, more than half the time.

**3. Waking Up Too Early:**

☐ 0   Most of the time, I awaken no more than 30 minutes before I need to get up.

☐ 1   More than half the time, I awaken more than 30 minutes before I need to get up.

☐ 2   I almost always awaken at least one hour or so before I need to, but I go back to sleep eventually.

☐ 3   I awaken at least one hour before I need to, and can't go back to sleep.

**During the past seven days...**

**4. Sleeping Too Much:**

☐ 0   I sleep no longer than 7–8 hours/night, without napping during the day.

☐ 1   I sleep no longer than 10 hours in a 24-hour period including naps.

☐ 2   I sleep no longer than 12 hours in a 24-hour period including naps.

☐ 3   I sleep longer than 12 hours in a 24-hour period including naps.

**5. Feeling Sad:**

☐ 0   I do not feel sad.

☐ 1   I feel sad less than half the time.

☐ 2   I feel sad more than half the time.

☐ 3   I feel sad nearly all of the time.

**Please complete either 6 or 7 (not both)**

**6. Decreased Appetite:**

☐ 0   There is no change in my usual appetite.

☐ 1   I eat somewhat less often or lesser amounts of food than usual.

☐ 2   I eat much less than usual and only with personal effort.

☐ 3   I rarely eat within a 24-hour period, and only with extreme personal effort or when others persuade me to eat.

**During the past seven days...**

### - OR -

**7. Increased Appetite:**

☐ 0    There is no change from my usual appetite.

☐ 1    I feel a need to eat more frequently than usual.

☐ 2    I regularly eat more often and/or greater amounts of food than usual.

☐ 3    I feel driven to overeat both at mealtime and between meals.

---

## Please complete either 8 or 9 (not both)

**8. Decreased Weight (Within the Last Two Weeks):**

☐ 0    I have not had a change in my weight.

☐ 1    I feel as if I have had a slight weight loss.

☐ 2    I have lost 2 pounds or more.

☐ 3    I have lost 5 pounds or more.

### - OR -

**9. Increased Weight (Within the Last Two Weeks):**

☐ 0    I have not had a change in my weight.

☐ 1    I feel as if I have had a slight weight gain.

☐ 2    I have gained 2 pounds or more.

☐ 3    I have gained 5 pounds or more.

---

**10. Concentration / Decision Making:**

☐ 0    There is no change in my usual capacity to concentrate or make decisions.

☐ 1    I occasionally feel indecisive or find that my attention wanders.

☐ 2    Most of the time, I struggle to focus my attention or to make decisions.

☐ 3    I cannot concentrate well enough to read or cannot make even minor decisions.

**During the past seven days...**

**11. View of Myself:**

☐ 0    I see myself as equally worthwhile and deserving as other people.

☐ 1    I am more self-blaming than usual.

☐ 2    I largely believe that I cause problems for others.

☐ 3    I think almost constantly about major and minor defects in myself.

**12. Thoughts of Death or Suicide:**

☐ 0    I do not think of suicide or death.

☐ 1    I feel that life is empty or wonder if it's worth living.

☐ 2    I think of suicide or death several times a week for several minutes.

☐ 3    I think of suicide or death several times a day in some detail, or I have made specific plans for suicide or have actually tried to take my life.

**13. General Interest**

☐ 0    There is no change from usual in how interested I am in other people or activities.

☐ 1    I notice that I am less interested in people or activities.

☐ 2    I find I have interest in only one or two of my formerly pursued activities.

☐ 3    I have virtually no interest in formerly pursued activities.

**14. Energy Level:**

☐ 0    There is no change in my usual level of energy.

☐ 1    I get tired more easily than usual.

☐ 2    I have to make a big effort to start or finish my usual daily activities (for example, shopping, homework, cooking, or going to work).

☐ 3    I really cannot carry out most of my usual daily activities because I just don't have the energy.

*(continued)*

**During the past seven days...**

**15. Feeling Slowed Down:**

☐ 0    I think, speak, and move at my usual rate of speed.

☐ 1    I find that my thinking is slowed down or my voice sounds dull or flat.

☐ 2    It takes me several seconds to respond to most questions and I'm sure my thinking is slowed.

☐ 3    I am often unable to respond to questions without extreme effort.

**During the past seven days...**

**16. Feeling Restless:**

☐ 0    I do not feel restless.

☐ 1    I'm often fidgety, wringing my hands, or need to shift how I am sitting.

☐ I    have impulses to move about and am quite restless.

☐ 3    At times, I am unable to stay seated and need to pace around.

### Center for Epidemiologic Studies Depression Scale (CES-D)

The CES-D is a 20-item measure of depressive symptoms. It is in the public domain and may be used without permission.

**Scoring and interpretation:** A total score is computed for the CES-D using the following steps. (Also, the companion website contains an Excel file, CESD.xls, that scores the CES-D.)

- Assign 0 to responses in the first column, 1 to responses in the second column, 2 to responses in the third column, and 3 to responses in the fourth column.
- Reverse score items 4, 8, 12, and 16.
- Add up the item responses (after reverse scoring items 4, 8, 12, and 16).

The total score has a potential range of values from 0 through 60, and higher scores indicate greater severity of depressive symptoms. Scores of 16 or more are in the problematic range. The RC equals 9.29 and the SEM equals 3.35 (based on a standard deviation of 8.65 and a coefficient alpha of .85). However, considerable research exists concerning the CES-D with different populations, so you should explore the possibility of computing the RC and SEM for reference populations relevant to your particular clients.

**Primary reference:**

Radloff, L. S. (1977), The CES-D Scale: A self-report depression scale for research in the general population. *Applied Psychological Measurement, 1*, 385–401.

**Recent reviews:**

Radloff, L. S., & Locke, B. Z. (2008). Center for Epidemiologic Studies Depression Scale (CES-D). In A. J. Rush Jr., M. B. First, & D. Blacker (Eds.), *Handbook of psychiatric measures* (2nd ed., pp. 506–508). Washington, DC: American Psychiatric Association.

Persons, J. B., & Fresco, D. M. (2008). Adult depression. In J. Hunsley & E. J. Mash (Eds.), *A guide to assessments that work* (pp. 96–120). New York: Oxford University Press.

**Figure A.2** • Center for Epidemiologic Studies Depression Scale (CES-D), NIMH

Below is a list of the ways you might have felt or behaved. Please tell me how often you have felt this way during the past week.

| | During the Past Week | | | |
| --- | --- | --- | --- | --- |
| | Rarely or none of the time (less than 1 day) | Some or a little of the time (1–2 days) | Occasionally or a moderate amount of time (3–4 days) | Most or all of the time (5–7 days) |
| 1. I was bothered by things that usually don't bother me. | ☐ | ☐ | ☐ | ☐ |
| 2. I did not feel like eating; my appetite was poor. | ☐ | ☐ | ☐ | ☐ |
| 3. I felt that I could not shake off the blues even with help from my family or friends. | ☐ | ☐ | ☐ | ☐ |
| 4. I felt I was just as good as other people. | ☐ | ☐ | ☐ | ☐ |
| 5. I had trouble keeping my mind on what I was doing. | ☐ | ☐ | ☐ | ☐ |
| 6. I felt depressed. | ☐ | ☐ | ☐ | ☐ |
| 7. I felt that everything I did was an effort. | ☐ | ☐ | ☐ | ☐ |
| 8. I felt hopeful about the future. | ☐ | ☐ | ☐ | ☐ |
| 9. I thought my life had been a failure. | ☐ | ☐ | ☐ | ☐ |
| 10. I felt fearful. | ☐ | ☐ | ☐ | ☐ |
| 11. My sleep was restless. | ☐ | ☐ | ☐ | ☐ |
| 12. I was happy. | ☐ | ☐ | ☐ | ☐ |
| 13. I talked less than usual. | ☐ | ☐ | ☐ | ☐ |
| 14. I felt lonely. | ☐ | ☐ | ☐ | ☐ |
| 15. People were unfriendly. | ☐ | ☐ | ☐ | ☐ |
| 16. I enjoyed life. | ☐ | ☐ | ☐ | ☐ |
| 17. I had crying spells. | ☐ | ☐ | ☐ | ☐ |
| 18. I felt sad. | ☐ | ☐ | ☐ | ☐ |
| 19. I felt that people disliked me. | ☐ | ☐ | ☐ | ☐ |
| 20. I could not get "going." | ☐ | ☐ | ☐ | ☐ |

SCORING: 0 for answers in the first column, 1 for answers in the second column, 2 for answers in the third column, 3 for answers in the fourth column. The scoring of positive items is reversed. Possible range of scores is 0 to 60, with the higher scores indicating the presence of more symptomatology.

### Geriatric Depression Scale-15 (GDS-15)

The 15-item GDS measures depressive symptoms in geriatric populations. Copies of the 15- and 30-item versions may be downloaded from http://www.stanford.edu/~yesavage/GDS.html. These measures are in the public domain and may be used without permission. Also, the GDS website contains a variety of other information about these measures.

**Scoring and interpretation:** A total score is computed for the GDS-15 using the following steps:

- Items 1, 5, 7, 11, and 13 indicate the presence of depression when answered "no." So, assign a value of 1 to each of these items if answered "no."
- Items 2, 3, 4, 6, 8, 9, 10, 12, 14, and 15 indicate the presence of depression when answered "yes." So, assign a value of 1 to each of these items if answered "yes."
- Add up the number of 1s.

The total score has a potential range of values from 0 through 15, and higher scores indicate more depressive symptoms. A score greater than 5 is suggestive of depression and should warrant a follow-up interview. Scores greater than 10 almost always indicate depression. The primary reference did not report a standard deviation or coefficient alpha for the GDS-15, so it wasn't possible to compute the RC and SEM. However, considerable research exists concerning the GDS-15 with different populations, so you should explore the possibility of computing the RC and SEM for reference populations relevant to your particular clients.

#### Primary reference (GDS-15):

Sheikh, J. I., & Yesavage, J. A. (1986). Geriatric Depression Scale (GDS): Recent evidence and development of a shorter version. *Clinical Gerontologist, 5*, 165–173.

#### Primary reference (GDS-30):

Yesavage, J. A., & Brink, T. L. (1983). Development and validation of a geriatric depression screening scale: A preliminary report. *Journal of Psychiatric Research, 17*, 37–49.

#### Recent reviews:

Allen, J., & Annells, M. (2009). A literature review of the application of the Geriatric Depression Scale, Depression Anxiety Stress Scales and Post-Traumatic Stress Disorder Checklist to community nursing cohorts. *Journal of Clinical Nursing, 18*, 949–959.

Lopez, M. N., Quan, N. M., & Carvajal, P. M. (2010). A psychometric study of the Geriatric Depression Scale. *European Journal of Psychological Assessment, 26*, 55–60.

Persons, J. B., & Fresco, D. M. (2008). Adult depression. In J. Hunsley & E. J. Mash (Eds.), *A guide to assessments that work* (pp. 96–120). New York: Oxford University Press.

Wancata, J., Alexandrowicz, R., Marquart, B., Weiss, M., & Friedrich, F. (2006). The criterion validity of the Geriatric Depression Scale: A systematic review. *Acta Psychiatrica Scandinavica, 114*, 398–410.

Yesavage, J. A., & Brink, T. L. Geriatric Depression Scale (GDS). In A. J. Rush Jr., M. B. First, & D. Blacker (Eds.), *Handbook of psychiatric measures* (2nd ed., pp. 524–526). Washington, DC: American Psychiatric Association.

---

**Figure A.3** • Geriatric Depression Scale-15 (GDS-15)

---

## MOOD SCALE
### (short form)

Choose the best answer for how you have felt over the past week:

1. Are you basically satisfied with your life? YES / NO

2. Have you dropped many of your activities and interests? YES / NO

3. Do you feel that your life is empty? YES / NO

4. Do you often get bored? YES / NO

5. Are you in good spirits most of the time? YES / NO

6. Are you afraid that something bad is going to happen to you? YES / NO

7. Do you feel happy most of the time? YES / NO

8. Do you often feel helpless? YES / NO

9. Do you prefer to stay at home, rather than going out and doing new things? YES / NO

10. Do you feel you have more problems with memory than most? YES / NO

11. Do you think it is wonderful to be alive now? YES / NO

12. Do you feel pretty worthless the way you are now? YES / NO

13. Do you feel full of energy? YES / NO

14. Do you feel that your situation is hopeless? YES / NO

15. Do you think that most people are better off than you are? YES / NO

---

## Penn State Worry Questionnaire—Past Week (PSWQ-PW)

The PSWQ-PW (Stöber & Bittencourt, 1998) is an adaptation of the PSWQ (Meyer, Miller, Metzger, & Borkovec, 1990). Both the PSWQ and the PSWQ-PW capture pathological worry as typical of clients diagnosed with generalized anxiety disorder (GAD). Whereas the PSWQ captures stable pathological worry as a trait-like person characteristic, the PSWQ-PW asks for pathological worry *during the past week*. With this, the PSWQ-PW captures pathological worry as a more momentary state and thus is very change-sensitive (see Stöber & Bittencourt, 1998). Therefore, the PSWQ-PW may be superior compared to the PSWQ when assessing changes in pathological worry, for example when monitoring treatment effects (Stöber & Bittencourt, 1998). The PSWQ-PW is copyrighted (© Stöber & Bittencourt) but may be used without permission.

**Scoring and interpretation:** A total score is computed for the PSWQ-PW using the following steps:

- Reverse score items 1, 3, 8, 10, and 11.
- Add up the item responses (after reverse scoring items 1, 3, 8, 10, and 11).

The total score has a potential range of values from 0 through 90, and higher values indicate greater pathological worry during the past week. The PSWQ-PW does not have a clinical cutting score to our knowledge. The RC equals 12.91 and the SEM equals 4.66 (based on a standard deviation of 15.52 and a coefficient alpha of .91).

**Primary reference (PSWQ-PW):**

Stöber, J., & Bittencourt, J. (1998). Weekly assessment of worry: An adaptation of the Penn State Worry Questionnaire for monitoring changes during treatment. *Behaviour Research and Therapy, 36,* 645–656.

**Recent review (PSWQ-PW):**

Gervais, N. J., & Dugas, M. J. (2008). Generalized anxiety disorder. In J. Hunsley & E. J. Mash (Eds.), *A guide to assessments that work* (pp. 254–274). New York: Oxford University Press.

**Primary reference (PSWQ):**

Meyer, T. J., Miller, M. L., Metzger, R. L., & Borkovec, T. D. (1990). Development and validation of the Penn State Worry Questionnaire. *Behaviour Research and Therapy, 28,* 487–495.

---

**Figure A.4** • Penn State Worry Questionnaire—Past Week (PSWQ-PW)

---

For each of the following statements, please indicate how often that statement was characteristic of you **during the past week.**

Answer categories:   0 = never
                     1 = very rarely        4 = often
                     2 = rarely             5 = very often
                     3 = sometimes          6 = almost always

---

| | |
|---|---|
| 1. If I didn't have enough time to do everything, I didn't worry about it. | 0 1 2 3 4 5 6 |
| 2. My worries overwhelmed me. | 0 1 2 3 4 5 6 |
| 3. I didn't tend to worry about things. | 0 1 2 3 4 5 6 |
| 4. Many situations made me worry. | 0 1 2 3 4 5 6 |
| 5. I knew I shouldn't have worried about things, but I just couldn't help it. | 0 1 2 3 4 5 6 |
| 6. When I was under pressure, I worried a lot. | 0 1 2 3 4 5 6 |
| 7. I was always worrying about something. | 0 1 2 3 4 5 6 |
| 8. I found it easy to dismiss worrisome thoughts. | 0 1 2 3 4 5 6 |
| 9. As soon as I finished one task, I started to worry about everything else that I had to do. | 0 1 2 3 4 5 6 |
| 10. I did not worry about anything. | 0 1 2 3 4 5 6 |
| 11. When there was nothing more I could do about a concern, I didn't worry about it anymore. | 0 1 2 3 4 5 6 |
| 12. I noticed that I had been worrying about things. | 0 1 2 3 4 5 6 |
| 13. Once I started worrying, I couldn't stop. | 0 1 2 3 4 5 6 |
| 14. I worried all the time. | 0 1 2 3 4 5 6 |
| 15. I worried about projects until they were all done. | 0 1 2 3 4 5 6 |

## Group Engagement Measure-27 (GEM-27)

The GEM was developed to measure the engagement of individual members of treatment groups along seven dimensions: (1) attendance, (2) contributing, (3) relating to worker, (4) relating with members, (5) contracting, (6) working on own problems, and (7) working on other members' problems (Macgowan, 1997, 2006). The original 37-item GEM is a leader-report measure of engagement for each group member, but it has been adapted successfully for use as a self-report measure. In addition, there is a 27-item version of the GEM that is reproduced in this appendix, and there is a 21-item version of the GEM that measures all but two of the seven dimensions (attendance and contracting) (Macgowan & Newman, 2005).

The GEM is copyrighted. For permission to use it contact:

Mark J. Macgowan, PhD, LCSW

Robert Stempel College of Public Health & Social Work

Florida International University

11200 SW 8th Street, GL 485

Miami, FL 33199

Tel: 305-348-5883

Email: Macgowan@fiu.edu
Academic website: http://swjpa.fiu.edu/faculty/macgowan/
http://www.EvidenceBasedGroupWork.com

**Scoring and interpretation:** A total score and seven subscale scores are computed for the GEM-27. To compute these scores, first reverse score items 15, 16, and 17. Then, for each subscale, add up the subscale item responses and divide by the number of items in the subscale that were completed. To compute the GEM-27 total score, add up all item responses and divide by the number of completed items.

The total score and each of the subscale scores have a potential range of values from 1 through 5. A higher total score indicates greater overall engagement, and higher subscale scores indicate greater engagement in each particular area. The GEM-27 does not have a clinical cutting score, and standard deviations are not available so it isn't possible to compute the RC or the SEM.

**Primary reference (GEM-27):**

Macgowan, M. J., & Newman, F. L. (2005). The factor structure of the Group Engagement Measure. *Social Work Research, 29*(2), 107–118.

**Primary references (GEM-37):**

Macgowan, M. J. (1997). A measure of engagement for social group work: The Groupwork Engagement Measure (GEM). *Journal of Social Service Research, 23*(2), 17–37.

Macgowan, M. J. (2006). The Group Engagement Measure: A review of its conceptual and empirical properties. *Journal of Groups in Addiction and Recovery, 1*(2), 33–52.

**Recent review:**

Macgowan, M. J. (2009). *Group Engagement Measure: Overview.* Unpublished manuscript, School of Social Work, Florida International University, Miami.

**Figure A.5** • Groupwork Engagement Measure (GEM-27)

## GROUPWORK ENGAGEMENT MEASURE (GEM-27)
### Mark J. Macgowan, Ph.D., L.C.S.W.

This measure assesses a group member's engagement in the early and middle stages of group development (it should not be completed for the first session). The measure is to be completed by the group leader for each member. This version of the GEM scores engagement over the past few consecutive sessions.

Please rate every statement to the best of your recollection—even if you are unsure of your choice. If you are stuck in a choice between two points in the rating scale, choose the first that comes to mind—it is often the most accurate. If you find you have no evidence to rate the member on a statement, leave it blank. As a guide, subscales that are missing more than half their items should be discarded.

To score the GEM, add up each item and divide by the number of subscale items to obtain a subscale score, which should be entered into the space provided. The following items are reverse-scored: 15–17. For example, if a member is given a score of 2 on item #16, it will be considered a 4 for scoring purposes. Likewise, if a member is given a 5, it will be considered a 1 for scoring purposes.

Leader(s) Name: _____     Member Name/ID: _____

Today's Date: _____     Session Numbers Rated: _____

---

Please use the following scale to rate each statement:

1-------------------2-------------------3-------------------4-------------------5

| Rarely or none of the time | A little of the time | Some of the time | A good part of the time | Most or all of the time |

---

| Statement | Rating (circle) |
|---|---|
| **I. Attending** | |
| 1. The member arrives at or before start time | 1 2 3 4 5 |
| 2. The member stays until the end of sessions or leaves only for important reasons | 1 2 3 4 5 |
| 3. The member does not hurry to leave at the end of sessions | 1 2 3 4 5 |
| *Attending Score (sum total divided by # of items completed):* | |
| **II. Contributing** | |
| 4. The member contributes his/her share of talk time (not too much, not too little) | 1 2 3 4 5 |
| 5. The member seems to follow and understand what others are saying | 1 2 3 4 5 |
| 6. The member responds thoughtfully to what **all** others are saying (not just one or two) | 1 2 3 4 5 |
| 7. The member verbally interacts with members on topics related to the group's purpose | 1 2 3 4 5 |
| 8. The member participates in group projects/activities | 1 2 3 4 5 |

*Contributing Score (sum total divided by # of items completed):*

Please use the following scale to rate each statement:

1------------------2--------------------3------------------4--------------------5

| Rarely or none of the time | A little of the time | Some of the time | A good part of the time | Most or all of the time |

| Statement | Rating (circle) |
|---|---|
| **III. Relating to worker** | |
| 9. The member follows guidance of the worker (e.g., discusses what worker wants group to discuss, is involved in activities suggested by worker)[1] | 1 2 3 4 5 |
| 10. The member shows enthusiasm about contact with worker (e.g., demonstrates interest in the worker, is eager to speak with worker)[1] | 1 2 3 4 5 |
| 11. The member supports work that the worker is doing with other members (e.g., by staying on topic or expanding on discussion)[1] | 1 2 3 4 5 |

*Relating to Worker Score (sum total divided by # of items completed):*

| Statement | Rating (circle) |
|---|---|
| **IV. Relating with members** | |
| 12. The member likes and cares for other members | 1 2 3 4 5 |
| 13. The member helps other group members to maintain good relations with each other (e.g., by encouraging members to work out interpersonal problems, by stopping unproductive arguments among members, by cheering up members, and so forth) | 1 2 3 4 5 |
| 14. The member helps and encourages other members | 1 2 3 4 5 |

*Relating with Members Score (sum total divided by # of items completed):*

| Statement | Rating (circle) |
|---|---|
| **V. Contracting** | |
| 15. The member expresses continual disapproval about the meeting times[2] | 1 2 3 4 5 |
| 16. The member expresses continual disapproval about the number of meetings[2] | 1 2 3 4 5 |
| 17. The member expresses continual disapproval about what the group members are doing together[2] | 1 2 3 4 5 |

*(continued)*

---

[1] Members might sometimes challenge the guidance of the worker. Thoughtful, constructive challenges are O.K.
[2] This statement refers to expressions of disapproval long after the issue has been resolved by other members.

*Contracting Score (sum total divided by # of items completed):*

## VI. Working on own problems

| | |
|---|---|
| 18. The member partializes problems and works on their parts | 1  2  3  4  5 |
| 19. The member makes an effort to achieve his/her particular goals | 1  2  3  4  5 |

Please use the following scale to rate each statement:

| 1 | 2 | 3 | 4 | 5 |
|---|---|---|---|---|
| Rarely or none of the time | A little of the time | Some of the time | A good part of the time | Most or all of the time |

| Statement | Rating (circle) |
|---|---|
| 20. The member works on solutions to specific problems | 1  2  3  4  5 |
| 21. The member tries to understand the things s/he does | 1  2  3  4  5 |
| 22. The member reveals feelings that help in understanding problems | 1  2  3  4  5 |

*Working on Own Problems Score (sum total divided by # of items completed):*

## VII. Working with others' problems

| | |
|---|---|
| 23. The member talks with (encourages) others in ways that help them focus on their problems[3] | 1  2  3  4  5 |
| 24. The member talks with (encourages) others in ways that help them partialize or specify their problems[3] | 1  2  3  4  5 |
| 25. The member talks with (encourages) others in ways that help them do constructive work on solving their problems[3] | 1  2  3  4  5 |
| 26. The member challenges others constructively in their efforts to sort out their problems[3] | 1  2  3  4  5 |
| 27. The member helps others achieve the group's purpose[3] | 1  2  3  4  5 |

*Working with Others' Problems Score (sum total divided by # of items completed):*

*TOTAL ENGAGEMENT SCORE (OUT OF # ITEMS COMPLETED):* _____

---

[3] To score high on this statement, the member's offer of help need not be received. The member is not to be held accountable for the behavior of other members.

## Parent Daily Report (PDR)

The current version of the PDR is a 30-item checklist of child behavior problems as reported by parents, typically during a brief telephone interview. At each assessment, parents are asked to report on the occurrence or nonoccurrence (not frequency) of 30 specific behaviors within the past 24 hours. The PDR was developed as an inexpensive, easy-to-administer, and relatively unobtrusive alternative to direct behavioral observation by outside observers that would avoid the needs for both aggregate recall over a number of days and estimates of the frequency of occurrence of specific behaviors.

The PDR is copyrighted. For permission to use it contact Dr. Patricia Chamberlain (pattic@oslc.org).

**Scoring and interpretation:** A total score is calculated for the PDR by adding up the number of problem behaviors reported (although other scoring methods have been reported). The total score has a potential range of values from 0 through 30, and higher scores indicate more problem behaviors. It's also possible to compute averages across days (e.g., a week or several days in a week) by adding up the daily totals and dividing by the number of days of observation. To our knowledge, the PDR does not have a clinical cutting score. The RC equals 4.50 and the SEM equals 1.62 (based on a standard deviation of 4.06 and coefficient alpha of .84).

**Primary reference:**

Chamberlain, P., Price, J. M., Reid, J. B., Landsverk, J., Fisher, P. A., & Stoolmiller, M. (2006). Who disrupts from placement in foster and kinship care? *Child Abuse & Neglect, 30*, 409–424.

**Recent review:**

Frick, P. J., & McMahon, R. J. (2008). Child and adolescent conduct problems. In J. Hunsley & E. J. Mash (Eds.), *A guide to assessments that work* (pp. 41–66). New York: Oxford University Press.

**Figure A.6** • Parent Daily Report (PDR) Telephone Log

| | # | Behavior | __/__ Mon | __/__ Tue | __/__ Wed | __/__ Thurs | __/__ Fri | __/__ Sat | __/__ Sun |
|---|---|---|---|---|---|---|---|---|---|
| | 1 | Argue | | | | | | | |
| | 2 | Back-talk | | | | | | | |
| | 3 | Wet | | | | | | | |
| | 4 | Competitive | | | | | | | |
| | 5 | Complain | | | | | | | |
| | 6 | Defiant | | | | | | | |
| | 7 | Destructive/vandalism | | | | | | | |
| | 8 | Fight | | | | | | | |
| | 9 | Irritable | | | | | | | |
| | 10 | Lie | | | | | | | |
| | 11 | Negative | | | | | | | |
| | 12 | Boisterous/rowdy | | | | | | | |
| | 13 | Not mind | | | | | | | |
| | 14 | Stay out late | | | | | | | |
| | 15 | Skip meals | | | | | | | |
| | 16 | Run away | | | | | | | |
| | 17 | Swear/use bad language | | | | | | | |
| | 18 | Drugs/alcohol | | | | | | | |
| | 19 | Tease/provoke | | | | | | | |
| | 20 | Depressed/sad | | | | | | | |
| | 21 | Sluggish | | | | | | | |
| | 22 | Jealous | | | | | | | |
| | 23 | Truant (skipped school) | | | | | | | |
| | 24 | Steal | | | | | | | |
| | 25 | Nervous/jittery | | | | | | | |
| | 26 | Short attention span | | | | | | | |
| | 27 | Daydream | | | | | | | |
| | 28 | Irresponsible | | | | | | | |
| | 29 | School problem | | | | | | | |
| | 30 | Inappropriate sexual activity | | | | | | | |

# Appendix B

## ONLINE AND PUBLISHED RESOURCES FOR STANDARDIZED SCALES

### Online Resources for Standardized Scales

A Collaborative Outcomes Resource Network (ACORN): https://psychoutcomes.org/bin/view/AcornOrg/WebHome

Behavioral Measurement Database Services, Health and Psychological Instruments (HaPI) database: http://www.ovid.com/site/catalog/DataBase/866.jsp

Buros Center for Testing: http://www.unl.edu/buros/

Catholic University of America, University Library: http://libraries.cua.edu/nurscoll/testmeas.html

Center for the Study and Prevention of Violence, Institute of Behavioral Science, University of Colorado at Boulder: http://ibs.colorado.edu/cspv/infohouse/vioeval/

Harvey Cushing, John Hay Whitney Medical Library, Yale University School of Medicine: http://www.med.yale.edu/library/reference/publications/tests.html

Mapi Research Institute, ProQolid (Patient-Reported Outcome and Quality of Life Instrument Database): http://proqolid.org/

Mental Health Statistics Improvement Program (MHSIP): http://www.mhsip.org/surveylink.htm#mhsipapprovedsurveys

National Institute on Alcohol Abuse and Alcoholism: http://pubs.niaaa.nih.gov/publications/Assesing%20Alcohol/factsheets.htm

National Library of Medicine, Health Services and Sciences Research Resources: http://www.nlm.nih.gov/nichsr/hsrr_search/

National Quality Measures Clearinghouse (NQMC): http://www.qualitymeasures.ahrq.gov/

Neurotransmitter.net: http://www.neurotransmitter.net/index.php

Patient-Reported Outcomes Measurement Information System (PROMIS): http://www.nihpromis.org/Web%20Pages/Goals.aspx?PageView=Shared

United States Department of Veterans Affairs, National Center for PTSD: http://www.ptsd.va.gov/professional/pages/assessments/list-trauma-exposure-measures.asp

University of Texas Library: http://www.lib.utexas.edu/subject/ss/psyc/test.html

University of Washington, Alcohol & Drug Abuse Institute: http://lib.adai.washington.edu/instrumentsearch.htm

### Reference Books for Standardized Scales Published Since 2000

Allen, J. P., & Wilson, V. B. (Eds.). (2003). *Assessing alcohol problems: A guide for clinicians and researchers* (Series 4) (2nd ed.). Washington, DC: U.S. Department of Health and Human Services, National Institutes of Health.

Allison, D. B., & Baskin, M. (2009). *Handbook of assessment methods for eating behaviors and weight-related problems: Measures, theory, and research* (2nd ed.). Thousand Oaks, CA: Sage.

Antony, M. M., & Barlow, D. H. (in press). *Handbook of assessment and treatment planning for psychological disorders* (2nd ed.). New York: Guilford Press.

Antony, M. M., Orsillo, S. M., & Roemer, L. (Eds.). (2001). *Practitioner's guide to empirically based measures of anxiety*. New York: Kluwer Academic/Plenum.

Baer, L., & Blais, M. A. (2009). *Handbook of clinical rating scales and assessment in psychiatry and mental health*. New York: Humana Press.

Bolton, B. F., & Parker, R. M. (2008). *Handbook of measurement and evaluation in rehabilitation* (4th ed.). Austin, TX: Pro-Ed.

Bowling, A. (2001). *Measuring disease: A review of disease-specific quality of life measurement scales* (2nd ed.). Philadelphia, PA: Open University Press.

Bowling, A. (2004). *Measuring health: A review of quality of life measurement scales* (3rd ed.). Philadelphia, PA: Open University Press.

Burn, B., & Payment, M. (2000). *Assessments A to Z: A collection of 50 questionnaires, instruments, and inventories.* San Francisco, CA: Jossey-Bass/Pfeiffer.

Burns, A., Lawlor, B., & Craig, S. (2004). *Assessment scales in old age psychiatry* (2nd ed.). London: Martin Dunitz.

Child Trends. (2003). *Conceptualizing and measuring "healthy marriages" for empirical research and evaluation studies: A compendium of measures (Part II).* Washington, DC: Author.

Chun, K. M., Organista, P. B., & Marin, G. (2003). *Acculturation: Advances in theory, measurement, and applied research.* Washington, DC: American Psychological Association.

Cone, J. D. (2001). *Evaluating outcomes: Empirical tools for effective practice.* Washington, DC: American Psychological Association.

Corcoran, J., & Walsh, J. (2010). *Clinical assessment and diagnosis in social work practice* (2nd ed.). New York: Oxford University Press.

Dahlberg, L. L., Toal, S. B., Swahn, M., & Behrens, C. B. (2005). *Measuring violence-related attitudes, beliefs and behaviors among youths: A compendium of assessment tools* (2nd ed.). Atlanta, GA: Centers for Disease Control and Prevention.

Dana, R. H. (2005). *Multicultural assessment: Principles, applications, and examples.* Mahwah, NJ: Erlbaum.

Donovan, D. M., & Marlatt, G. A. (Eds.). (2005). *Assessment of addictive behaviors* (2nd ed.). New York: Guilford Press.

Fayers, P. M., & Machin, D. (2007). *Quality of life: The Assessment, analysis, and interpretation of patient-reported outcomes* (2nd ed.). New York: John Wiley.

Feindler, E. L., Rathus, J. H., & Silver, L. B. (2003). *Assessment of family violence: A handbook for researchers and practitioners.* Washington, DC: American Psychological Association.

Finch, E., Brooks, D., Stratford, P. W., & Mayo, N. E. (2002). *Physical rehabilitation outcome measures: A guide to enhanced clinical decision making* (2nd ed.). Hamilton, ON: B. C. Decker.

Fischer, J., & Corcoran K. (2007a). *Measures for clinical practice: Vol. 1. Couples, families, children* (4th ed.). New York: Oxford.

Fischer, J., & Corcoran, K. (2007b). *Measures for clinical practice: Vol. 2. Adults* (4th ed.). New York: Oxford.

Frank-Stromborg, M., & Olsen, S. J. (2004). *Instruments for clinical health-care research* (3rd ed.). Sudbury, MA: Jones and Bartlett.

Gallo, J. J., Bogner, H. R., Fulmer, T., & Paveza, G. J. (Eds.). (2006). *Handbook of geriatric assessment* (4th ed.). Gaithersburg, MD: Aspen.

Gitlin, L. N. (2006). *Physical function in older adults: A comprehensive guide to its meaning and measurement.* Austin, TX: Pro-Ed.

Goldman, B. A., & Mitchell, D. F. (2002). *Directory of unpublished experimental mental measures.* Washington, DC: American Psychological Association.

Grisso, T. (2003). *Evaluating competencies* (2nd ed.). Hingham, MA: Guilford.

Grisso, T., Vincent, G., & Seagrove, D. (2005). *Mental health screening and assessment in juvenile justice.* New York: Guilford Press.

Hersen, M. (2004). *Psychological assessment in clinical practice.* New York: Brunner-Routledge.

Hersen, M. (Ed.). (2006a). *Clinician's handbook of adult behavioral assessment.* St. Louis, MO: Academic Press.

Hersen, M. (Ed.). (2006b). *Clinician's handbook of child behavioral assessment.* St. Louis, MO: Academic Press.

Hersen, M. (Ed.). (2007). *Handbook of psychological assessment, case conceptualization, and treatment.* New York: Wiley.

Hersen, M., & Bellack, A. S. (Eds.). (2002). *Dictionary of behavioral assessment techniques* (2nd ed.). Clinton Corners, NY: Percheron Press.

Hunsley, J., & Mash, E. J. (Eds.). (2008). *A guide to assessments that work.* New York: Oxford University Press.

IsHak, W. W., Burt, T., & Sederer, L. (2002). *Outcome measurement in psychiatry: A critical review.* Washington, DC: American Psychiatric Publishing.

Johnson, D. (2010). *A compendium of psychosocial measures: Assessment of people with serious mental illness in the community.* New York: Springer.

Jordan, C., & Franklin, C. (Eds.). (2003). *Clinical assessment for social workers: Quantitative and qualitative methods* (2nd ed.). Chicago: Lyceum.

Kamphas, R. W., & Frick, P. J. (2005). *Clinical assessment of child and adolescent personality and behavior.* New York: Springer.

Kane, R. L., Kane, R. A., & Eells, M. (Eds.). (2004). *Assessing older persons: Measures, meaning, and practical applications.* New York: Oxford University Press.

Kellerman, H., & Burry, A. (2007). *Handbook of psychodiagnostic testing* (4th ed.). New York: Springer.

Kelley, M. L., Noell, G. H., & Reitman D. (2002). *Practitioner's guide to empirically based measures of school behavior.* Hingham, MA: Guilford.

Kennedy, J. A. (2003). *Fundamentals of psychiatric treatment planning* (2nd ed.). Washington, DC: American Psychiatric Publishers.

Keyser, D. J., & Sweetland, R. C. (Eds.). (2005). *Test critiques: Volume XI.* Austin, TX: Pro-Ed.

Lester, P. E., & Bishop, L. K. (2000). *Handbook of tests and measurement in education and the social sciences* (2nd ed.). Lanham, MD: Scarecrow Press.

Lichtenberg, P. A. (Ed.). (in press). *Handbook of assessment in clinical gerontology* (2nd ed.). Burlington, MA: Academic Press.

Lopez, S. J., & Snyder, C. R. (Eds.). (2003). *Positive psychological assessment: A handbook of models and measures.* Washington, DC: American Psychological Association.

Maddox, T. (2008). *A comprehensive reference for assessments in psychology, education, and business* (6th ed.). Austin, TX: Pro-Ed.

Maruish, M. E. (Ed.). (2004a). *The use of psychological testing for treatment planning and outcomes assessment: Vol. 1. General considerations* (3rd ed.). Hillsdale, NJ: Erlbaum.

Maruish, M. E. (Ed.). (2004b). *The use of psychological testing for treatment planning and outcomes assessment: Vol. 2. Instruments for children and adolescents* (3rd ed.). Hillsdale, NJ: Erlbaum.

Maruish, M. E. (Ed.). (2004c). *The use of psychological testing for treatment planning and outcomes assessment: Vol. 3. Instruments for adults* (3rd ed.). Hillsdale, NJ: Erlbaum.

Mash, E. J., & Barkley, R. A. (2007). *Assessment of childhood disorders* (4th ed.). New York: Guilford Press.

McDowell, I. (2006). *Measuring health: A guide to rating scales and questionnaires* (3rd ed.). New York: Oxford University Press.

Mowder, B. A., Rubinson, F., & Yaski, A. E. (Eds.). (2009). *Evidence-based practice in infant and early childhood psychology.* Hoboken, NJ: John Wiley.

Murphy, L. L., Plake, B. S., & Spies, R. A. (2006). *Tests in print VII.* Lincoln, NE: Buros Institute of Mental Measurements.

Naar-King, D. A., Ellis, M. A., & Frey, M. L. (2003). *Assessing children's well-being: A handbook of measures.* Mahwah, NJ: Lawrence Erlbaum.

Nader, K. (2007). *Understanding and assessing trauma in children and adolescents: Measures, methods, and youth in context.* New York: Routledge.

Nangle, D. W., Hansen, D. J., Erdley, C. A., & Norton, P. J. (Eds.). (2010). *Practitioner's guide to empirically based measures of social skills.* New York: Springer.

National Institute for Mental Health England (NIMHE). (2009). *Mental health outcomes compendium.* London: Department of Health. Retrieved from http://www.dh.gov.uk/en/Publicationsandstatistics/Publications/PublicationsPolicyAndGuidance/DH_093316

Nezu, A. M., Ronan, G. F., Meadows, E. A., & McClure, K. S. (Eds.). (2000). *Practitioner's guide to empirically based measures of depression.* New York: Springer.

Ogles, B. M., Lambert, M. J., & Fields, S. A. (2002). *Essentials of outcome assessment.* New York: John Wiley & Sons.

Paniagua, F. A. (2005). *Assessing and treating culturally diverse clients: A practical guide* (3rd ed.). Thousand Oaks, CA: Sage.

Perkinson, R. R. (2004). *Treating alcoholism: Helping your clients find the road to recovery.* Hoboken, NJ: John Wiley.

Rathus, J. H., & Feindler, E. L. (2004). *Assessment of partner violence: A handbook for researchers and practitioners.* Washington, DC: American Psychological Association.

Redman, B. K. (2003). *Measurement tools in patient education* (2nd ed.). New York: Springer.

Reynolds, C. R., Kamphaus, R. W., & Hendry, C. N. (Eds.). (2003). *Handbook of psychological and educational assessment of children: Intelligence, aptitude, and achievement* (2nd ed.). New York: Guilford Press.

Roberts, A. R., & Yeager, K. R. (Eds.). (2003). *Evidence-based practice manual: Research and outcome measures in health and human services.* Oxford: Oxford University Press.

Rush, A. J., Jr., First, M. B., & Blacker, D. (Eds.). (2008). *Handbook of psychiatric measures* (2nd ed.). Washington, DC: American Psychiatric Association.

Sajatovic, M., & Ramirez, L. F. (2003). *Rating scales in mental health* (2nd ed.). Cleveland: Lexi-Comp.

Salek, S. (2007). *Compendium of quality of life instruments: Vol 7*. Hampshire, England: Euromed Communications Ltd.

Sattler, J. M., & Hoge, R. D. (2006). *Assessment of children: Behavioral, social, and clinical foundations* (5th ed.). Austin, TX: Pro-Ed.

Smith, S. R., & Handler, L. (2006). *The clinical assessment of children and adolescents: A practitioner's handbook*. Hillsdale, NJ: Erlbaum.

Sperry, L. (Ed.). (2004). *Assessment of couples and families: Contemporary and cutting edge strategies*. London: Routledge.

Spies, R. A., Plake, B. S., Geisinger, K. F., & Carlson, J. F. (2010). *The eighteenth mental measurements yearbook*. Lincoln: Buros Institute, University of Nebraska.

Stanhope, M., & Knollmueller, R. N. (2000). *Handbook of community-based and home health nursing practice: Tools for assessment, intervention, and education* (3rd ed.). St. Louis, MO: Mosby.

Strickland, O. L., & Dilorio, C. (Eds.). (2003a). *Measurement of nursing outcomes: Vol. II. Client outcomes and quality of care* (2nd ed.). New York: Springer.

Strickland, O. L., & Dilorio, C. (Eds.). (2003b). *Measurement of nursing outcomes: Vol. III. Self-care and coping* (2nd ed.). New York: Springer.

Suzuki, L. A., & Ponterotto, J. G. (Eds.). (2008). *Handbook of multicultural assessment: Clinical, psychological, and educational applications* (3rd ed.). San Francisco: Jossey-Bass.

Thomlison, B. (2007). *Family assessment handbook: An introduction and practical guide to family assessment* (2nd ed.). Belmont, CA: Thomson Higher Education.

Thompson, M. P., Basile, K. C., Hertz, M. F., & Sitterle, D. (2006). *Measuring intimate partner violence victimization and perpetration: A compendium of assessment tools*. Atlanta, GA: Centers for Disease Control and Prevention.

Touliatos, J., Perlmutter, B. F., Straus, M. A., & Holden, G. W. (2001). *Handbook of family measurement techniques*. Newbury Park, CA: Sage.

Trauer, T. (2010). *Outcome measurement in mental health*. Cambridge: Cambridge University Press.

Turk, D. C., & Melzak, R. (Eds.). (in press). *Handbook of pain assessment* (3rd ed.). New York: Guilford Press.

Verhulst, F. C., & van der Ende, J. (2006). *Assessment scales in child and adolescent psychiatry*. Oxon: Informa.

Wall, J. E., & Walz, G. R. (2004). *Measuring up: Assessment issues for teachers, counselors, and administrators*. Austin, TX: Pro-Ed.

Walters, S. J. (2010). *Quality of life outcomes in clinical trials and health-care evaluation: A practical guide to analysis and interpretation*. New York: Wiley.

Watson, J. (2001). *Assessing and measuring caring in nursing and health sciences*. New York: Springer.

Wilson, J. P., & Keane, T. M. (2004). *Assessing psychological trauma and PTSD*. New York: Guilford Press.

# Glossary

**A-B design:** two-phase single-case design consisting of a pre-intervention baseline phase (A) followed by an intervention phase (B).

**A-B-A design:** three-phase single-case design consisting of a pre-intervention baseline phase ($A_1$); an intervention phase (B); and a second baseline phase ($A_2$) in which the intervention is withdrawn to determine if the outcome reverses to the initial baseline pattern.

**A-B-A-B design:** four-phase single-case design consisting of a pre-intervention baseline phase ($A_1$); an intervention phase ($B_1$); a second baseline phase ($A_2$) in which the intervention is withdrawn to determine if the outcome reverses to the initial baseline pattern; and a reintroduction of the intervention ($B_2$) to see whether the initial intervention effects are replicated. Also known as a *reversal* or *withdrawal* design.

**A-B-BC design:** three-phase single-case design consisting of a pre-intervention baseline (A); an intervention phase (B); and a second intervention phase in which a new intervention (C) is added to the first intervention in response to the failure of the first intervention to produce sufficient improvement in the outcome.

**A-B-C design:** three-phase single-case design consisting of a pre-intervention baseline (A); an intervention phase (B); and a second intervention phase (C) in which a new intervention is introduced in response to the failure of the first intervention to produce sufficient improvement in the outcome.

**Accountability:** obligation of an individual to other individuals based on a social or legal contract to justify his or her actions; the processes and procedures through which a professional justifies and takes responsibility for professional activities and decisions; and extent to which a person is answerable to another (e.g., a supervisor or official review body) for his or her behaviors, decisions, or judgments, especially in a professional capacity.

**Adverse effect:** harmful, undesired, inadvertent intervention effect. Also known as an *iatrogenic effect*. See also *Side effect*.

**Alternative explanations:** plausible reasons for a relationship between an intervention and an outcome, other than that the intervention caused the outcome. Also known as *alternative hypotheses*. The ability to rule out alternative hypotheses is a requirement for inferring that one variable (intervention) caused another (outcome).

**Alternative hypotheses:** See *Alternative explanations*.

**Ambiguous temporal precedence:** potential threat to internal validity in which it is not clear whether one variable (e.g., intervention) occurred before or after another (e.g., outcome), making it difficult to distinguish the cause from the effect. The ability to establish that one variable (e.g., intervention) coincided with or occurred before another (e.g., outcome) is a requirement for inferring that one variable caused another.

**Analogue situation:** contrived circumstances designed to elicit a sample of behavior that is representative of behavior that occurs in the natural environment. See also *Enactment analogue*, *Paper-and-pencil analogue*, and *Role-playing analogue*.

**Anchor:** brief (usually) explicit labels, descriptions, or examples used to define points or numbers on a rating scale (e.g., 1, poor; 2, fair; 3, good; 4, very good; 5, excellent).

**A-phase:** See *Baseline phase*.

**Ascending baseline:** See *Trend*.

**Assessment:** systematic collection, organization, and interpretation of data related to a client's functioning in order to make decisions or recommendations about intervention or other services.

**Attribute:** quality or property of a person, object, or event (e.g., attributes of people include abilities, attitudes, and behaviors).

**B+ design:** single-case design (arguably, since there isn't repeated measurement during baseline) consisting of one pre-intervention outcome measurement followed by an intervention phase (B) during which the outcome is measured repeatedly.

**B-A-B design:** three-phase single-case design beginning with the intervention phase ($B_1$), followed by the withdrawal of the intervention (A) to determine if the outcome changes in the absence of the intervention, and reintroduction of the intervention ($B_2$) to see whether the initial intervention effects are replicated.

**Baseline phase:** period of time during which an outcome is measured repeatedly in the absence of an intervention in order to (1) describe the naturally occurring pattern of outcome data (e.g., level, trend, variability) and (2) determine the effect of an intervention on that outcome. Typically symbolized by the letter A.

**Behavior:** what people do (e.g., expressions of criticism and contempt), in contrast to what people have (e.g., depression). It includes how people move and what they say, think, and feel. See also *Behavior product*, *Covert behavior*, and *Overt behavior*.

**Behavior product:** effects or results of behaviors, not the behaviors themselves (e.g., number of cigarette butts in an ashtray as a product of smoking cigarettes).

**Behavioral skills training:** intervention designed to facilitate an individual's behavior in interacting and communicating with others.

**Bias:** tendency to see and interpret information consistently with an emotional preference or preconceived expectation; in research, unknown or unacknowledged error created during the conceptualization, design, measurement, sampling, procedure, or interpretation of findings.

**B-only design:** single-case design (arguably) consisting of an intervention phase (B) during which the outcome is measured repeatedly.

**B-phase:** See *Intervention phase*.

**Carryover effect:** lingering effect of one intervention phase on later phases (e.g., a child receives praise for raising his hand in class and retains that skill in a subsequent phase focused on rewarding him for cooperating with his classmates).

**Case conceptualization/formulation:** integration of a client's circumstances with knowledge of theory of human behavior or change, including hypotheses about the mechanisms that are causing and maintaining problems and the plan for intervening with them in a particular client.

**Causal ambiguity:** uncertainty about which of several events or processes caused an outcome.

**Causal inference:** conclusion based on evidence and reasoning that one variable (e.g., intervention) causes another (e.g., outcome).

**Cause:** a variable (e.g., intervention) that produces an effect or is responsible for events or results (e.g., outcome).

**Client:** individual, couple, family, group, organization, or community seeking assistance with a problem from a helping professional. Also known as a *case*. Clients also may be referred to as *patients* in medical settings and psychiatric settings or *residents* in assisted living facilities, independent living facilities, and nursing homes.

**Client log or structured diary:** systematic observation and recording by a person of his or her behavior or other experiences and the the conditions under which these behaviors or other experiences occur.

**Clinically significant improvement:** change that occurs when a client's measured functioning on a standardized scale is in the dysfunctional range before intervention (e.g., greater than 5 on the QIDS-SR) and in the functional range after intervention (e.g., 5 or below on the QIDS-SR), and that the change is reliable.

**Coefficient alpha:** statistic typically used to quantify the internal-consistency reliability of a standardized scale. Also known as *Cronbach's alpha* and, when items are dichotomous, *Kuder-Richardson 20*, *KR20*, or *KR-20*.

**Cognitive behavior therapy:** a psychotherapeutic approach that aims to solve problems concerning dysfunctional emotions, behaviors, and cognitions through a goal-oriented, systematic procedure.

**Composite score:** score that combines results from two or more related items or other measures using a specified formula (e.g., percentage of items answered correctly on a statistics test).

**Concept:** abstraction that symbolizes a class of people (e.g., female), objects (e.g., chair), or events (e.g., baseball game) that have one or more characteristics in common.

**Conceptual definition:** definition that assigns meaning to a concept in terms of other concepts, such as in a dictionary, instead of in terms of the activities or operations used to measure it. (Contrast with *Operational definition*.)

**Concurrent validity:** degree to which scores on a measure can predict a contemporaneous criterion. (Contrast with *Predictive validation*.) See also *Criterion validity*.

**Condition:** environmental arrangement (e.g., baseline or intervention) in effect at a given time in a single-system design (e.g., in an A-B-A-B design, there are two conditions: baseline and intervention).

**Condition change line:** dashed vertical line drawn upward from the horizontal axis on a single-system design line graph that shows the point when a change is made from one condition (e.g., baseline) to the next (e.g., intervention).

**Confirmation bias:** tendency to gather evidence that confirms one's preconceptions by emphasizing or pursuing supporting evidence while dismissing or failing to seek contradictory evidence.

**Construct:** complex concept (e.g., intelligence, well-being, depression) that is inferred or derived from a set of interrelated attributes (e.g., behaviors, experiences, subjective states, attitudes) of people, objects, or events; typically embedded in a theory; and oftentimes not directly observable but measured using multiple indicators.

**Construct validity:** degree to which scores on a measure can be interpreted as representing a given construct, as evidenced by theoretically predicted patterns of associations with measures of related and unrelated variables, group differences, and changes over time; accuracy of conclusions based on evidence and reasoning about the degree to which cause and effect variables as operationalized in a study represent the constructs of interest (e.g., does an intervention as implemented or an outcome as measured contain all of the relevant features and exclude irrelevant features). See also *Convergent validity* and *Discriminant validity*.

**Content validity:** degree to which questions, behaviors, or other types of content represent a given construct comprehensively (e.g., the full range of relevant content is represented, and irrelevant content is not).

**Control/placebo group:** group of participants in an experiment who are exposed to control conditions (such as a placebo or waiting list), rather than the experimental condition (such as an intervention).

**Convergent validity:** degree to which scores derived from a measure of a construct are correlated in the predicted way with other measures of the same or related constructs or variables. (Contrast with *Discriminant validity*.) See also *Construct validity*.

**Correlation:** statistic which indicates whether and how two variables are related. A correlation has a potential range from $-1.0$ to $+1.0$. A *positive correlation* means that people with higher values on one variable tend to have higher values on another variable. A *negative correlation* means that people with lower values on one variable tend to have higher values on another variable. A correlation of 0 means there's no linear relationship between two variables. The absolute value of a correlation (i.e., the actual number, ignoring the plus or minus sign) indicates the strength of the relationship—the larger the absolute value, the stronger the relationship.

**Count:** number of times a behavior occurs. Also known as *frequency*.

**Covert behavior:** behavior that occurs within individuals and therefore cannot be observed by others, at least directly. (Contrast with *Overt behavior*.)

**Criterion validity:** degree to which scores on a measure can predict performance or status on another measure that serves as a standard (i.e., the criterion, sometimes called a *gold standard*). See also *Concurrent validity* and *Predictive validity*.

**Critical thinking:** application of logical principles, rigorous standards of evidence, and careful reasoning to the analysis and discussion of data, claims, beliefs, or issues.

**Culture:** distinctive values, customs, beliefs, knowledge, art, history, institutions, and language shared by a particular social group at a particular time and place.

**Cut scores:** specific predetermined numerical values along a continuum of scores that are used to separate people into categories with distinct substantive interpretations (e.g., clinically depressed or not) and to make decisions (provide treatment for depression or not). Also known as *cutting scores, cutoff scores,* and *clinical cutting scores*.

**Cyclical data pattern:** variable outcome data that exhibit a sequence of alternating patterns (e.g., upward and downward trends).

**Data:** a collection of quantitative or qualitative facts used to provide information, draw conclusions, or make decisions.

**Data path:** solid lines connecting consecutive data points within a condition in a single-case design line graph.

**Data pattern:** a particular arrangement of data in terms of level, trend, variability, cyclicity, overlap, immediacy, permanency, and practical significance.

**Data point:** intersection of a time period and a numerical value of the measure used to quantify the outcome in a single-case design line graph.

**Data series:** set of related data points plotted on a single-case design line graph (e.g., data for one outcome, such as percentage completed assignments, or data from one source, such as a single teacher).

**Descending baseline:** See *Trend*.

**Deteriorating baseline:** See *Deteriorating trend*.

**Deteriorating trend:** overall direction of a data path within a phase is moving in an undesirable direction (e.g., descending if higher values of the outcome are desirable, and ascending if lower values of the outcome are desirable). (Contrast with *Improving trend*.)

**Diagnosis:** classification of individuals based on a disease, disorder, abnormality, or set of characteristics; in psychiatry usually based on the *Diagnostic and Statistical Manual of Mental Disorders* (American Psychiatric Association, 2000).

***Diagnostic and Statistical Manual of Mental Disorders* (DSM):** publication of the American Psychiatric Association (2000) that provides criteria for the classification of mental disorders (e.g., substance-related disorders, schizophrenia and other psychotic disorders, mood disorders, anxiety disorders), including specific symptoms that must be present (and for how long) and absent for a particular diagnosis and additional information about each disorder (e.g., subtypes and/or specifiers, numerical codes and other information for recording diagnoses, associated features and disorders, specific culture, age, and gender features, prevalence, course, familial pattern, and differential diagnosis). *DSM* was designed for use in clinical, educational, and research settings by health and mental health professionals.

**Dimension:** quantitative quality or property (i.e., attribute) of a person, object, or event (e.g., height, length, and width are dimensions of an object).

**Direct observation:** observation of overt behavior by outside observers.

**Discriminant validity:** degree to which scores derived from a measure of a construct are uncorrelated with, or otherwise distinct from, theoretically dissimilar or unrelated constructs or other variables. (Contrast with *Convergent validity*.) See also *Construct validity*.

**Dropout:** unplanned termination of an intervention by the client, usually without notice to the helping professional.

**Duration:** length of time that a specific behavior occurs.

**Effect:** change in one variable (e.g., outcome) that occurred at least in part as the result of another variable (e.g., intervention).

**Effect size:** measure of the strength of the relationship between variables (e.g., effect of an intervention on an outcome, as quantified by any one of a number of different statistics).

**Effectiveness:** extent to which an intervention works when implemented under routine practice conditions (i.e., in the context of everyday real-world service delivery). (Contrast with *Efficacy*.)

**Efficacy:** extent to which an intervention works when implemented under ideal conditions (i.e., closely controlled scientific conditions). (Contrast with *Effectiveness*.)

**Enactment analogue:** type of analogue situation in which the client interacts in the agency or clinical setting with people he or she has difficulty interacting with in the natural environment. See also *Paper-and-pencil analogue* and *Role-playing analogue*.

**Ethics:** principles of morally right conduct accepted by a person or group or considered appropriate to a discipline or field.

**Evaluation:** systematic investigation of the value, quality, or importance of something (e.g., intervention) or someone (e.g., student, employee) in relationship to a set of standards (e.g., intervention goals and objectives). See also *Case-level evaluation, Explanatory evaluation, Formative evaluation, Impact assessment, Outcome evaluation, Practice evaluation, Program evaluation,* and *Summative evaluation*.

**Evaluation/research design:** overall plan that describes all of the elements of a research or evaluation study, and ideally the plan allows the researcher or evaluator to reach valid conclusions (e.g., questions or hypotheses to be addressed, number and types of participants to be included, number and types of variables to be studied, collection and analysis of data).

**Event-contingent sampling:** observation and recording of information in response to predefined events or situations. (Contrast with *Interval-contingent sampling* and *Signal-contingent sampling*.)

**Evidence:** external objective support for an argument, idea, hypothesis, or intervention based on research or other explicit standards.

**Expectancy effect:** influence on client outcomes of the client's anticipation of the effects of the intervention.

**Explanatory evaluation:** evaluation designed to determine why an intervention does or does not work as intended, including an understanding of the conditions under which the intervention does or does not work as intended.

**External validity:** accuracy of conclusions based on evidence and reasoning about how well a causal relationship applies across or beyond the people, settings, treatment variables, and measurement variables that were studied (e.g., extent to which a causal relationship between an intervention and outcome is the same with different people).

**Extraneous variable:** variable that is associated with the independent variable inadvertently influences the outcome, and consequently makes it difficult to determine the effect of the intervention on the outcome (e.g., an unknown event that occurs during intervention but not baseline and causes the pattern of outcome data to change from baseline to intervention). Also known as a *confound* or *confounding variable*, and such a result is said to be *confounded*.

**Face validity:** degree to which a measure of a construct or other variable appears to measure a given construct in the opinion of clients, other respondents, and other users of the measure.

**Falsification:** deliberate process of seeking information to discount or disprove a hypothesis or theory.

**Fatigue effect:** deterioration in an outcome caused by fatigue associated with repeated measurement of the outcome (e.g., a mother who is self-recording each instance of time-out with her preschooler reduces those time-outs to avoid recording the behavior). (Contrast with *Practice effect*.)

**Feedback:** ongoing systematic information provided to a practitioner, client, or other person or group regarding a client's outcomes for the purpose of improving those outcomes.

**Fidelity:** See *Intervention fidelity*.

**Follow-up phase:** period of time after an intervention has ended during which outcome data are collected to determine the extent to which a client's progress has been maintained. Also known as a *maintenance phase*.

**Formative evaluation:** evaluation conducted during the course of a program to provide ongoing feedback used to continuously improve the program while it is underway. Formative evaluation includes intervention monitoring in order to assess how well the intervention is being implemented (fidelity), outcome monitoring in order to assess how well program goals are being met, or both program and outcome monitoring. (Contrast with *Summative evaluation*.)

**Global rating:** single rating based on a rater's integration of information about numerous factors (e.g., global rating of change, improvement, or social functioning).

**Goal:** general and abstract statement of a desired outcome for which an intervention is implemented (e.g., reduce or alleviate depression). (Compare to *Objective*.)

**Goal line:** dashed line in a single-system design line graph that represents an objective as quantified by the outcome measure

and provides a visual aid that can be used to monitor and evaluate client progress.

**Google Docs:** free web-based word processor, spreadsheet, presentation, form, and data storage service that allows users to create, edit, and share documents online.

**Helping professional:** social worker, psychologist, psychiatrist, counselor, nurse, physical and occupational therapist, or other allied health care or social service professional.

**History effect:** potential threat to internal validity in which change in an outcome could be misinterpreted as an intervention effect, when in fact it is caused by an external event that occurs at the same time as the intervention (e.g., a student who has trouble completing his homework for a new teacher improves his performance as he becomes accustomed to her and her expectations, and the improvement is misinterpreted as being due to the rewards he earns working with a social worker).

**Horizontal axis (X-axis):** in a line graph, a solid horizontal line perpendicular to the vertical axis that represents, from left to right, the chronological progression of equal time periods (week 1, 2, 3, etc.) or other units (e.g., intervention sessions).

**Hypothesis:** empirically testable proposition about a fact, behavior, or relationship, usually based on theory.

**Iatrogenic effect:** unintended negative effect of a treatment or intervention.

**Idiographic:** study of an individual person or case focused on description and understanding of unique and lawful characteristics, qualities, and responses of that person or case. (Compare to *Nomothetic*.)

**Immediacy of change:** amount of time it takes for a change in level, trend, or variability to occur after a condition change (e.g., baseline to intervention).

**Implementation:** activities involved in delivery of an intervention, including intended and unintended activities, and activities that did and did not occur.

**Implementation assessment:** evaluation designed to describe and assess the extent to which an intervention is being implemented as originally designed and planned (fidelity). Also known as *process evaluation*.

**Improving baseline:** See *Improving trend*.

**Improving trend:** overall direction of a data path within a phase is moving in the desired direction (e.g., descending if lower values of the outcome are desirable and ascending if higher values of the outcome are desirable). (Contrast with *Deteriorating trend*.)

**Inferential thinking:** thinking that seeks the broader or deeper meaning of specific facts; in intervention, thinking about patterns in client behavior, causes of behavior or behavior change, and other broad issues; sometimes called *reading between the lines*.

**Instrumentation effect:** potential threat to internal validity in which an apparent change in an outcome could be misinterpreted as an intervention effect, when in fact it is caused by a change in how the outcome is measured (e.g., an older man's weight stabilizes when he begins weighing at his physician's office rather than at home).

**Intermediate goal/objective:** smaller goals or objectives that must be achieved in order to reach the ultimate goal.

**Internal-consistency reliability:** degree to which responses to a set of items on a standardized scale measure the same construct consistently.

**Internal validity:** accuracy of conclusions based on evidence and reasoning about causal relationships between variables (e.g., extent to which an intervention, as opposed to other factors, caused a change in an outcome).

**Interobserver reliability:** See *Inter-rater reliability.*

**Inter-rater reliability:** degree of consistency in ratings or observations across raters, observers, or judges (e.g., a second opinion from a health care professional, judges in an Olympic competition). Also known as *interobserver* or *interjudge* reliability or agreement.

**Interresponse time:** length of time between the occurrence of two successive instances of the same behavior (e.g., amount of time between completing two tasks or between two thoughts).

**Interval-contingent sampling:** observation and recording of information at predefined times each day. (Contrast with *Event-contingent sampling* and *Signal-contingent sampling.*)

**Intervention:** specific planned action by a helping professional and client, designed to achieve a goal or otherwise bring about beneficial change or prevent an undesirable outcome in a targeted client problem. Also referred to as a *treatment* when the intervention is designed to relieve a pathological or otherwise undesirable condition.

**Intervention adherence:** extent to which the client follows a prescribed intervention regimen. Also known as *treatment adherence.*

**Intervention effect:** portion of an outcome change that can be attributed uniquely to an intervention rather than to other influences.

**Intervention fidelity:** extent to which an intervention is implemented as designed and planned. Also known as *treatment integrity* and *procedural fidelity.*

**Intervention monitoring:** continual systematic documentation and tracking of the fidelity with which an intervention is implemented in order to ensure that the intervention is implemented with fidelity.

**Intervention phase:** period of time during which an intervention is implemented while an outcome is measured repeatedly.

**Intervention plan:** prescribed steps for intervening devised by the helping professional in collaboration with the client, after completion of assessment. May be written in contract form. Also known as a *treatment plan.*

**Item:** statement, question, problem, task, or other individual element of a measure used to elicit a response.

**Latency:** length of time it takes for a behavior to occur in relation to some stimulus (e.g., amount of elapsed time between a parent asking a child to go to bed and the time the child gets into bed). Also known as *response latency.*

**Level:** value on the vertical axis around which a series of outcome data converge.

**Line graph:** graph that connects successive data points (e.g., status of an outcome at a particular time) with lines to show changes in the value of a variable (e.g., client outcomes), usually over time.

**Magnitude:** strength, intensity, or force of a behavior or other event.

**Maintenance phase:** See *Follow-up phase.*

**Maturation effect:** potential threat to internal validity in which change in an outcome could be misinterpreted as an intervention effect, when in fact it is caused by naturally occurring changes in clients over time (e.g., a toddler's tantrums diminish not in response to an intervention, but due to maturing out of the terrible twos, or a child outgrows enuresis).

**Measurement:** systematic process that involves assigning labels (usually numbers) to characteristics of people, objects, or events using explicit and consistent rules so, ideally, the labels accurately represent the characteristic measured.

**Measurement errors:** discrepancies between measured and actual (true) values of a variable caused by flaws in the measurement process (e.g., characteristics of clients or other respondents, measurement conditions, properties of measures). See also *Random measurement errors* and *Systematic measurement errors.*

**Measurement instrument:** specific measurement tool (e.g., a specific standardized self-report scale measuring depression).

**Measurement method:** class of measurement procedures (e.g., standardized self-report scales).

**Measurement plan:** overall strategy used to measure a client's outcomes, including the methods and instruments used, as well as how to obtain the information, who can best provide the information, and when, where, and how often the information should be collected.

**Measurement validity:** general term for the degree to which accumulated evidence and theory support interpretations and uses of scores derived from a measure. See also *Concurrent validity*, *Construct validity*, *Content validity*, *Convergent validity*, *Criterion validity*, *Discriminant validity*, *Face validity*, *Predictive validity*, and *Sensitivity to change.*

**Median:** measure of central tendency that divides a distribution of values in half when the values are arranged in numerical order (or the average of the middle two values in a set with an even number of values).

**Meta-analysis:** quantitative method of synthesizing the findings of multiple studies by combining the effect sizes of the studies into a single effect size (or range).

**Method bias:** relationships in data resulting solely from the particular type of measurement procedure or data source.

**Multidimensional scale:** scale that measures two or more distinct but related attributes or constructs, and measures of the different attributes or constructs are referred to as *subscales.* (Contrast with *Unidimensional scale.*) Also known as *multifactorial scales.*

**Multiple baseline across behaviors (problems) design:** single-case design that begins with a baseline during which two or more problems are measured at the same time for a single client in a particular setting. Baseline is followed by the application of the intervention to one problem with baseline conditions remaining in effect for other problems, then the intervention is applied sequentially to the remaining problems to see whether intervention effects are replicated across different problems.

**Multiple baseline across settings design:** single-case design that begins with a baseline during which the same problem is measured for a single client in two or more settings at the same time. Baseline is followed by the application of the intervention in one setting while baseline conditions remain in effect for other settings, then the intervention is applied sequentially across the remaining settings to see whether intervention effects are replicated across different settings.

**Multiple baseline across subjects (clients) design:** single-case design that begins with a baseline during which the same problem is measured for two or more clients at the same time in a particular setting. Baseline is followed by the application of the intervention to one client while baseline conditions remain in effect for other clients, then the intervention is applied sequentially to remaining clients to see whether intervention effects are replicated across different clients.

**Multiple baseline designs:** See *Multiple baseline across behaviors (problems) design*, *Multiple baseline across settings design*, and *Multiple baseline across subjects (clients) design*.

**Nomothetic:** study of groups of people or cases for the purpose of discovering general principles or laws that characterize the average person or case. (Compare to *Idiographic*.)

**Norm:** single value or distribution of values that represent the performance of a normative group and serve as the basis of comparison and interpretation for scores derived from a measure (e.g., an individual's percentile rank on the ACT, SAT, GRE, or similar measure based on the distribution of scores in a normative group). See also *Normative group* and *Reference population*.

**Normative group:** representative sample of a reference population used to estimate norms for that population and, more generally, used to develop and test standardized measures. Also known as a *standardization group* or *standardization sample*.

**Objective:** (noun) specific and concrete statement detailing a desired outcome of an intervention along with measurable criteria used to define and evaluate client success (e.g., to reduce the level of depression on a particular standardized scale to below a certain score, a benchmark). Operational definition of a goal. (adjective) judgments that are relatively less influenced by personal feelings, beliefs, experiences, interpretations, or other biases or prejudices.

**Observer drift:** unintended change over time in the way an observer measures a behavior due, for example, to changes in how the observer interprets the original definitions of the behavior.

**Operational definition:** definition that assigns meaning to a concept in terms of the activities or operations used to measure it, ideally in a way that contains relevant features of the concept and excludes irrelevant features. (Contrast with *Conceptual definition*.)

**Order effect:** result due to the order in which different interventions are administered (e.g., a couple may be more successful in an intervention designed to increase their pleasant time together each day if they first complete an intervention designed to increase their reflective listening). Also known as a *sequence effect*.

**Outcome:** status of a client's problem along some dimension (e.g., frequency, severity) at some point in time (e.g., before, during, or after intervention). (Compare to *Goal*, which is a statement of the desired—not actual—status of a client's problem.) Final status of a client's problem along some dimension (e.g., frequency, severity). (Compare to *Outcome measure*.)

**Outcome change:** difference between outcome levels at different times.

**Outcome evaluation:** evaluation undertaken to determine the change in client outcomes, if any, resulting from an intervention. (Contrast with *Progress monitoring*, also known as *outcome monitoring*, which is used to determine if satisfactory progress is made toward achieving client goals, but does not attempt to attribute observed changes to the intervention.)

**Outcome-informed practice:** practice in which you measure your client's outcomes at regular, frequent, predesignated intervals, in a way that is sensitive to and respectful of the client; monitor those outcomes to determine if your client is making satisfactory progress; and modify your intervention plan as needed along the way by using this practice-based evidence, in concert with evidence-based practice, to improve your client's outcomes.

**Outcome measure:** tool used to measure the status of a client's problem along some dimension. Operational definition of an outcome. Sometimes a measured outcome is referred to as an *indicator*.

**Outcome monitoring:** See *Progress monitoring*.

**Outcomes management:** the process of using data about client outcomes to determine the continuation, alteration, or termination of an intervention.

**Overlap:** degree to which data in adjacent phases share similar quantitative values—the more the overlap, the less the difference between adjacent phases, and the less the overlap, the greater the difference.

**Overt behavior:** behavior that can be observed by others (at least theoretically). (Contrast with *Covert behavior*.)

**Paper-and pencil analogue:** type of analogue situation in which the client is asked to respond orally or in writing to a situation presented in written form. See also *Enactment analogue* and *Role-playing analogue*.

**Phase:** period of time within a single-system design (e.g., in an A-B-A-B design, there are four phases: two baseline and two intervention).

**Practice effect:** improvement in an outcome caused by repeated measurement of the outcome (e.g., taking multiple practice exams may improve a student's score on the Graduate Record Exam simply because he or she becomes familiar with the format of the exam). (Contrast with *Fatigue effect*.)

**Practice-based evidence:** in this book, evidence about the effectiveness of an intervention for a particular client based on that client's outcomes.

**Predictive validity:** degree to which scores on a measure can predict a criterion measured at a future point in time. (Contrast with *Concurrent validity*.) See also *Criterion validity*.

**Presenting problem:** problem offered by a client as a reason for seeking services.

**Problem:** specific situation, condition, or concern that needs to be addressed in order to achieve a desired goal, including difficulties or deficiencies to be remediated or prevented as well as assets and strengths to be enriched.

**Progress monitoring:** frequent, regular, systematic measurement and tracking of a client's outcome(s) in order to determine if the client is making satisfactory progress toward achieving goals. (Contrast with *Outcome evaluation*, which attempts to attribute observed changes to the intervention.) Also known as *outcome monitoring*.

**Random measurement errors:** discrepancies between measured and actual (true) values of a variable that are equally likely to be higher or lower than the actual values because they are caused by chance fluctuations in measurement. They are caused by flaws in the measurement process and they tend to cancel each other out and average to zero but they increase the variability of measured values. Also known as *unsystematic* measurement errors. (Contrast with *Systematic measurement errors*.)

**Randomized controlled trial (RCT):** type of experiment commonly used in testing the efficacy or effectiveness of interventions in which research participants are assigned randomly to groups (e.g., treatment, control) and outcomes are compared across groups to determine intervention effects. Also known as a *randomized clinical trial* when used in clinical research. (See the CONSORT [Consolidated Standards of Reporting Trials] website http://www.consort-statement.org that provides recommendations for reporting RCTs.)

**Rate:** count per a unit of time.

**Rating:** systematic estimation of some attribute of a person, object, or event along some dimension (e.g., magnitude or degree) using a numerical scale (i.e., a score).

**Rating scale:** measurement instrument used to elicit a rating.

**Raw score:** score in its original, untransformed, observed units of measurement (e.g., number of correct items on a test before being converted to a percentage correct, grade, percentile rank, or standard score).

**Reactivity:** degree to which measurement procedures produce changes in what is being measured.

**Reference population:** population of people for which a measure is intended and from which a normative group is sampled and norms are created.

**Regression effect:** potential threat to internal validity in which change in an outcome could be misinterpreted as an intervention effect, when in fact it is caused by the tendency of an individual with unusually high or low scores on a measure to subsequently have scores closer to the mean (e.g., clients who are depressed frequently seek help when they have hit bottom, and their scores are likely to improve somewhat in the following weeks, even without intervention). Also known as *regression toward the mean*.

**Reinforcement:** in operant conditioning, any consequence of a behavior that causes an increase in the probability of that response occurring in the future.

**Relevant other:** an individual who is an important part of another individual's social network.

**Reliability:** general term for the consistency of measurements, and *unreliability* means inconsistency caused by random measurement errors. See also *Internal-consistency reliability*, *Inter-rater reliability*, and *Test–retest reliability*.

**Reliable change:** change in a score from one time to another that is more than expected just from random measurement error.

**Reliable deterioration:** deterioration in a score from one time to another that is more than expected just from random measurement error.

**Reliable improvement:** improvement in a score from one time to another that is more than expected just from random measurement error.

**Representative sample:** subset of observations (e.g., people, situations, times) that has characteristics similar to or typical of observations of the population from which the sample was selected.

**Response category:** point on a rating scale that represents the degree, magnitude, or intensity of an outcome.

**Reverse-worded item:** item for which smaller numbers indicate a higher score on the measured variable because the item is worded to mean the opposite of the measured variable (e.g., If a standardized scale is used to measure depression, and a higher score on the measure indicates greater depression, an example of a reverse-worded item would be "I am happy"; 0, rarely or none of the time; 1, some or little of the time; 2, occasionally or a moderate amount of the time; 3, most or all of the time).

**Role-playing analogue:** type of analogue situation in which the client is asked to visualize a situation in the natural environment and his or her response to it, or to act out situations with the practitioner or others (e.g., in group therapy) role-playing relevant people. See also *Enactment analogue* and *Paper-and-pencil analogue*.

**Sampling:** selection of a subset of a population for the purpose of drawing conclusions about the entire population; implies selection procedures (e.g., random selection) designed to result in a subset with characteristics that are equal to those of the population, within a specified level of probability.

**Scientific method:** standardized group of procedures for testing scientific laws through construction and testing of predictions based on hypotheses; procedures emphasize experimental manipulation of variables and elimination of alternative explanations for outcomes.

**Score:** generic term for a number derived from a measure that represents the quantity or amount of an attribute or observation (e.g., number of times a behavior is observed, percentage correct on a test, value obtained from a standardized scale).

**Scoring:** procedure by which data from a measure are used to produce a score (e.g., number of times a behavior occurs or value on a standardized scale) or category (e.g., diagnostic category).

**Scoring formula:** a mathematical rule by which data from a measure are used to produce a score (e.g., sum or average of responses to items on a multi-item standardized scale).

**Self-monitoring:** systematic observation and recording by a person of his or her behavior or other experiences.

**Self-report measure:** instrument used by a respondent to assess his or her own behaviors, feelings, thoughts, or other experiences or attributes.

**Sensitivity to change:** degree to which a measure detects genuine change in the variable measured. Also known as *responsiveness to change*.

**Sequence effect:** See *Order effect*.

**Side effect:** any unintended intervention effect, adverse or otherwise. See also *Adverse effect*.

**Signal-contingent sampling:** observation and recording of information at random times, typically signaled by an electronic device (e.g., smartphone). (Contrast with *Event-contingent sampling* and *Interval-contingent sampling*.)

**Single-case design:** family of research and evaluation designs characterized by the systematic repeated measurement of a client's outcome(s) at regular, frequent, predesignated intervals under different conditions (baseline and intervention), and the evaluation of outcomes over time and under different conditions in order to monitor client progress, identify intervention effects, and more generally, learn when, why, how, and the extent to which client change occurs. Also known as *single-subject designs, single-system designs, N = 1 designs,* or sometimes *time series* or *interrupted time series designs*.

**Slope:** typical amount of change in an outcome from day to day, week to week, or whatever unit is involved.

**Social skills training:** intervention designed to facilitate an individual's behavior in interacting and communicating with others.

**Stable baseline:** pattern of baseline data that exhibits relatively little variability over time and little or no trend.

**Standard error of measurement (SEM):** estimate of the degree of random measurement error (i.e., unreliability) in scores derived from a measure that can be used to determine the range of values within which an individual's true score is likely to fall.

**Standardization:** use of identical procedures to collect, score, interpret, and report results of a measure in order to assure that differences over time or among different people are due to the variable being measured and not due to different measurement procedures; process used to establish norms or uniform procedures for a measure.

**Standardized scale:** measurement method that uses uniform procedures to collect, score, interpret, and report numerical results; usually has norms and empirical evidence of reliability and validity; typically includes multiple items aggregated into one or more composite scores; and frequently used to measure constructs.

**Statistical conclusion validity:** accuracy of conclusions based on evidence and reasoning about the presence, direction, and strength of relationships between variables (e.g., outcome is different during baseline than intervention). The ability to establish that one variable (e.g., intervention) is related to another (e.g., outcome) is a requirement for inferring that one variable caused another.

**Success:** accomplishment of the client's goals.

**Summative evaluation:** evaluation undertaken after an intervention has been completed to examine a program's ultimate impact in order to determine the extent to which the program was effective in achieving its goals.

**Systematic measurement errors:** discrepancies between measured and actual (true) values of a variable that are more likely to be higher or lower than the actual values of the variable. They are caused by flaws in the measurement process and they lead to over- or underestimates of the actual values of a variable. Also known as *bias* in measurement. (Contrast with *Random measurement errors*.)

**Template:** master version of a document with a predesigned format (e.g., line graphs formatted with standard single-case design conventions).

**Testing effect:** potential threat to internal validity in which change in an outcome could be misinterpreted as an intervention effect, when in fact it is caused by repeated measurement of the outcome (e.g., a pretest about health behaviors may sensitize a client to the need to make changes in diet and exercise). See also *Fatigue effect* and *Practice effect*.

**Test–retest reliability:** degree to which scores on a measure are consistent over time.

**Threats to internal validity:** reasons why it might be partly or completely wrong (i.e., invalid) to conclude that one variable (e.g., an intervention) caused another (e.g., an outcome). See also *Ambiguous temporal precedence, History effect, Instrumentation effect, Maturation effect, Regression effect,* and *Testing effect*.

**Treatment plan:** See *Intervention plan*.

**Trend:** overall direction of a data path within a phase or across phases of a single-case design line graph: (1) no trend; (2) negative trend (also referred to as a *descending* or *decelerating* trend because values are decreasing over time); and (3) positive trend (also referred to as an *ascending* or *accelerating* trend because values are increasing over time). See also *Deteriorating trend* and *Improving trend*.

**Triangulation:** engineering term that describes a process of collecting data from several different nearby locations to verify the location of a geographical point; in assessment, emphasizes collection of data from several sources and using different methods and procedures.

**Unidimensional scale:** scale that measures a single attribute or construct (e.g., depression). (Contrast with *Multidimensional scale*.)

**Validity:** general term for the degree to which accumulated evidence and theory support particular interpretations of test scores, or other measurements, for certain purposes. See also *Concurrent validity, Construct validity, Content validity, Convergent validity, Criterion validity, Discriminant validity, Face validity, Predictive validity,* and *Sensitivity to change*.

**Values:** different quantities of a variable (e.g., different levels of depression).

**Variability:** degree to which data points deviate from (or dispersed relative to) the overall trend.

**Variable:** characteristics that can take on different values for different people, objects, or events (different values of depression for different people), or different values for the same people, objects, or events at different times (different values of depression for the same person at different times).

**Variable baseline:** pattern of baseline outcome data that do not fall within a relatively small range of values (i.e., they are variable).

**Vertical axis (Y-axis):** in a line graph, a solid vertical line perpendicular to the horizontal axis that starts at the left end of the horizontal axis, and represents a range of numerical values of the outcome measure with equal intervals representing equal quantities and lower to higher values arranged from bottom to top.

**Visual analysis:** systematic process for interpreting results of single-case design data that involves the visual examination of graphed data within and between different conditions (e.g., baseline, intervention) in terms of level, trend, variability, cyclicity, overlap, immediacy, permanency, and practical significance.

# References

Achenbach, T. M., & Rescorla, L. A. (2000). *Manual for ASEBA preschool forms and profiles*. Burlington: University of Vermont, Research Center for Children, Youth, and Families.

Achenbach, T. M., & Rescorla, L. A. (2001). *Manual for ASEBA school-age forms and profiles*. Burlington: University of Vermont, Research Center for Children, Youth, and Families.

Ahluwalia, M. K. (2008). Multicultural issues in computer-based assessment. In L. A. Suzuki & J. G. Ponterotto (Eds.), *Handbook of multicultural assessment: Clinical, psychological, and educational applications* (3rd ed., pp. 92–106). San Francisco: Jossey-Bass.

Aisenberg, E. (2008). Evidence-based practice in mental health care to ethnic minority communities: Has its practice fallen short of its evidence? *Social Work, 53*, 297–306.

Albers, G., Echteld, M. A., de Vet, H. C. W., Onwuteaka-Philipsen, B. D., van der Linden, M. H. M., & Deliens, L. (2010). Evaluation of quality-of-life measures or use in palliative care: A systematic review. *Palliative Medicine, 24*, 17–37.

Al-Krenawi, A., & Graham, J. R. (2000). Culturally sensitive social work practice with Arab clients in mental health settings. *Health and Social Work, 25*, 9–22.

Allen, J. (2010). Personality assessment with American Indians and Alaska Natives: Instrument considerations and service delivery style. *Journal of Personality Assessment, 70*, 17–42.

Alter, C., & Egan, M. (1997). Logic modeling: A tool for teaching critical thinking in social work practice. *Journal of Social Work Education, 33*, 85–102.

American Educational Research Association, American Psychological Association, and National Council on Measurement in Education. (1999). *Standards for educational and psychological testing*. Washington, DC: American Educational Research Association.

American Psychiatric Association. (2000). *Diagnostic and statistical manual of mental disorders* (4th ed., Text rev.). Washington, DC: Author.

American Psychological Association Presidential Task Force on Evidence-Based Practice. (2006). Evidence-based practice in psychology. *American Psychologist, 61*, 271–285.

Andrews, B. (2007). Doing what counts. *Human Givens Journal, 14*, 32–37.

Anker, M. G., Duncan, B. L., & Sparks, J. A. (2009). Using client feedback to improve couple therapy outcomes: A randomized clinical trial in a naturalistic setting. *Journal of Consulting and Clinical Psychology, 77*, 693–704.

Antle, B. F., Barbee, A. P., Christensen, D. N., & Martin, M. H. (2008). Solution-based casework in child welfare: Preliminary evaluation research. *Journal of Public Child Welfare, 2*, 197–227.

Armstrong, A. W., Watson, A. J., Makredes, M., Frangos, J. E., Kimball, A. B., & Kvedar, J. C. (2009). Text-message reminders to improve sunscreen use: A randomized, controlled trial using electronic monitoring. *Archives of Dermatology, 145*, 1230–1236.

Arnold, L. E., Vitiello, B., McDougle, C., Scahill, L., Shah, B., Gonzalez, N. M., et al. (2003). Parent-defined target symptoms respond to risperidone in RUPP autism study: Customer approach to clinical trials. *Journal of the American Academy of Child and Adolescent Psychiatry, 42*, 1443–1450.

Austrian, S. G. (2009). Guidelines for conducting a biopsychosocial assessment. In A. R. Roberts (Ed.), *Social workers' desk reference* (2nd ed., pp. 376–380). New York: Oxford University Press.

Avina, C. (2008). The use of self-monitoring as a treatment intervention. In W. T. O'Donohue & N. A. Cummings (Eds.), *Evidence-based adjunctive treatments* (pp. 207–222). Burlington, MA: Academic Press.

Bachar, E., Canetti, L., Yonah, I., & Bonne, O. (2004). Group versus individual supportive-expressive psychotherapy for chronic, symptomatically stabilized outpatients. *Psychotherapy Research, 14*, 244–251.

Baer, D. M., Harrison, R., Fradenburg, L., Petersen, D., & Milla, S. (2005). Some pragmatics in the valid and reliable recording of directly observed behavior. *Research on Social Work Practice, 15*, 440–451.

Baker, L. R., Stephens, F., & Hitchcock, L. (2010). Social work practitioners and practice evaluation: How are we doing? *Journal of Human Behavior in the Social Environment, 20*, 963–973.

Barkham, M., Hardy, G. E., & Mellor-Clark, J. (Eds.). (2010). *Developing and delivering practice-based evidence*. Oxford, UK: John Wiley & Sons.

Barkham, M., Mellor-Clark, J., Connell, J., Evans, C., Evans, R., & Margison, F. (2010). Clinical Outcomes in Routine Evaluation (CORE)—The CORE measures and system: Measuring, monitoring, and managing quality evaluation in the psychological therapies. In M. Barkham, G. E. Hardy, & J. Mellor-Clark (Eds.), *Developing and delivering practice-based evidence* (pp. 175–220). Oxford, UK: John Wiley & Sons.

Barlow, D., Nock, M., & Hersen, M. (2009). *Single case experimental designs: Strategies for studying behavior for change* (3rd ed.). Boston: Pearson.

Barratt, M. (2003). Organizational support for evidence-based practice within child and family social work: A collaborative study. *Child and Family Social Work, 8,* 143–150.

Barrett, M. S., Chua, W. J., Crits-Christoph, P., Gibbons, M. B., & Thompson, D. (2008). Early withdrawal from mental health treatment: Implications for psychotherapy practice. *Psychotherapy Theory, Research, Practice, Training, 45,* 247–267.

Barton, E. E., Reichow, B., & Wolery, M. (2007). Guidelines for graphing data with Microsoft® and PowerPoint™. *Journal of Early Intervention, 29,* 320–336.

Battle, C. C., Imber, S. D., Hoehn-Saric, R., Stone, A. R., Nash, E. R., & Frank, J. D. (1966). Target complaints as criteria of improvement. *American Journal of Psychotherapy, 20,* 184–192.

Bauer, S., Lambert, M. J., & Nielsen, S. L. (2004). Clinical significance methods: A comparison of statistical techniques. *Journal of Personality Assessment, 82,* 60–70.

Benca, R., & Lichstein, K. L. (2008). Sleep disorders measures. In A. J. Rush Jr., M. B. First, & D. Blacker (Eds.), *Handbook of psychiatric measures* (2nd ed., pp. 649–666). Washington, DC: American Psychiatric Association.

Berlin, S. B., & Marsh, J. C. (1993). *Informing practice decisions.* New York: Macmillan.

Berman, P. S. (2010). *Case conceptualization and treatment planning.* Los Angeles: Sage.

Bickman, L. (2008). A measurement feedback system (MFS) is necessary to improve mental health outcomes. *Journal of the American Academy of Child and Adolescent Psychiatry, 47,* 1114–1119.

Bickman, L., Riemer, M., Lambert, E. W., Kellwy, S. D., Breda, C., Dew, S. E., et al. (Eds.). (2010). *Manual of the peabody Treatment progress battery* (2nd ed.) [Electronic version]. Nashville, TN: Vanderbilt University. Retrieved from http://peabody.vanderbilt.edu/ptpb/

Bird, H. R., Canino, G., Rubio-Stipec, M., & Ribera, J. C. (1987). Further measures of the psychometric properties of the children's global assessment scale. *Archives of General Psychiatry, 44,* 821–824.

Bisman, C. (2004). Social work values: The moral core of the profession. *British Journal of Social Work, 34,* 109–123.

Bloom, M., Fischer, J., & Orme, J. G. (2009). *Evaluating practice: Guidelines for the accountable professional* (6th ed.). Boston: Allyn & Bacon.

Bloom, M., & Orme, J. G. (1993). Ethics and the single subject design. *Journal of Social Service Research, 18,* 161–180.

Bohanske, R. T., & Franczak, M. (2010). Transforming public behavioral health care: A case example of consumer-directed services, recovery, and the common factors. In B. L. Duncan, S. D. Miller, B. E. Wampold, & M. A. Hubble (Eds.), *The heart and soul of change: Delivering what works* (2nd ed., pp. 299–322). Washington, DC: American Psychological Association.

Bolen, R. M., & Hall, J. C. (2007). Promoting and sustaining evidence-based practice managed care and evidence-based practice: The untold story. *Journal of Social Work Education, 43,* 463–479.

Bronfenbrenner, U. (1977). Toward an experimental ecology of human development. *American Psychologist, 32,* 513–531.

Brown, G. S., & Minami, T. (2010). Outcomes management, reimbursement, and the future of psychotherapy. In B. L. Duncan, S. D. Miller, B. E. Wampold, & M. A. Hubble (Eds.), *The heart and soul of change: Delivering what works* (2nd ed., pp. 267–297). Washington, DC: American Psychological Association.

Brown, L. S. (2006). The neglect of lesbian, gay, bisexual, and transgendered clients. In J. C. Norcross, L. E. Beutler, & R. F. Levant (Eds.), *Evidence-based practices in mental health: Debate and dialogue on the fundamental questions* (pp. 346–353). Washington, DC: American Psychological Association.

Busseri, M. A., & Tyler, J. D. (2004). Client-therapist agreement on target problems, working alliance, and counseling outcome. *Psychotherapy Research, 14,* 77–88.

Butler, G., Fennell, M., & Hackmann, A. (2008). *Cognitive-behavioral therapy for anxiety disorders: Mastering clinical challenges.* New York: Guilford.

Buxton, A. R. M., Rodger, S., Cummings, A. L., & Leschied, A. W. (2006). The change process in clients with high needs. *Canadian Journal of Counseling, 40,* 32–47.

Campbell, J. A. (1988). Client acceptance of single-system evaluation procedures. *Social Work Research & Abstracts, 24,* 21–22.

Campbell, J. M., & Herzinger, C. V. (2010). Statistics and single subject research methodology. In D. L. Gast (Ed.), *Single subject research methodology in behavioral sciences* (pp. 417–453). New York: Routledge.

Chamberlain, P., Price, J. M., Reid, J. B., Landsverk, J., Fisher, P. A., & Stoolmiller, M. (2006). Who disrupts from placement in foster and kinship care? *Child Abuse & Neglect, 30,* 409–424.

Chamberlain, P., & Reid, J. B. (1987). Parent observation and report of child symptoms. *Behavioral Assessment, 9,* 97–109.

Chapleski, E. E., Lamphere, J. K., Kaczynski, R., Lichtenberg, P. A., & Dwyer, J. W. (1997). Structure of a depression measure among American Indian elders: Confirmatory factor analysis of the CES-D scale. *Research on Aging, 19,* 462–486.

Chorpita, B. F., Bernstein, A., & Daleiden, E. L. (2008). Driving with roadmaps and dashboards: Using information resources to structure the decision models in service organizations. *Administration and Policy in Mental Health, 35,* 114–123.

Clark, J. P., & Alvarez, M. E. (Eds.). (2010). *Response to intervention: A guide for school social workers.* New York: Oxford University Press.

Clark, J. P., & Gilmore, J. (2010). Tier 3 intensive individualized interventions. In J. P. Clark & M. E. Alvarez (Eds.), *Response to intervention: A guide for school social workers* (pp. 131–153). New York: Oxford University Press.

Cnaan, R. A., & Dichter, M. E. (2008). Thoughts on the use of knowledge in social work practice. *Research on Social Work Practice, 18,* 278–284.

Collins, P. M., Kayser, K., & Platt, S. (1994). Conjoint marital therapy: A practitioner's approach to single-system evaluation. *Families in Society: The Journal of Contemporary Human Services, 75,* 131–141.

Combs-Orme, T. D., & Orme, J. G. (1986). Reliability of self-reported child abuse and neglect in a general population survey. *Social Work Research & Abstracts, 22,* 19–21.

Cooper, J. O., Heron, T. E., & Heward, W. L. (2007). *Applied behavior analysis* (2nd ed.). Upper Saddle River, NJ: Pearson.

Corcoran, J. (2005). *Building strengths and skills. A collaborative approach to working with clients.* New York: Oxford University Press.

Corcoran, J., & Walsh, J. (2010). *Clinical assessment and diagnosis in social work practice.* New York: Oxford University Press.

Cortes, D. E., Gerena, M., Canino, G., Aguilar-Gaxiola, S., Febo, V., Magana, C., et al. (2007). Translation and cultural adaptation of a mental health outcome measure: The BASIS-R. *Culture, Medicine and Psychiatry, 31,* 25–49.

Council on Social Work Education. (2008). *2008 EPAS handbook.* Retrieved from http://www.cswe.org/Accreditation/Handbook.aspx

Cox, L. E. (2009). Predictors of medication adherence in an AIDS clinical trial: Patient and clinician perspectives. *Health and Social Work, 34,* 257–264.

Crockett, L. J., Randall, B. A., Shen, Y., Russell, S. T., & Driscoll, A. K. (2005). Measurement equivalence of the Center for Epidemiological Studies Depression Scale for Latino and Anglo adolescents: A national study. *Journal of Consulting and Clinical Psychology, 73*(1), 47–58.

Currie, S. R. (2008). Sleep disorders. In J. Hunsley & E. J. Mash (Eds.), *A guide to assessments that work* (pp. 535–550). New York: Oxford University Press.

Dausch, B. M., Miklowitz, D. J., & Richards, J. A. (1996). Global Assessment of Relational Functioning Scale (GARF), II: Reliability and validity in a sample of families of bipolar patients. *Family Process, 35,* 175–189.

Del Carmen, M. G., & Joffe, S. (2005). Informed consent for medical treatment and research: A review. *The Oncologist, 10,* 636–641.

Di Noia, J., & Tripodi, T. (2008). *Single-case design for clinical social workers* (2nd ed.). Washington, DC: National Association of Social Workers.

Dick, R. W., Beals, J., Keane, E. M., & Manson, S. M. (1994). Factorial structure of the CES-D among American Indian adolescents. *Journal of Adolescence, 17,* 73–79.

Dieckhaus, K. D., & Odesina, V. (2007). Outcomes of a multifaceted medication adherence intervention for HIV-positive patients. *AIDS Patient Care and STDs, 21,* 81–91.

Dixon, M. R., Jackson, J. W., Small, S. L., Horner-King, M. J., Lik, N. M. K., Garcia, Y., & Rosales, R. (2009). Creating single-subject design graphs in Microsoft Excel™ 2007. *Journal of Applied Behavior Analysis, 42,* 277–293.

Donaldson, S. I., Christie, C. A., & Mark, M. M. (Eds.). (2009). *What counts as credible evidence in applied research and evaluation practice?* Thousand Oaks, CA: Sage.

Dougherty, L. R., Klein, D. N., Olino, T. M., & Laptook, R. S. (2008). Depression in children and adolescents. In J. Hunsley & E. J. Mash (Eds.), *A guide to assessments that work* (pp. 69–95). New York: Oxford University Press.

Duncan, B. L. (2011). *The partners for change outcome management System (PCOMS): Administration, scoring, and interpretation manual update for the Outcome and Session Rating Scales.* Chicago, IL: The Heart and Soul of Change Project.

Duncan, B. L., Miller, S. D., & Sparks, J. A. (2004). *The heroic client: A revolutionary way to improve effectiveness through client-directed, outcome-informed therapy* (Rev. ed.). San Francisco: Jossey-Bass.

Duncan, B. L., Miller, S. D., Sparks, J. A., Claud, D. A., Reynolds, L. R., Brown, J., & Johnson, L. D. (2003). The session rating scale: Preliminary psychometric properties of a "working" alliance measure. *Journal of Brief Therapy, 3,* 3–12.

Duncan, B. L., Miller, S. D., Wampold, B. E., & Hubble, M. A. (Eds.). (2010). *The heart and soul of change: Delivering what works* (2nd ed.). Washington, DC: American Psychological Association.

Dworkin, R. H., Turk, D. C., Wyrwich, K. W., Beaton, D., Cleeland, C. S., Farrar, J. T., et al. (2008). Interpreting the clinical importance of treatment outcomes in chronic pain clinical trials: IMMPACT recommendations. *Journal of Pain, 9,* 105–121.

Edgington, E. S. (1983). Response-guided experimentation. *Contemporary Psychology, 28,* 64–65.

Eigenmann, C. A., Colagiuri, R., Skinner, T. C., & Trevena, L. (2009). Are current psychometric tools suitable for measuring outcomes of diabetes education? *Diabetic Medicine, 26,* 425–436.

Elmquist, J. M., Melton, T. K., Croarkin, P., & McClintock, S. M. (2010). A systematic overview of measurement-based care in the treatment of childhood and adolescent depression. *Journal of Psychiatric Practice, 16,* 217–234.

Eyberg, S. (2010). *Parent child interaction training* (Version 2.1). Miami, FL: Child Study Laboratory. Retrieved from http://pcit.phhp.ufl.edu/

Eyberg, S. M., & Pincus, D. (1999). *The Eyberg Child Behavior Inventory and Sutter-Eyberg Student Behavior Inventory:* Professional manual. Lutz, FL: Psychological Assessment Resources.

Eysenck, H. J. (1952). The effects of psychotherapy: An evaluation. *Journal of Consulting and Clinical Psychology, 60,* 659–663.

Farrimond, S. J., & Leland, L. S., Jr. (2006). Increasing donations to supermarket foodbank bins using proximal prompts. *Journal of Applied Behavior Analysis, 39,* 249–251.

Feindler, E. L., & Gerber, M. (2008). TAME: Teen anger management education. In C. W. LeCroy (Ed.), *Handbook of evidence-based treatment manuals for children and adolescents* (2nd ed., pp. 139–169). New York: Oxford University Press.

Fernandez, K., Boccaccini, M. T., & Noland, R. M. (2007). Professionally responsible test selection for Spanish-speaking clients: A four-step approach for identifying and selecting translated tests. *Professional Psychology: Research and Practice, 38,* 363–374.

Ferron, J., & Jones, P. K. (2006). Tests for the visual analysis of response-guided multiple-baseline data. *The Journal of Experimental Education, 75,* 66–81.

Fischer, J. (1973). Is casework effective? A review. *Social Work, 18,* 5–21.

Fischer, J. (2009). *Toward evidence-based practice: Variations on theme.* Chicago, IL: Lyceum Books.

Fischer, J., & Corcoran, K. (2007a). *Measures for clinical practice and research: Vol. 1. Couples, families, and children* (4th ed.). New York: Oxford University Press.

Fischer, J., & Corcoran, K. (2007b). *Measures for clinical practice and research: Vol. 2. Adults* (4th ed.). New York: Oxford University Press.

Franklin, C., & Jordan, C. (2003). An integrative skills assessment approach. In C. Jordan & C. Franklin (Eds.), *Clinical assessment for social workers: Quantitative and qualitative methods* (2nd ed., pp. 1–52). Chicago, IL: Lyceum Books.

Franklin, C., Kim, J. S., & Tripodi, S. J. (2009). A meta-analysis of published school social work practice studies: 1980–2007. *Research on Social Work Practice, 19,* 667–677.

Fraser, M. W., Richman, J. M., Galinsky, M. J., & Day, S. H. (2009). *Intervention research: Developing social programs.* New York: Oxford University Press.

Friman, P. C. (2009). Behavior assessment. In D. Barlow, M. Nock, & M. Hersen (Eds.), *Single case experimental designs: Strategies for studying behavior for change* (3rd ed., pp. 99–134). Boston, MA: Allyn & Bacon.

Furman, R. (2009). Ethical considerations of evidence-based care. *Social Work, 54,* 82–84.

Furr, R. M., & Bacharach, V. R. (2008). *Psychometrics: An introduction.* Thousand Oaks, CA: Sage.

Furukawa, T. A. (2010). Assessment of mood: Guides for clinicians. *Journal of Psychosomatic Research, 68*(6), 581–589.

Gambrill, E. (2005). *Critical thinking in clinical practice. Improving the quality of judgments and decisions* (2nd ed.). Hoboken, NJ: John Wiley & Sons.

Garb, H. N. (2005). Clinical judgment and decision making. *Annual Review of Clinical Psychology, 1,* 67–89.

Garvin, C. D. (2009). Developing goals. In A. R. Roberts (Ed.), *Social workers' desk reference* (2nd ed., pp. 521–526). New York: Oxford University Press.

Gast, D. L. (Ed.). (2010). *Single subject research methodology in behavioral sciences.* New York: Routledge.

Gast, D. L., & Spriggs, A. D. (2010). Visual analysis of graphic data. In D. L. Gast (Ed.), *Single subject research methodology in behavioral sciences* (pp. 199–233). New York: Routledge.

Gaus, V. L. (2007). *Cognitive-behavioral therapy for adult Asperger syndrome.* New York: Guilford.

Gilgun, J. (2005). The four cornerstones of evidence-based practice in social work. *Research on Social Work Practice, 15,* 52–61.

Ginsburg, G. S., Baker, E. V., Mullaney, B. C., Barlow, A., Goklish, N., Hastings, R., et al. (2008). Depressive symptoms among reservation-based pregnant American Indian adolescents. *Maternal and Child Health Journal, 12,* 110–118.

Gold, S., & Marx, B. P. (2006). Analogue and virtual reality assessment. In M. Hersen (Ed.), *Clinicians handbook of child behavioral assessment* (pp. 82–102). St. Louis, MO: Academic Press.

Goldman, H. H., Skodol, A. E., & Lave, T. R. (1992). Revising Axis V for DSM-IV: A review of measures of social functioning. *American Journal of Psychiatry, 149,* 1148–1156.

Graham, J. R., Bradshaw, C., & Trew, J. L. (2010). Cultural considerations for social service agencies working with Muslim clients. *Social Work, 55,* 337–346.

Graybeal, C. T. (2007). Evidence for the art of social work. *Families in Society: The Journal of Contemporary Social Services, 88,* 513–523.

Greenberg, R. P., Constantino, M. J., & Bruce, N. (2006). Are patient expectations still relevant for psychotherapy process and outcome? *Clinical Psychology Review, 26,* 657–678.

Greene, R. R., & Jones, S. H. (2007). Chapter 1: Introduction. *Journal of Human Behavior in the Social Environment, 14,* 1–30.

Greenhalgh, J. (2009). The applications of PROs in clinical practice: What are they, do they work, and why? *Quality of Life Research, 18,* 115–123.

Grehan, P., & Moran, D. J. (2005). Constructing single-subject reversal design graphs using Microsoft Word: A comprehensive tutorial. *Behavior Analyst Today, 6,* 235–242.

Gross, D., Fogg, L., Young, M., Ridge, A., Cowell, J., Sivan, A., & Richardson, R. (2007). Reliability and validity of the Eyberg Child Behavior Inventory with African-American and Latino parents of young children. *Research in Nursing & Health, 30,* 213–223.

Gupta, R. (1999). The revised caregiver burden scale: A preliminary evaluation. *Research on Social Work Practice, 9,* 508–520.

Hannan, C., Lambert, M. J., Harmon, C., Nielsen, S. L., Smart, D. W., & Shimokawa, K. (2005). A lab test and algorithms for identifying clients at risk for treatment failure. *Journal of Clinical Psychology: In Session, 61,* 155–163.

Harmon, S. C., Lambert, M. J., Smart, D. M., Hawkins, E., Nielsen, S. L., Slade, K., & Lutz, W. (2007). Enhancing outcome for potential treatment failures: Therapist-client feedback and clinical support tools. *Psychotherapy Research, 17,* 379–392.

Hartman, A. (1995). Diagrammatic assessment of family relationships. *Families in Society: The Journal of Contemporary Human Services, 76,* 111–122.

Hawkins, E. J., Lambert, M. J., Vermeersch, D. A., Slade, K., & Turtle, K. (2004). The effects of providing patient progress information to therapists and patients. *Psychotherapy Research, 14,* 308–327.

Hektner, J. M., Schmidt, J. A., & Csikszentmihalyi, M. (2007). *Experience sampling: Measuring the quality of everyday life.* Thousand Oaks, CA: Sage.

Hepworth, D. H., Rooney, R. H., Rooney, G. D., Strom-Gottfried, K., & Larsen, J. A. (2006). *Direct social work practice. Theory and skills.* Belmont, CA: Brooks/Cole.

Hicks, C. L., von Baeyer, C. L., Spafford, P., van Korlaar, I., & Goodenough, B. (2001). The Faces Pain Scale—Revised: Toward a common metric in pediatric pain measurement. *Pain, 93,* 173–183.

Hodge, D. R. (2006). Spiritually modified cognitive therapy: A review of the literature. *Social Work, 51,* 157–166.

Hofvander, B., Delorme, R., Chaste, P., Nyden, A., Wentz, E., Stahlberg, O., et al. (2009). Psychiatric and psychosocial problems in adults with normal-intelligence autism spectrum disorders. *BMC Psychiatry, 9,* 35–43.

Houle, T. T. (2009). Statistical analyses for single-case experimental designs. In D. Barlow, M. Nock, & M. Hersen (Eds.), *Single case experimental designs: Strategies for studying behavior for change* (3rd ed., pp. 271–305). Boston: Pearson.

Howe, D. (2002). Relating theory to practice. In M. Davies (Ed.), *The Blackwell companion to social work* (2nd ed., pp. 81–87). Oxford: Blackwell Publishing.

Hubble, M. A., Duncan, B. L., Miller, S. D., & Wampold, B. E. (2010). Introduction. In B. L. Duncan, S. D. Miller, B. E. Wampold, & M. A. Hubble (Eds.), *The heart and soul of change: Delivering what works* (2nd ed., pp. 23–46). Washington, DC: American Psychological Association.

Hudson, W. W. (1997). *The WALMYR assessment scale scoring manual*. Tallahassee, FL: WALMYR.

Hudson, W. W., & Faul, A. C. (1998). *The clinical measurement package: A field manual* (2nd ed.). Tallahassee, FL: WALMYR.

Huff, D. (1954). *How to lie with statistics*. New York: W. W. Norton.

Hunsley, J., & Mash, E. J. (2008). *A guide to assessments that work*. New York: Oxford University Press.

Jackson, K. F., & Hodge, D. R. (2010). Native American youth and culturally sensitive interventions: A systematic review. *Research on Social Work Practice, 20*, 260–270.

Jacobson, N. S., Follette, W. C., & Revenstorf, D. (1984). Psychotherapy outcome research: Methods for reporting variability and evaluating clinical significance. *Behavior Therapy, 15*, 336–352.

Jacobson, N. S., Roberts, L. J., Berns, S. B., & McGlinchey, J. B. (1999). Methods for defining and determining the clinical significance of treatment effects: Description, application, and alternatives. *Journal of Consulting and Clinical Psychology, 67*, 300–307.

Janosky, J. E., Leininger, S. L., Hoerger, M. P., & Libkuman, T. M. (2009). *Single subject designs in biomedicine*. New York: Springer.

Johnston, J. M., & Pennypacker, H. S. (2009). *Strategies and tactics of behavioral research* (3rd ed.). New York: Routledge.

Jordan, C., & Franklin, C. (2003). *Clinical assessment for social workers: Quantitative and qualitative methods* (2nd ed.). Chicago, IL: Lyceum Books.

Jordan, C., & Franklin, C. (Eds.). (2011). *Clinical assessment for social workers: Quantitative and qualitative methods* (3rd ed.). Chicago: Lyceum.

Kadushin, A., & Harkness, D. (2002). *Supervision in social work*. New York: Columbia University Press.

Kahng, S. W., Chung, K. M., Gutrshall, K., Pitts, S. C., Kao, J., & Girolami, K. (2010). Consistent visual analyses of intrasubject data. *Journal of Applied Behavior Analysis, 43*, 35–45.

Kamper, S., Maher, C. G., & Mackay, G. (2009). Global rating of change scales: A review of strengths and weaknesses and considerations for design. *The Journal of Manual & Manipulative Therapy, 17*, 163–170.

Kane, R. L., Kane, R. A., & Eells, M. (Eds.). (2004). *Assessing older persons: Measures, meaning, and practical applications*. New York: Oxford University Press.

Kaye, J. L. (2001). *Target complaints as a measure of outcome in psychotherapy with the depressed elderly*. Unpublished doctoral dissertation, Pacific Graduate School of Psychology, Palo Alto, CA.

Kazdin, A. E. (2008). Evidence-based treatments and delivery of psychological services: Shifting our emphases to increase impact. *Psychological Services, 5*, 201–215.

Kazdin, A. E. (2011). *Single-case research designs: Methods for clinical and applied settings* (2nd ed.). New York: Oxford University Press.

Keller, H. (2003). Socialization for competence: Cultural models of infancy. *Human Development, 46*, 288–311.

Kellett, S. (2007). A time series evaluation of the treatment of histrionic personality disorder with cognitive analytic therapy. *Psychology and Psychotherapy: Practice and Research, 80*, 389–405.

Kelley, M. L., & Jurbergs, N. (2009). Daily report cards: Home-based consequences for classroom behavior. In A. Akin-Little, S. G. Little, M. A. Bray, & T. J. Kehle (Eds.), *Behavioral interventions in schools: Evidence-based positive strategies* (pp. 221–230). Washington, DC: American Psychological Association.

Kellow, J. T., & Willson, V. L. (2008). Setting standards and establishing cut scores on criterion-referenced assessments: Some technical and practical considerations. In J. W. Osborne (Ed.), *Best practices in quantitative methods* (pp. 15–28). Los Angeles: Sage.

Kennedy, C. H. (2005). *Single-case designs for educational research*. Boston, MA: Allyn & Bacon.

Kirk, S. A., & Reid, W. J. (2002). *Science and social work: A critical appraisal*. New York: Columbia University Press.

Kivlighan, D. M., Multon, K. D., & Patton, M. J. (2000). Insight and symptom reduction in time-limited psychoanalytic counseling. *Journal of Counseling Psychology, 47*, 50–58.

Kraus, D., & Castonguay, L. G. (2010). Treatment Outcome Package (TOP)—Development and use in naturalistic settings. In M. Markham, G. E. Hardy, & J. Mellor-Clark (Eds.), *Developing and delivering practice-based evidence* (pp. 155–174). Oxford, UK: John Wiley & Sons.

Kuyken, W., Padesky, C. A., & Dudley, R. (2009). *Collaborative case conceptualization: Working effectively with clients in cognitive-behavioral therapy*. New York: Guilford Press.

Lambert, M. J. (2007). Presidential address: What we have learned from a decade of research aimed at improving psychotherapy outcome in routine care. *Psychotherapy Research, 17*, 1–14.

Lambert, M. J. (2010a). *Prevention of treatment failure: The use of measuring, monitoring, and feedback in clinical practice*. Washington, DC: American Psychological Association.

Lambert, M. J. (2010b). Yes, it is time for clinicians to routinely monitor treatment outcome. In B. L. Duncan, S. D. Miller, B. E. Wampold, & M. A. Hubble (Eds.), *The heart and soul of change* (2nd ed., pp. 239–266). Washington, DC: American Psychological Association.

Lambert, M. J., & Barley, D. E. (2001). Research summary on the therapeutic relationship and psychotherapy outcome. *Psychotherapy: Theory, Research, Practice, Training, 38*, 357–361.

Lambert, M. J., Harmon, C., Slade, K., Whipple, J. L., & Hawkins, E. J. (2004). Providing feedback to psychotherapists on their patients' progress: Clinical results and practice suggestions. *Journal of Clinical Psychology, 61*, 165–174.

Lambert, M. J., & Ogles, B. M. (2009). Using clinical significance in psychotherapy outcome research: The need for a common procedure and validity data. *Psychotherapy Research, 19*, 493–501.

Lambert, M. J., Whipple, J. L., Bishop, M. J., Vermeersch, D. A., Gray, G. V., & Finch, A. E. (2002). Comparison of empirically-derived and rationally-derived methods for identifying patients at risk for treatment failure. *Clinical Psychology and Psychotherapy, 9*, 149–164.

Lambert, M. J., Whipple, J. L., Hawkins, E. J., Vermeersch, D. A., Nielsen, S. L., & Smart, D. W. (2003). Is it time for clinicians to routinely track patient outcome? A meta-analysis. *Clinical Psychology Scientific Practice, 10,* 288–301.

Lambert, M. J., Whipple, J. L., Smart, D. W., Vermeersch, D. A., Nielsen, S. L., & Hawkins, E. J. (2001). The effects of providing therapists with feedback on patient progress during psychotherapy: Are outcomes enhanced? *Psychotherapy Research, 11,* 49–68.

Lang, R., Regester, A., Lauderdale, S., Ashbaugh, K., & Haring, A. (2010). Treatment of anxiety in autism spectrum disorders using cognitive behaviour therapy: A systematic review. *Developmental Neurorehabilitation, 13,* 53–63.

Lau, A. S. (2006). Making the case for selective and directed cultural adaptations of evidence-based treatments: Examples from parent training. *Clinical Psychology Science and Practice, 13,* 295–310.

Lilienfeld, S. O. (2007). Psychological treatments that cause harm. *Perspectives on Psychological Science, 2,* 53-70.

Linn, M. (1988). Rapid Disability Rating Scale-2 (RDRS-2). *Psychopharmacology Bulletin, 24,* 799–800.

Linn, M., & Linn, B. (1982). The Rapid Disability Rating Scale-2. *Journal of the American Geriatrics Society, 30,* 378–382.

Littell, J. H., Corcoran, J., & Pillai, V. (2008). *Systematic reviews and meta-analysis.* New York: Oxford University Press.

Lutz, W., Stulz, N., & Kock, K. (2009). Patterns of early change and their relationship to outcome and follow-up among patients with major depressive disorders. *Journal of Affective Disorders, 118,* 60–68.

Luyben, P. D. (2009). Applied behavior analysis: Understanding and changing behavior in the community—A representative review. *Journal of Prevention & Intervention in the Community, 37,* 230–235.

Lyons, J. S. (2009). *Communimetrics: A communication theory of measurement in human service settings.* New York: Springer.

Macgowan, M. J. (1997). A measure of engagement for social group work: The Groupwork Engagement Measure (GEM). *Journal of Social Service Research, 23,* 17–37.

Macgowan, M. J. (2006). The Group Engagement Measure: A review of its conceptual and empirical properties. *Journal of Groups in Addiction and Recovery, 1,* 33–52.

Macgowan, M. J. (2008). *A guide to evidence-based group work.* New York: Oxford University Press.

Macgowan, M. J., & Newman, F. L. (2005). The factor structure of the Group Engagement Measure. *Social Work Research, 29,* 107–118.

Malgady, R. G., & Colon-Malgady, G. (2008). Building community test norms: Considerations for ethnic minority populations. In L. A. Suzuki & J. G. Ponterotto (Eds.), *Handbook of multicultural assessment: Clinical, psychological, and educational applications* (3rd ed., pp. 34–51). San Francisco: Jossey-Bass.

Mano, K. E. J., Davies, W. H., Klein-Tasman, B. P., & Adesso, V. J. (2009). Measurement equivalence of the Child Behavior Checklist among parents of African American adolescents. *Journal of Child and Family Studies, 18,* 606–620.

Manolov, R., Solanas, A., & Leiva, D. (2010). Comparing "visual" effect size indices for single-case designs. *Methodology, 6,* 49–58.

Marshall, S., Haywood, K., & Fitzpatrick, R. (2006). Impact of patient-reported outcome measures on routine practice: A structured review. *Journal of Evaluation in Clinical Practice, 12,* 559–568.

Martin, L. R., Haskard-Zolnierek, K. B., & DiMatteo, M. R. (2010). *Health behavior change and treatment adherence: Evidence-based guidelines for improving healthcare.* New York: Oxford University Press.

McBeath, B., Briggs, H. E., & Aisenberg, E. (2010). Examining the premises supporting the empirically supported intervention approach to social work practice. *Social Work, 55,* 347–357.

McDowell, I. (2006). *Measuring health: A guide to rating scales and questionnaires* (3rd ed.). New York: Oxford University Press.

McGoldrick, M., Gerson, R., & Shellenberger, S. (1999). *Genograms: Assessment and intervention* (2nd ed.). New York: W.W. Norton & Company.

McMurtry, S. L., Rose, S. J., & Cisler, R. A. (2008). Brief screening instruments. In A. R. Roberts (Ed.), *Social workers' desk reference* (2nd ed., pp. 358–370). New York: Oxford University Press.

Mechling, L., & Gast, D. L. (2010). Ethical principles and practices. In D. L. Gast (Ed.), *Single subject research methodology in behavioral sciences* (pp. 32–56). New York: Routledge.

Meier, S. T. (2003). *Bridging case conceptualization, assessment and intervention.* Thousand Oaks, CA: Sage.

Meier, S. T. (2008). *Measuring change in counseling and psychotherapy.* New York: Guilford Press.

Meyer, M. S. (2001). Why they don't come back: A clinical perspective on the no-show client. *Clinical Social Work Journal, 29,* 325–339.

Meyer, T. J., Miller, M. L., Metzger, R. L., & Borkovec, T. D. (2008). Penn State Worry Questionnaire (PSWQ). In A. J. Rush Jr., M. B. First, & D. Blacker (Eds.), *Handbook of psychiatric measures* (2nd ed., pp. 556–558). Washington, DC: American Psychiatric Association.

Miller, S. D., Duncan, B. L., Sorrell, R., & Brown, G. S. (2005). The partners for change outcome management system. *Journal of Clinical Psychology: In Session, 61,* 199–208.

Mintz, J., & Kiesler, D. J. (1982). Individualized measures of psychotherapy outcome. In P. C. Kendall & J. N. Butcher (Eds.), *Handbook of research methods in clinical psychology* (pp. 491–534). New York: John Wiley & Sons.

Mizrahi, T., & Davis, L. (Eds.). (2008). *Encyclopedia of social work* (20th ed.). New York: NASW Press and Oxford University Press.

Mokkink, L. B., Terwee, C. B., Stratford, P. W., Alonso, J., Patrick, D. L., Riphagen, I., et al. (2009). Evaluation of the methodological quality of systematic reviews of health status measurement instruments. *Quality of Life Research, 18,* 313–333.

Montalvo, F. (2009). Ethnoracial gap in clinical practice with Latinos. *Clinical Social Work Journal, 37,* 277–286.

Morgan, D. L., & Morgan, R. K. (2009). *Single-case research methods for the behavioral and health sciences.* Los Angeles: Sage.

Mullen, E. J., Dumpson, J., & Associates. (1972). *Evaluation of social intervention.* San Francisco: Jossey-Bass.

Mullen, E. J., & Streiner, D. L. (2004). The evidence for and against evidence-based practice. *Brief Treatment and Crisis Intervention, 4,* 111–121.

Muran, J. C., & Barber, J. P. (2011). *The therapeutic alliance: An evidence-based guide to practice.* New York: Guilford.

Myles, B. S., Ferguson, H., & Hagiwara, T. (2007). Using a personal digital assistant to improve the recording of homework assignments by an adolescent with Asperger syndrome. *Focus on Autism and Other Developmental Disabilities, 22,* 96–99.

National Association of Social Workers. (2008). *Code of ethics of the National Association of Social Workers.* Washington, DC: Author (Original work published 1996).

Nelsen, J. C. (1994). Ethics, gender, and ethnicity in single-case research and evaluation. *Journal of Social Service Research, 18,* 139–152.

Nezu, A. M., & Nezu, C. M. (Eds.). (2008). *Evidence-based outcome research: A practical guide to conducting randomized controlled trials for psychosocial interventions.* New York: Oxford University Press.

Nickerson, R. S. (1998). Confirmation bias: A ubiquitous phenomenon in many guises. *Review of General Psychology, 2,* 175–220.

Norcross, J. C., Beutler, L. E., & Levant, R. F. (Eds.). (2006). *Evidence-based practices in mental health: Debate and dialogue on the fundamental questions.* Washington, DC: American Psychological Association.

Nugent, W. R. (2009). Meta-analysis as a research synthesis methodology: Cause for concern. *Journal of Social Service Research, 35,* 181–192.

Nugent, W. R. (2010). *Analyzing single system design data.* New York: Oxford University Press.

O'Hare, T. (2005). *Evidence-based practices for social workers: A multidisciplinary approach.* Chicago, IL: Lyceum Books.

O'Hare, T. (2009). *Essential skills of social work practice: Assessment, intervention, and evaluation.* Chicago, IL: Lyceum Books.

Ogles, B. M., Lambert, M. J., & Fields, S. A. (2002). *Essentials of outcome assessment.* New York: John Wiley & Sons.

Okawa, J. B. (2008). Considerations for the cross-cultural evaluation of refugees and asylum seekers. In L. A. Suzuki & J. G. Ponterotto (Eds.), *Handbook of multicultural assessment: Clinical, psychological, and educational applications* (3rd ed., pp. 165–194). San Francisco: Jossey-Bass.

Okiishi, J. C., Lambert, M. J., Eggett, D., Nielsen, L., & Dayton, D. D. (2006). An analysis of therapist treatment effects: Toward providing feedback to individual therapists on their clients' psychotherapy outcome. *Journal of Clinical Psychology, 62,* 1157–1172.

Olkin, R., & Taliaferro, G. (2006). Evidence-based practices have ignored people with disabilities. In J. C. Norcross, L. E. Beutler, & R. F. Levant (Eds.), *Evidence-based practices in mental health: Debate and dialogue on the fundamental questions* (pp. 353–359). Washington, DC: American Psychological Association.

Padilla, A. M., & Borsato, G. N. (2008). Issues in culturally appropriate psychoeducational assessment. In L. A. Suzuki & J. G. Ponterotto (Eds.), *Handbook of multicultural assessment: Clinical, psychological, and educational applications* (3rd ed., pp. 5–21). San Francisco: Jossey-Bass.

Parker, R. I., Cryer, J., & Byrns, G. (2006). Controlling baseline trend in single-case research. *School Psychology Quarterly, 21,* 418–443.

Parker, R. I., & Hagan-Burke, S. (2007). Single case research results as clinical outcomes. *Journal of School Psychology, 45,* 637–653.

Parker, R. I., Vannest, K. J., & Brown, L. (2009). The improvement rate difference for single-case research. *Exceptional Children, 75,* 135–150.

Parsonson, B. S., & Baer, D. M. (1986). The graphic analysis of data. In A. Poling & R. W. Fuqua (Eds.), *Research methods in applied behavior analysis: Issues and advances* (pp. 157–186). New York: Plenum Press.

Patrick, P. D., Mozzoni, M., & Patrick, S. T. (2000). Evidence-based care and the single-subject design. *Infants and Young Children, 13,* 60–73.

Pawson, R. (2002). Evidence-based policy: In search of a method. *Evaluation, 8,* 157–180.

Persons, J. B. (2008). *The case formulation approach to cognitive-behavior therapy.* New York: Guilford Press.

Polowy, C. I., Morgan, S., Bailey, W. D., & Gorenberg, C. (2008). Confidentiality and privileged communication. In T. Mizrahi & L. Davis (Eds.), *Encyclopedia of social work* (20th ed., pp. 408–415). New York: NASW Press and Oxford University Press.

Proctor, E. K. (1990). Evaluating clinical practice: Issues of purpose and design. *Social Work Research & Abstracts, 26,* 32–40.

Proctor, E. K., & Rosen, A. (1983). Problem formulation and its relation to treatment planning. *Social Work Research & Abstracts, 19,* 22–28.

Proctor, E. K., & Rosen, A. (2003). The structure and function of social work practice guidelines. In A. Rosen & E. K. Proctor (Eds.), *Developing practice guidelines for social work intervention* (pp. 108–127). New York: Columbia University Press.

Proctor, E. K., & Rosen, A. (2008). From knowledge production to implementation: Research challenges and imperatives. *Research on Social Work Practice, 18,* 285–291.

Quinn, C. C., Clough, S. S., Minor, J. M., Lender, D., Okafor, M. C., & Gruber-Baldini, A. (2008). WellDoc mobil diabetes management randomized controlled trial: Change in clinical and behavioral outcomes and patient and physician satisfaction. *Diabetes Technology & Therapeutics, 10,* 160–168.

Radloff, L. S. (1977). The CES-D Scale: A self-report depression scale for research in the general population. *Applied Psychological Measurement, 1,* 385–401.

Radloff, L. S., & Lock, B. Z. (2008). Center for Epidemiologic Studies Depression Scale (CES-D). In A. J. Rush Jr., M. B. First, & D. Blacker (Eds.), *Handbook of psychiatric measures* (2nd ed., pp. 506–508). Washington, DC: American Psychiatric Association.

Reamer, F. G. (2009). *The social work ethics casebook: Cases and commentary.* Washington, DC: NASW Press.

Reese, R. J., Norsworthy, L. A., & Rowlands, S. R. (2009). Does a continuous feedback system improve psychotherapy outcome? *Psychotherapy Theory, Research, Practice, Training, 46,* 418–431.

Reid, W. J. (2003). Knowledge for direct social work practice: An analysis of trends. *Social Service Review, 76,* 6–33.

Rhodes, K. W., Cox, M. E., Orme, J. G., Coakley, T., Buehler, C., & Cuddeback, G. S. (2006). *Casey Home Assessment Protocol (CHAP): User's manual* (2nd ed.). Knoxville: University of Tennessee, Children's Mental Health Services Research Center.

Richey, C. A., Blythe, B. J., & Berlin, S. B. (1987). Do social workers evaluate their practice? *Social Work Research & Abstracts, 23*, 14–20.

Riley-Tillman, T. C., & Burns, M. K. (2009). *Evaluating educational interventions: Single-case design for measuring response to intervention*. New York: Guilford Press.

Roberts, A. R. (Ed.). (2009). *Social workers' desk reference*. New York: Oxford University Press.

Rodgers, A. Y., & Potocky, M. (1997). Evaluating culturally sensitive practice through single-system design: Methodological issues and strategies. *Research on Social Work Practice, 7*(3), 391–401.

Romano, E., & De Luca, R. V. (2006). Evaluation of a treatment program for sexually abused adult males. *Journal of Family Violence, 21*, 75–88.

Rooney, R. H. (2009). *Strategies for work with involuntary clients* (2nd ed.). New York: Columbia University Press.

Rosen, A., & Proctor, E. K. (Eds.). (2003). *Developing practice guidelines for social work intervention*. New York: Columbia University Press.

Rosqvist, J., Sundsmo, A., MacLane, C., Cullen, K., Norling, D. C., Davies, M., & Maack, D. (2006). Analogue and virtual reality assessment. In M. Hersen (Ed.), *Clinicians handbook of adult behavioral assessment* (pp. 43–62). St. Louis, MO: Academic Press.

Ross, S. W., & Horner, R. H. (2009). Bully prevention in positive behavior support. *Journal of Applied Behavior Analysis, 42*, 747–759.

Royse, D., Thyer, B. A., & Padgett, D. K. (2010). *Program evaluation: An introduction* (5th ed.). Belmont, CA: Wadsworth.

Rubin, A. (2008). *Practitioner's guide to using research for evidence-based practice*. Hoboken, NJ: John Wiley & Sons.

Rush, A. J., Bernstein, I. H., Trivedi, M. H., Carmody, T. J., Wisniewski, S., Mundt, J. C., et al. (2006). An evaluation of the Quick Inventory of Depressive Symptomatology and the Hamilton Rating Scale for Depression: A sequenced treatment alternatives to relieve depression trial report. *Biological Psychiatry, 59*, 493–501.

Rush, A. J., Jr., First, M. B., & Blacker, D. (Eds.). (2008). *Handbook of psychiatric measures* (2nd ed.). Washington, DC: American Psychiatric Association.

Rush, A. J., Trivedi, M. H., Ibrahim, H. M., Carmody, T. J., Arnow, B., Klein, D. N., et al. (2003). The 16-item Quick Inventory of Depressive Symptomatology (QIDS), Clinician Rating (QIDS-C), and Self-Report (QIDS-SR): A psychometric evaluation in patients with chronic major depression. *Biological Psychiatry, 54*, 573–583.

Saggese, M. L. (2005). Maximizing treatment effectiveness in clinical practice: An outcome-informed, collaborative approach. *Families in Society: Journal of Contemporary Social Services, 86*, 558–564.

Sapyta, J., Riemer, M., & Bickman, L. (2005). Feedback to clinicians: Theory, research, and practice. *Journal of Clinical Psychology: In Session, 61*, 145–153.

Satake, E. B., Jagaroo, V., & Maxwell, D. L. (2008). *Handbook of statistical methods: Single subject design*. San Diego: Plural Publishing.

Schaefer, B. A., Koeter, M. W. J., Wouters, L., Emmelkamp, P. M. G., & Schene, A. H. (2003). What patient characteristics make clinicians recommend brief treatment? *Acta Psychatrica Scandinavica, 107*, 188–196.

Scriven, M. (2009). Demythologizing causation and evidence. In S. I. Donaldson, C. A. Christie, & M. M. Mark (Eds.), *What counts as credible evidence in applied research and evaluation practice?* (pp. 134–152). Thousand Oaks, CA: Sage.

Shadish, W. R., Cook, T. D., & Campbell, D. T. (2002). *Experimental and quasi-experimental designs for generalized causal inference*. New York: Houghton Mifflin.

Shaffer, D., Gould, M. S., Brasic, J., Ambrosini, P., Fisher, P., Bird, H., & Aluwahlia, S. (1983). A Children's Global Assessment Scale (CGAS). *Archives of General Psychiatry, 40*, 1228–1231.

Shear, M. K., Brown, T. A., Barlow, D. H., Money, R., Sholomskas, D. E., Woods, S. W., et al. (1997). Multicenter collaborative panic disorder severity scale. *American Journal of Psychiatry, 154*, 1571–1575.

Shear, M. K., Brown, T. A., Barlow, R., Money, D. E., Sholomskas, D. E., Woods, S. W., et al. (2008). Panic Disorder Severity Scale (PDSS). In A. J. Rush, Jr., M. B. First, & D. Blacker (Eds.), *Handbook of psychiatric measures* (2nd ed., pp. 542–543). Washington, DC: American Psychiatric Association.

Sheikh, J. I., & Yesavage, J. A. (1986). Geriatric Depression Scale (GDS): Recent evidence and development of a shorter version. *Clinical Gerontologist, 5*, 165–173.

Shimokawa, K., Lambert, M. J., & Smart, D. W. (2010). Enhancing treatment outcome of patients at risk of treatment failure: Meta-analytic and mega-analytic review of a psychotherapy quality assurance system. *Journal of Consulting and Clinical Psychology, 78*, 298–311.

Sigmon, S. T., & LaMattina, S. M. (2006). Self-assessment. In M. Hersen (Ed.), *Clinicians handbook of adult behavioral assessment* (pp. 145–164). St. Louis, MO: Academic Press.

Sikkes, S. A. M., de Klerk, E. S. M. D. L., Pijnenburg, Y. A. L., Scheltens, P., & Uitdehaag, B. M. J. (2009). A systematic review of instrumental activities of daily living scales in dementia: Room for improvement. *Journal of Neurology, Neurosurgery, and Psychiatry, 80*, 7–12.

Sivan, A. B., Ridge, A., Gross, D., Richardson, R., & Cowell, J. (2008). Analysis of two measures of child behavior problems by African American, Latino, and non-Hispanic Caucasian parents of young children: A focus group study. *Journal of Pediatric Nursing, 23*, 20–27.

Slade, K., Lambert, M. J., Harmon, S. C., Smart, D. W., & Bailey, R. (2008). Improving psychotherapy outcome: The use of immediate electronic feedback and revised clinical support tools. *Clinical Psychology and Psychotherapy, 15*, 287–303.

Snyder, D. K., Heyman, R. E., & Haynes, S. N. (2008). Couple distress. In J. Hunsley & E. J. Mash (Eds.), *A guide to assessments that work* (pp. 439–463). New York: Oxford University Press.

Solomon, P., Cavanaugh, M. M., & Draine, J. (2009). *Randomized controlled trials: Design and implementation for community-based psychosocial interventions*. New York: Oxford University Press.

Spies, R. A., Plake, B. S., Geisinger, K. F., & Carlson, J. F. (2010). *The eighteenth mental measurements yearbook*. Lincoln: Buros Institute, University of Nebraska.

Spriggs, A. D., & Gast, D. L. (2010). Visual representation of data. In D. L. Gast (Ed.), *Single subject research methodology in behavioral sciences* (pp. 166–198). New York: Routledge.

Springer, D. W., & Tripodi, S. J. (2009). Assessment protocols and rapid assessment instruments with troubled adolescents. In A. R. Roberts (Ed.), *Social workers' desk reference* (2nd ed., pp. 385–389). New York: Oxford University Press.

Staudt, M. (1997). Pseudoissues in practice evaluation: Impediments to responsible practice. *Social Work, 42*, 99–106.

Stemler, S. E., & Tsai, J. (2008). Best practices in interrater reliability: Three common approaches. In J. W. Osborne (Ed.), *Best practices in quantitative methods* (pp. 29–49). Los Angeles: Sage.

Stinson, J. N., Kavanagh, T., Yamada, J., Gill, N., & Stevens, B. (2006). Systematic review of the psychometric properties, interpretability and feasibility of self-report pain intensity measures for use in clinical trials in children and adolescents. *Pain, 125*, 143–157.

Stöber, J., & Bittencourt, J. (1998). Weekly assessment of worry: An adaptation of the Penn State Worry Questionnaire for monitoring changes during treatment. *Behaviour Research and Therapy, 36*, 645–656.

Stone, A. A., Shiffman, S., Atienza, A. A., & Nebeling, L. (Eds.). (2007). *The science of real-time data capture: Self-reports in health research*. New York: Oxford University Press.

Strandbygaard, U., Thomsen, S. F., & Backer, V. A. (2010). Daily SMS reminder increases adherence to asthma treatment: A three-month follow-up study. *Respiratory Medicine, 104*, 166–171.

Strauss, B., Burlingame, G. M., & Bormann, B. (2008). Using the CORE-R battery in group psychotherapy. *Journal of Clinical Psychology: In Session, 64*, 1225–1237.

Streiner, D. L., & Norman, G. R. (2008). *Health measurement scales: A practical guide to their development and use* (4th ed.). New York: Oxford University Press.

Sue, S., & Zane, N. (2006). Ethnic minority populations have been neglected by evidence-based practices. In J. C. Norcross, L. E. Beutler, & R. F. Levant (Eds.), *Evidence-based practices in mental health: Debate and dialogue on the fundamental questions* (pp. 329–337). Washington, DC: American Psychological Association.

Suzuki, L. A., & Ponterotto, J. G. (Eds.). (2008). *Handbook of multicultural assessment: Clinical, psychological, and educational applications* (3rd ed.). San Francisco: Jossey-Bass.

Taylor, C. B. (Ed.). (2010). *How to practice evidence-based psychiatry: Basic principles and case studies*. Washington, DC: American Psychiatric Association.

Taylor, C. B., & Gray, G. E. (2010). What is evidence-based psychiatric practice? In C. B. Taylor (Ed.), *How to practice evidence-based psychiatry: Basic principles and case studies* (pp. 3–11). Washington, DC: American Psychiatric Association.

Terwee, C. B., Bot, S. D. M., de Boer, M. R., van der Windt, D. A. W. M., Knol, D. L., Dekker, J., et al. (2007). Quality criteria were proposed for measurement properties of health status questionnaires. *Journal of Clinical Epidemiology, 60*, 34–42.

Thomas, R., & Zimmer-Gembeck, M. J. (2007). Behavioral outcomes of Parent-Child Interaction Therapy and Triple P-Positive Parenting Program: A review and meta-analysis. *Journal of Abnormal Child Psychology, 35*, 475–495.

Thyer, B. A., & Myers, L. L. (2007). *A social worker's guide to evaluating practice outcomes*. Alexandria, VA: Council on Social Work Education.

Toseland, R. W., & Rivas, R. F. (2009). *An introduction to group work practice* (6th ed.). Boston: Allyn & Bacon.

Tran, T. V. (2009). *Developing cross-cultural measurement*. New York: Oxford University Press.

Trivedi, M. H., Ibrahim, M., Biggs, M., Crimson, L., Wilson, M. G., Toprac, E., et al. (2004). The Inventory of Depressive Symptomatology, Clinician Rating (IDS-C) and Self-Report (IDS-SR), and the Quick Inventory of Depressive Symptomatology, Clinician Rating (QIDS-C) and Self-Report (QIDS-SR) in public sector patients with mood disorders: A psychometric evaluation. *Psychological Medicine, 34*, 73–82.

Trottera, C. (1999). Don't throw the baby out with the bath water—In defence of problem solving. *Australian Social Work, 52*, 51–55.

Utsey, S. O., & Bolden, M. A. (2008). Cross-cultural considerations in quality-of-life assessment. In L. A. Suzuki & J. G. Ponterotto (Eds.), *Handbook of multicultural assessment: Clinical, psychological, and educational applications* (3rd ed., pp. 299–318). San Francisco: Jossey-Bass.

Van Camp, C. M., Vollmer, T. R., Goh, H. L., Whitehouse, C. M., Reyes, J., Montgomery, J. L., & Borrero, J. C. (2008). Behavioral parent training in child welfare: Evaluations of skills acquisition. *Research on Social Work Practice, 18*, 377–391.

Vannest, K. J., Harrison, J. R., Temple-Harvey, K., Ramsey, L., & Parker, R. I. (2010). Improvement rate differences of academic interventions for students with emotional and behavioral disorders. *Remedial and Special Education, 20*, 1–14.

Varela, R. E., Sanchez-Sosa, J. J., Biggs, B. K., & Luis, T. M. (2008). Anxiety symptoms and fears in Hispanic and European American children: Cross-cultural measurement. *Journal of Psychopathology Behavioral Assessment, 30*, 132–145.

Vidotto, G., Ferrario, S. R., Bond, T. G., & Zotti, A. M. (2010). Family Strain Questionnaire—Short form for nurses and general practitioners. *Journal of Clinical Nursing, 19*, 275–283.

Wampold, B. E. (2010). The research evidence for common factors models: A historically situated perspective. In B. L. Duncan, S. D. Miller, B. E. Wampold, & M. A. Hubble (Eds.), *The heart and soul of change: Delivering what works* (2nd ed., pp. 49–81). Washington, DC: American Psychological Association.

Warren, J. S., Nelson, P. L., Mondragon, S. A., Baldwin, S. A., & Burlingame, G. M. (2010). Youth psychotherapy change trajectories and outcomes in usual care: Community mental health versus managed care settings. *Journal of Consulting and Clinical Psychology, 78*, 144–155.

Watkins, D. C., Hudson, D. L., Caldwell, C. H., Siefert, K., & Jackson, J. S. (2011). Discrimination, mastery, and depressive symptoms among African American men. *Research on Social Work Practice, 21*, 269–277.

Watson, D. L., & Tharp, R. G. (2007). *Self-directed behavior* (9th ed.). Belmont, CA: Thomson Wadsworth.

Weisz, J. R., Chorpita, B. F., Frye, A., Ng, M. Y., Lau, N., Bearman, S. K., Hoagwood, K. E. (2011). Youth top problems: Using idiographic, consumer-guided assessment to identify treatment needs and to track change during psychotherapy. *Journal of Consulting and Clinical Psychology, 79*(3), 369–380.

Whipple, J. L., Lambert, M. J., Vermeersch, D. A., Smart, D. W., Nielsen, S. L., & Hawkins, E. J. (2003). Improving the effects of psychotherapy: The use of early identification of treatment failure and problem-solving strategies in routine practice. *Journal of Counseling Psychology, 50*, 59–68.

Whitbeck, L. B., McMorris, B. J., Hoyt, D. R., Stubben, J. D., & LaFromboise, T. (2002). Perceived discrimination, traditional practices, and depressive symptoms among American Indians in the upper Midwest. *Journal of Health and Social Behavior, 43*, 400–418.

Wolery, M., Busick, M., Reichow, B., & Barton, E. E. (2010). Comparison of overlap methods for quantitatively synthesizing single-subject data. *The Journal of Special Education, 44*, 18–28.

Worthen, V. E., & Lambert, M. J. (2007). Outcome oriented supervision: Advantages of adding systematic client tracking to supportive consultations. *Counselling and Psychotherapy Research, 7*, 48–53.

Wright, J. H., Turkington, D., Kingdon, D. G., & Basco, M. R. (2009). *Cognitive-behavior therapy for severe mental illness: An illustrated guide.* Washington, DC: American Psychiatric Association.

Ximenes, V. M., Manolov, R., Solanas, A., & Quera, V. (2009). Factors affecting visual inference in single-case designs. *The Spanish Journal of Psychology, 12*, 823–832.

Yesavage, J. A., & Brink, T. L. (1983). Development and validation of a geriatric depression screening scale: A preliminary report. *Journal of Psychiatric Research, 17*, 37–49.

Yesavage, J. A., & Brink, T. L. (2008). Geriatric Depression Scale (GDS). In A. J. Rush, Jr., M. B. First, & D. Blacker (Eds.), *Handbook of psychiatric measures* (2nd ed., pp. 524–526). Washington, DC: American Psychiatric Association.

Yoder, P., & Symons, F. (2010). *Observational measurement of behavior.* New York: Springer.

# Index